Visual FoxPro Programming Basics

About the Authors

Tom Stearns is a computer consultant in Salt Lake City, Utah, specializing in Xbase work. He has led training seminars in FoxPro and is a freelance product reviewer for *LAN Times* magazine.

Leonard Stearns, an electrical engineer, has 40 years of experience in designing computers, comp systems, and control systems.

Visual FoxPro Programming Basics

Tom Stearns
Leonard Stearns

Osborne **McGraw-Hill**

Berkeley New York St. Louis San Francisco Auckland Bogotá Hamburg London Madrid Mexico City
Milan Montreal New Delhi Panama City Paris São Paulo Singapore Sydney Tokyo Toronto

Osborne **McGraw-Hill**
2600 Tenth Street
Berkeley, California 94710
U.S.A.

For information on translations or book distributors outside of the U.S.A., or to arrange bulk purchase discounts for sales promotions, premiums, or fundraisers please write to Osborne **McGraw-Hill** at the above address.

Visual FoxPro Programming Basics

1234567890 DOC 99876

ISBN 0-07-882092-8

Publisher
Lawrence Levitsky

Acquisitions Editor
Cynthia Brown

Project Editor
Claire Splan

Copy Editor
Judy Ziajka
Dennis Weaver

Proofreader
Pat Mannion

Computer Designer
Roberta Steele

Illustrator
Roberta Steele

Quality Control Specialist
Joe Scuderi

Cover Design
Ted Mader Associates

We dedicate this book to our mothers:

Elaine and Rose

Contents at a Glance

Contents

Acknowledgments

We do not have enough pages to express our appreciation individually to all the people who have helped us along the way and ultimately made this book possible. We know who you are, as you do, and we thank you from the bottoms of our hearts. However, without the kindness and generosity of *one* individual this book would not exist. That person is Cindy Brown, Osborne\McGraw-Hill Managing Editor. She taught us how to write a book as we wrote this one, and in many ways it is as much her book as it is ours. Thank you, Cindy. You were truly wonderful.

Thanks to all the folks at Osborne for their help in producing this book: Claire Splan, Project Editor, who managed the editing and production process, and made sure the pieces fit together; Judy Ziajka, our gracious and talented copyeditor; and all the people in the Production Department who were responsible for the design and layout of the finished pages. We also owe very special thanks to Gretchen Schaffer of Microsoft's public relations firm, Waggener Edstrom. Gretchen is the account executive responsible for promoting Visual FoxPro and she never let us down when we needed advance information or the latest pre-release Visual FoxPro code and documentation. If it were not for Gretchen's generosity in providing us with whatever we needed, even before it was released, we would still be writing this book. We also thank her and Microsoft for permission to use, in our appendixes, some material directly from the Visual FoxPro help files.

Finally, we thank our wives, Sharon and Jan, and our families for their encouragement and forbearance throughout this adventure of writing our first book. Leonard thanks his dear friend, Steve Spencer, M.D., for professional understanding and personal friendship over the years—not to speak of keeping him alive and healthy. We both thank our good friend Brad Shimmin for his advice and support, and for introducing us to Osborne\McGraw-Hill.

Introduction

Visual FoxPro is a dynamic new relational database development environment that both new programmers and seasoned developers will find friendly, accommodating, and extremely powerful. By providing an integrated development environment with full-featured object-oriented tools, Visual FoxPro makes it possible for almost anyone to quickly and easily create full-featured applications.

We wrote *Visual FoxPro Programming Basics* with three main objectives:

- First, as the title suggests, to teach the *basic* programming essentials necessary to begin using Visual FoxPro quickly and productively—whether you are a beginner or an experienced Xbase programmer.
- Second, to explain and illustrate these essentials by using no-frills examples and exercises that produce immediate tangible results you can begin using right away.
- Third, to demonstrate some fundamental concepts that are not usually addressed in basic texts on computer programming.

By covering fundamental *concepts* in addition to teaching you how to use Visual FoxPro, we hope, without going overboard, to open the door to some powerful ideas you may find both interesting and extremely helpful:

- **Data Normalization:** A simple, powerful strategy that improves the reliability and efficiency of database design.
- **Referential Integrity (RI):** Straightforward, elegant rules and strategy for enforcing data consistency at the database level.
- **Modality:** A window or form is modal if it retains the focus until you explicitly close it. It is modeless if it does not require that you close it before switching to another form or window. Generally, Windows applications are best designed when they are modeless.

Although the above concepts are familiar to most professional programmers, they are seldom discussed in the context of a *basic* programming text. We feel that is a mistake. The earlier you are exposed to straightforward professional concepts, the sooner your programs will begin performing at their potential. We hope to teach you, along with how to use Visual FoxPro, some strategies and procedures that will help make you a better programmer in your "real-world" work environment—regardless of whether you use Visual FoxPro or another development platform. The principals of sound planning and analysis are independent of your programming language or the objectives of a given application.

Our general approach in teaching Visual FoxPro is to select small, simple examples that illustrate broader capabilities and enable you to begin immediately using Visual FoxPro's visual tools *as we cover them.*

- Part I is an overall introduction to Visual FoxPro in which we highlight and discuss the major new features such as: object orientation, rapid application development, and data independence.
- Part II presents an elementary overview of Visual FoxPro by developing simple programmatic examples of fundamental operations.
- Part III examines and illustrates programming complex data relationships and the Visual FoxPro tools that greatly simplify program design.
- Part IV covers more advanced programming topics, such as data normalization, menus, and data-driven controls.
- Part V is an introduction to SQL and client server database techniques using Visual FoxPro tools.
- Part VI includes four appendixes, covering the differences between FoxPro 2.6 and Visual FoxPro 3.0, running existing FoxPro2.6 resources, a Visual FoxPro language overview, and Visual FoxPro reserved words.

As the book progresses from Part I through Part VI, you integrate what you learn by creating and refining more and more elegant routines and procedures, until you have mastered the basics of Visual FoxPro. This book is not intended as the definitive work on Visual FoxPro. Instead, we hope it will be a painless way for almost anyone, novice or professional, to *begin* productively using this truly powerful programming platform.

In case you are wondering, your authors are father and son. Tom is the son and Leonard is the father. We hope you enjoy our book.

part 1

Visual FoxPro—Gateway to Rapid Growth

1

The Visual FoxPro Environment

Visual FoxPro may be the world's first major revolution to arrive in a shrink-wrapped box. Microsoft's new incarnation of our old friend FoxPro is capable of building one-to-many database applications, complete with multiple custom screens and multiple custom printed reports, without you having to write more than a few lines of program code.

However, this does not mean you won't be writing any more code, because you *will* need to write some code when you create meaningful custom Visual FoxPro applications. For a given project, you will write less code, simpler code, and code that will, line for line, accomplish a whole lot more. The next few chapters teach you how quickly you can put Visual FoxPro to work; but transitioning into this powerful new automated product can be much quicker and easier if we first overview its main features.

Introducing Visual FoxPro 3.0

Visual FoxPro 3.0 helps you create better visual applications more easily, more quickly, and more reliably than ever before—*and with less debugging.* Productivity increases dramatically because your new projects become extensions and expansions of resources you have already developed, debugged, and catalogued as Visual FoxPro *reusable* self-contained modules. With Visual FoxPro's move to object orientation, FoxPro at last fulfills its promise to deliver a truly integrated visual development environment.

Following Visual FoxPro's object-oriented strategy, you verify the functionality of each program component *as you create it*; and once you have created all the functional components of an application, you are ready to compile them into a sophisticated visual application and save them as fully functional self-contained resources for instant use in future projects. You will discover that, with Visual FoxPro's help and relatively few lines of simple straightforward code, you can quickly transform existing modal programs into truly modeless event-driven visual applications that perform seamlessly in the Windows environment.

Visual FoxPro does not *mandate* that you exercise its powerful object-oriented features. Although Visual FoxPro preserves your option to continue writing top-down procedural Xbase code just as you did in the earlier incarnations of FoxPro, pursuing this outmoded programming strategy is akin to running a 100-MHz Pentium with only 4 megs of memory and no hard drive or mouse. It just doesn't make sense.

Getting Started with Visual FoxPro

After you install Visual FoxPro, just double-click its icon in the Windows Program Manager. When Visual FoxPro starts for the first time, a new empty project appears on your main screen in Visual FoxPro's Project Manager window, as shown in Figure 1-1. You can create new projects at any time, simply by selecting File, New, and Project. This action commands the Project Manager to create a new project with a name you specify.

1

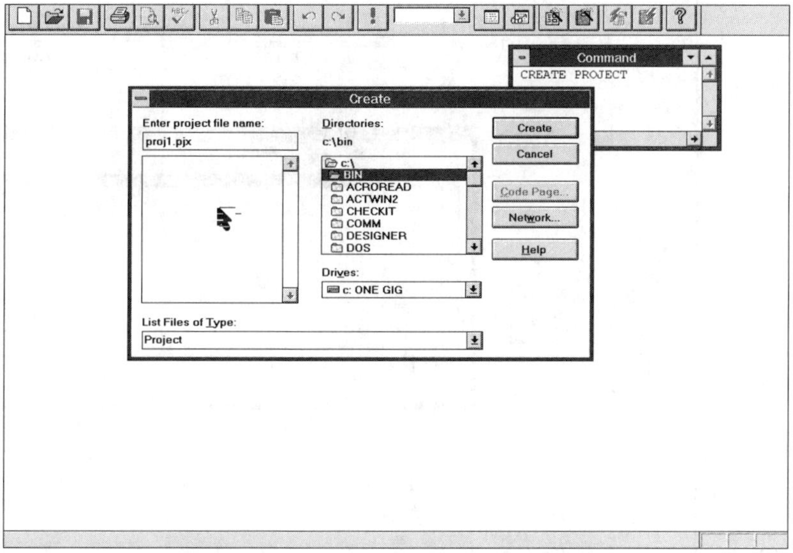

Project Manager—Visual FoxPro's nerve center
Figure 1-1.

Introducing the Project Manager

The Project Manager is Visual FoxPro's control center for building projects and viewing and managing project files. Project Manager is invaluable early in the development process, during design, and during modification and test of individual application components. You will also rely on it throughout the completion stages as you integrate and compile your applications for distribution or for your own use. The Project Manager presents an organized hierarchical view of a project's components. To examine a particular type of file or object, you choose the six tabs that contain your project's data. Let's briefly look at two important tabs and see what they contain.

Data Tab The data tab displays your project data: databases, tables, queries, and views. Figure 1-2 shows how the Project Manager looks with the data tab selected. You will begin working with the elements contained in the data tab in Chapter 6.

Documents Tab The Documents tab displays the project's documents that you use when working with data: forms, reports, and labels. Figure 1-3 shows how the Project Manager looks with the Documents tab selected. You will begin working with the project elements contained in the Documents tab in Chapter 11.

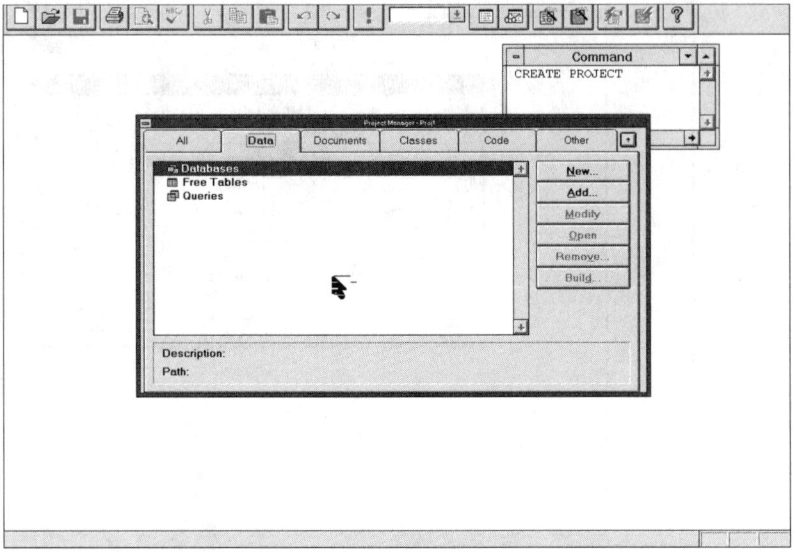

Project Manager's Data tab
Figure 1-2.

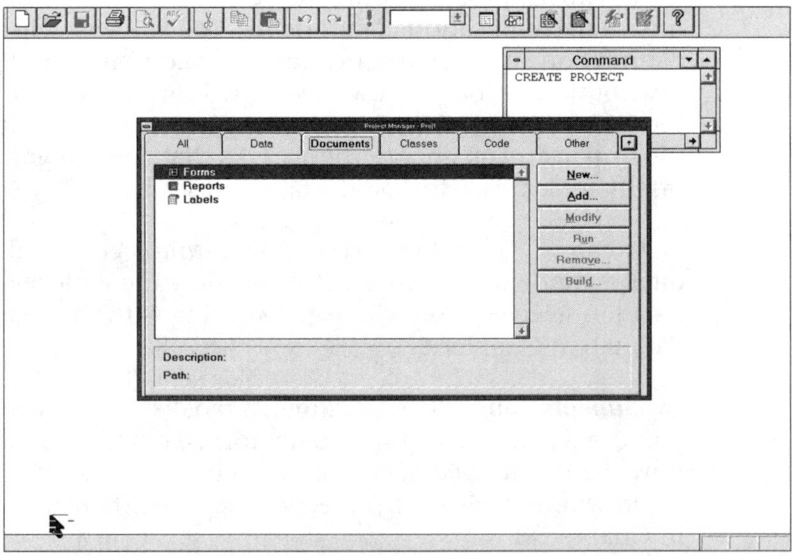

Project Manager's Documents tab
Figure 1-3.

Tip: Before you can use the Project Manager, you have to add existing files or create new ones. For example, if you are moving a set of existing .dbf files into a project, just click Free Tables in the data tab and click add to add them to your project.

As we work through the following chapters, you will learn that the Project Manager has many more useful features than we have covered in this overview. However, you will get a sense of what it can do when you begin working in the Visual FoxPro integrated environment.

Visual FoxPro Designers

In addition to the features we discussed earlier, Visual FoxPro's Project Manager also affords quick, easy access to Visual FoxPro's automated Designers. Designers make quick work of creating tables, forms, databases, queries, and reports. Let's take a brief look at some of Visual FoxPro's Designers and what they will do for you.

Table Designer The Table Designer assists you in creating and modifying free tables, database tables, fields, and indexes. This tool helps you design into your applications such advanced features as validation rules and default values. When you open the Table Designer, three options appear at the top as long as a data table remains open. Figure 1-4 shows how the Table Designer looks after you open it to create a new table. See Chapter 6 for a thorough treatment of this designer.

Database Designer Visual FoxPro's Database Designer displays the tables, views, and relationships contained in your database. When you are working in the Database Designer, Visual FoxPro displays both the Database menu and the Database Designer toolbar. Each data table appears in a sizable window, which lists its fields and, if any, its indexes. This Designer graphically represents persistent relationships by drawing connecting lines between the indexes that connect the related tables. Figure 1-5 shows the Database Designer with some Visual FoxPro sample files.

Data Environment Designer Visual FoxPro's Data Environment Designer helps you visually create and modify the data environment of your forms, formsets, and reports. The Data Environment Designer window gives you access to the Data Environment menu, the Properties window, and the Visual FoxPro Code window. Using these tools, you can manipulate your application's data environment and its objects. An application's data environment allows you graphically to define the source for data used in

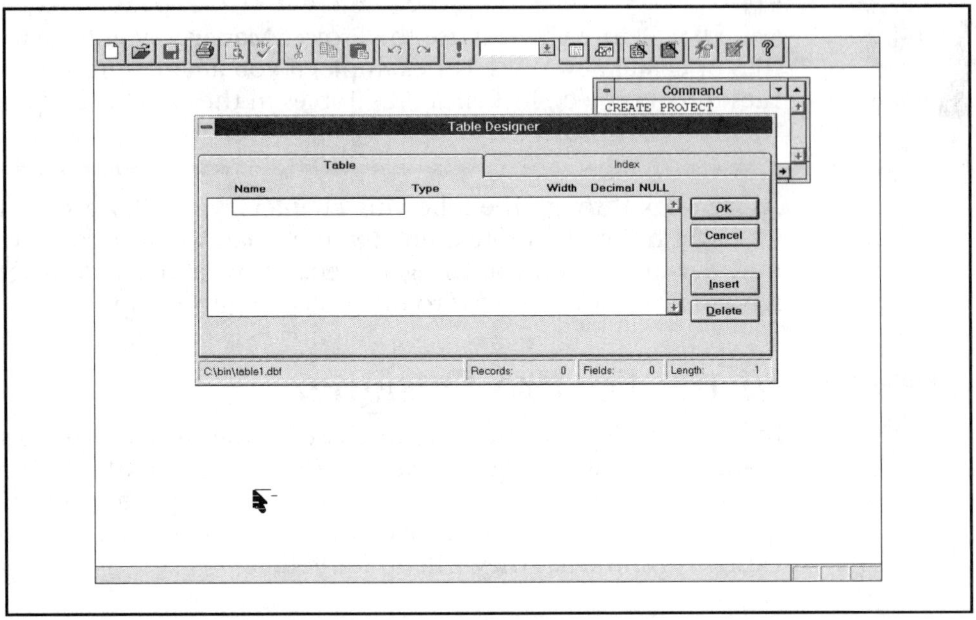

Table Designer
Figure 1-4.

forms and reports. Data sources include databases, tables, views, and relationships. The data environment is saved automatically with associated

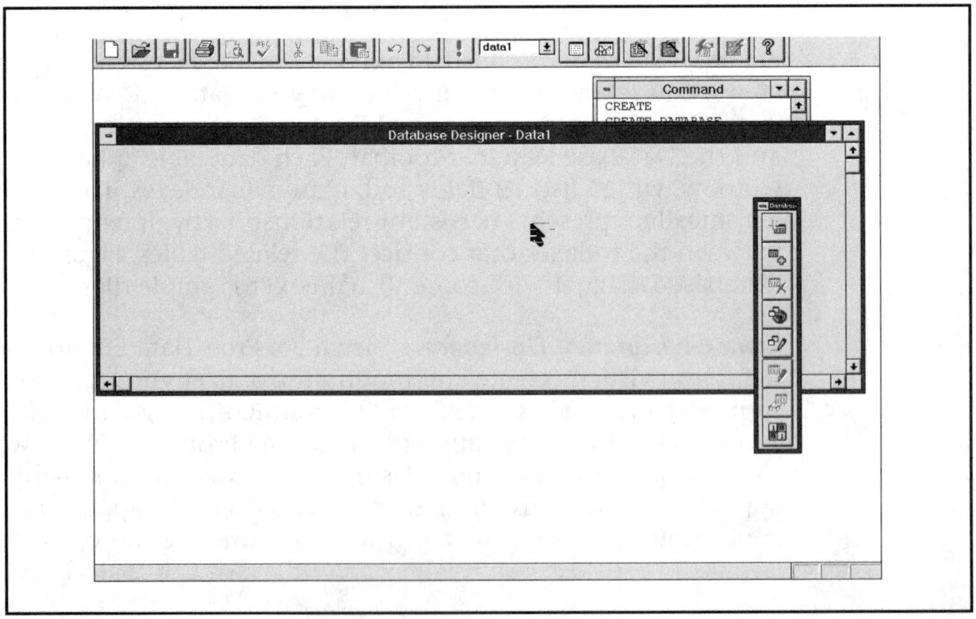

Database Designer
Figure 1-5.

forms and reports. You can modify the data environment using the Report Designer or Form Designer. Once you define the data environment, Visual FoxPro automatically opens the appropriate tables and views when a file is opened and closes them when that file is closed or released. Using Visual FoxPro's Data Environment Designer, you can perform the following operations graphically without writing a line of code:

- Add tables and views to a data environment
- Insert fields and tables from the data environment simply by dragging them to your forms and reports
- Remove tables from a data environment
- Establish data environment relationships
- Modify data environment relationships
- Set the data environment

Form Designer Visual FoxPro's Form Designer allows you visually to create and modify your forms and formsets. A formset is, in this context, an object comprising one or more forms that you can manipulate as a unit. Forms and formsets are objects that have their own unique properties, events, and methods. When using the Form Designer, Visual FoxPro displays a special Form menu and makes available three powerful tools: A Form Controls toolbar, a Form Designer toolbar, and a control Properties window. Figure 1-6 shows the Visual FoxPro Form Designer with the Properties window and the three toolbars.

Visual FoxPro's highly automated Form Designer helps you to do the following:

- Create forms
- Modify forms
- Customize forms
- Add controls to forms
- Run and test a form's functionality
- Save forms

See Chapter 7 for a thorough treatment of this designer.

Label Designer The Label Designer enables you visually to create and modify labels. When you activate the Label Designer window, Visual FoxPro automatically displays the Report menu and the Report Controls toolbar. The Label Designer is almost identical to the Report Designer in that it uses

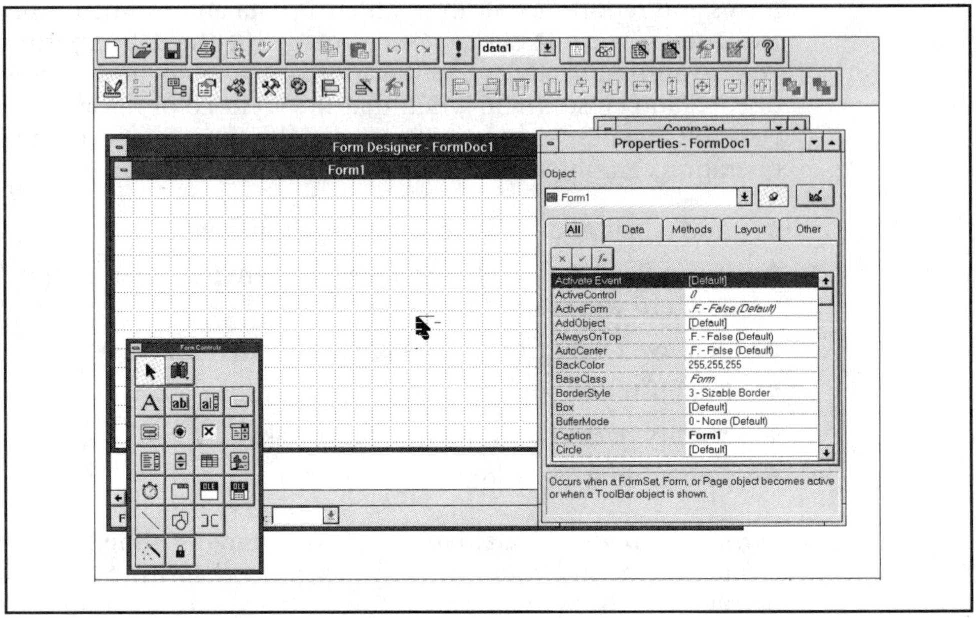

Form Designer with Properties window and toolbars showing **Figure 1-6.**

the same menus and toolbars. The only difference is that the Label Designer automatically defines the page and its columns depending on the layout of the label you select or design. You can quickly create a label layout simply by clicking Quick Report on the Report menu. You can perform the following automated operations using the Label Designer:

- Create labels
- Add label controls
- Specify Label Sizes
- Create label layouts, such as mailing labels
- Create mailing labels using the Label Wizard

Menu Designer The automated Menu Designer helps you create Visual FoxPro menus and submenus. Using the Menu Designer, you can easily design custom menus for your applications or for Visual FoxPro. The Quick Menu feature greatly facilitates creating a new menu. Figure 1-7 shows the Menu Designer. See Chapter 16 for a thorough treatment of this designer.

Query Designer and View Designer The Query Designer and View Designer allow you to create and modify SQL queries and views. When one of these designers is active, Visual FoxPro displays a special Query Menu and

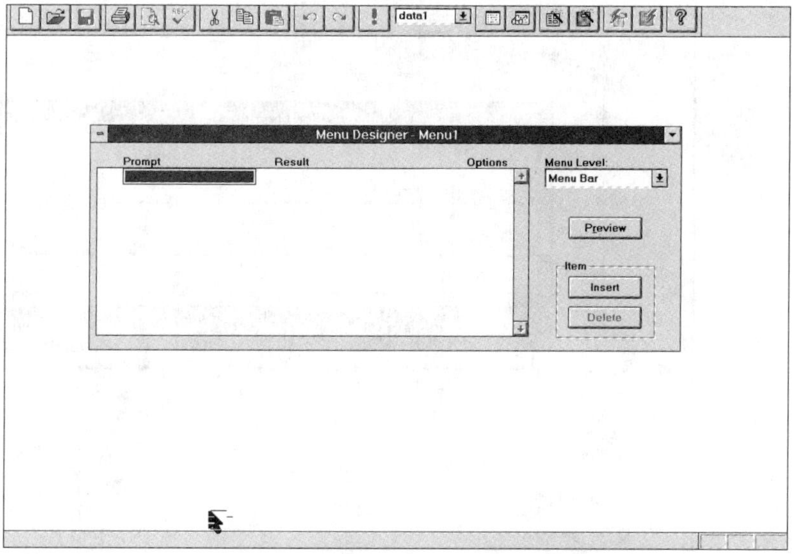

Menu Designer
Figure 1-7.

Query Toolbar or View Designer Toolbar, depending on the tool you are using. See Chapter 20 for a thorough treatment of this designer.

Report Designer The Visual FoxPro Report Designer helps you visually create and modify reports. When you activate the Report Designer, Visual FoxPro displays a special Report menu and Report Controls toolbar. You can quickly and easily create a report layout by clicking Quick Report on the Report menu. Quick Report then prompts you for input describing the fields and layout you want to create. Figure 1-8 shows the Report Designer with its Report Controls toolbar. See Chapter 9 for a thorough treatment of this designer.

The automated Report Designer helps you to quickly and easily perform the following operations:

- Create a report using the New Report feature
- Create a report using the Report Wizard
- Control report output
- Specify report pages
- Design custom reports
- Place report controls into custom reports

See Chapter 9 for a thorough treatment of this designer.

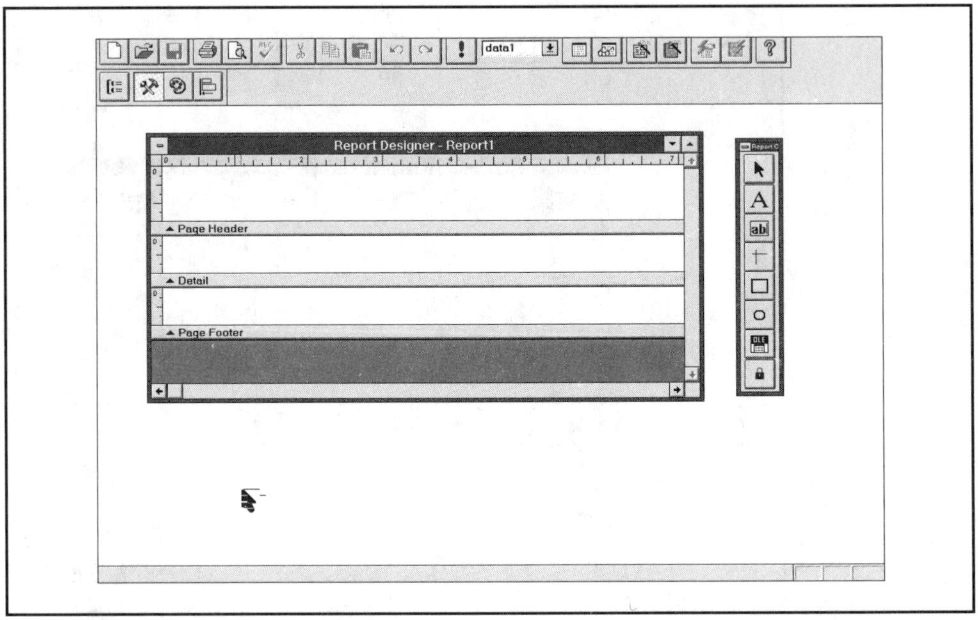

Report Designer
Figure 1-8.

Visual FoxPro Windows

Visual FoxPro provides a variety of special-purpose windows to make application development and management more convenient. We will cover most of these windows in subsequent chapters.

Browse Window The Visual FoxPro Browse window, which is very similar to the FoxPro 2.6 Browse window, displays the active data table's records, views, or queries.

Code Window Use the Visual FoxPro Code window to write, display, and edit custom code for Visual FoxPro forms, events, and methods. Visual FoxPro allows you to open as many Code windows as you need; therefore, you can easily reuse, edit, copy, and paste code from different entities in your project. To open a Code window, such as the one shown in Figure 1-9, all you have to do is double-click a form or form control while in Form Designer or double-click an event or method when you are working in a Properties window. This action has the same effect as clicking the Code command in the View menu.

Visual FoxPro's Code window allows you to conveniently select the current form, form set, data environment, toolbar objects, and any control on your current form. If you need to edit a control's properties, just click that control from the list and the appropriate code edit window appears. If you need help

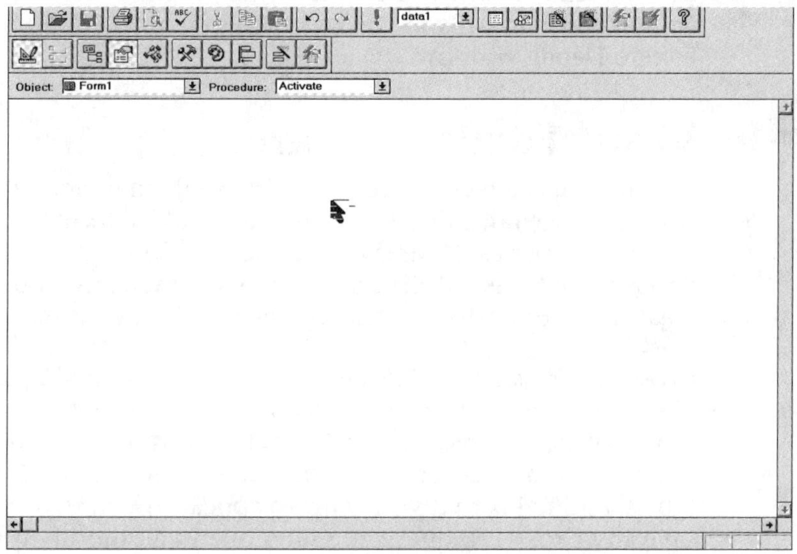

Code window
Figure 1-9.

on command syntax while working in the Code window, just type the keyword of interest and press F1 to immediately receive context-sensitive online Help. You can also select an event in the Procedure box, then press F1 for helpful online information about the selected event. See Chapter 15 for a discussion of how this window is used.

Command Window The Visual FoxPro Command window is actually a system window, very similar in function to the FoxPro 2.6 (and earlier) Command window. However, there is a nice improvement; when you click Visual FoxPro menu commands, the Command window instantly displays any language elements executed by that menu command. As you could in FoxPro 2.6, you can also type Visual FoxPro commands directly into the Command window for immediate execution.

Debug Window The Visual FoxPro Debug window allows you to test functions, view variables, view properties, and check expressions at run time. You can view selected program data as each command executes. You just select Debug from the Tools menu and the Debug window appears on the Visual FoxPro main screen. Either in the development environment or in real time, Debug presents a dynamic view of variable and function return values. Debug presents information for your examination in two panes: The left pane is editable, allowing you to insert the names of variables or expressions you wish to monitor. The values of these variables appear automatically in the right pane as the program executes, and the values update automatically as their variables change. Figure 1-10 shows the Visual FoxPro Debug window.

Visual FoxPro Wizards

Wizards are interactive programming tools that facilitate accomplishing common programming tasks, such as creating forms, formatting reports, and setting up queries. By answering questions prompted by a Wizard, or choosing options within a series of wizard screens, you tell the wizard to create a file or perform a task consistent with your responses.

Cross-Tab Wizard The Visual FoxPro Cross-Tab Wizard allows you to create, in spreadsheet format, a convenient cross-tab query to display the results of SQL queries. This wizard, like most of the others, prompts you with questions as a brief series of steps. All you need to do is specify the databases, tables, and fields that you want to appear in your Cross-Tab query. You can save any Cross-Tab query and later open and modify it (like any other query) using the Visual FoxPro Query Designer. Using the wizard, you can select Save and Run Cross-Tab Queries and the wizard will conveniently display results in a Browse window.

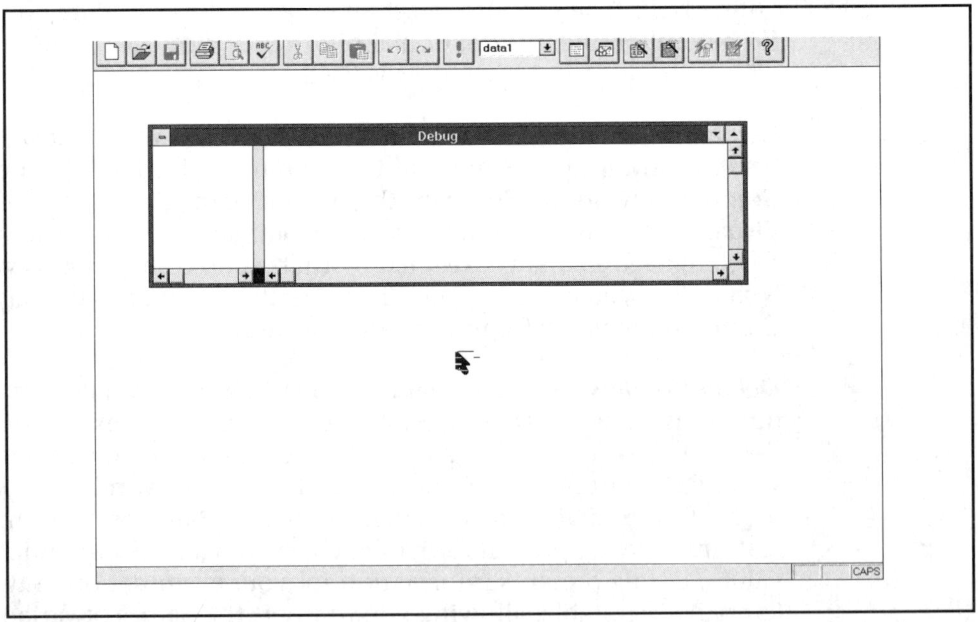

Debug window
Figure 1-10.

Form Wizard The Visual FoxPro Form Wizard allows you to visually and easily create custom Visual FoxPro forms using multiple data tables. The wizard prompts you with simple questions as a brief series of steps in which you specify the tables and fields you want to use in creating Visual FoxPro controls that will bring your form to life. The size of forms generated by the Form Wizard is variable. After saving a form created in the Form Wizard, you can open and modify it in the Form Designer at any time. See Chapter 7 for a thorough treatment of this designer.

One-To-Many Form Wizard This wizard is very similar to the Form Wizard except that it creates Visual FoxPro forms using two related data tables. After you save the form with the wizard, you can open and modify it like any other form in the Form Designer.

Graph Wizard Using Microsoft Graph, the Graph Wizard allows you to create graphs from data contained in any Visual FoxPro data table. The wizard prompts you with simple questions as a brief series of steps in which you specify tables and fields that you need to display in your graphs. This wizard is not fast, so with larger tables it will take the wizard noticeably longer to process your graph. However, the power of this tool is worth the relatively small amount of time you will invest in using it. The wizard can create graphs in a variety of attractive and useful styles. Picture buttons facilitate easily choosing a style that meets your application's needs.

Group/Total Report Wizard The Group/Total Report Wizard allows you to easily create Visual FoxPro summary reports. This wizard prompts you with a series of simple questions and automatically creates the expressions that determine how your data is to be grouped on the report. The wizard can very effectively help you to use data grouping to categorize and sort information, making it easier to read and understand. After you save a report generated by this wizard, you can later open and modify it in the Report Designer as easily as any other report.

Import Wizard The Visual FoxPro Import Wizard greatly simplifies importing virtually any data from other file formats into your Visual FoxPro data tables. This wizard prompts you with simple questions as a brief series of steps in which you may specify source files and whether you want to create new files or append the imported data into existing data tables. After importing data into a Visual FoxPro table, you can view it by opening the table and browsing it.

Label Wizard The Label Wizard allows you to create labels from a Visual FoxPro data table using a generous selection of provided standard label types. After you save a label created by the wizard, you can open and modify it as you would any other label in the Label Designer.

Mail Merge Wizard The Mail Merge Wizard creates a Visual FoxPro data source for a Microsoft Word merged document or an appropriate text file useable by any other word processor. You need to have installed Microsoft Word version 6.0 if you choose to select the Microsoft Word 6.0 option. If you wish to create a text file, the wizard prompts you to assure that the file is saved, such that you can later access the file using another word processor.

Pivot Table Wizard A pivot table is an interactive worksheet tool that facilitates summarizing and analyzing data from existing tables. It allows you to save a pivot table directly in Microsoft Excel or you can add pivot tables as embedded objects in your forms. You are required to install Microsoft Excel with Microsoft Query before you can create a Visual FoxPro pivot table. The pivot table will contain a column for each unique value that exists in the field that you drag to the Column box. Pivot tables comprise a row for each unique value of any field you drag to the wizard's Row box. If you create an Excel pivot table, the wizard will display your pivot table in Microsoft Excel. If you create new form containing an embedded pivot table option, the wizard creates a new form containing your embedded pivot table and opens it in the Form Designer.

Query Wizard The Query Wizard creates SQL queries in which you can specify databases, tables, and fields that you want to include in a query. You can select fields from multiple tables and views. After you save queries created using the wizard, you can later open and modify them as you can any query in the Query Designer. See Chapter 20 for a thorough treatment of this designer.

Remote View Wizard The Remote View Wizard creates views using remote ODBC data in which you can specify databases, tables, and fields required in your view. After you save remote views, you can later open and modify them in the View Designer, as with any other view.

Report Wizard The Report Wizard creates reports using a single table. After you save a report, you can open it in the Report Designer and modify it as in any other report. See Chapter 9 for a thorough treatment of this designer.

Table Wizard The Table Wizard creates tables based on Visual FoxPro table structures. With this wizard, you can select a table that fits your application from a list of sample tables. You can create customized table structures and fields as the wizard guides you through the process. At a later time, after the wizard has saved a table, you can modify it using the Table Designer. If one or more databases are open when you run the wizard, it automatically adds the new table to the current database. If no databases are open, the wizard creates a free table. See Chapter 6 for a thorough treatment of this designer.

Visual FoxPro Builders

Visual FoxPro Builders are convenient, easy-to-use tools that simplify creating and modifying forms and controls. Each builder comprises a set of tabs allowing you to access and set the properties of selected objects. Builders are for forms, many form controls, formatting controls, and for establishing referential integrity within database tables. Figure 1-11 shows an example of the often used Combo Box Builder. Other Visual FoxPro Builders are

- Command Group Builder
- Edit Box Builder
- Form Builder
- Grid Builder
- Option Group Builder
- Text Box Builder
- AutoFormat Builder
- Referential Integrity Builder

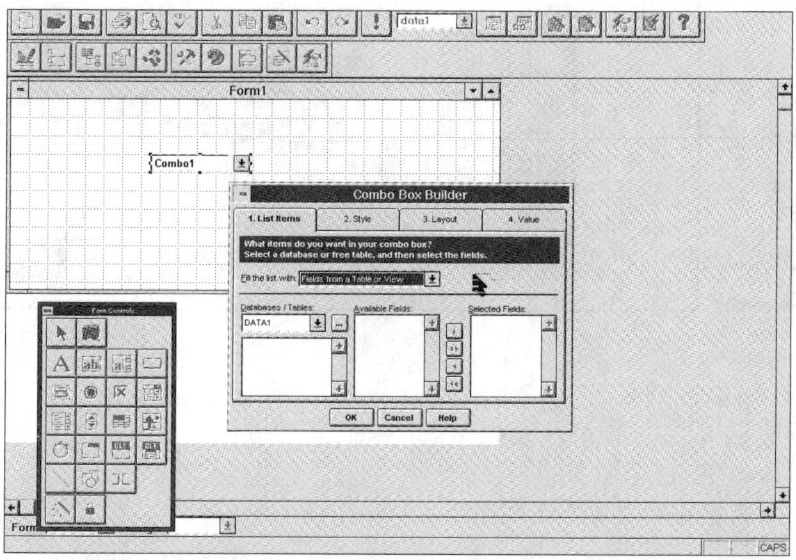

Combo Box Builder
Figure 1-11.

Much like Visual FoxPro wizards, builders are convenient, fast, and effective. The builder asks a series of questions about the control you are adding to your form or modifying. It then automatically sets the control's properties to change or modify its functionality as you specify. For example, if you add a new text box to a form, the builder asks you to specify which style of text box you prefer and which table's field it will display. Figure 1-12 shows an example of the Text Box Builder.

After you save a data table, you can later open it in the Table Designer and modify its structure as with any other table. New tools and methods empower you to produce applications heretofore beyond any reasonable expectation. The dramatic and exciting improvements we are about to explore arise directly from implementation of the concepts of object-oriented programming and its handmaiden, event-driven programming.

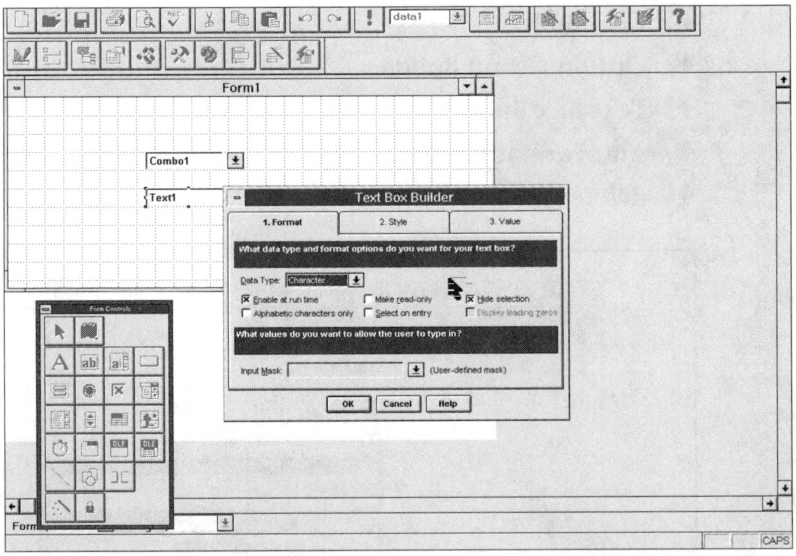

Text Box Builder
Figure 1-12.

2

Programming with Class: A Painless Introduction to Object-Oriented Programming

This chapter introduces essential principles programmers need to know before using Visual FoxPro. When you understand these principles and grasp the enormous benefits they deliver, you will know why Visual FoxPro and virtually all other important development platforms are shifting to object orientation.

What is Object Orientation?

Broadly speaking, the primary difference between procedural programming and object-oriented programming is that procedural programming requires the programmer to fit the real-world problem to the programming language. Object-oriented programming attempts to fit the programming environment to the real-world problem.

Object orientation refocuses the programmer's vision from how a programming language works to object models that perform programmatic functions. Rather than focusing on how each piece of program code interacts with the rest of the program and with the system, object-oriented programmers focus on creating objects that model real-world problems that the program needs to solve. Visual FoxPro objects are self-contained models which encapsulate data that represents the real-world problem, *plus* the programmatic functionality the objects need to manipulate data effectively and efficiently.

As in procedural programming, object-oriented programming involves both analysis and design. Analysis, the first step in developing *any* program, focuses on the real-world problems and how best to model them. Design focuses on defining objects that represent, or map, the real-world problems, as well as how objects relate to each other and to the system. As a practical matter, the disciplines of analysis and design always overlap. Most programmers perform both analysis and design as a simultaneous, somewhat blurred process. However, all too often this approach gives analysis the short shrift and, as an inevitable consequence, programmers and their programs suffer and sometimes fail.

Visual FoxPro's Shift to Object Orientation

Visual FoxPro moves familiar, often arduous, procedural coding chores from the programmer's domain into a largely invisible underlying systemic process. This work, better managed by a computer anyway, ranges in pleasantness from a mild case of hives to oral surgery. By relieving developers and programmers of unnecessary busywork, Visual FoxPro promotes greater programming efficiency and enhanced productivity. In the bargain, programmers acquire a new array of extraordinary tools and features that stagger the imagination. With Visual FoxPro's shift to object orientation, Microsoft relegates procedural programming, with all its warts and excess baggage, to antiquity.

You can approach Visual FoxPro as if it were an entirely new application that just happens to recognize the FoxPro Xbase language, because that's what it is. Visual FoxPro's object-oriented approach is no more a mere extension of the FoxPro language than space travel is an extension of the oxcart. In fact, platforms that have already moved to the object-oriented model recognize many different languages, including BASIC. Successful new implementations such as Visual FoxPro are appearing almost daily.

If you are a FoxPro or Xbase programmer, when you move to Visual FoxPro, you do not lose any of your equity in the Xbase language. It is still alive and well, embedded within Visual FoxPro. However, instead of being the *whole thing*, the familiar FoxPro Xbase language is now only part of a much bigger, more powerful, and easier-to-use environment. Knowing FoxPro or any Xbase language gives you a head start on learning Visual FoxPro. On the other hand, if you don't already know FoxPro or another Xbase language, learning it in the Visual FoxPro environment will be much easier than ever before.

Before launching into the nuts and bolts of putting Visual FoxPro's greatly enriched environment to work, take some time to explore its new features and concepts. In this chapter you will become familiar with:

- Classes
- Subclasses
- Inheritance
- Objects
- Containers
- Controls
- Events

You will also learn the fundamental differences between Visual FoxPro's object-oriented, event-driven infrastructure and the procedural programming strategy of previous FoxPro incarnations.

By the end of this chapter, you should be familiar with Visual FoxPro's object-oriented environment and understand its basic tools. Be mindful that the material in this chapter is the key to effectively using Visual FoxPro's powerful new capabilities. If it is still unclear to you at the end of this chapter, review the discussions of classes, inheritance, and objects.

Why Visual FoxPro Shifted to Object Orientation

Why would Microsoft advance another new programming approach when we seem already to have more than enough? Shifting gears to a new language or programming environment every few years has stressed and irritated programmers almost to distraction. Sometimes, as in the case of C, programming went the right way; and sometimes, as in the case of Prolog, it went the wrong way and programmers had to backtrack. Yet there can be no doubt that the present trend toward object-oriented programming and away from procedural programming is right. In this chapter, you will discover why Visual FoxPro's object-oriented strategy is the only way to go in the mid-1990s; in fact, it brings so many benefits that we cannot reasonably take any other direction.

Few of us could now endure the applications we thought were so marvelous only ten years ago. Even running at the Mach speeds of today's computing hardware, those programs just cannot measure up to the performance we now take for granted. But computing as we know it today did not arise as a product *only* of advancing hardware technology. This current crop of elegant applications deliver higher performance in part because computer hardware is faster and has more memory. However, the greatest gains have arisen from new programming strategies that leverage this increased computing power into a great deal more than just raw speed. Two driving forces, hardware performance and systems strategy, are inexorably linked—each feeding on the other's growth and success to deliver extraordinarily powerful performance. A communion of cooperative endeavors such as this, yielding results far exceeding the sum of their individual contributions, is called *synergy*.

Object-oriented programming and, by extension, Visual FoxPro are examples of synergistically advancing new strategies and programmatic models that leverage increased computing power into explosive advances in the realm of user productivity. Conversely, these same expanding programmatic resources feed back into the hardware design process and yield even higher-performance computers.

Ultimately, the major benefit for programmers and application developers is the disappearance of programming tedium and drudgery into the background of internal, and hidden, computer processes. This is the answer to the question, "Why object-oriented programming?"

What Is Object-Oriented Programming?

Despite its ponderous moniker, object-oriented programming is a stunningly elegant and successful paradigm that programmers never grow weary of using. If computer science were a religion, Bjarne Soustrup surely would be one of its saints, and Bell Laboratories its holy grail. Although more suitable designations beg to embellish Bell Lab's famous creation, we may be destined to choke on that ungainly nine-syllable monster for a long time.

However, for a moment let's be bold and consider one promising and very appropriate alternative: class. This pleasantly succinct word brings appropriately to mind an image of elegance. And wouldn't you know: class is exactly what object-oriented programming and Visual FoxPro are all about. Their fundamental premise, as you soon shall see, is nothing less than class!

Historical Perspective

Although not everyone has noticed, object-oriented programming is already the dominant programmatic giant of the 1990s, with no serious challengers in sight. Only a few years ago, computing power sufficient to support this elegant concept simply was not available in the desktop computing world. What happened during the past few decades to produce today's giant and the hardware needed to implement it?

With the development of C and Pascal, the 1970s ushered in a new approach and the era of *structured* programming. This strategy went a long way toward organizing the chaotic spaghetti programming legacy of FORTRAN, BASIC, and COBOL. C became the dominant structured programming language of the 1980s and brought with it new levels of order, discipline, and productivity.

The 1980s saw the emergence of another, even more elegant, vision: object-oriented programming. Today, C++, with its object-oriented extensions, dominates the programming scene. Most emerging major systems and applications, such as Visual FoxPro, are written in C++ and share its substantial benefits.

However, *procedural* programming dominated the mainstream for almost 50 years, since the 1930s when Alan Turing advanced the conceptual archetype of modern computing strategy. His concept, called Turing's Machine, was a purely procedural model.

Later, in the 1940s and 1950s, John VonNeumann designed the first successful *functional* computer model, which we still use today in all but the most exotic computing machines. His concept, called *VonNeumann architecture*, is based largely, if not entirely, upon Turing's procedural model. Thus, procedural programming became so firmly established at the very birth of modern computing that it would endure, unchallenged, for half a century.

After a half-century of dominance, the procedural paradigm is so deeply ingrained in our creative process that other approaches seem unnatural and even mind-bending. Most programs in existence today are structured procedural programs because almost all programming during the past fifty years has been procedural. We have a name for outmoded programs that are still in use: We call them *legacy programs*. The overwhelming majority of programs now in everyday use all over the world are in this category.

However, another factor may explain why procedural programming seems more natural to most people than the newer, more holistic, object-oriented approach. Traditional thinking processes, especially in our Western culture, are procedural, sequential, and algorithmic. This may be in part our heritage from the Golden Age in Greece, where Western philosophy emerged and where the predominant reasoning strategies of the Western world were born out of Aristotle's syllogism—which is *the* prototype procedural program. In a deeper sense, it may be simply the way most people's conscious minds work. Object-oriented programming is more representative of the way the inner mind seems to function.

Note: Within the past three decades a growing number of respectable scientists and mathematicians are advancing a strong case that bivalent Aristotelian logic may be the Achilles' heel of modern mathematics and physics. Their multivalent alternative: Fuzzy Logic. Though still extremely controversial, it is gaining momentum among scientists and engineers around the world, especially in Japanese industry where it is enormously successful in a wide range of applications from high-speed transit systems to video camcorders.

For these reasons, people now need to prepare for a paradigm shift. The world you are about to enter may at first seem strange, but it will be worth a little struggle. It advances another, *perhaps better,* way of seeing things and developing computer programs.

Visual FoxPro Classes, Objects, and Events

Visual FoxPro's object-oriented design and object-oriented programming are a substantial departure from traditional procedural programming. Instead of focusing on the flow of program code from the beginning of a program to its end, object orientation focuses on *objects* and, as we discuss later in this chapter, *events.*

Classes and Objects

Objects are the fundamental building blocks of Visual FoxPro. Object modules are self-contained program elements that have both internal private functionality accessible only by the object and external public functionality accessible by the program.

Visual FoxPro offers an elegant mechanism for creating reusable code packages. These packages, or *classes,* serve as blueprints for creating and propagating objects. Properly understood and used, Visual FoxPro classes afford programmers the means to create and propagate new objects with great simplicity and near-flawless precision.

Understanding Classes

Through the concept of *classes,* object-orientation brings an entirely new dimension to program clarity, reliability, and ease of maintenance. Class is the fundamental building block of Visual FoxPro. Class defines all the properties, events, and methods that determine how an object looks and behaves. **Unlike procedural programming, which treats data and algorithms as separate entities, object-oriented programming emphasizes the integration of data with the operations performed on that data**. Whereas procedural programs try to fit the problem to the programming language, object-oriented programs, through the concept of classes, attempt to match the program environment to the structure of the problem. As a Visual FoxPro programmer, your principal objective is to design classes comprising properties and methods that accurately embrace program objectives.

Class is Visual FoxPro's abstract blueprint that specifies properties and methods that comprise real objects. These ready-made blueprints simplify the creation of objects because each new object automatically inherits the entire definition embodied in its base class.

Objects are sometimes called *instances* of their base class, and programmers frequently speak of *instantation* when creating objects because they are creating a real instance of an abstract class blueprint. Consider a simple and familiar example of instantation. Class Automobile can define a four-wheeled vehicle. Object Ford can then be a real instance (or instantation) of class Automobile.

The important distinction you need to understand is that *classes* are abstract blueprints or definitions from which objects are created. *Objects* are real programmatic entities or instances of their class definitions.

Tip: Understanding classes and objects is absolutely essential to harnessing the power of Visual FoxPro. Remember: Because classes are abstract, they exist in your source code, but not in any run-time programmatic sense. Classes are a programming tool that enable you effortlessly to create the objects that *do* exist in the run-time world.

Class abstraction lets you ignore the inner complexities of familiar objects, thus allowing you to focus only on those features you need to use. When you drive an automobile, for example, you don't need to know how the engine and transmission work. You can drive safely and efficiently while the automobile's inner complexity remains hidden. You need neither to see it, nor even be aware that it exists.

Object-oriented programming affords the same benefit, because class definitions give you the option of declaring functions as either *private* (hidden) or *public* (visible). Thus, the internal functionality users do not need to access directly can be kept invisible and protected.

Because object-oriented programming makes it very convenient to incorporate existing classes into new programs, your investment in designing robust, reliable classes pays long-term dividends. Programmers can easily plug these tried and tested classes into future applications to simplify development and increase reliability. Visual FoxPro contains a variety of class libraries that include almost every class needed for such tasks as creating fully functional Windows programs, managing data, and performing I/O operations.

Leveraging Class Power with Subclasses

Creating a new class can be, and usually is, amazingly simple: Start with the definition of an existing class whose object is similar to what you need, then customize this definition to create a new *subclass*. Subclasses relieve you of tedious, repetitive coding and improve reliability through *inheritance:* Each new subclass automatically inherits all the features and functionality of its base class, plus any extended controls and features you add. For example, from the base class of a basic automobile, you can create an endless variety of cars that inherit all the functionality of the basic automobile plus the extended functionality you elect to encapsulate in each subclass. Beginning with the base class Automobile, you can create convertibles, Indy racers, sports cars, motor homes, and any other subclass you can imagine. Figure 2-1 illustrates the concept of subclasses.

Visual FoxPro subclass inheritance not only simplifies the creation of new classes and objects, it enables much easier program maintenance. For example, if new legislation requires anti-lock brakes on all cars, you can simply modify your base class Automobile to incorporate anti-lock brakes. All derivative subclasses automatically inherit anti-lock brakes along with all the methods and properties designed into the base class modification incorporating anti-lock brakes. Figure 2-2 illustrates the concept of inheritance.

Inheritance also simplifies debugging. In object-oriented programming, nearly all bugs occur in class definitions. With inheritance, when programmers debug their applications, modifications automatically propagate to all subclasses based upon the bug-infested class. This feature can greatly reduce your workload and at the same time increase program reliability.

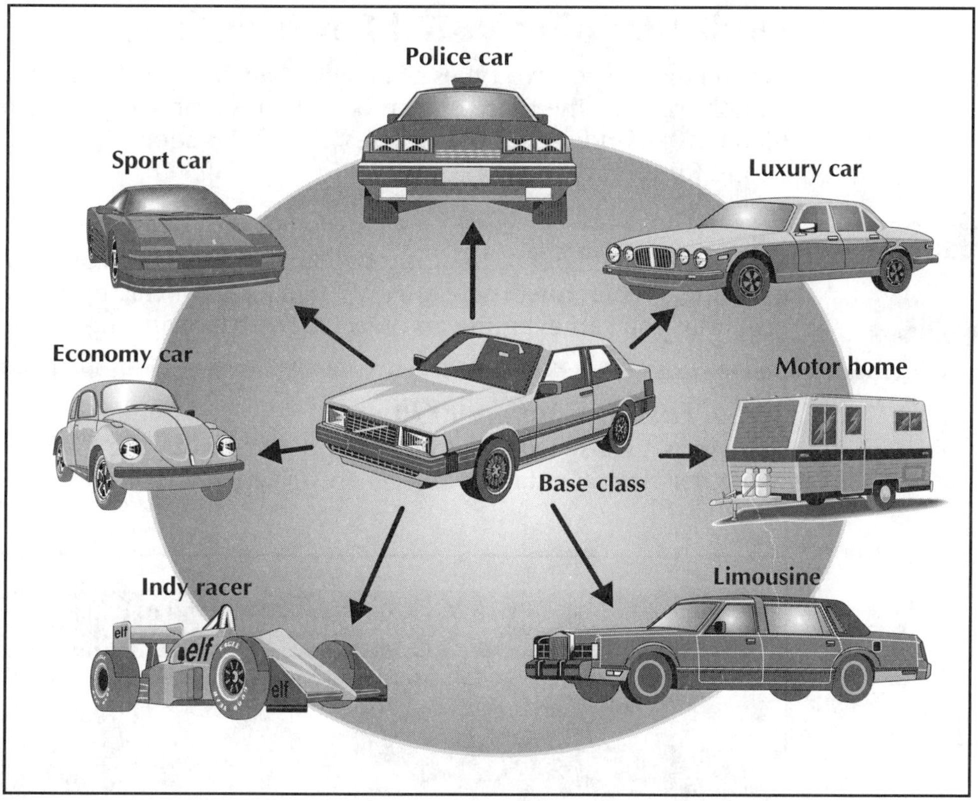

From the base class, you can create subclasses
Figure 2-1.

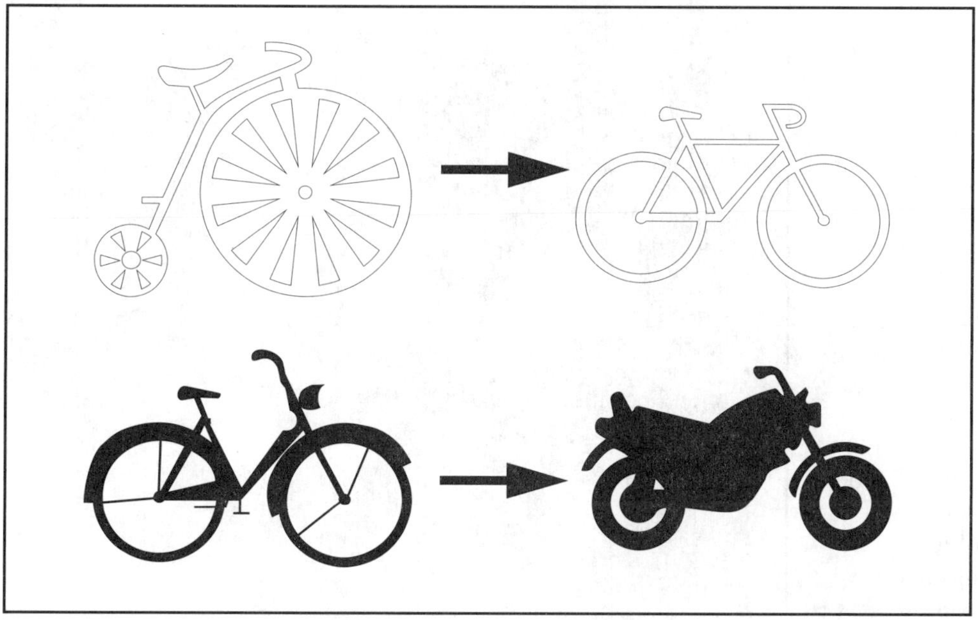

Inheritance simplifies code maintenance
Figure 2-2.

Understanding Visual FoxPro Objects

Visual FoxPro uses two types of objects: *containers* and *controls*. In this section we examine these objects and their relationship to Visual FoxPro's hierarchy of underlying base classes. Figure 2-3 shows the hierarchy of base classes for each type of object.

Tip: Visual FoxPro has only two kinds of objects: controls and containers. Therefore, there are only two kinds of classes. Remember: The only way you can examine an object is by first examining base class.

Visual FoxPro Container Objects

Containers are a special type of object derived from the Visual FoxPro container class. Container objects are designed to contain other objects as

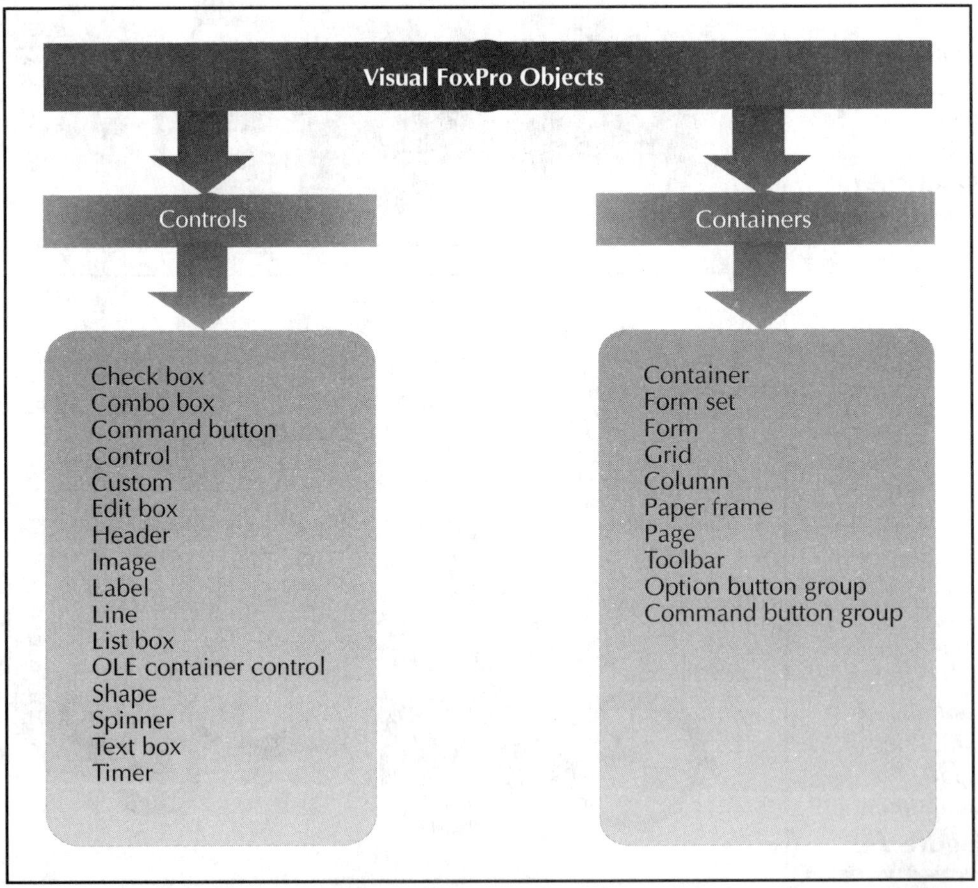

Hierarchy of Visual FoxPro base classes and their relationship to control and container objects

Figure 2-3.

shown in Table 1. They can contain other container objects, and they can also contain control objects. Figure 2-3 lists the available container objects. These container objects will be familiar to experienced Windows users, although identifying them as container objects may be unfamiliar. Table 2-1 lists the contents of each container object.

Visual FoxPro Control Objects

Controls are objects derived from the control class. These objects can be manipulated at design time or at run time; but unlike containers, the elements that make up controls cannot be accessed or modified individually. They are, of necessity, more securely encapsulated than containers. For this reason, controls are less flexible than containers. Figure 2-3 lists the available control objects. Again, many of these controls will be familiar to experienced Windows users.

Visual FoxPro control objects are the principal means of user interaction with programs. By moving, dragging, and clicking appropriate controls on Visual FoxPro forms, users manipulate data and execute the programmatic tasks embedded in the control objects.

Users can install two types of controls in Visual FoxPro forms: controls that are bound to data in tables and controls that are not bound. When users manipulate bound controls, they are limited either to selecting or storing data in a data source, which can be a table field, cursor field, or variable. Users can bind an object to Visual FoxPro data by setting the object's ControlSource property.

Container	Contents
Container	Any controls
Form set	Forms and toolbars
Form	Page frames, any controls, containers
Grid	Grid columns
Column	Column headers, form sets, grid columns, toolbars, and any objects except forms
Paper frame	Pages
Page	Any controls and containers
Toolbar	Any controls and page frames
Option button group	Option buttons
Command button group	Command buttons
Control	Any controls

Contents of Each Visual FoxPro Container
Table 2-1.

If the user does not set a control's ControlSource property, a value the user chooses is stored only as a property setting. The value is not saved or stored beyond the lifetime of the control.

Visual FoxPro controls are flexible and easy to use. However, be sure to use a consistent approach when selecting and using controls. Users will find your applications easier to use and understand if you design controls to respond in a logical and predictable manner.

The functionality you need to build into your programs will usually fall into one or more of the following categories:

- Accepting input that is not predetermined
- Accepting input that is predefined
- Accepting input in a specified range
- Providing users with the means to perform specific actions
- Performing actions at specified intervals
- Responding to events

Tip: Remember that the Visual FoxPro libraries provide hundreds of ready-to-use objects—all you need to begin designing powerful Visual FoxPro applications.

Visual FoxPro Events

The Visual FoxPro event model enables programmers to design true modeless operation into their applications. Simply stated, modeless operation makes it possible, for example, to coordinate multiple forms automatically and to run multiple instances of a form simultaneously.

Note: A window or form is modeless if the user does not have to close it before switching to another form or window. Conversely, a window or form is modal if the user is required to close it before switching to another one.

Visual FoxPro's event handling system automatically triggers event code in response to, among other things, a user's action. For example, Visual FoxPro automatically processes code written for a click event whenever a user clicks a control. All you have to do is tell Visual FoxPro, *through the control object's class definition*, what you want to happen when that control is clicked, and then it will happen without your having to write any additional code. You can also use objects that trigger event code in response to system events, such as with timer controls.

Most Visual FoxPro objects recognize the base events shown in Table 2-2.

Visual FoxPro's Event-Driven Programming

Only the recent proliferation of high-performance computers and the object-oriented paradigm made the next step in programming, Visual FoxPro's event-driven strategy, possible *and necessary*. By relying upon events instead of procedures to direct a program's focus, programmers and developers can create truly modeless operations.

With event-driven programming, you don't have to manage everything the computer is doing. Mainly, you only have to worry about recognizing and

Event	When triggered
Load	When a form or formset is loaded into memory
Unload	When a form or formset is released from memory
Init	When an object is created
Destroy	When an object is destroyed
Click	When the user clicks an object using the primary mouse button
DblClick	When the user double-clicks an object using the primary mouse button
RightClick	When the user clicks an object using the secondary mouse button
GotFocus	When the object receives the focus either by user action, such as a button click, or program code using the SetFocus method
LostFocus	When the object loses the focus either by user action, such as a button click, or program code using the SetFocus method
KeyPress	When the user presses and releases a key
MouseDown	When the user presses a mouse button while the mouse is over an object
MouseUp	When the user releases a mouse button while the mouse is over an object
InteractiveChange	When an object's value is changed interactively
ProgrammaticChange	When an object's value is changed by program action

Visual FoxPro Core Events
Table 2-2.

handling events; such as mouse movement, serial I/O, and disk I/O. The systemic infrastructure invisibly maintains control of the computer, watches for the events you define, and responds according to the event handlers you write and embed in Visual FoxPro objects.

Your Visual FoxPro programs will manage some activities, such as event response, very differently than earlier versions of FoxPro, and some of your most dreaded programming travail will vanish in the wake of your new event-driven paradigm. In Chapter 5 you will learn more about the nature and anatomy of Visual FoxPro events.

3

Data Independence

Data is the essence of most business programming, the life-blood of business. Who a company's customers are is data. How much inventory a company has and where it is located is data, as is the cost of the inventory and what it should sell for. The computer age has ushered in the data age, and people now take the instant availability of data for granted.

Storing and sifting data is the task that Visual FoxPro is designed to perform. Database programmers and administrators have seen that as the access to data expands, old methods of handling this data become obsolete. Not long ago, every phone call had to be manually connected by one or more operators sitting at telephone company switchboards. Can you imagine what it would take to place all phone calls now using this method? Similarly, as databases have expanded, the old means of accessing them no longer work. Consider how the ability to store data has increased the demands to access this data.

Companies first automated their invoicing, and before long they had huge databases containing customer, contact, invoice, payment, inventory, warehouse, and supplier records. Then companies put all this information on a network. Now not only the accounting department, but the purchasing, shipping, sales, and manufacturing departments are online. Often, the data tools that worked fine for a hundred customers and a thousand inventory items do not work well for thousands of customers and tens of thousands of items. Data access slows, and response times grow from annoying to infuriating. Some users even resort to that old technology—the pencil and paper.

Into this fray have come the database servers. Products such as those from Oracle and Sybase make the case for concentrating database power in the server and letting users, the clients, simply access it. Instead of every user's computer needing the power to perform the most complex database tasks, user workstations can be tailored to perform simpler display and data entry operations.

Until recently, however, switching to a more attractive database server has meant reinventing the programs used on the server from scratch. In addition, the programs needed to be redebugged and the users retrained. This overhead has been an insurmountable obstacle for many companies.

Visual FoxPro addresses this challenge with its open database connectivity (ODBC) drivers. Figure 3-1 shows how users can connect to virtually any data source from Visual FoxPro using the standard FoxPro data manipulation language.

Overview

Only a few years ago, after you had selected your compiler, libraries, and interactive tools, you were left with little choice in data sources; you had to run what would work with your other tools, and that was that. If you needed to combine data on an Oracle server with FoxPro data, you had few, if any, choices. Usually, you used a utility to download the relevant Oracle data, then put it into a FoxPro (DBF) table, and then work on it. The problems

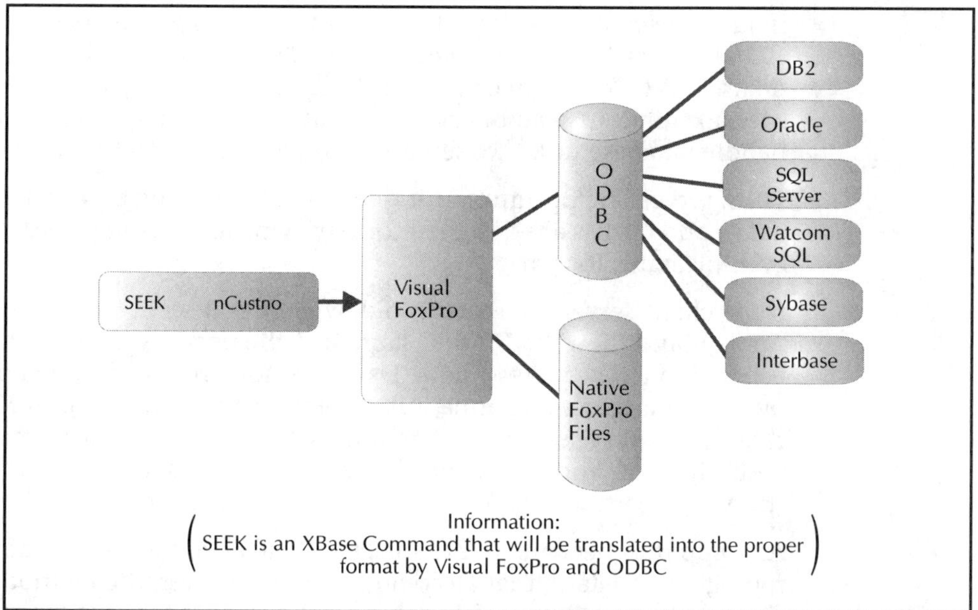

Open database connectivity lets you connect to different data sources with a common language
Figure 3-1.

3

with this method are several: You do not operate on live data but only on a snapshot of the data at the time it was downloaded. This method can also be quite slow; when you want some simple information, downloading an entire table is cumbersome. In addition, you have to learn another data manipulation language, know the Xbase syntax for working with the Xbase standard, DBF data tables, and know the SQL syntax to get the Oracle data.

With Visual FoxPro, not only can you pick your data source, but you can mix multiple sources to suit your needs. You can use some data from a departmental Oracle server, some from the corporate mainframe running IBM's DB2, and some from a local DBF file; with Visual FoxPro it's simple. Best of all, you can access these data sources with the same data manipulation language. Older versions of FoxPro and dBASE supported SQL statements but operated on a DBF-style file. These provided the power of SQL *statements* but not the power of SQL *servers*.

What Is the Client/Server Model?

The *client/server* model is both a new way to solve data access problems and a model that has been in use since the early days of computing. The first computers all used the client/server approach, though the term itself wasn't used. The server was the mainframe, and the teletype terminals or punched-card readers were the clients.

In fact. the central notion of the client/server model is spelled out in the 1776 book *An Inquiry into the Nature and Causes of the Wealth of Nations* by Adam Smith. The key concept of the model is simply the division of labor, or specialization: instead of each workstation needing the processing power to handle database tasks, let servers be made optimal to that task.

Thus, servers are optimized for disk activity—sorting and managing data—and clients are designed for retrieving and displaying data in a usable, even pleasant, format.

If the client/server approach is old, why does it seem like a new idea? The Apple II and then the IBM PC launched the personal computing age and ushered in a new view of data. Data was not a report dropped on your desk by the management information systems department. It was live information that you could use to run a "what if" with Lotus 1-2-3, print mailing labels with dBASE II, and create form letters with Wordstar. Users broke free from the MIS department, and the client/server approach declined.

As computers became ubiquitous, the local area network became the repository of data so that all could share it. However, the methods for accessing data stored on a personal computer are not ideal for accessing data stored on a network. This problem has been masked by faster network protocols, software, and hardware, but data needs have grown even faster. Thus, the client/server model is making a comeback.

Visual FoxPro and the Client/Server Model

The term "client/server" is used in several ways, but in this book, it refers to a database client and server arrangement. In this model, the client requests data, such as a list of all the customers in California, from the server. The client does not need to know how the data is stored or retrieved; it simply needs to know how to ask for it. The server, on the other hand, does not need to know how the information will be used; it just needs to know how to get it and send it to the client. The power of this arrangement is that you can tailor the hardware to meet the different needs of clients and servers.

An alternative to the client/server approach is a peer arrangement, where the file server is just a repository of data, and each workstation accesses the data directly. With this arrangement, however, to speed up your queries and transactions you need to upgrade each workstation. With the client/server model, you can simply upgrade the database server. Even old hardware can provide speedy access because it does not directly access the data but relies on the server to do so.

A few examples will help clarify the use and benefits of the client/server model.

Example of Using a Database Server to Filter Data

The Xbase language, which includes Visual FoxPro, has a command that is little used today: SET FILTER. This command is very useful, but it is slow. FoxPro's Rushmore technology has increased its speed somewhat, but not enough. Running a command such as

```
SET FILTER TO BALANCE > 0
```

can bring your application to its knees, and maybe your network, too.

Note: The command SET FILTER TO affects a data table. It retrieves only the records that meet the specified condition (BALANCE > 0). Because each record must be examined for the condition, it can be very sluggish if the table is large or the condition excludes a large percentage of the records. If the records are on a network, each one has to be passed over the wire to the workstation, creating a lot of traffic and slowing other traffic. The procedure is like searching a candy bin for only the red jellybeans; if the bin has a lot of candy, or if there are few red jellybeans, your search for each one can be slow.

The slow operation of this command is unfortunate because with this single command you can exclude records that you don't want..

If you use a database server, however, you can simply issue the command to request the records, and instead of sending each record along the network for the workstation to examine, the server searches the database and retrieves the correct records for you. The only records sent over the network are the ones that meet the specified conditions. The server thus saves network resources and reduces the need to upgrade to the latest, speediest personal computers. Using the server also frees the workstation, or client, from having to know the details of how the data is stored, processed, and shared.

Example Applying the Client/Server Model to Auto Repair

To underscore the principles of the client/server model, here is one more example. One day you notice an ominous pool of fluid under your car, so you call your mechanic, who calls a towing company to dispatch a tow truck for your car. Later you get the news: your car needs a new water pump, the garage will order one, and you will have your car back that afternoon. Sure enough, later that same day you get your car back, new water pump in place and no more leaks, and your checkbook one check lighter. Figure 3-2 illustrates this transaction.

Getting your car fixed
Figure 3-2.

Now look at this example in client/server, or division of labor, terms. The first client/server transaction is from you to your mechanic when you call to say that your car needs to be repaired. In the second transaction, the mechanic is a client asking the towing company, the server, to bring your car to the shop. Then the original server, the mechanic, applies expertise to the problem to determine that the water pump is broken and needs to be replaced.

In the third transaction, the mechanic, originally the server, again acts as a client, calling the parts shop and asking for a new water pump. Then the mechanic again applies expertise to replace the ailing pump and the lost fluid. Finally, the original server, the mechanic, reports back to you, the client, that the requested task has been successfully completed. Figure 3-3 shows this same transaction in client/server form.

Notice the leverage you applied to solve your problem. You used the resources of three servers—the mechanic, tow truck driver, and parts person—by simply issuing a request to fix your car. You didn't need to know a socket from a sledge hammer. You didn't need to know how to operate a tow truck. You didn't need to know how to read a parts catalog or find a part in the warehouse.

Benefits of Visual FoxPro's Data Independence

The use of database servers frees the FoxPro environment from the default Xbase data file format, providing several key advantages. In particular, Visual FoxPro can take advantage of the benefits of scalability, referential integrity, and security.

Scalability and security address issues of databases that are growing in size or use. Referential integrity is a tool for ensuring that your databases remain free of improper records.

Scalability

By providing, as much as possible, a standard interface for all data sources, you can scale your data sources to suit your needs. For instance, during development you may want to run your program using a data subset stored in FoxPro format. With this operation, you can check your programs against sample data without affecting the real, or live, data.

When you deploy your application, you may want to use a Microsoft SQL server or a mainframe running IBM's DB2. With few, if any, changes to your code, you just call a different driver. Thus, you can run database tasks against live data on a SQL server using native Xbase commands such as SKIP and SEEK.

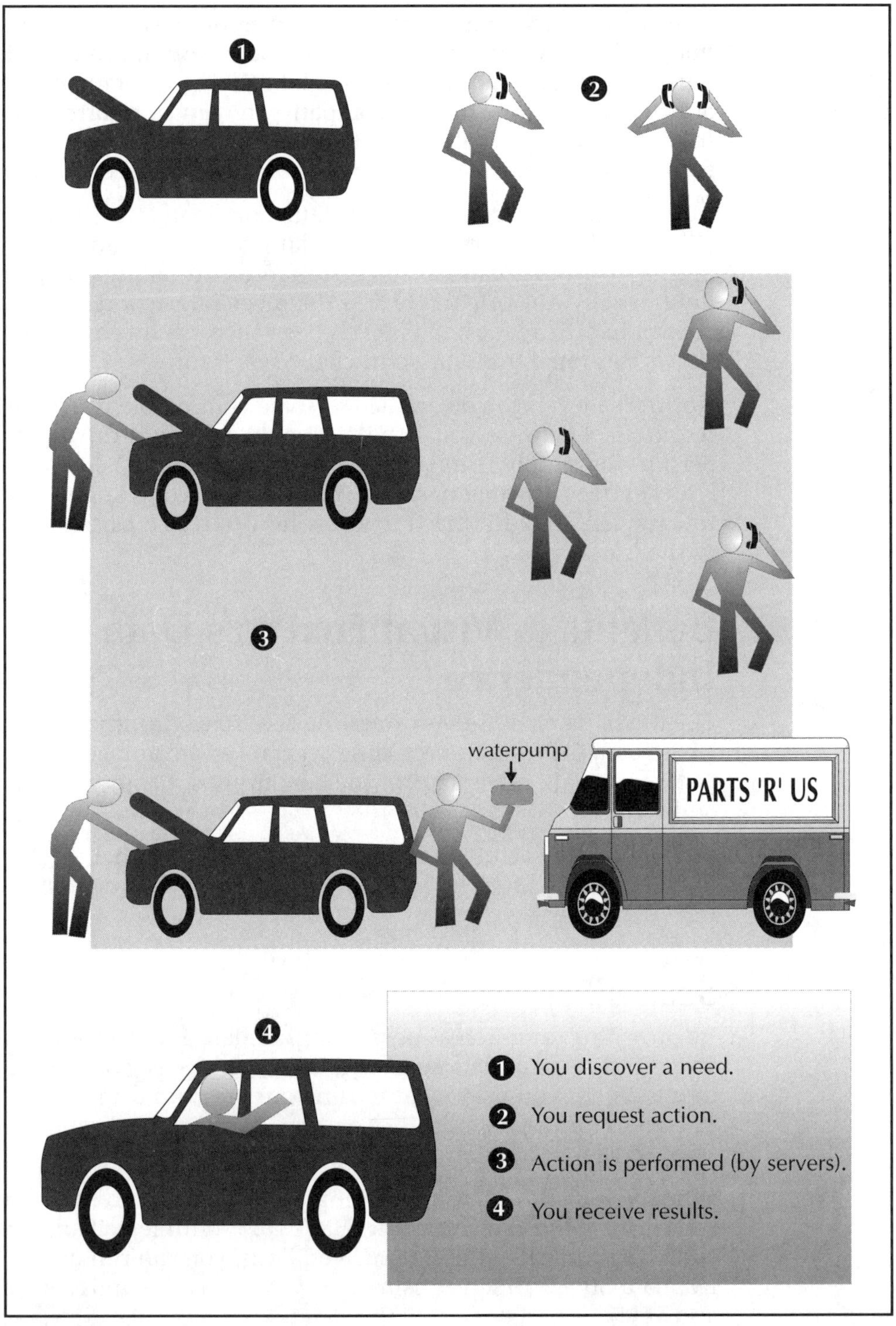

Getting your car fixed client/server style
Figure 3-3.

This is scalability, the power to tailor your data servers to fit your needs. As your data processing needs grow you only need to beef up your servers to handle the load. Servers can range from DOS based to mainframe hosted. Scalability leaves room for growth. If your requirements start small, as they may when your company is new, you can use the native Visual FoxPro format. As your needs grow with your business, you can move to a database server with little effort. In fact, Visual FoxPro Professional comes with a wizard that makes migration to Microsoft's SQL server simple. Just answer the questions, and the wizard converts your data to the SQL server format. Your code, though, remains unchanged.

Security

As an enterprise grows, a lot of confidential information is placed online: for instance, employee records, customer information, and financial data. With traditional PC-based products such as FoxPro, the information is right there in the open, and anyone with access to the file server volume that stores the data can open the files in any number of programs and have a look. Because files are readily available, they also can be easily stolen, and file read permission, which all users need for legitimate access, makes files easy to copy.

The security tools of SQL servers free you from the drudgery of coding security into your program. Using management tools supplied with your server, you can quickly set up and maintain a high level of security. For example, servers such as Oracle's have security built in. Security information is stored right in the database so that even if a person copies data, the user must have the appropriate password to view it.

Servers also control security when the server itself is the only process that has access to the data volume. In this case, users cannot access the raw files—only the server can. This arrangement is analogous to a bank's: You don't go into the vault and get money yourself. Instead, you go to a teller who determines whether you have the appropriate permissions (you are a signatory on the account) and the account contains enough money to cover the check. Then the teller gives you your money. Indeed, because data is the life-blood of many businesses, securing it can be as important as securing money in a bank.

As companies grow, they often overlook the importance of data security. However, as what was a three- or four-person company where everybody knew each other well becomes a company with a hundred employees and regular turnover, the wise organization must be sure that its crucial data resources are secure.

Referential Integrity

Xbase-type tools do not have *referential integrity*. Referential integrity is a way for the database server to enforce relationships in your data. For example, suppose you have a customer table with the usual customer information and a sales representative table with one entry for each salesperson. You want to enforce the following rule: each customer must be assigned to a valid sales representative.

To ensure that this rule is applied, each customer record must include a code that identifies a salesperson in the sales representative table. Before a new customer can be entered, a valid sales representative must be assigned. In addition, before a sales representative can be deleted, all of that person's customers must be reassigned. Referential integrity is a tool for defining these relationships and the proper actions needed to maintain them. If the database handles these rules, you are freed from the grueling task of coding them into your programs. Further, interactive users are protected too. For example, if a user tries to assign an invalid sales representative code in an interactive session, such as in the Visual FoxPro command line, they are warned, and the transaction is not allowed.

SQL Overview

Structured query language, or SQL, stems from a paper published in 1970 by Dr. E. F. Codd, an IBM researcher, on the mathematical properties of a relational database. At the time, the idea of using a common value to relate tables of data was new and in competition with other models for handling data. Since that time, relational database management systems (RDBMS) have won the battle of models. SQL is a language that understands how to relate data in the relational format.

Xbase is, in fact, relational. However, this assertion is sure to generate heated arguments whenever database programmers gather. Data can be related by common values, but the DBMS engine does not know about these relationships and cannot enforce them. Instead, such relationships must be enforced programmatically. In 1985, to counter confusion over the use of the term "relational," Dr. Codd published his 12 rules for a relational database. No current database follows all 12 rules. Adherents of SQL who can spout Codd's rules like the Ten Commandments blanch at the notion that Xbase is relational, but it is argument for argument's sake—Xbase is relational; just don't say so too loudly.

With Visual FoxPro, whether you use Xbase or SQL is up to you. Visual FoxPro's data independence lets you choose which language you use. Are you familiar with Xbase and want to ease slowly into SQL? Fine. Do you prefer to skip SQL altogether, or do you want to bypass Xbase and get right down and wrestle with SQL? Either is fine, too. Data independence in Visual FoxPro is in the grand tradition of freedom; do it whatever way you want.

4

Rapid Application Development

Coming of age in the last few years, rapid application development has struck Visual FoxPro full force. What is rapid application development, how did it develop, and why is it now so important? This chapter discusses these topics as well as the implementation of rapid application development in Visual FoxPro.

With rapid application development, our trilogy of buzzwords (including object orientation and client/server) is now complete. However, the fact that rapid application development is a buzzword should not deter you from recognizing its value. Here, you will learn what it is and what its implementation in Visual FoxPro does for you.

The History of Rapid Application Development

This section presents a brief history of rapid application development, including its relationship to fourth-generation languages (4GLs).

The Early Years

The first digital computers were programmed directly in binary code—that is, using the base-2 system, with digits 1 and 0 (or true and false). The programmer converted programming instructions by hand to binary code and then later converted the computer output—strings of 1s and 0s—back to comprehensibility.

However, even programmers do not find binary code very easy to use. The prosaic number 12, for example, is 1100 in binary format. But computers "think" in binary code, so programmers had to learn it. The first big jump in programmer productivity came with the idea of grouping binary digits into a higher-base number system. A translator was created that converted octal (base 8, numbers 0 to 7) or hexadecimal (base 16, numbers 0 to 9 and letters A to F) values to binary values and then converted the computer's binary output back to octal or hexadecimal format. Thus, the binary code 1100 (the decimal number 12) became the more easily managed 14 in octal code or C in hexadecimal code. Octal and hexadecimal values still were not as familiar as decimal values and confusion was possible, but they were much more convenient than binary values.

Assemblers were the next rapid application development tools. These enabled programmers to use *opcodes*—mnemonics such as MOV for the move instruction and SUB for subtraction—instead of octal or hexadecimal notation. The assembler translated this language—properly called assembly language, not assembler, as it is sometimes called—into the binary codes the computer uses.

Surely the notion of assembly language as a tool for rapid application development will strike a humorous chord in some. However, rapid application development is relative. Assembly language raised programmer productivity several fold; though it seems silly now, it provided rapid application development in its day.

The languages of the BASIC era supplanted assembly language as rapid application development tools, leading to today's object-oriented languages. Interestingly, BASIC returned as a means to rapid application development with Microsoft's Visual BASIC.

Rapid Application Development Now

The ability to visually design program screens and other program elements marks rapid application development today. Until the popularity of graphical user interfaces (GUIs) such as Microsoft's Windows 3*x*, programmers usually coded screens by hand. This process became much more difficult with the advent of graphical interfaces. Higher-resolution displays have dramatically increased the amount of data that a screen can display. Instead of DOS text mode's 25 rows of 80 characters each (2,000 unique positions), today's high-resolution displays can address from 640 pixels by 480 pixels (over 300,000 positions) to 1,600 pixels by 1,280 pixels (over two million positions). Because programmers cannot count on any particular display size, they must make sure that dialog boxes are not too small at the highest resolutions nor too large at the lower resolutions. In addition, the format of a standard Windows application requires much more screen data, frames, title bars, minimize buttons, and so forth than for non-GUI programs.

Visual BASIC brought modern rapid application development tools to the fore, not because BASIC is such a powerful language, though Microsoft has souped it up considerably, but because it offers visual design tools to ease development tasks. It allows programmers to offer user-friendly, and often user-demanded, Windows programs without getting lost in the minutiae of the Windows interface.

Visual FoxPro enters this arena heavily armed with visual design tools—screens, menus, databases, and reports, to name just a few. It adds these on top of the powerful FoxPro data capabilities, thus providing a powerful business programming tool.

4GL

You will see references to fourth-generation languages (4GLs) in discussions of Visual FoxPro and other programs of its ilk. An explanation of 4GL helps illuminate the concept of rapid application development.

Fourth-generation languages have been the coming thing for some time. C and Pascal are considered third-generation languages, BASIC and COBOL are second-generation languages, and machine code and assembly language are first-generation languages.

The goal of fourth-generation languages is to leverage computer power to make programming less wearisome and bug-prone from the programmer's perspective and better and quicker from the user's perspective. Although object orientation is not necessary to fourth-generation languages, the idea of abstraction is central to both. Instead of using a bottom-up approach fostered by a machine-code lineage, fourth-generation languages take a step or two back and look at processes on a higher level. Instead of seeing the pistons and crankshafts of a third-, second-, or first-generation language, 4GLs want programmers to see the engine; that is, 4GLs want programmers to apply their programming talent at a higher level.

Look at the following example, which examines the process of getting ready to go out the door in the morning:

```
Is it raining?
     If so, put rain coat on
Is it snowing?
     If so, put parka on
Is it cool?
    If so, put sweater on
Etc...
Go out
```

Now look at this process from a 4GL perspective:

```
Dress appropriately
Go out
```

The complexity is hidden from view; the person simply must dress appropriately and go out. Fourth-generation languages can be less efficient than previous generations; for instance, a person may live in Florida, but the process will still check to see if it is snowing. This is one reason why fourth-generation languages have only recently taken hold. Until recently, programmers did not have processing power to "waste." They needed to, or felt they needed to, optimize procedures; if a person lives in Florida, a program must not bother to check for snow.

Also, until recently the level of complexity expected in a program was low enough that re-inventing the wheel each time was not too costly. For instance, checking the weather each day and acting accordingly was a simpler process than creating a tool to automate the process. Sometimes it is easier to do a thing in a familiar way than to learn a new, possibly better, way.

The irony is that a fourth-generation language is not a *language* anymore; it is an environment. Visual BASIC is clearly a fourth-generation language, but it is the tools, not the second-generation language, BASIC, that makes it so.

The confusion over the word "language" has caused the adoption of a more precise term: rapid application development.

Visual FoxPro and Rapid Application Development

Visual FoxPro has leapt into rapid application development with both feet. Virtually every aspect of program operation can be designed visually. However, this wasn't always so.

Previous Versions of FoxPro

FoxPro 1.*x*, a DOS-only product, had a limited and unintuitive screen drawing tool. Its banded report writer was a little better. Its language, an Xbase dialect, supported some sophisticated abstraction; that is, a single command accomplished a lot. As a rapid application development tool, however, it left a lot wanting.

FoxPro version 2.*x* made a big move toward the rapid application development concept. With the release of Windows versions 2.5 and 2.6, FoxPro offered screen and report tools that behaved as Windows users expected, helping to overcome the curse of rapid application development: tools that are difficult to use.

Getting Your Feet Wet

The best way to see how Visual FoxPro confronts rapid application development is to jump right in. Look at Figure 4-1, which shows the basic design screen for forms.

This figure shows the visual nature of Visual FoxPro, starting with the blank Form1. The toolbar shows many of the items you can put on your form. For example, to place a text box (like a traditional Xbase SAY/GET, used to display and enter a single data element) on the form, click the icon as shown and then click a location on the form. Figure 4-2 shows the text box placed on a form.

You can size the text box by clicking the border boxes and dragging the border to the desired size. You can also use the Properties window shown at the right side of Figure 4-2 to change the characteristics of the selected object. The LEFT property is selected. In Figure 4-3, the box is moved to the left from position 60 to 20.

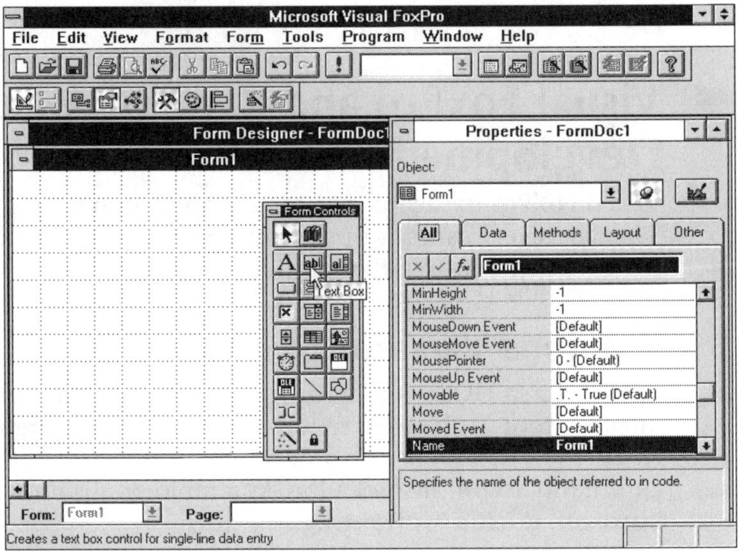

A blank form on the Forms page with the Properties window and Forms toolbar

Figure 4-1.

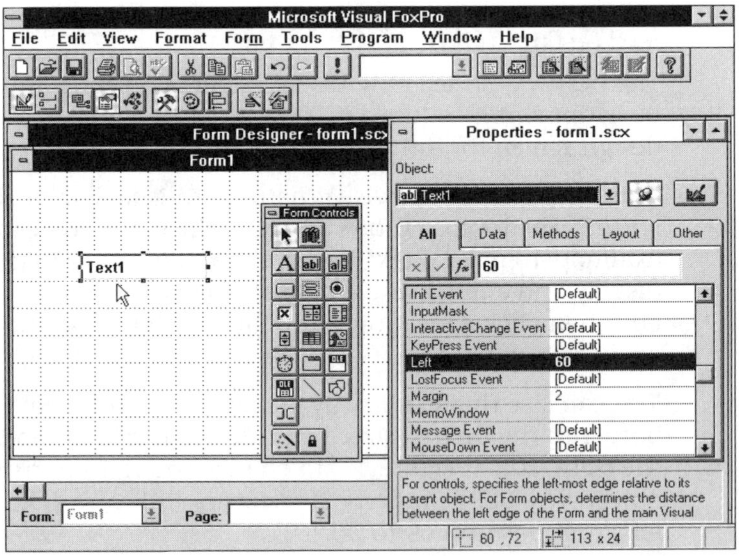

The text box placed on the form

Figure 4-2.

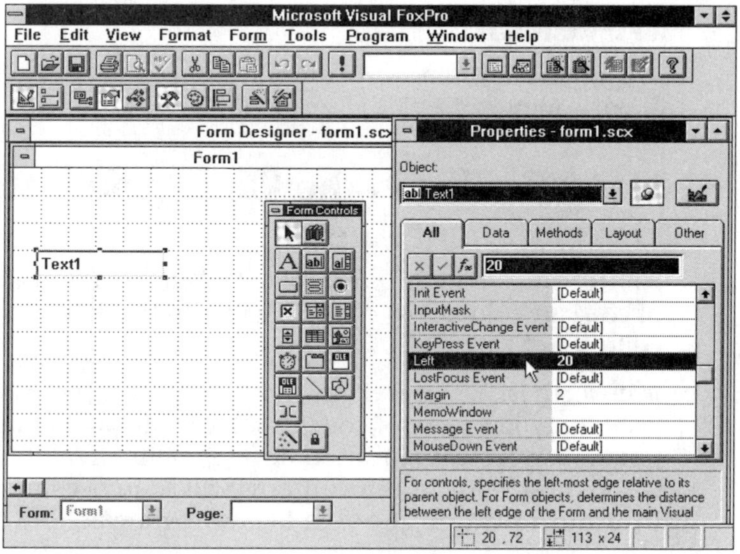

Moving the box to the left
Figure 4-3.

You can also visually move the text box by grabbing it using the mouse and moving it. You will see the LEFT property change to reflect the new position.

Using Wizards

Wizards are Microsoft's name for another rapid application development idea: automation of repetitive tasks. For instance, tables, queries, and reports are the stuff of database applications. Creating them can be time consuming, but often they are straightforward, almost boilerplate elements.

Why not let a tool make some sensible, or at least common, choices, ask you some questions, and create these elements automatically? This is the idea behind a wizard. Wizards also handle simple but little-used functions. Do you really want to become an expert on sending data to Excel using Window's object linking and embedding (OLE)? OLE is really a straightforward task with little to decide, an ideal candidate for a wizard.

Wizards, then, put a simple face on tasks that are not difficult but that can be made simpler. Automatic dishwashers may have seemed superfluous when they were introduced; washing dishes is not that big a deal. Now they are widely considered indispensable. So it is with wizards. Creating a table is not difficult, by why not make life easier with a wizard?

Programming for Rapid Application Development

We finish our discussion of rapid application development with some notes about coding.

Hand Coding in the Rapid Application Development Age

So here you are in the visual age. Old-timers who can spout page after page of code are told not to code by hand, to break the bonds of their program editors and enter the brave, new world.

Is it worth it? Yes, it is. If you are a long-time programmer, you may find it faster to type a piece of code to solve some problem than to face the new, unfamiliar, rapid application development environment. Nevertheless, face it you must. What is difficult now will soon become second nature. Remember switching to your latest program editor? It will be worth it.

Programming without Writing a Single Line of Code?

Many new tools, including Visual FoxPro, boast to some degree that you don't need to program them, that "no coding is required." The image they leave is that even neophytes can sit down at 8 A.M. and be whipping out classy, powerful applications by the morning coffee break.

This just isn't so. While you do not need to be a programmer, and tools like Visual FoxPro have made programming experience even less of a requirement, you still need the mental tools. You need to know how to define the problem, design the solution, and use the tools you have to find the solution.

Visual FoxPro provides an excellent set of tools for creating powerful, classy applications. The other two requirements—defining the problem and designing the solution—are more habits of the mind than anything else. Although the external manifestation of programming is the use of the tools, it is really the mindset that makes a successful programmer.

5

Event Management and Modeless Operation

Object behavior and events are not difficult subjects to understand. However, you need to be prepared to examine these concepts that, at first, may be unfamiliar. Understanding object behavior requires examination of concepts that are very different from the fundamental concepts that govern procedural programming. Assimilating the basics need not be difficult, but it can be unless you are willing to approach the task with an open mind and an appetite to learn challenging new ideas. Objects bring new life to Visual FoxPro's object orientation, and events are their heartbeat.

Object behavior, simply defined, is how an object is manipulated and how it responds to specific manipulations. Object behavior is defined in terms of events and states.

Events arise from both object behavior and systemic processes, such as clock ticks. Events make it possible for programmers to achieve truly modeless program operation. This chapter elaborates on the nature of events and shows how understanding and managing them greatly simplifies the programmer's job of designing modeless operation into Visual FoxPro applications.

Note: Recall that Chapter 2 introduced the term "modeless" and explained that a window or form is modeless if the user does not have to close it before switching to another form or window. Conversely, a program is modal if the user is required to close a form or window before switching to another.

You will learn to recognize, model, and implement events in the Visual FoxPro environment, but first you need a clear conceptual understanding of what constitutes an event and why events are essential elements of modeless program operation. You will begin by examining the broader meaning of events and then narrow your focus to better understand the programmatic nature of event recognition and processing in Visual FoxPro.

What Is an Event?

In science as in life, events are commonplace: A star explodes, ejecting primordial fragments from which new stars eventually are born. Cosmic dust coalesces into stars, giving rise to new galaxies. Aunt Sophie arrives on a plane from Minneapolis. Someone clicks a mouse button. These are all examples of events; however, only the latter is representative of those you will need to focus on in your study of Visual FoxPro.

An event, simply defined, is any change in the state or condition of an object. State changes can be as subtle as minute changes in a relationship between two Visual FoxPro objects or as dramatic as a supernova. It is only when state changes are important enough to warrant your attention that programmers think of them as events. An event, then, as discussed in this book, is a change in the state of an object that has a bearing on a program's mission or purpose. Keep in mind that this definition does not attempt to model the reality of events; it simply models the way we perceive them.

Figure 5-1 shows the relationship between events and processes: Events are changes, and processes are agents of change.

Events Arise from State Changes

It is impossible to understand events without examining a relatively new, but now fundamental, programming concept: states. All events arise from processes that bring about state changes. It is these state changes that people *perceive* as events. For example, the thermostat in your house has two important relationships: First, it has a relationship with the furnace in that it turns the heat on and off by controlling a switch. Second, it has a relationship with the air temperature in your house in that it monitors the air temperature.

Using the previous definition of an event, you know that whenever the air temperature changes even a fraction of a degree, that change is an event because the relationship between the thermostat and the air temperature changed. However, you don't want the furnace to go on and off every time the temperature changes a fraction of a degree. For example, when you set

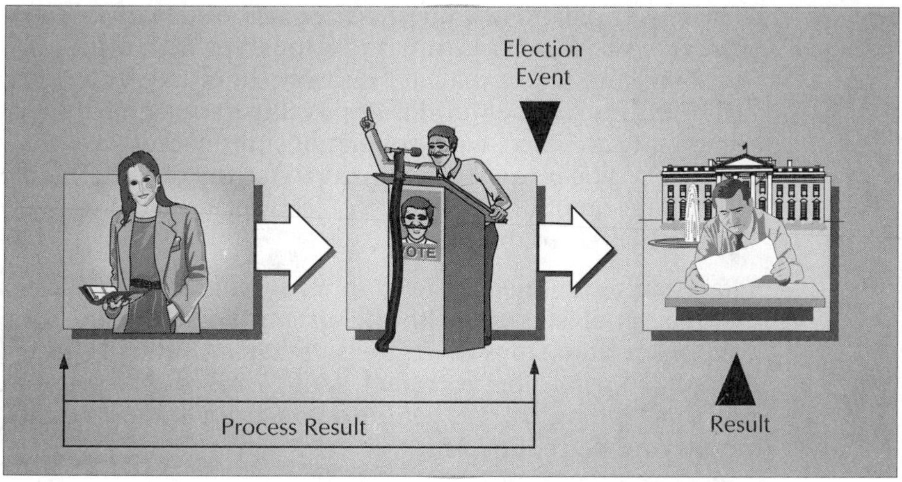

Events and processes
Figure 5-1.

the dial to 70°F, you want the thermostat to ignore all temperature changes unless the temperature falls below the setting. If the temperature does fall below the setting, you want the thermostat to switch on the furnace. The thermostat obediently watches the temperature and does nothing until it drops below your setting. Events are happening, but the thermostat does nothing until the conditions it is monitoring fit the rule programmed into the unit. This rule—in this case, "switch on the heat at 70°F"—is called a *trigger rule.*

Now that you understand events as *noteworthy* changes in the states of objects, you need to know a little more about states and how states change.

What Is a State?

Clearly, programmers and developers need an intimate understanding of the concept of state before they can appreciate the full programmatic value and potential of Visual FoxPro events—so give your undivided attention for a few moments to the concept of state.

The state is important for the following reasons:

- State is central to the definition of an event.
- Events are central to determining how objects behave.
- How objects behave is central to the structure of Visual FoxPro's object orientation.

The most fundamental question about the state of an object is whether the object exists. If it exists, it has relationships with other objects that define its existence. An object that *only* exists without having a relationship with anything else in the world is impossible to imagine. In fact, logic prohibits imagining an object with no relationships because as soon as you imagine an object, you create a relationship with the object. Therefore, the more important question is: How do objects relate to themselves, to each other, and to the rest of the world?

State, simply defined, is the combined relationships of a Visual FoxPro object with other objects and with the system. Therefore, the sum total of an object's relationships determines its state. Although this is a grossly simplified definition, it is an elegant global foundation for understanding the concept. Again, this definition does not attempt to model reality but to model our perception of it.

Tip: Relationships between objects can change either in a binary (on-off) sense or in a quantitative (how much) sense to create events.

States and Time

Visual FoxPro events, by definition, are time related because they occur *when* an object's state changes. Because an object's state is the sum total of all its relationships with other objects, it is *time* that allows you to map an object's changing states into meaningful events. Otherwise, without considering time, you could know only an object's *total state:* that is, the sum total of all relationships during the object's existence. If events did not occur or were not of interest in the Visual FoxPro environment, time would not be a programmatic factor.

States and Objects

You need to understand clearly that a state is not an object. States are mappings of relationships whereas objects are conceptual models of things. For example, the term "stockholder" can describe a state, but it can also describes a *type* of object. Which, then, are we talking about—a state or a type—when we use such a term?

Although states and object types can have the same or similar names, they are not the same thing. The distinction between states and objects is critical, and it can easily become blurred. For example, if there is an object of type person who owns another object of type stock, then "stockholder" describes a *state* of the object person. Logic suggests—but does not dictate—that you could create a third object of type stockholder that embodies stock ownership as one of its *inherent* properties. In other words, Visual FoxPro allows a stockholder to be an object type or a relationship of an object with another object called stock. Figure 5-2 illustrates this concept.

Objects, States, and Triggers

Triggers are the functional manifestation of Visual FoxPro events. Understanding triggers is the foundation of effectively implementing one of Visual FoxPro's most powerful object-oriented features: event-driven programming. A *trigger* is the link between an event and a programmatic

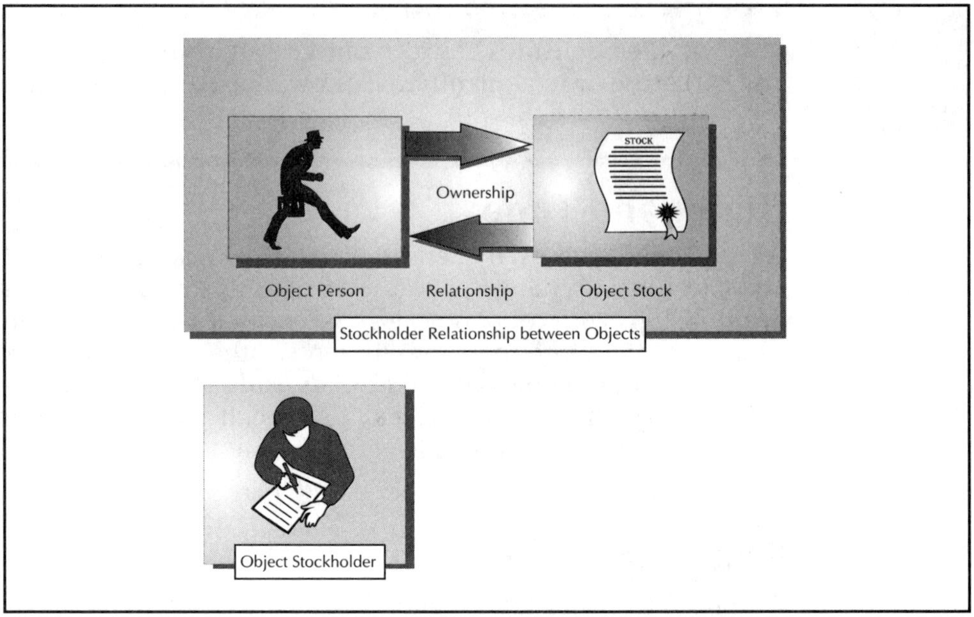

Object state versus object type
Figure 5-2.

process. Understanding this essential relationship is the key to using events easily and effectively when you develop Visual FoxPro applications. Event handling, or event code, is the term used when programmers design specific processes that determine whether a unique event triggers a response as well as what response or responses it triggers. Visual FoxPro provides a rich set of built-in trigger rules, and it is these rules that are the foundation of modeless operation.

Triggers arise from cause-and-effect relationships. Cause and effect is one of life's most familiar relationships. Almost from birth, we learn by recognizing the cause-and-effect relationships that produce noteworthy events in our lives. One important lesson we learn is that events trigger reactions that can have consequences ranging from insignificant to massive.

Triggers are managed by trigger rules, which are cause-and-effect links that specify the set of conditions required before an event can generate a trigger. For example, clicking a mouse button is an event; but for this event to produce a response, the cursor has to be in a predefined position, such as over a check box; otherwise, the click produces no response. If the cursor is not in a position programmatically defined to produce a response, the click event is without programmatic meaning. Figure 5-3 shows how a trigger rule dictates event response.

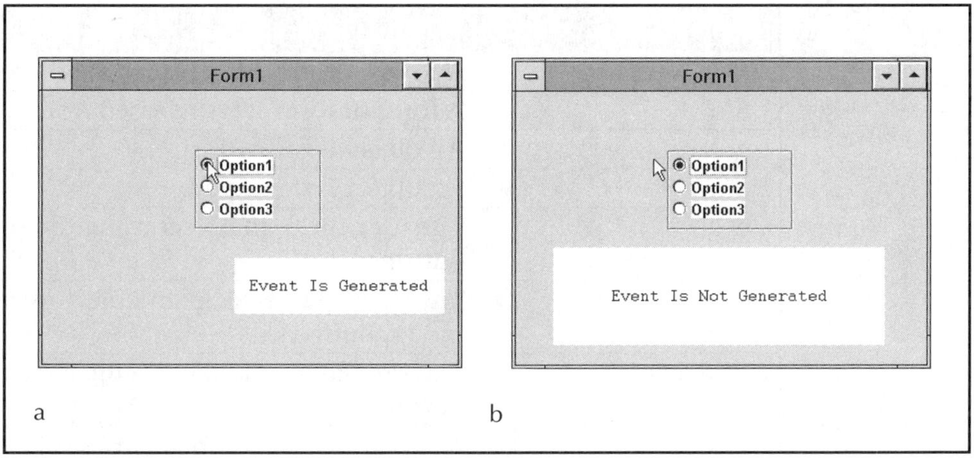

Events and trigger responses
Figure 5-3.

Events In the Visual FoxPro Programming Environment

Visual FoxPro automatically triggers built-in event code in response to a rich set of pre-defined user actions. For example, the system automatically processes click event code every time a user clicks a control. Rules that determine whether an event generates a trigger are built into the Visual FoxPro control classes. These ready-to-use classes provide virtually the entire set of Windows modeless features that programmers can implement in their applications *without writing a single line of extra code.* Using library classes as models, programmers can derive custom classes to implement their own unique special-purpose objects.

Tip: Containers do not process events associated with controls contained within them. If no event code is implemented for a control, Visual FoxPro checks higher up the class hierarchy to determine if event code exists. If such code is found, Visual FoxPro automatically implements it.

Most Visual FoxPro controls are designed to generate standardized triggers in response to a core set of events. The core set represents the minimum events that controls recognize. Most controls greatly expand this set, and a few do not include all core events. Visual FoxPro Help gives a complete description of these events. Table 5-1 lists the core events and tells when each is triggered.

Event	When Triggered
Load	A form or form set is loaded into memory.
Unload	A form or form set is released from memory.
Init	An object is created.
Destroy	An object is destroyed.
Click	The user clicks an object using the primary mouse buttons.
DblClick	The user double-clicks an object using the primary mouse buttons.
RightClick	The user clicks an object using a secondary mouse button.
GetFocus	The object receives the focus by either a user action, such as clicking a button, or program code using the SetFocus method.
LostFocus	The object loses the focus by either a user action, such as clicking a button, or program code using the SetFocus method.
KeyPress	The user presses and releases a key.
MouseDown	The user presses a mouse button while the mouse is over the object.
MouseUp	The user releases a mouse button while the mouse is over the object.
InteractiveChange	An object's value is changed interactively.
ProgrammaticChange	An object's value is changed by programmatic action.

Visual FoxPro Core Events
Table 5-1.

Containers, Objects, and Events

When users interact with an object in any way—by tabbing to it, clicking it, moving a cursor over it, and so on—events are triggered. Every object triggers events independently and uniquely, regardless of whether the object is contained by another object. For example, if a user clicks a control, such as a radio button, contained in a form, the form's click event is not triggered—only the control's click event is triggered.

Unless you assign or associate code with an event, nothing will happen *even if the event occurs.* Visual FoxPro provides a simple way to add code to be executed when an event occurs. You do this in the Form Designer's code window. In Part 3, you will learn to use the Form Designer to associate event code with your custom controls.

part 2

Data Management Concepts

6

Creating and Indexing a Single Table Database

This chapter introduces data tables and shows you how to create and modify your own tables using both Visual FoxPro's manual Table Designer and its automated Table Wizard. You will create a data table, modify it, and integrate it into a single table database. You will learn about indexing and learn how to work with and customize existing tables, including .dbf files created in other versions of FoxPro.

Visual FoxPro's Expanded Definition of a Database

Before the release of Visual FoxPro, an Xbase program's basic data structure was the *database*, often referred to by its file extent as *.dbf*. In Visual FoxPro, this familiar structure is now called a *data table*. Data tables don't really differ from the databases of old, except in name, and they have the same *.dbf* file extent as when they were called databases. The main difference is that Visual FoxPro enlarged the database concept, allowing programmers conveniently to create groups of related data tables and make their relationships *persistent*. Data tables, however, do not have to be related, nor do they have to be members of a database. Conversely, a database cannot exist unless it contains at least one table.

What Is a Persistent Relationship?

Visual FoxPro expands its definition of the familiar term "database" to describe a family of data *tables* that can be linked together by relationships that *persist* whenever such tables are used. However, don't be misled by the expanded concept. A database is still a database, and in that sense, little is changed except terminology. In a broader and more important sense, however, Visual FoxPro's expansion of the database concept, *allowing persistent relationships between tables*, opens the door to more flexible program design, simpler program maintenance, and programs with greater overall reliability and referential integrity (which Chapter 3 examined in depth).

Note: Relationship persistence is a powerful concept that arises from Visual FoxPro's object orientation. Persistence is the quality of a relationship that allows it to survive the operation that created it.

Visual FoxPro tables that are not members of a database are called *free tables*. Programmers and developers can manipulate free tables the same way they manipulate tables that are members of a database. The only difference is that the relationships of free tables are not persistent; that is, the relationships do not remain after the operations that created them are completed. You may find it convenient to think of free tables exactly the way you thought of databases before Microsoft introduced the expanded concept of a database.

What Is a Visual FoxPro Data Table?

Data tables are groups of similar data stored in a common structure. The unit of this structure is the data *record*. Visual FoxPro tables can contain any number of records, which organize and store their data in containers called data *fields*.

Visual FoxPro uses the *relational database* strategy for storing data in data tables that can be linked to other tables through common data fields. These common fields are often called *key fields*, or simply *keys*. Because data tables and keys are fundamental to Visual FoxPro, it is important that you understand them completely.

Visual FoxPro Data Types

All fields in a data table are assigned data types at the time they are created. The types of data stored in these fields must match the assigned data types. You can assign any of the data types listed in Table 6-1 to a Visual FoxPro data field.

Data Type	Description	Example
Character	Alphanumeric text	Name or address
Currency	Monetary units	Cost or sales price
Numeric	Numbers	Quantity, weight, distance
Float	Same as numeric	
Double	Double-precision number	Number expressed to a high degree of precision.
Integer	Whole numbers (no fractional part)	Line number
Date	Month, day, and year	November 11, 1918
DateTime	Same as date plus hours, minutes, and seconds	November 11, 1918 13:23:12
Logical	True or false, yes or no	Check box
Memo	Character text of unspecified length	Notes
General	OLE	Worksheet

Visual FoxPro Data Types
Table 6-1.

Creating a New Table with Visual FoxPro

Visual FoxPro makes it easy to create new data tables and modify existing ones. You can create or change tables in two ways: by using the *Table Designer* or the *Table Wizard*. The Table Wizard provides a more automatic process than the Table Designer. In this chapter, you will learn to create and index new data tables using both methods.

Whether you use the Table Designer or Table Wizard to create your data tables, you need to be mindful of four essential principles:

- Fields must be large enough to accommodate any data that may be assigned to them.
- Numeric fields and float fields must have the appropriate number of decimal places.
- Data field types must match the types of data you plan to store in them.
- You must check the Null check box if you want a field to accept the null value.

Using Visual FoxPro's Table Designer

You will now create a Visual FoxPro data table using the Table Designer. You can best get the feel of creating data tables by using the Table Designer because it uses a more manual procedure than the Table Wizard. After mastering data table design using the Table Designer, you will use the more automatic Table Wizard and create the same table using the wizard's convenient step-by-step prompting.

Your first step after launching Visual FoxPro is to bring up the New dialog box by selecting New from the File menu. When the New dialog box appears, click the Table button and then click New File as shown in Figure 6-1.

In the Create dialog box, enter the new table's name and select the directory where you want to store it. In this example, name the table *contacts.dbf*. Then select Create to display the Table Designer. Now you can begin creating your table by typing **lastname**, the name of the first field, as shown in Figure 6-2.

Accept the default field type, Character, but increase the field length to 20 either by typing the number in the edit box or by using the spin buttons attached to the box.

You will usually design tables with more than one field; so you need to add a few more fields and create a table that contains a useful body of information.

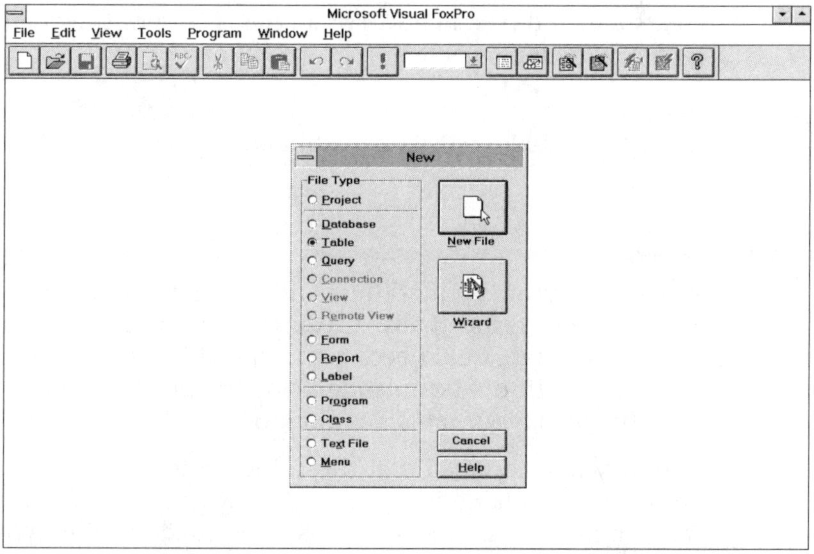

Creating a new data table in Visual FoxPro
Figure 6-1.

Click the outlined blank area below the lastname field name that you just entered. Now type **firstname**, the name of your second field. Accept the default field type; but this time change the length to 15. Now your table contains two fields—one to store last names, and one to store first names—and the Table Designer screen looks like Figure 6-3.

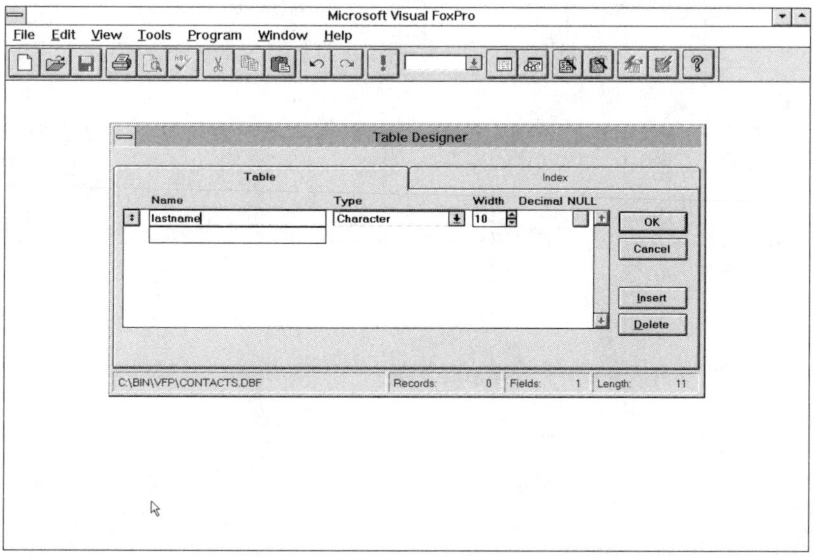

The Table Designer
Figure 6-2.

Complete the table design by creating four more fields: address, city, state, and postalcode. For all fields, accept the default field type, Character.

Tip: Visual FoxPro does not allow spaces in field names.

When you create your address and city fields, change their widths to 80 and 30 characters, respectively, because streets and cities can have very long names. The state field needs a width of 15 characters to accommodate all state names. In the postalcode field, accept the default width, 10. After you have finished, your table should look like Figure 6-4.

You may have noticed that the Table Designer lets you conveniently select among the available field types, field widths, and decimal values when you create a new field. This feature is also available when you modify fields in an existing table. You may also have noticed that the Table Designer provides two tabs: Table and Index. Thus far, you have used the Table portion of the Table Designer. The Index portion allows you to create indexes associated with your table. After entering a few records in your new table, you will explore Visual FoxPro's index feature.

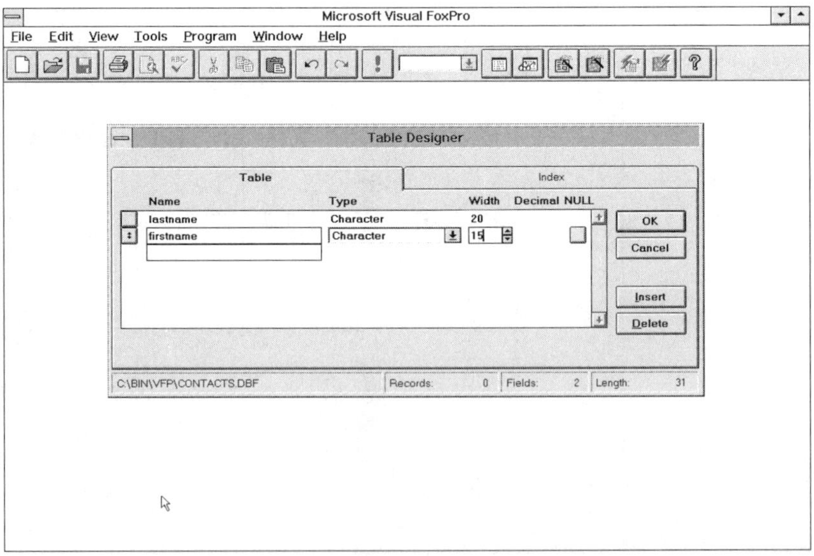

Creating successive fields in the Table Designer

Figure 6-3.

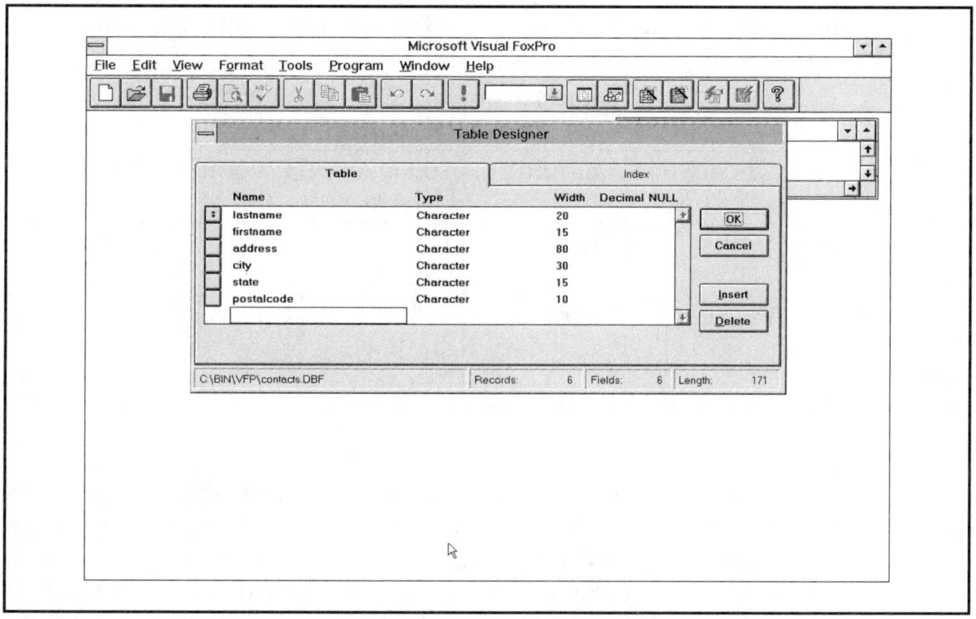

The Table Designer with six fields
Figure 6-4.

Entering Data in a New Data Table

When you finish creating the six fields, select OK, and the Input Records Now dialog box will appear. Click Yes to enter the five records shown in Table 6-2 into *contacts.dbf.*

Continue entering the data until you have entered all five records. When you finish, press ENTER. Visual FoxPro will store your new data table, *contacts.dbf,* with the five records for future use. When you finish entering the records in Table 6-2, your data table will look like Figure 6-5.

Now is a good time to see how *contacts.dbf* looks using the Visual FoxPro *browse* feature. To open the Browse window and view your table, click View and then Browse and Contacts.

Visual FoxPro's browse feature provides a convenient way to examine and modify your data tables. You will examine this feature more closely after you have constructed a larger table that will allow you to better exercise all its features, but right now you can see how easy it is to add a new record to your table using the Visual FoxPro Browser.

Click the empty row just below the last record you just created and enter **Stone** in the lastname column. If you can't enter text in the lastname box, you are not in append mode. Click View and click Append Mode and then enter the last name. Your screen should look like Figure 6-6.

Five Records In *contact.dbf*
Table 6-2.

Applegood	Jane	2334 Main St.	Ogden	Utah	84123
Zigfeld	Morris	18762 Orange St.	Queens	New York	10036
Underwood	Mathilda	169 E. Lake Ave.	Colombus	Ohio	43221
White	Alice	1224 Forest St.	Dallas	Texas	72892
Parker	Elaine	14500 Elmlawn Dr.	Corsicana	Texas	75111

Continue entering data in all the fields to fill out your sixth record. That is all you have to do to create a data table and add to it. If you want to modify a record, simply click the field you want to modify while you are in Browse and change it. For example, to change Mr. Zigfeld's name to Mr. *Zigfield;* just click Zigfeld and change the name to Zigfield. That's all there is to it.

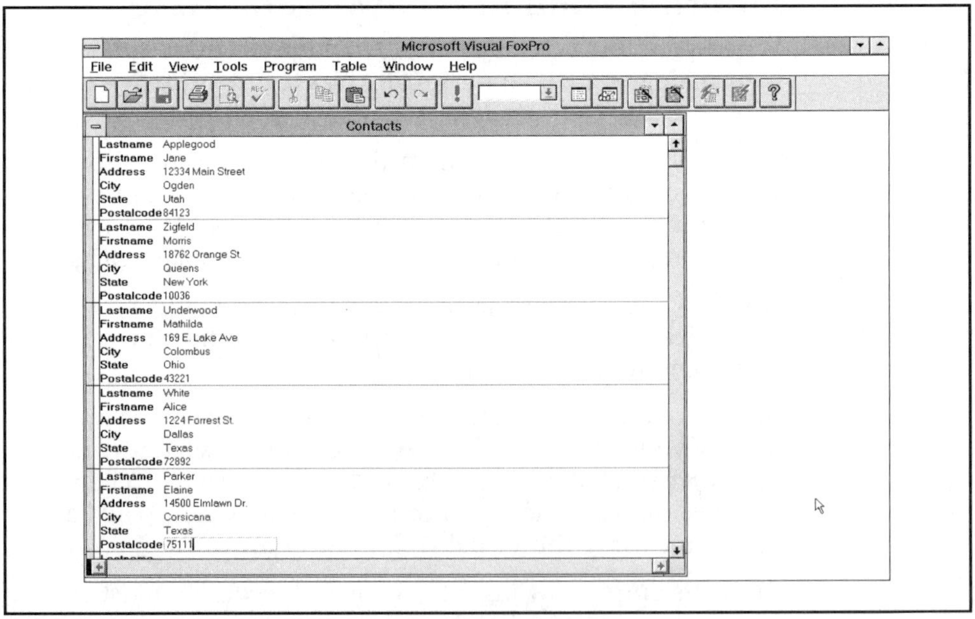

The data table with five records entered
Figure 6-5.

Using Visual FoxPro's Table Wizard

Just when you think things couldn't get any easier, along comes Visual FoxPro's Table Wizard to challenge your optimism. Actually, the Table Wizard may or may not be easier for you to use. It provides a nice step-by-step procedure, but the new Table Designer is so efficient that the Table Wizard may not have much more to offer. You can be the judge, because now you will re-create the table you created with the Table Designer, this time using the Table Wizard.

Begin by launching the Table Wizard. If the Browse screen is still active, press ESCAPE to get rid of it. Browse automatically saves your changes when you leave it. Then click Tools, Wizards, and Table to open the Table Wizard.

The Table Wizard is very straightforward, and since you already know how to create a table, the procedure will be familiar. You will be performing the same procedures as when you used the Table Designer, except this time you will be prompted at each step.

Visual FoxPro's Table Wizard has a built-in set of table structures to simplify and speed up table design. The left scroll box labeled Sample Tables contains

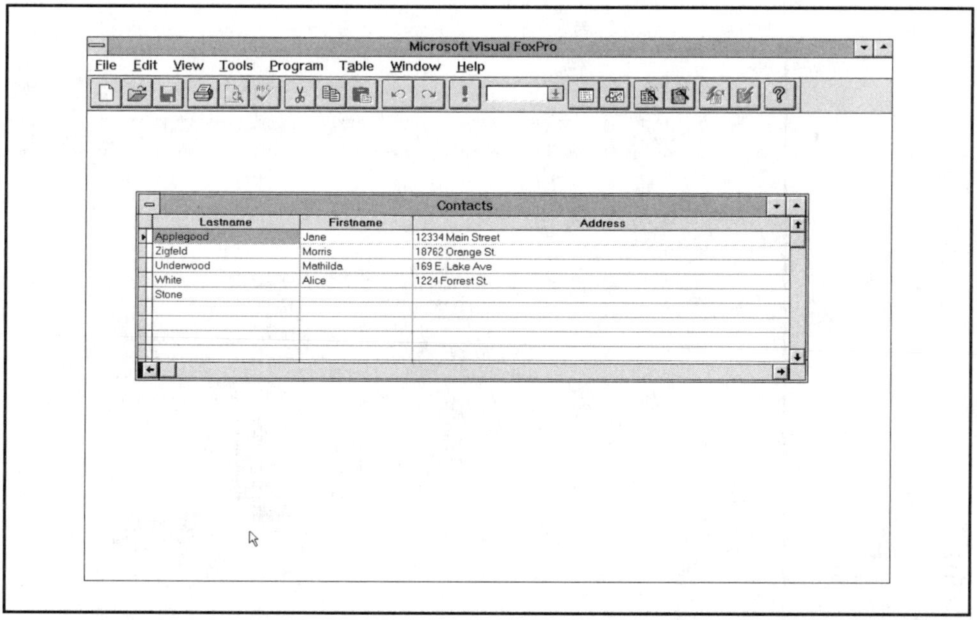

Using the browse feature to add a record
Figure 6-6.

a list of table descriptions to choose from. Scroll down to Customers and double-click. The middle scroll box, labeled Available Fields, changes to show the predesigned fields in Visual FoxPro's Customers sample table.

Because you are going to duplicate the table you just created in the Table Designer, you have more choices than you need. First click lastname to highlight it. Your screen should now look like Figure 6-7.

Notice the four buttons arranged vertically to the right of the Available Fields box. You will use the top two buttons to move fields from the Available Fields box into the Selected Fields box. The top button moves only the highlighted field, and the second button moves all available fields. The bottom two buttons move fields out of the Selected Fields box should you change your mind after making a selection. The button with a single arrow moves one field at a time, and the button with a double arrow moves all fields at once.

Click the top button to move the lastname field to the selected box. You have now added lastname to your table. Add firstname, address, city, state, and postalcode, one at a time, clicking the right arrow button each time to move the field to the selected column. When you are finished, your screen will look like Figure 6-8.

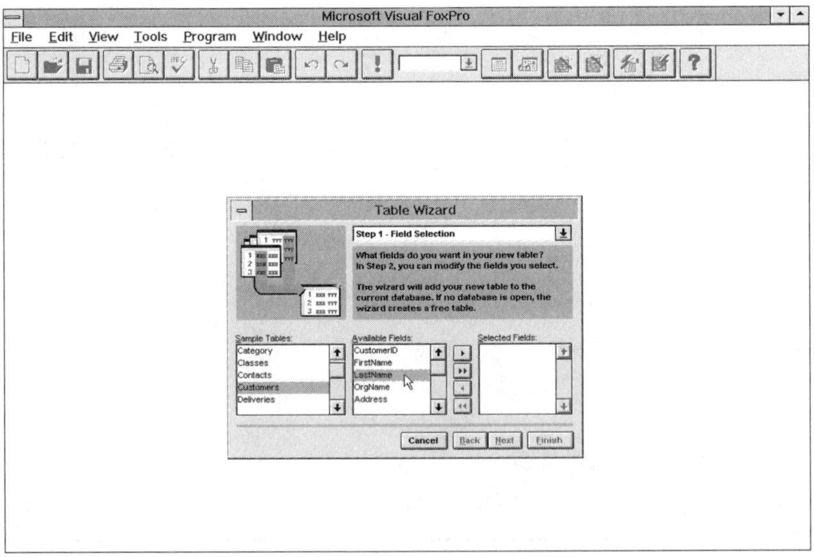

The Table Wizard
Figure 6-7.

Click Next at the bottom of the Table Wizard dialog box to display the Step 2 dialog box, where you will set the properties for each of your data fields. Click through the fields and verify that the default fields correspond to the ones you created with the Table Designer. You will notice that all are the same, except the state field. Change this field and click Next. This takes you to the Index dialog box. Creating an index in the Table Wizard is as easy as clicking check boxes. Note that the grid in the center of the current dialog box displays the fields of your table, with check boxes to the left. The order in which you check the boxes establishes the sort order. Therefore, if you check lastname, then check firstname; the sort order of your index will be lastname+firstname. This is what you want; therefore, check lastname, then firstname, in that order. Above the Fieldname grid is a list box labeled Primary Key. This is darkened because it is not applicable unless you are indexing in a one-to-many relationship.

Click Next to advance to the Finish dialog box, then click the center radio button. Click Finish and the Save dialog box will ask you for a filename for your data table. Enter **contacts.dbf** and click Save. The Browser automatically appears, displaying your new data table as in Figure 6-9.

Your new table, *contacts.dbf*, is identical to the table you created earlier using the Table Designer. Whether you use the Table Designer or the Table Wizard is largely a matter of preference. The results, as you can see, are the same.

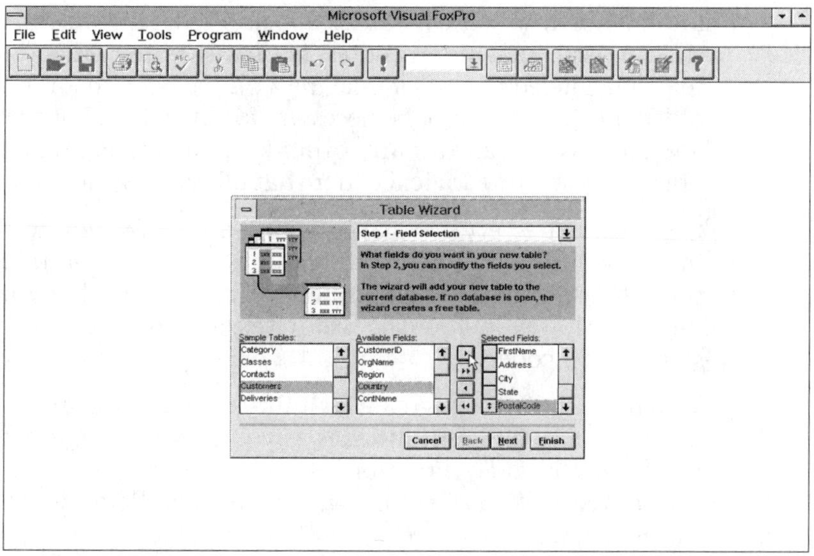

The Table Wizard with the fields added
Figure 6-8.

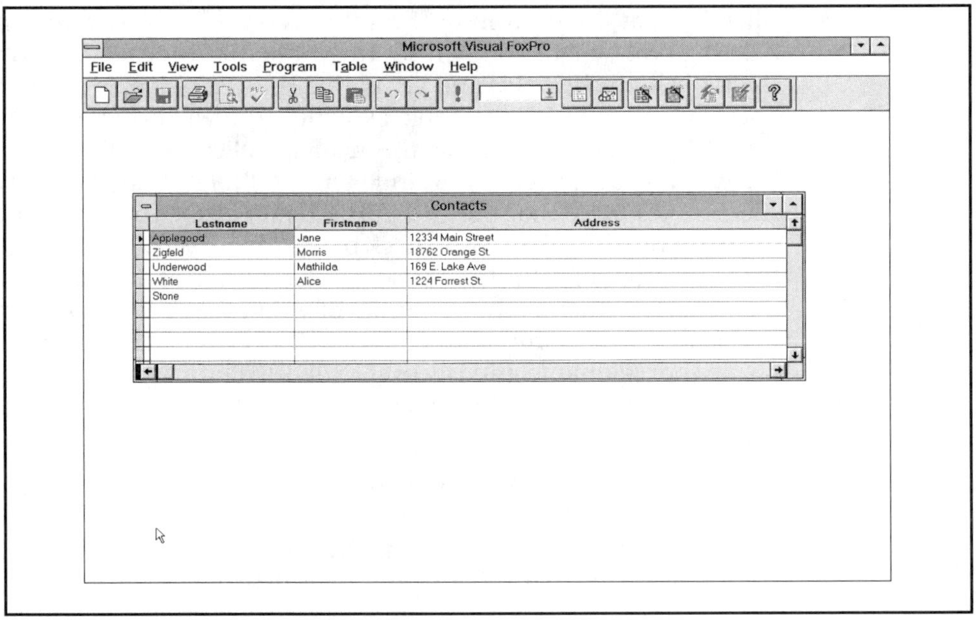

The Browser with the new table
Figure 6-9.

What Is Indexing?

Now that you know how to create a data table, let's take a look at indexing. In everyday life, indexes are everywhere. Your address book, your file cabinet, and the telephone book are common examples of indexes. Indexing simply organizes information into some predefined logical order that makes the information items easier to find. Imagine an address book with entries listed in the random order that you entered them—or imagine a phone book that is not in alphabetical order. Indexing may not be necessary for small lists, but a large array of names and addresses or almost any other kind of data is unmanageable if it is not organized in some logical order that allows easy access.

Computers are very good at indexing and allow you to organize data tables in many different ways so you can find information in different ways based on different needs. For example, everyone is familiar with alphabetical indexes. However, you can also index names on the basis of a person's city, state, or zip code.

Visual FoxPro affords great flexibility in indexing and allows a single table to have as many different indexes as you need. Using indexes, you can quickly rearrange Visual FoxPro tables so you can easily access information based on the contents of any field in your table. Such fields are called key fields, or simply keys.

Tip: You can use combinations of fields as your index keys. For example, you may later make several entries in *mytable1.dbf* with the same last name and different first names, as when you enter the names of members of the same family. If you index on lastname plus firstname, your table organizes all the people with the same last name in the correct order of their first names.

Creating a Visual FoxPro Index

Creating a Visual FoxPro index is easy. Begin with your table displayed in browse mode, as you just left it. Click View and then Table Designer, and you will see the familiar Table Designer dialog box with your table loaded.

Earlier, when you first started using the Table Designer, you used one of the two tabs at the top of the screen: Table. Now click the Index tab to expose the Index page of the Table Designer. Then type **contact** under Name, as in Figure 6-10, to name the index file you are about to create.

Notice that some options pop up as soon as you start typing in the name box. For now, accept the default field type, Regular. Click the small button to the right of the Expression box to bring up the Expression Builder and, in the Fields list, double-click lastname. The lastname field name moves into

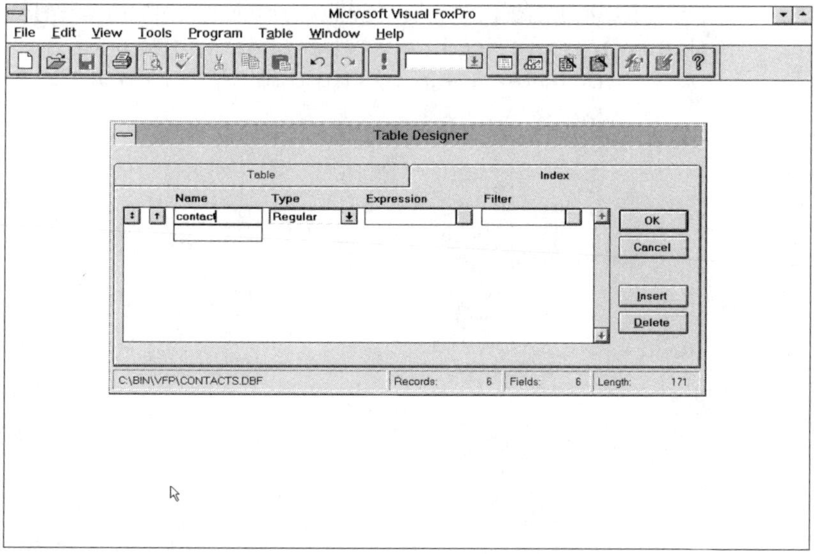

The index page
Figure 6-10.

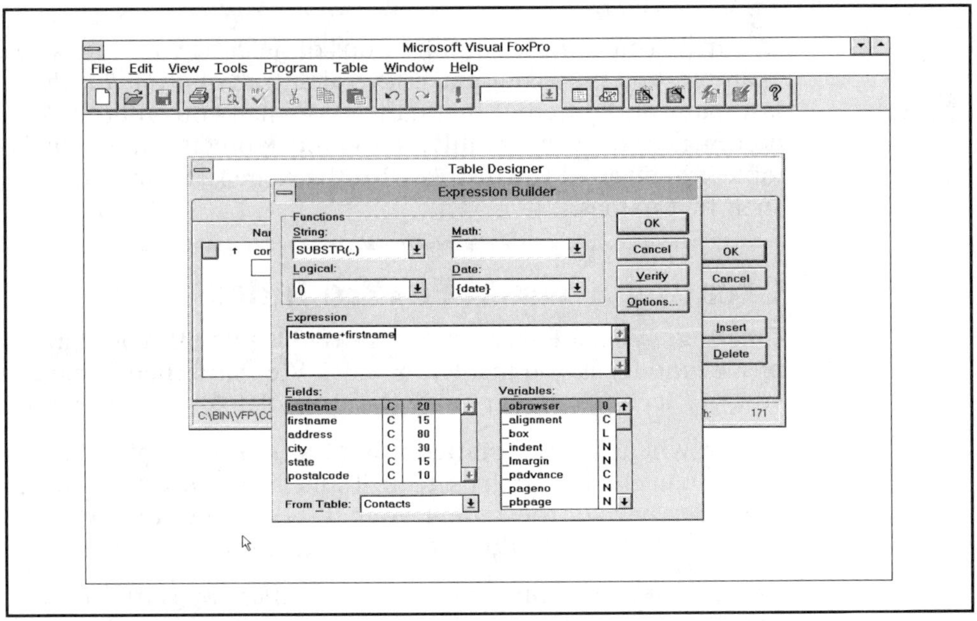

The Expression Builder window
Figure 6-11.

the Expression list. Click the Expression list, type +, and double-click firstname in the Fields list. At this point, you have created an index named contacts and your screen should look like Figure 6-11.

You just created your first Visual FoxPro index. You probably noticed some options you didn't use in the Expression Builder window. You'll learn about them all, as you need to use them later in the book. For now, you have used only those features that you need to do the job at hand.

7

Creating a Visual FoxPro Form

You are about to discover how incredibly easy it is to design a Visual FoxPro form that is both effective and visually pleasing. Visual FoxPro forms allow programmers to give users a familiar interface for viewing, entering, and manipulating data. However, Visual FoxPro forms are more that just user interfaces—they embrace a powerful set of objects capable of responding to both user events and system events.

Visual FoxPro forms give programmers tools for performing data management operations more easily and more intuitively than ever before.

In the last chapter you learned how easy it is to design custom data tables using Visual FoxPro. Designing custom forms is no more difficult. You can choose to use the Form Wizard or Form Designer alone, or you can use a combination of the Form Wizard and Form Designer. In designing Visual FoxPro forms, you will find that it is often more convenient first to use the Form Wizard to create your form's initial layout, and then switch to the Form Designer and modify the layout to look exactly the way you want it.

You will know how to use all three methods of creating forms by the time you complete this chapter. This chapter discusses the following topics:

- Designing a form
- Creating a form
- Selecting and placing objects
- Manipulating objects

In the course of the chapter, you will create a custom form for entering, accessing, and modifying your data table, using powerful Visual FoxPro controls. Your ability to create and work with custom forms will prepare you for the next big step—organizing data into custom reports—which you will take in Chapter 9.

What Is a Visual FoxPro Form?

Forms are Visual FoxPro container objects that have their own unique properties, events, and methods. Forms contain the controls you need to design functionality into your applications.

In Chapter 2 you learned that form objects are derived from the *container* class. As containers, *forms* can be the parent objects of other objects, such as the controls you place in your forms. For example, a form is the parent of a radio button object you insert in that form. You will soon see that this concept is more difficult to think about than actually to understand and use in Visual FoxPro.

Designing a Visual FoxPro Form

Visual FoxPro's powerful Form Designer allows you conveniently to design both the containers and the controls your programs require. Using the Form Designer, you can set your form's properties, events, and methods; then include the controls your form needs and set their properties using the Visual FoxPro Properties window.

Visual FoxPro Form Set and Form Container Classes
Table 7-1.

Container	Objects Allowed in Container
Column	Headers and controls
Form set	Forms and toolbars
Form	Page frames, grids, and controls
Page	Grids and controls

When you design a new form, you establish its functionality by:

- Setting your form's properties
- Adding the appropriate controls
- Setting your control's properties
- Writing event code

Visual FoxPro provides two kinds of container classes: form containers (including form set containers) and base containers. Table 7-1 lists the form containers and the kinds of objects they can contain.

In addition to the forms and form sets listed in Table 7-1, Visual FoxPro provides four *base container classes.* Table 7-2 lists these base container classes and the kinds of objects they can contain.

Tip: The difference between form containers and base containers is that base containers are used to organize the control objects and container objects that you place within other containers, such as forms.

Tip: Base containers can exist only within form containers, and you use them when you need to group controls within your forms. For example, you can include a group of related option buttons in an option button group to simplify their management and manipulation.

Visual FoxPro Base Container Classes
Table 7-2.

Container	Objects Allowed in Container
Command button group	Command buttons
Grid	Columns
Option button group	Options
Page frame	Pages

Creating a New Visual FoxPro Form

It is often more convenient to begin creating a new form by first using the Form Wizard. You will try that strategy now and use the Form Wizard to create a new form that will allow users to view and modify your data table, *mytable1.dbf*.

Setting the Visual FoxPro Form Options

Before you begin creating your first Visual FoxPro form, make sure your form options are properly set. Launch Visual FoxPro and close any projects that appear on your main screen. On the main menu bar, click Tools and then Options to bring up the Options dialog box. The Options dialog box comprises ten pages, as indicated by the ten tabs along the top of the page frame. Click the Forms tab to display the Form Options page.

In the Grid box, enable Grid Lines and Snap to Grid. If these check boxes do not already contain X's, click the boxes to place X's in them. Set both Horizontal Spacing (pixels) and Vertical Spacing (pixels) to 6. Be sure that Show Position is enabled; then set Tab Ordering to By List and Scale Units to Pixels.

The next option setting, Maximum Design Area, can be tricky because the setting that works best depends on your computer's display configuration. Try setting Maximum Design Area to 1280x1024 and see how it works. If you have trouble displaying the Form Designer with this setting, try the other available settings until you find the right one for your display. Figure 7-1 shows the Form Options page when you have completed the settings.

At the bottom of the Options dialog box, click Set as Default and then Save. Visual FoxPro's main screen reappears.

Using the Form Wizard to Begin Creating the New Form

On the Visual FoxPro main screen, click Tools, then Wizards, and then Form. When the Wizard Selection dialog box appears, double-click Form Wizard to bring up the Form Wizard dialog box with Step 1 displayed.

First, you need to tell the wizard that you want to use *contacts.dbf*. Click the ellipsis button (that's the small button with three dots (**...**) to the right of the Databases/Tables box) to launch the Windows Open dialog box. Locate the directory where you stored *contacts.dbf* and double-click it. This action places your data table in the wizard's Databases/Tables box and places its fields in the Available Fields box just to the right, as in Figure 7-2.

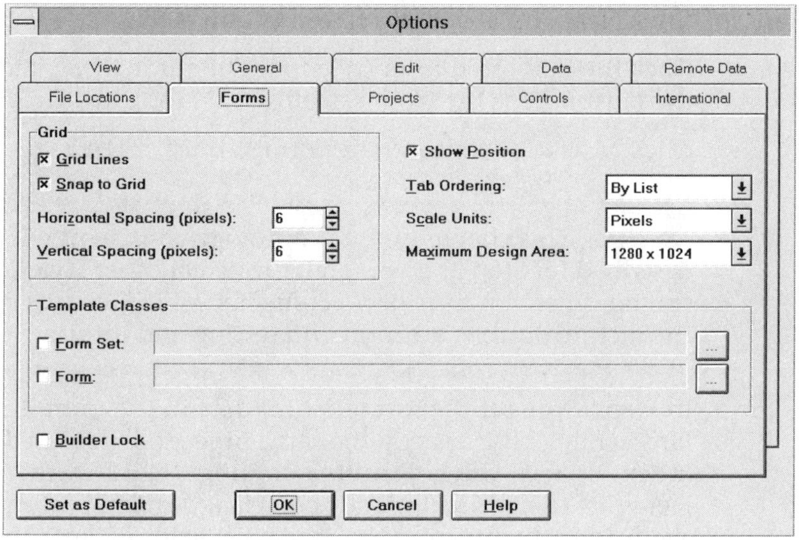

The completed Form Options page

Figure 7-1.

Between the Available Fields box and the Selected Fields box is a vertical row of small buttons. You need to include all the table's fields, so click the button labeled with a double right arrow (>>). Clicking this button automatically moves all of your table's fields into the Selected Fields box. The single right arrow (>) allows you to select the fields you want, one at a

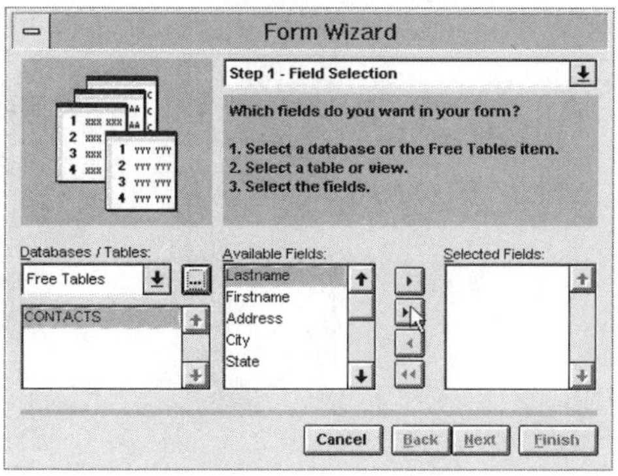

The Form Wizard Step 1 screen

Figure 7-2.

time. The left arrows allow you to remove fields from the Selected Fields box. Click Next and advance to Form Wizard's Step 2.

Click the Embossed form style to highlight it. Then click Picture Buttons in the Button Type list. Your screen should look like Figure 7-3.

Click Next to advance to the Form Wizard's Step 3.

Tip: This chapter uses terminology consistent with the settings described for Step 2. If you prefer to select other styles, go ahead. Doing so should cause you little or no confusion or difficulty. However, for most users the picture buttons are more interesting and intuitive than the other choices.

In Step 3, you set the sort order for data in the form. If this step seems familiar, it is. It is exactly the same procedure you used to create an index—in fact, you *are* creating an index. Click Lastname in the Available Fields list to highlight it and then click the Add button. This action moves the field Lastname from the Available Fields list into the Selected Fields list. Next, click Firstname to move this field into the Available Fields list, then click the Ascending button and Next.

You have now informed the wizard that you want to sort your table first on the Lastname and then on the Firstname field, in ascending order. This means, for example, that if your database includes two people, Alice and Sam, whose last names both are Smith, Visual FoxPro will sort them with the last names in alphabetical order, and Alice Smith will appear ahead of Sam Smith.

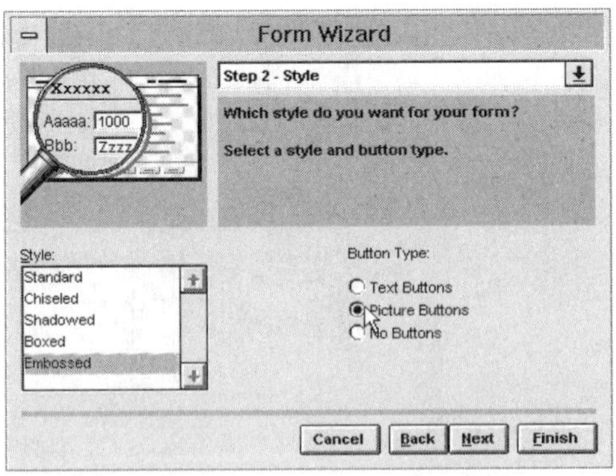

The Form Wizard Step 2 screen
Figure 7-3.

You've now reached the Form Wizard's Finish step. Click the bottom radio button to tell the wizard that you want to place the new table in the Table Designer. Click Finish to display the Windows Save As dialog box. Select the directory in which you want to save your form and enter *contacts.scx* as the form name. When you select the filename, the Form Wizard creates a new Visual FoxPro form according to your instructions. Then the Form Wizard launches the Form Designer and places your new form, *contacts.scx*, in it. Your screen should now look like Figure 7-4.

If your screen doesn't look like Figure 7-4, try moving the form window labeled *mytable1* to the center of the Form Designer screen as it appears in the figure. If you can't do this, click Tools, click Options, and select the Option dialog box's Form tab and try different Maximum Design Area settings. One of the available choices should cure the problem.

If your Form Designer screen does not display the three toolbars—Form Controls, Form Designer, and Layout—click View, select these toolbars, and arrange them as in Figure 7-4 or in any convenient positions.

Examining Your New Form

Examine your new form and see what Visual FoxPro's Form Wizard did for you. First, it inserted six *text boxes* in your form, each containing one of the

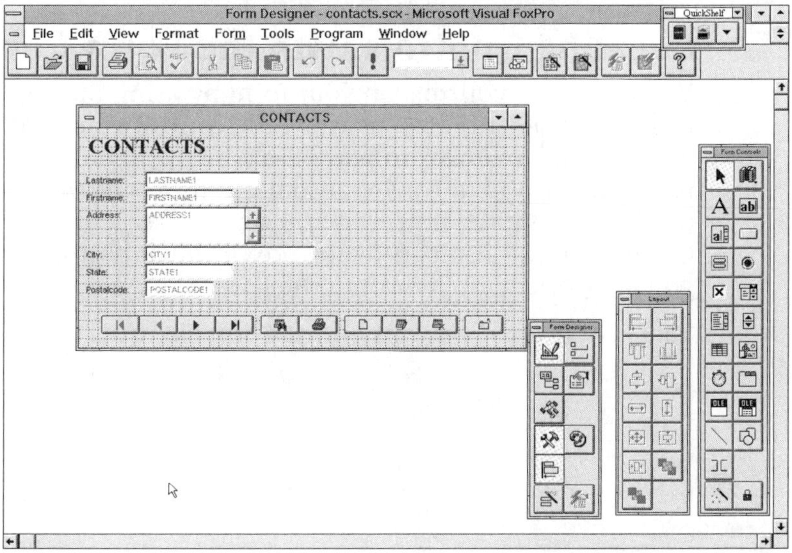

The Form Designer with the *contacts.scx* form displayed

Figure 7-4.

fields you selected in the Form Wizard dialog box. It also inserted six *labels,* one describing each field text box.

Notice that the wizard automatically arranged your form's controls into a surprisingly orderly group. This may not be the grouping you want, but it is a very nice start and much easier than building the same form from scratch in the Form Designer.

Along the bottom of the new form, the wizard automatically inserted ten Visual FoxPro controls needed to manipulate your data table. These controls form a Visual FoxPro *control group.* These buttons are sometimes called *VCR buttons* because when you label them with pictures, they look similar to the control buttons on a VCR.

Note: The Add/Save Record button in your form's VCR button control group shows a page with its upper-right corner turned down. This is the New Record Button. As soon as you click this button, the picture changes to a floppy disk, denoting that it is now the button you click to save a new record after you've created it. This button is a simple but elegant example of an event-driven control: When you first click the control (the VCR button), its save event code is executed; then its picture changes, and its event code changes to *add,* to match the new picture. When you click the control the second time, it executes the *add* event code and reverts back to its prior *save* state. This process is called *toggling.* Such a strategy allows programmers to use a single control for multiple purposes when such use makes sense, as it clearly does in this example.

Creating Controls with the Form Controls Toolbar

You can create controls on your form by using the Form Controls toolbar. Click the toolbar button to select the control you want, position the pointer on the form, and click to place the control. You can also drag most controls to size them. Visual FoxPro automatically opens this toolbar when you open the Form Designer; however, you can display it at any time by selecting Controls in the Toolbars dialog box. Toolbar buttons are not enabled unless you are working on a form in the Form Designer.

Table 7-3 lists the buttons on the Form Controls toolbar.

Button	Description
Select Objects	Resizes and moves controls.
View Classes	Selects and displays a registered Visual FoxPro class library.
Label	Creates a label control to show text the user can't change.
Text Box	Creates a text box control to hold a single line of text.
Edit Box	Creates an edit box control to hold multiple lines of text.
Command Button	Creates a command button control to execute a command.
Command Group	Creates a command group control to group related commands.
Option Group	Creates an option group control to display multiple options from which the user can select one.
Check Box	Creates a check box control to allow users to choose between true or false or to choose any or all of a list of multiple options.
Combo Box	Creates a combo box control to create a drop-down combination or list box where users can select one from a list of items or enter text manually.
List Box	Creates a list box control to display a scrollable list from which users can select one item.
Spinner	Creates a spinner control to accept numeric input within a specified range.
Grid	Creates a grid control to display information in a spreadsheet grid.
Image	Displays a graphic image.
Timer	Responds to timer events at specified intervals; invisible at run time.
Page Frame	Displays controls in multiple-page format.
OLE Container	Adds OLE objects to a form.

Buttons on the Form Control Toolbar
Table 7-3.

Button	Description
OLE Bound Control	Binds OLE controls to a general field; however, as with OLE containers, users can add OLE objects to an application.
Line	Draws a variety of line styles only at design time.
Shape	Draws a variety of shapes only at design time.
Separator	Inserts space between toolbar controls.
Builder Lock	Opens the builder for a new control the user adds to the form.
Button Lock	Adds more than one control of the same type without the user's having to click the control button on the toolbar more than once.

Buttons on the Form Control Toolbar (*continued*)
Table 7-3.

Using the Form Designer to Reorganize the Form Layout

Using the Form Designer, you can arrange your form's objects into any order you find pleasing. You can move a form's objects either individually or in groups.

Form Designer Toolbar

Visual FoxPro automatically displays the Form Designer toolbar with the Form Designer. Table 7-4 lists the buttons in this toolbar.

Reorganizing Your Form's Layout

Now touch up the labels on your form and make them a little clearer. If you need to make your form larger to accommodate these changes, just click on a corner and drag the form to the size you want.

First move the six text boxes to make room to expand the text in your labels. You can move these objects individually, but that's not as convenient as moving them as a group. You can select multiple objects in two ways: Click each object you want to select while holding down the SHIFT key, or select a group using the mouse. Here you will use the mouse because it's more convenient.

Click the mouse just above and to the left of your top text box, labeled Lastname, and drag it down and to the right until the mouse box encloses all six text boxes. Release the button and notice that all six text boxes are now

Button	Description
Design Mode	Switches between tab order mode and design mode.
Tab	Displays form objects conveniently for setting the tab order.
Data Environment	Displays Visual FoxPro's Data Environment Designer.
Properties Window	Displays property settings for the selected object.
Code Window	Displays code for the selected object for viewing and editing.
Form Controls Toolbar	Shows or hides the Form Controls toolbar.
Color Palette Toolbar	Shows or hides the Color Palette toolbar.
Layout Toolbar	Shows or hides the Layout toolbar.
Form Builder	Launches the Form Builder.
Auto Format	Applies a style to a form's controls. At least one control must be selected to enable the Auto Format button.

Buttons on the Form Designer Toolbar
Table 7-4.

selected. Click inside any of the boxes you selected and drag the group about a half inch to the right. Your screen should look like Figure 7-5.

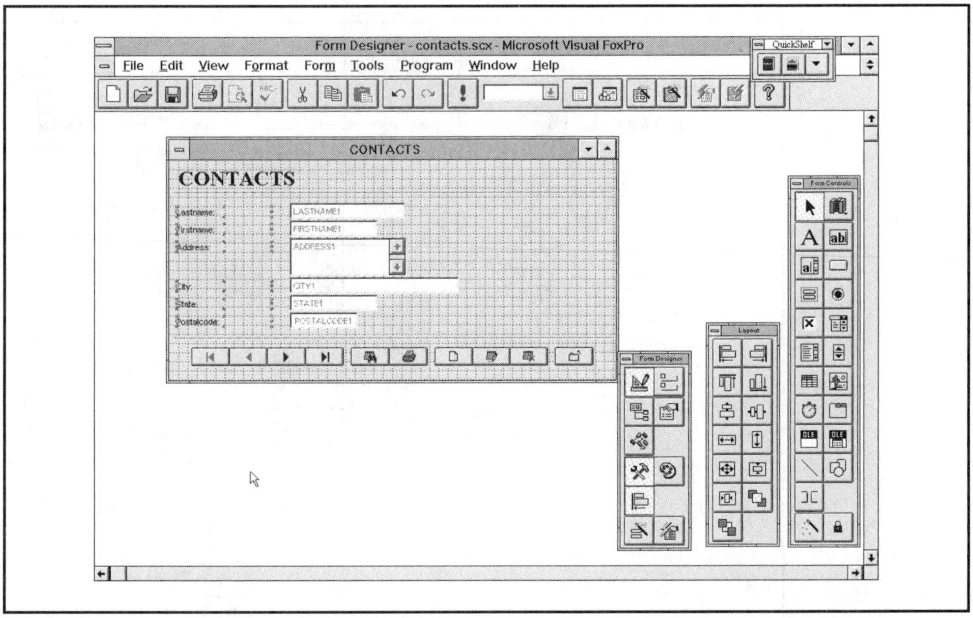

The form with the text boxes moved to the right
Figure 7-5.

Click the right mouse button on the Lastname label box. This action displays the Visual FoxPro Properties dialog box. Note that the Properties dialog box comprises five pages of properties information, as indicated by the five tabs at the top of each page. The Properties dialog box allows you to customize the properties of any object in your form.

Click the Layout tab and then click Caption to highlight it. Your screen should look like Figure 7-6.

Click the text box above the page tabs. The text box now contains the word "Last." Insert the words **Last Name** in its place and press ENTER to accept this new caption.

Now change the captions of the next two labels to **First Name** and **Street Address**, respectively. If any of the label fields are not large enough to contain the new caption, just stretch it again, like before, until it is large enough. If you need to, move the text boxes more to the right. Your screen should look like Figure 7-7.

Test Driving Your New Form

Now see how the new form works. Click Form in the main menu and then click Run Form. Click Yes when the Save Changes dialog box appears, and

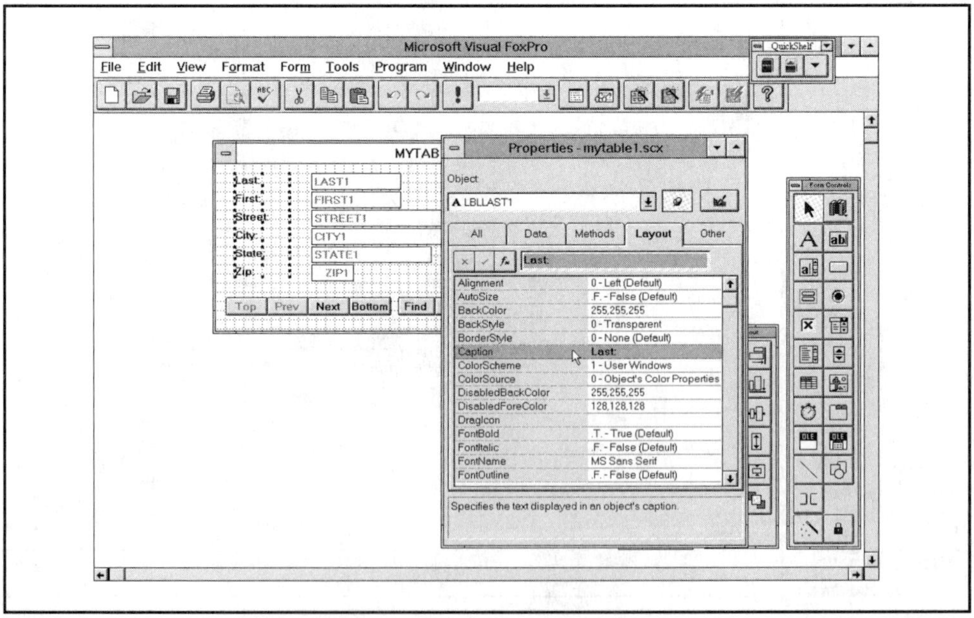

The Properties dialog box
Figure 7-6.

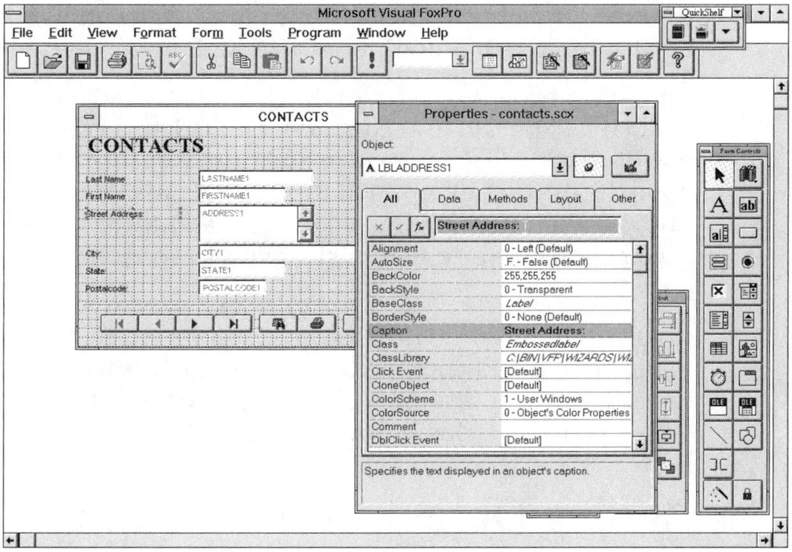

The Properties dialog box with changed labels
Figure 7-7.

Visual FoxPro will run the form inside the Form Designer and allow you to test it. Your screen should look like Figure 7-8.

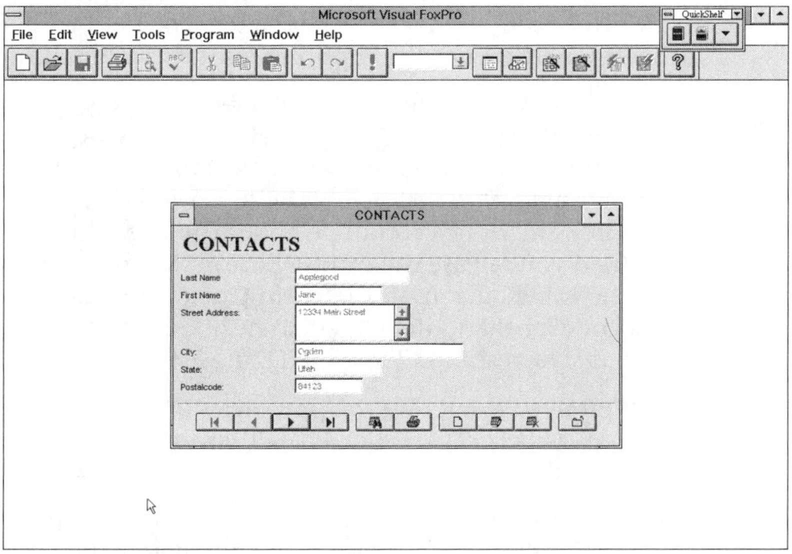

The form in the Form Designer
Figure 7-8.

Notice that the form begins with the first record in your table showing. Use the navigation buttons at the bottom of your form to move around the table and examine it, but don't use the Add, Edit, or Delete button yet.

Your form allows users to do much more than navigate and examine the data table. You can also edit, add, and delete records. Try it. Click the Add button, and Visual FoxPro appends a new record to the table and displays blank fields on the form. Fill in the fields with any information you choose. You can then click the Save button to add this new record to your table or, if you change your mind, click Revert to abandon the new record. Here, click Save.

If you decide after saving that you don't want to keep the record, just navigate to it and click Delete. This action brings your table back to the way it was when you first started running the form. Click Exit to close the form. When your form closes, you will return to the Visual FoxPro main screen.

Adding Objects to Your Form

Enter the Form Designer to do a little more work on your form. Click File in the main menu and then click Open. This action displays the Windows Open dialog box. Select Form in the List Files of Type box at the bottom of the dialog box and double-click your form's filename to launch the Form Designer with your form loaded.

It is extremely easy to add or remove objects in Visual FoxPro's Form Designer. You will add a new field to the form, but first you need to add another field to the data table. Add a new field, Homephone, to your data table. Make sure to make it a character type field with a length of 15 to accommodate all necessary phone number information.

Reopen the form in the Form Designer by selecting File and Open so you can add a new text box to display the Homephone field on your form. In the Form Controls toolbox, click the Text Box control button. Move the cursor, but don't drag it, to just below the lower-left corner of the Postalcode text box. Click and drag a rectangle about the size you want your new text box to be. When you release the mouse button, the new text box will appear. Next, click the Label button on the Form Objects toolbar. Then click below the Postalcode label and drag a rectangle about the shape you want the label to be. Your screen should look like Figure 7-9.

Now you need to modify the properties of the new box. Right-click the new label box, Label2. Then click Properties in the drop-down menu to open the Properties dialog box.

Click the Layout tab in the Properties dialog box and scroll down to the row marked Caption and click it. In the box below the row of tabs, change the

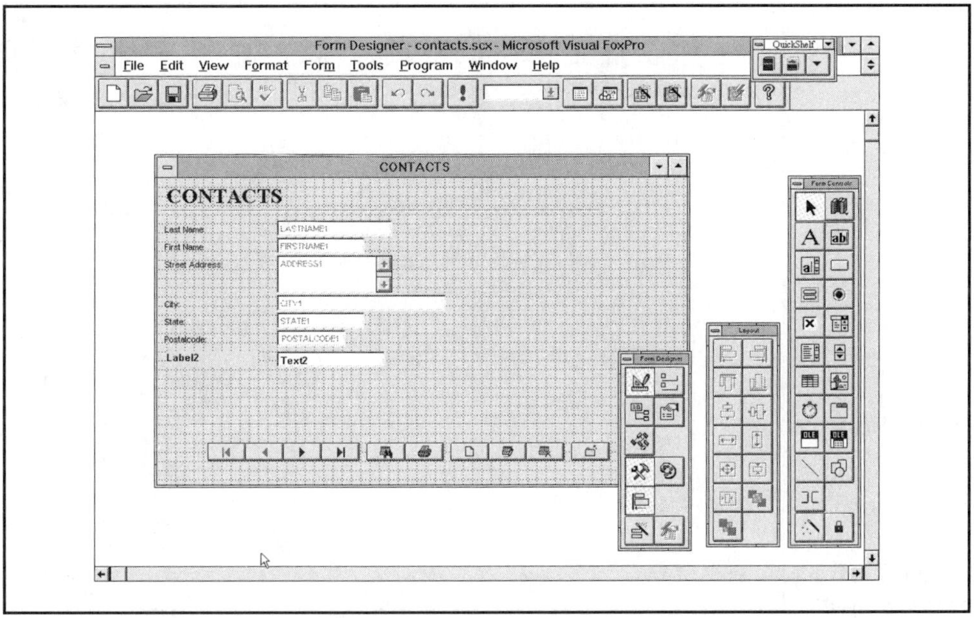

The form with a new text box added
Figure 7-9.

entry to **Home Phone** and press ENTER to accept the new label. Next, click the new text box on the right and notice that the Properties dialog box is now focused on that text box. Right-click the text box and click Builder in the drop-down menu to launch the Visual FoxPro Text Box Builder.

The Text Box Builder contains three pages. Click the Values tab and then click the small button with three dots (...) to display the Windows Open dialog box. Double-click the data table filename and click OK.

Now all that remains is to change the name of the new text box to reflect the field it contains. Click the Other tab in the Properties dialog box and click the Name row. Type **HOMEPHONE** in the edit box and press ENTER to accept it. Your screen should look like Figure 7-10.

Run your form again now and add a few phone numbers to try out your new field.

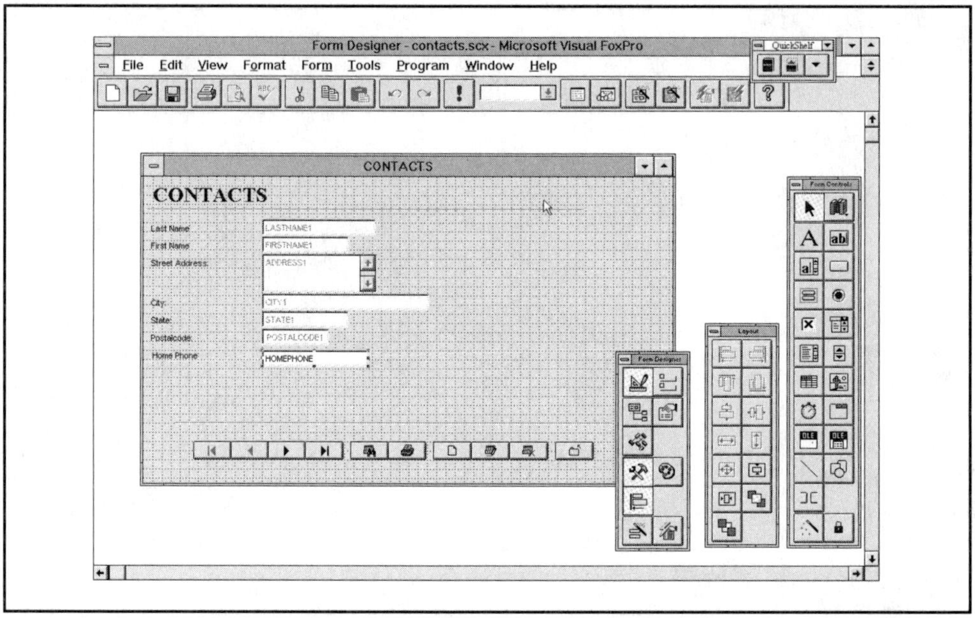

The form with Homephone added

Figure 7-10.

8

Understanding and Using Visual FoxPro Controls

In Chapter 5 you learned the basic principles that underlie Visual FoxPro controls, and in the intervening chapters you used controls to design a simple form and a simple report. Thus far, however, the focus has been more on using control functionality and less on manipulating and modifying controls. In this chapter, you will focus on the latter.

Manipulating Controls

You can manipulate Visual FoxPro controls in several important ways. You can

- Align them using tools on the Layout toolbar.
- Set their foreground and background colors using the Palette toolbar.
- Size and position them by dragging them in the Form Designer window.
- Set their properties using the Properties window.

You can manipulate Visual FoxPro controls at design time or run time; but you cannot individually access or modify the elements that make up the control. This is because controls are more securely encapsulated than containers to protect the integrity of their programmatic functions.

Tip: The primary tools for manipulating all form controls reside in the Properties window.

Selecting the Right Control

Because Visual FoxPro controls are both versatile and powerful, a variety of controls can be configured to accomplish the same task. However, you need to use a consistent approach in selecting and designing controls to avoid confusing the people who use your applications. For example, labels and lines have click events just like command buttons; however, experienced Windows users do not ordinarily expect to click labels or lines to execute actions, as they do with command buttons. When you design functionality into your forms, this functionality will usually take one or more of the following forms:

- Accepting unique user input that cannot be predefined or derived
- Accepting limited user input, such as input within a specified range
- Providing predefined user choices and options
- Displaying data or information
- Performing predetermined actions at specified intervals
- Performing predefined actions at the user's discretion

Working with Controls

Launch Visual FoxPro and open *contacts.scx* in the Form Designer. You will now create a new control on your form and start learning to manipulate its properties using the Properties window.

First, click the ListBox icon on the Form Controls toolbar. Then click any empty spot on the right side of your form to drop in the list box control. Size and position your new list box to look like Figure 8-1.

List Control Properties and Methods

Table 8-1 lists the most common list object properties.

Because list boxes display multiple items that are always visible, you can easily set up the list box on your form to scroll through and display all the names in your data table. The quickest and easiest way to set up a list box is with the Visual FoxPro List Box Builder.

Launch the List Box Builder by right-clicking the new list box and then click Builder to launch the Visual FoxPro List Box Builder. Note that the List Box

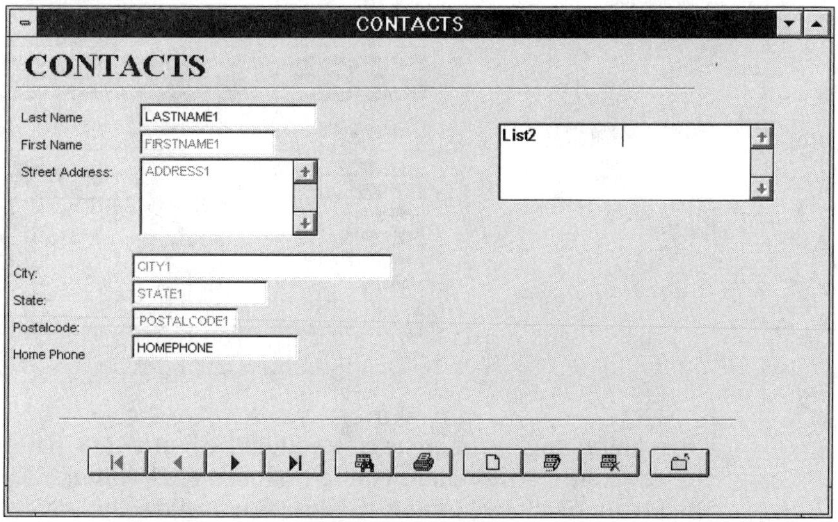

The new list box on the form

Figure 8-1.

Property	Description
ColumnCount	Defines the number of columns displayed in the object
ControlSource	Specifies where the object's data is stored
MoverBars	Determines whether mover bars appear at the left of listed items to allow rearrangement of item order
MultiSelect	Specifies whether more than one item can be selected at one time
RowSourceType	Defines the source of data supplied in a row of listed items

Common List Object Properties
Table 8-1.

Builder anticipates that you may want to use the *contacts.dbf* table and automatically (one might say *intuitively*) makes the appropriate fields available. Move the Lastname field and then the Firstname field into the Selected Fields box. Then click the Style tab at the top of the List Box Builder. In the Styles dialog box, click Three Dimensional, select 3 Rows, and click the Layout tab. Your screen should look like this:

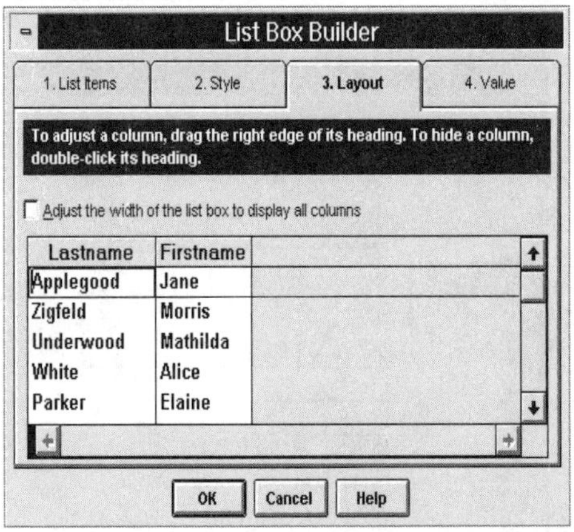

This dialog page is okay as is, so click the Value tab. Then click the arrow on the right side of the Field Name box and click *contacts.lastname* to complete the setup. Click OK to exit the List Box Builder.

You have now set up the list box to display Lastname and Firstname from your data table so you can scroll through the names using the spin buttons at the right of the box. Don't forget to save your form.

Now run your form by clicking the Run button. Try scrolling through the names using the new list box and familiarize yourself with this new control. Notice that you can highlight an entry in the box by clicking it, but nothing happens. You'll see how to fix this shortly, and at the same time you will add a very convenient feature to your form that will allow quick access to a specific record.

Your form should now look like Figure 8-2.

When you have finished exploring your new creation, take a moment to examine the Visual FoxPro Properties window for this new control. First, close your running form and return to the Form Designer. Then launch the Properties window by right-clicking the new list box. Click Properties, and your screen displays the Properties window shown in Figure 8-3.

Bound Data

The term *bound data* refers to an object-oriented feature of Visual FoxPro that allows you permanently to associate a control with a data item. This data can be in the form of a variable, a table, a record, or a cursor field. When you interact with control objects, the values you enter or select are stored in the data source to which the object is bound. You can specify whether an

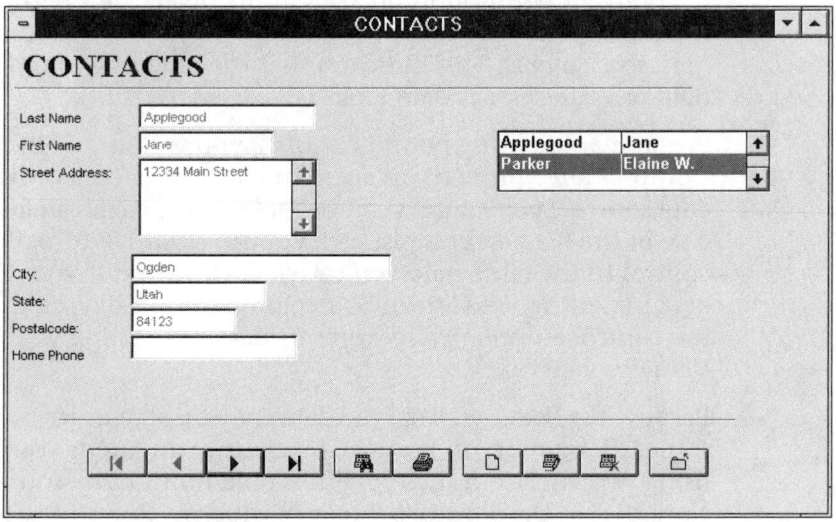

The form with the completed list box
Figure 8-2.

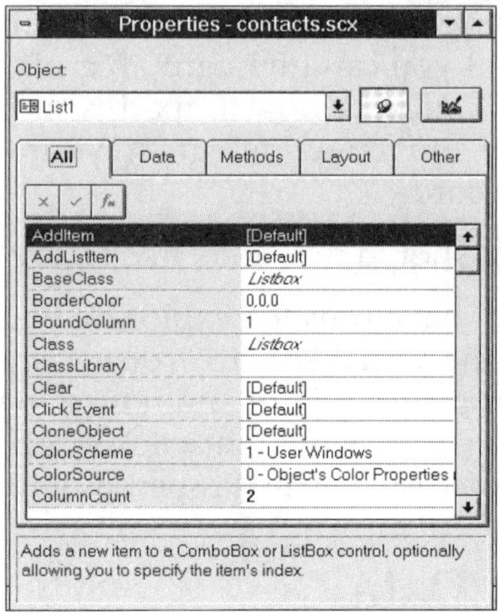

The Properties window
Figure 8-3.

object's data values are stored in a variable, table field, record field, or cursor field by setting the control's ControlSource property.

This action of permanently associating a control with specific data is called *binding* a control to its data. In the case of the list box you just created, the wizard bound your control to the data fields you selected during your interaction with the wizard's dialog boxes. The location of the data to which the object is bound now appears in the object's Properties window. Click the Data tab in the Properties window and note that the control source is *contacts.lastname*. This indicates that the object is bound to the Lastname field of your *contacts* data table.

When manipulating bound controls, you are limited by the control's ControlSource property to accessing or storing data only in the specified data source. Such sources can be table fields, cursor fields, or variables. In the case of the list box you just created, the wizard automatically bound this control to the table field you selected. However, if you don't bind a control's data by setting the ControlSource property (or having the wizard do it), then the control automatically stores its data as a setting in the control's internal Value property.

Because list boxes arrange the data they display in rows, you need to specify some information on how the rows are configured. You accomplish this using two entries in the Properties box: RowSource and RowSourceType. Note that in the control's Property window, RowSourceType is set to Fields, and RowSource specifies the fields you instructed the wizard to display in the list box in the order in which you specified them.

Adding Event Code to an Object

The Form Designer's Code Edit window allows you to attach your own event code to a Visual FoxPro object. For example, you can add the convenience of being able to quickly select a record by double-clicking a line in the list box you just created, rather than having to use the VCR buttons to scroll through the data table. You add this feature by adding double-click event code to the list box.

Because the new list box is already bound to your data table's Lastname record, when you select a record in this object, Visual FoxPro's record pointer automatically moves to that record. Thus, to view the entire contents of a record on your form, all you need to do is refresh the text boxes on the form that you created in Chapter 6. Each of these seven text boxes is already bound to a field of your data table—that's why they automatically display the current record as you move from record to record using the VCR buttons. The VCR buttons have built-in event code to refresh the records. However, your list box does not; therefore, you need to add the code using the Code Edit window.

Adding the event code you need is simple using Visual FoxPro's Table Designer and the Code Edit window. First, double-click the list box to launch the Code Edit window. It appears with the ListBox object selected in the Object box at the top of the window. Click the right arrow on the Procedure box and select DblClick by double-clicking it. Now type **thisform.refresh** on the main screen. Your screen should look like this:

The event code you just entered refreshes the entire form each time you double-click the list box. Because the list box automatically moves the Visual FoxPro record pointer when you click a line of its displayed data, the form displays the new record when the double-click event triggers your refresh command.

To see how this operation works, exit from the Code Edit window and click the Bang button to run your form. Observe how the event code you added to your list box increases the convenience of your form. When you double-click an entry in the list box, your form is updated automatically to display all the fields in that record.

By now, you should be starting to see why controls are the most versatile and complex objects in Visual FoxPro's arsenal of object-oriented tools. You will come back to controls again and again in future chapters to see more of the functionality and power they place at your disposal.

Controls as Containers

Controls *can* contain other objects. However, because controls, unlike containers, *do not allow access to the objects within them,* you cannot access these embedded controls individually. For example, if you create a control object containing two text box controls and two label controls and then add this control object to your form, you cannot manipulate the text boxes and labels individually, either at design time or run time. When you embed objects in controls, be sure you will not have to access them at some later time in the design process.

Control Functionality

You have now learned all the basic principles you need to create and manipulate virtually any control in Visual FoxPro's extensive control library. In creating one simple control, you have been introduced to the subject of control properties and manipulation. The fundamentals of all Visual FoxPro controls are the same. Control manipulation is easy if you carefully plan what each control needs to accomplish and then use Visual FoxPro's tools to create and manage your controls.

The following sections detail the functionality of some key controls that you have used thus far or will use in Parts 3, 4, and 5. Now is a good time to familiarize yourself with these controls, while their underlying principles of operation are fresh in your mind.

Check Boxes

Check boxes let the user select between two choices such as yes and no; true and false; or red and yellow. When a choice is selected, an X appears in the check box. The CheckBox Caption property specifies any text that appears beside the check box. The Picture property can be used to specify an image for a check box. Key properties of a check box always appear in its Properties window, allowing you to change them conveniently. A check box can have one of three possible states, with a corresponding number—0, 1, or 2—stored in its Value property, as follows:

- No or false (unchecked) = 0
- Yes or true (checked) = 1
- Null (dimmed) = 2

Text Boxes

A text box allows users to add or edit data stored in any non-memo data field. You can manipulate the text in a text box by changing the Value property. If you set the ControlSource property, the displayed value is stored in both the text box's Value property and the table or cursor field you specify in the ControlSource property. For example, if a text box is named Text1 and its ControlSource property is set to Contact.Lastname, then whatever is stored in the Lastname field of the customer table will appear in the text box and can be accessed programmatically by testing Text1.Value.

Edit Boxes

Edit boxes hold multiple lines of text, in contrast to text boxes, which hold only one line of text. Otherwise, edit boxes are functionally the same as text boxes. Edit boxes are best used to facilitate the editing of text stored in long character fields or in memo fields.

Spinners

You use a spinner control to select from a range of numeric values. You spin through the values by clicking the up or down arrow on the spinner bar or by typing a value in the spinner box. The KeyBoardHighValue and SpinnerHighValue properties of spinner objects specify the maximum numeric values you can enter in the spinner box from the keyboard or select by clicking the spinner buttons. The KeyBoardLowValue and SpinnerLowValue properties allow you to specify the minimum numeric values you can enter in the spinner box from the keyboard or select by clicking the spinner buttons.

Drop-Down List Boxes and Combo Boxes

Drop-down list boxes and combo boxes provide lists of options and information:

- List boxes display multiple items, with all items always visible.
- Combo boxes display only one item; however, the user can enter a value or click the box's down button to scroll to additional items.

If the ControlSource property of one of these controls is set to a field in a table, the value you choose from the list is written back into the table. If an item in the list matches the value in the control's ControlSource field, then the item is selected as the record pointer. You specify a combo box's style by changing the control's Style property.

Timers

Timer controls trigger timer events at regular intervals, independent of user interaction. The control's timing interval determines how often the timer fires its trigger. Alone, it does not measure elapsed time.

Tip: All timer controls have to be associated either with a form or with the _SCREEN object.

The timer's Interval property specifies the number of milliseconds between timer events. Unless disabled, timers continue to trigger timer events at roughly equal intervals. The timer's Interval property has some limitations:

- The length of the timer interval is limited to between 0 and 2,147,483,647 milliseconds. This means the longest programmable interval is 596.5 hours, or just a little more than 24 days.
- Visual FoxPro does not guarantee that timer intervals will elapse exactly on time. Therefore, to facilitate accuracy, your timer's event code should check the system clock periodically, rather than try to keep track of accumulated time internally.
- The system produces only 18 clock interrupts (ticks) per second, so even though the timer's Interval property is programmatically measured in milliseconds, the true interval precision is less than one-eighteenth of a second.
- Under conditions of heavy demand on the system, such as long iterative loops, long numerical calculations, or protracted input-output operations, your timer cannot be relied on to trigger events as the Interval property specifies. Use the timer control with extreme care for critical timing functions.

Images

Image controls add *.bmp* pictures to your form. These controls have all the properties, events, and methods that other controls have, and like other controls, image controls can be changed by the user dynamically at run time. Interaction with images is accomplished by clicking, double-clicking, and dragging. Previous versions of FoxPro allowed image controls to be bound with a General field; Visual FoxPro does not. In Visual FoxPro, this functionality is available only if you use the OLE-bound control.

Shapes

Visual FoxPro uses the shape control's Curvature property to set the corner radius. Valid settings are 0 (rectangle) through 99 (ellipse). (This control replaces the rectangle and rounded rectangle controls in previous versions of FoxPro for Windows.)

Lines

Like other Visual FoxPro controls, the line control also has properties, events, and methods. In FoxPro for Windows, lines could be only horizontal or vertical. In Visual FoxPro, they can connect any two points on a form.

Labels

Functionally, labels are similar to text boxes, with these main differences:

- Labels cannot have a data source.
- Labels cannot be edited directly by a user.
- Users cannot use the TAB key to move into a label.

Option Buttons and Option Button Groups

Visual FoxPro initially provides two buttons by default when you create an option button group. If you want more buttons or fewer, change the control's ButtonCount property. Right-click an object and choose Edit from the shortcut menu to manipulate individual elements of either an option button or option button group.

Note: If a button's control source is a character field, when you choose the button, its Caption property is written in the field. If the control source is numeric, the number of the option button selected is written in the field.

9

Creating a Visual FoxPro Report

Visual FoxPro's report design features provide programmers with convenient run-time methods for extracting, organizing, and presenting data as hard-copy reports. You should be aware, though, that although Visual FoxPro's report generating capabilities are more than adequate, they differ little from those of FoxPro for Windows 2.6.

If you are familiar with the FoxPro 2.6 report generator, you may choose to skip this chapter.

In Chapter 7 you learned how easily you can create a Visual FoxPro form. In this chapter you will discover how easily you can design a Visual FoxPro report that is both informative and visually pleasing. You can design Visual FoxPro reports using the Report Wizard, the Report Designer, or a combination of the two. Although the Visual FoxPro Report Designer and Report Wizard lack many of the elegant object-oriented visual features otherwise implemented in Visual FoxPro, you will have no trouble designing first-class reports capable of satisfying all your needs. Visual FoxPro retains all of FoxPro's traditional capabilities for designing reports using inline code, but adds new automated design features. This chapter focuses on these new features.

Even though you will learn in this chapter how to use Visual FoxPro's basic automated features to create a report, this chapter does not discuss the most powerful and convenient features of Visual FoxPro report design: one-to-many relationships. However, experimenting and familiarizing yourself with Visual FoxPro's reporting features now will set the groundwork for what you will learn in Chapter 10.

When designing reports you can use either the Visual FoxPro Report Designer, as shown in Figure 9-1, or Report Wizard, much as you did when

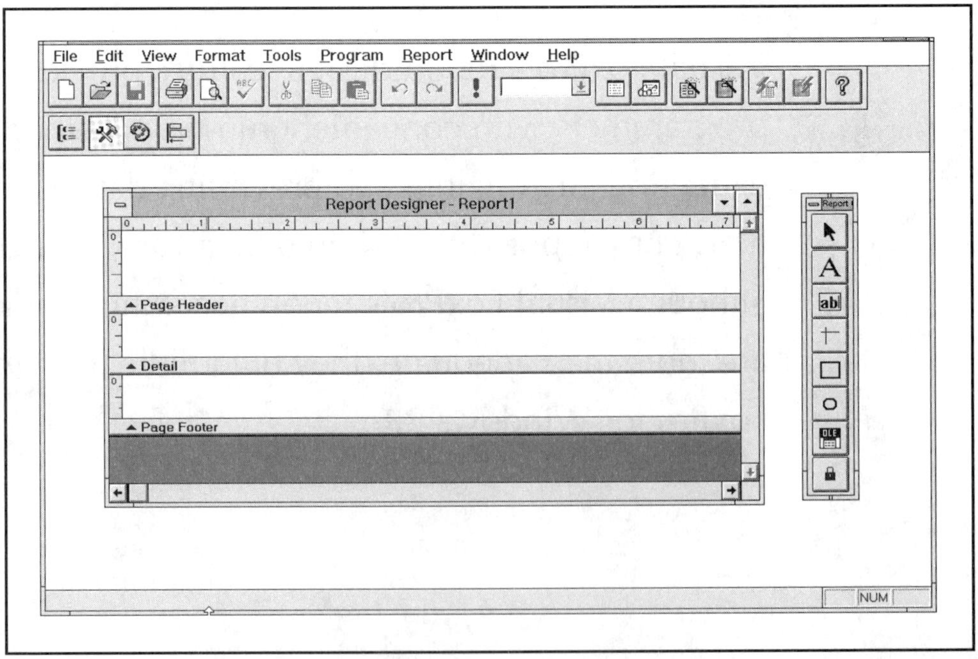

The Visual Foxpro Report Designer
Figure 9-1.

designing custom forms in the previous chapter. Creating useful, even complex, Visual FoxPro reports is surprisingly simple when you use the Report Designer and Report Wizard—much easier, faster, and more reliable than using inline code, except in unusual circumstances.

This chapter discusses the following topics:

- Designing and creating a single-table report
- Selecting and placing report objects
- Manipulating report objects

In the course of this chapter, you will use the Report Wizard to create a Visual FoxPro custom report for accessing and printing data from your simple data table, *contacts.dbf*, and learn how to manipulate the Visual FoxPro controls available in the Report Designer. Your ability to create and work with single-table custom reports prepares you for the next big step in data management and reporting: organizing data into one-to-many custom reports using multiple data tables.

Why Use Visual FoxPro's Report Designer?

Because report generators perform the task of organizing repetitive data and managing a host of programming work, many programmers have, in the past, found them to be nonintuitive. Programmers are accustomed to managing these tasks with hand-coded procedures. Early report generators tended to be clumsy and all too often were unreliable and ineffective. Visual FoxPro's report generator, however, will serve you well if you invest a little time in learning to use it.

When you use the Report Designer, you have to tell it how you want to keep track of page headers, page numbers, dates, column headers, data tables, footers, and so on. Programmers accustomed to hand-coding these procedures know what a frustrating and time-consuming job it can be—and when the coding is done, debugging the report is slow death by torture.

Sadly, early automated report generators—including the one in FoxPro 1.0—were so frustrating that many programmers continued to use hand coding. Visual FoxPro, however, at last offers a reliable reporting tool. The Report Designer is what its previous incarnations promised to be but were not. Once you are familiar with using this tool, you will be glad you invested the time and energy so you can delegate the uninteresting drudgery of coding and debugging complex reports to Visual FoxPro's Report Designer.

Designing a Visual FoxPro Report with the Report Wizard

When you design a Visual FoxPro report, you are simply formatting a printed page, or pages, that organizes and contains information you have generated and stored in Visual FoxPro. The process is straightforward once you master a few simple procedures. You learned in Chapter 7 that Visual FoxPro forms are container objects with elegantly sophisticated object-oriented features. In this chapter, you will see that Visual FoxPro report design is extremely useful and powerful; however, it does not require the level of sophistication demanded by most other data management operations. For example, when generating reports, you don't need to be as concerned with object properties, events, and methods.

Visual FoxPro's Report Wizard automatically generates data reports in a variety of attractive formats based on the data table or tables you specify. The more powerful Report Designer allows you to establish data relationships, format pages, add or delete fields, create captions, and arrange and group your data.

As with Visual FoxPro form design, it is often most convenient to begin designing your report by letting the Wizard build the initial format based on the data and other criteria you specify. Then you can use the Report Designer to rearrange and embellish the wizard's skeletal report to suit your needs. As a general rule, this strategy is not only easier and faster; it usually creates reports that require less debugging later.

Using the Visual FoxPro Report Wizard

Begin by creating a simple Visual FoxPro report using the *contacts.dbf* data table that you created in Chapter 6. Click Tools, Wizards, and then Report to launch the Report Wizard. Your screen should look like Figure 9-2.

Click Report Wizard to highlight it and then click OK. On the Field Selection screen, click the small button to the right of the Databases/Tables window to bring up the Windows Open dialog box so you can select your data table. Double-click *contacts.dbf* to select it. Click the Select All button to tell the wizard you want your report to include all fields in the selected table. The wizard will move all fields into the Selected Fields box. Click Next. The Report Wizard Style dialog box lists three styles, denoted by three radio buttons in the center of the box, as shown in Figure 9-3.

Click the bottom radio button to select Presentation. Then click Next to move to the Report Wizard Layout dialog box. Accept the default setting of 1 column and under Field Layout click the Rows radio button. Accept the

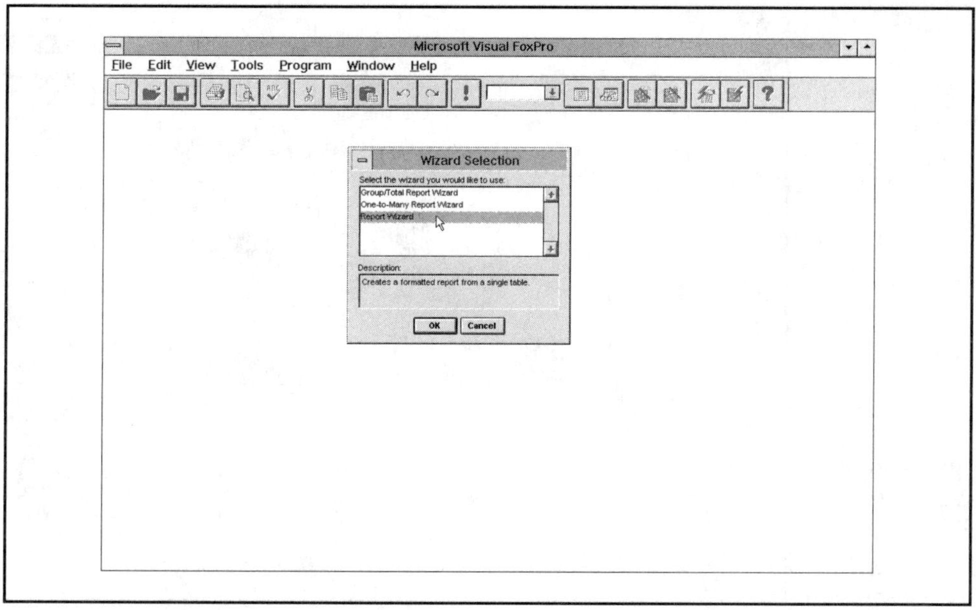

The Report Wizard Selection screen
Figure 9-2.

default orientation of Portrait. Then click Next to move to the Sort Order dialog box, where you specify how your report's data will be indexed. Highlight Lastname and click the Add button. Highlight Firstname and click the Add

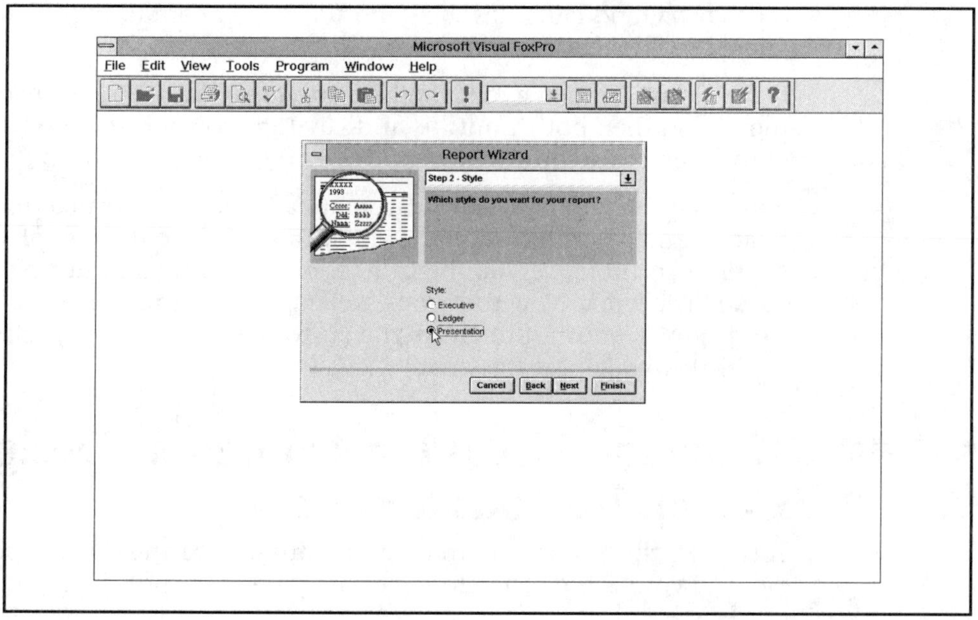

Report Wizard Style dialog box
Figure 9-3.

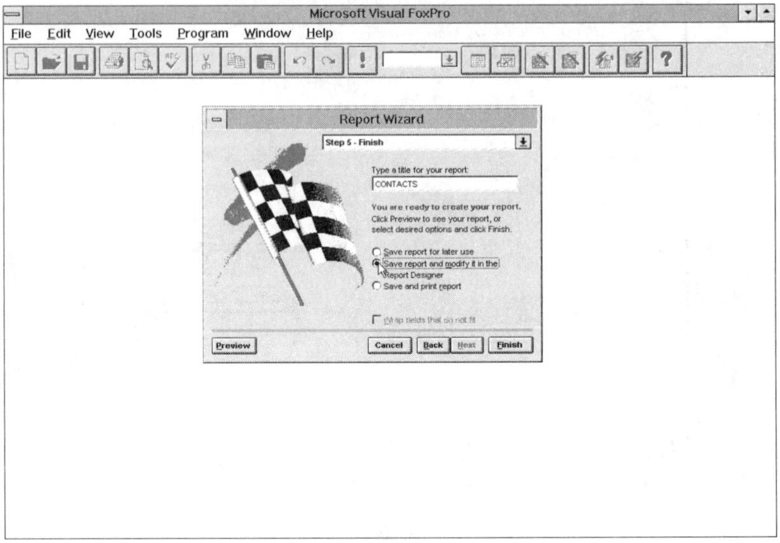

The Report Wizard Finish dialog box
Figure 9-4.

button again to sort on Lastname+Firstname. Click Next to move to the wizard's Finish dialog box. Your screen should look like Figure 9-4.

Select the center radio button, accept the remaining default settings, and click Finish. In the Windows Save As dialog box, accept the default filename, *contacts.frx*, and click Save. The wizard now generates your new report, *contacts.frx*, and launches the Report Designer containing the report, as shown in Figure 9-5.

If the Controls and Layout toolbars are not visible, click View on the main menu and then both Controls and Layout. Position the toolbars at any convenient place on the screen.

Note that the Report Wizard automatically gave the form a title, page header, and column headers, and it arranged the data, complete with the captions it "thought" you might like, in an orderly manner. Not a bad start for so little work. Now that your skeletal form is in the Report Designer, you can begin to polish it to create the custom form you want, using the more sophisticated Report Designer.

Using the Visual FoxPro Report Designer to Customize Your Report

Although the wizard is extremely helpful in creating quick reports, it cannot *yet* read your mind. Therefore, you may need to spruce up and tune your wizard-generated report using the more sophisticated Report Designer. Correctly used, Visual FoxPro's Report Designer gives programmers the ability to accomplish almost any reporting task they can perform with hand coding, only they can do it faster and with far less debugging. Here, you will only scratch the surface of Visual FoxPro's Report Designer, but in Parts 3 and 4 you will build upon this work and learn some powerful procedures for automatically linking multiple data tables and designing reliable and extremely complex business reports. Before delving into the Visual FoxPro Designer, you need to know a little more about what it can do for you and how it works.

Tip: Remember that you can also use the Report Designer to create Visual FoxPro reports from scratch. The procedures you learn working with the wizard-generated report will enable you to create new reports, if you wish, starting with a blank Report Designer screen, although you may not often find it either necessary or desirable to do so.

Anatomy of the Visual FoxPro Report Designer

The Visual FoxPro Report Designer provides bands to help you in designing reports that contain repeating data sets over many pages. Understanding

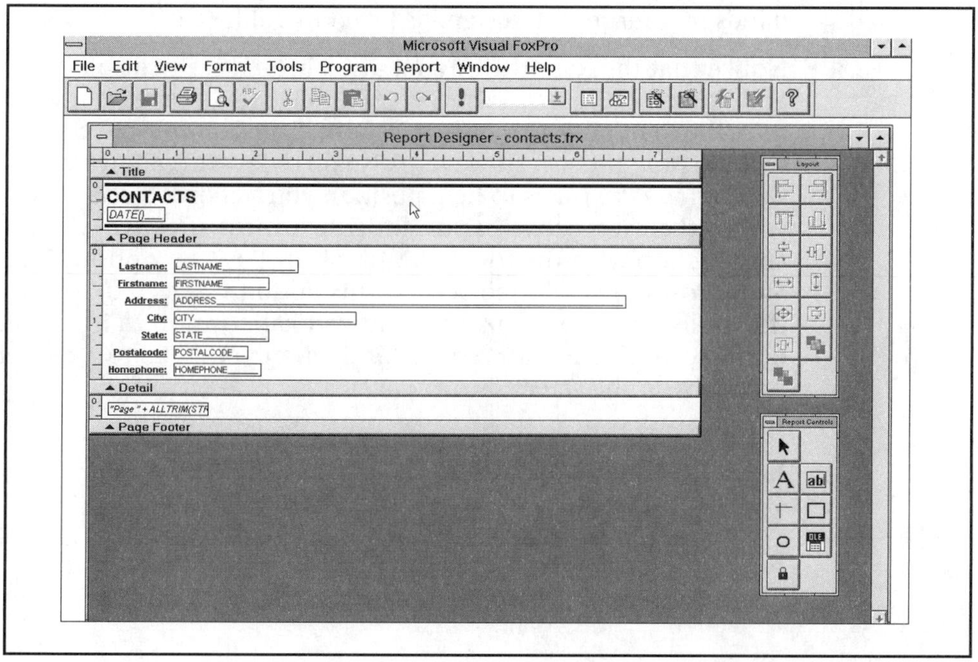

The Visual FoxPro Report Designer containing *contacts.frx*
Figure 9-5.

Band	Printed	Typical Contents
Column Header	Once per column	Column title
Column Footer	Once per column	Summary, totals
Group Header	Once per group	Preface to following data
Group Footer	Once per group	Calculated values for group data
Title	Once per report	Title, date, and page number
Summary	Once per report	Grand totals or text such as "Grand Totals"
Ruler	Not printed	N/A

Optional Report Generator Bands
Table 9-1.

these bands is essential to designing and organizing your data reports. By default, the Report Designer displays three bands when you launch it: Page Header, Detail, and Page Footer. Gray separator bars appear at the bottom of each band. The new report now on your screen contains these three bands, plus one more, a Title band, that the Wizard automatically included. The gray bars positioned between each band display the band's type designation next to a small blue arrow. This blue arrow indicates that the report band is *above*, not below, the gray separator bar. You can include a variety of useful bands in your report design, as listed in Table 9-1.

Notice that the Report Designer also automatically displays both vertical and horizontal rulers. When you launch the designer, these rulers are set to inches, which is the system default. The examples in this book will use only inches. However, Visual FoxPro also allows you to use pixels. You can use the rulers to help position your report objects more precisely within their respective bands. Rulers are most effective when used in conjunction with the View Menu's Show Position option. Check to be sure Show Position is selected. When this option is selected, Visual FoxPro shows the mouse cursor's horizontal and vertical position in inches at the bottom of the screen. This feature is helpful when you need to position objects precisely on the screen.

Using the Report Controls Toolbar

The Report Controls toolbar, as shown in the following illustration, appears automatically when you open the Report Designer.

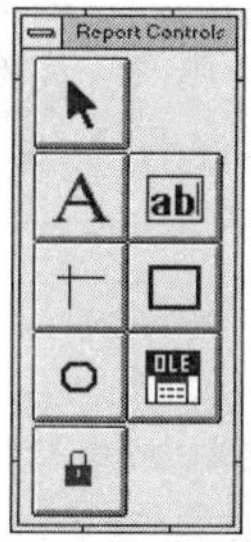

Place additional controls on your report using the control buttons located on the Report Controls toolbar. Click any control you want to place in your report, position the pointer where you want the control to appear, and click again to place the control. You can also drag some controls to the size you need. Double-click any control on your report to display its Properties dialog box.

The Report Controls toolbar contains the control buttons listed in Table 9-2.

Using the Report Designer to Tune Your Report

Now return your attention to the Report Designer screen, as shown in the following illustration. Note that in the Detail band, the wizard placed a label

Button	Description
Select Objects	Resizes and moves controls. After you create a control, the Select Objects button is activated automatically.
Label	Creates a label control to place text.
Field	Creates a field container control to display the contents of a table field, a memory variable, or any other expression.
Line	Draws a variety of line styles on your report at design time.
Rectangle	Draws rectangles on your report.
Rounded Rectangle	Draws rectangles with rounded corners and elliptical shapes.
Picture/OLE Bound Control	Displays a picture or the contents of a general data field.
Button Lock	Allows you to add multiple controls of the same type without clicking the control button each time.

Control Buttons in the Report Controls Toolbar
Table 9-2.

in front of each of your fields, and that each field with its label occupies one line. You will make the layout a little easier to use by rearranging the fields and changing some field properties.

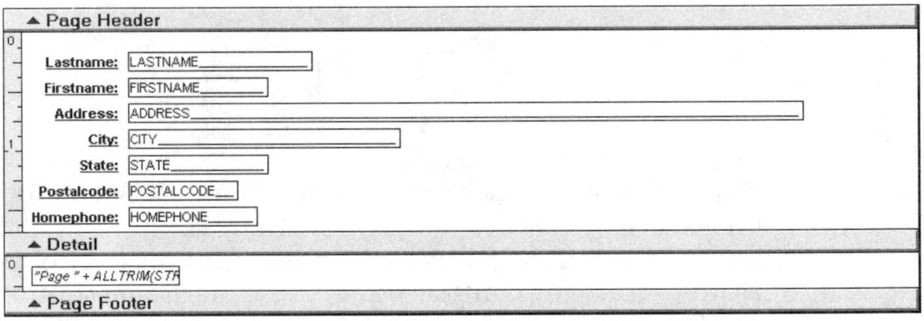

First, since the field information on your simple report is self-explanatory, you can remove the field labels without loosing any functionality. The easiest way to remove the labels is by selecting them all at once, as a block, by placing the cursor just above and to the left of the label Lastname and dragging it to a point just below and to the right of the label Homephone.

When you release the mouse button, all labels in the Detail band are selected simultaneously. Press the DELETE key to make all the labels disappear. If you make a mistake and delete something you don't want to delete, click the Undo button to undo the last deletion and then repeat the deletion procedure with the correct items selected.

Tip: The Undo button, at the top of the screen, shows a counterclockwise blue arrow. You can use this button to undo most operations immediately after you have executed them. It can save you a lot of work.

Your last delete operation left a gap at the left side of the band, so now select all of the field controls the same way you selected the labels and drag them to the left to the gap. Your screen should now look like Figure 9-6.

You can arrange the information in several ways to make it more useful. First try grouping some related fields, such as Firstname and Lastname, and City, State, and Postalcode, on single lines. Begin by dragging the Firstname and Lastname fields to position them as in Figure 9-7.

Was it difficult to perfectly align the fields when you moved them? This is where the Layout toolbar comes in handy. Select both the Firstname and Lastname fields. Then click the Align Bottom Edges button on the Layout toolbar. Now these fields should be perfectly aligned horizontally. Finish

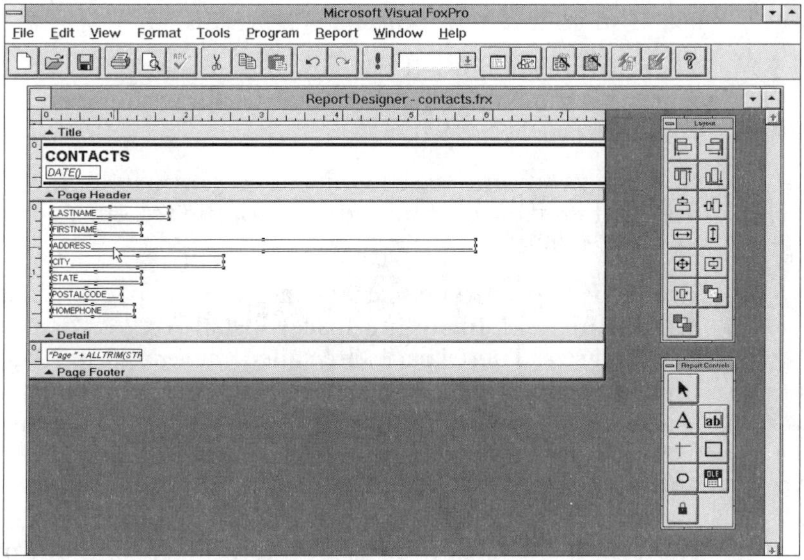

The Report Designer screen with the bands deleted
Figure 9-6.

your rearrangement by moving the Address field up to fill the gap left by the Firstname field you just moved up a line. Then arrange City, State, and

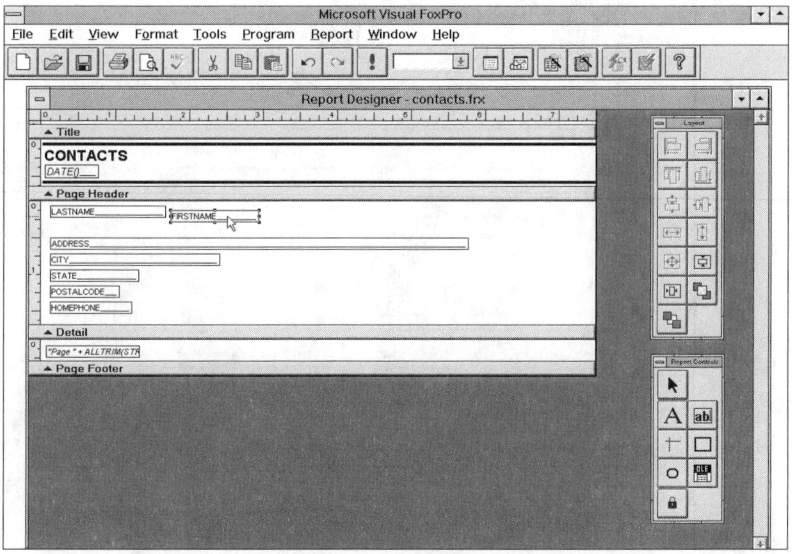

Dragging Firstname to the same line as Lastname
Figure 9-7.

Postalcode below the Address field and move Homephone up into the empty space, so your report looks like Figure 9-8.

Your rearrangement left a large white space at the bottom of the Detail band. Eliminate it by dragging the gray bar below the band upward until the excess white space is removed.

Now is a good time to see how your report will look when printed. Just click the Print Preview button at the top of the screen. Your preview should look like Figure 9-9.

The fields appear to be scattered around the page because you are printing each entire field, including spaces Visual FoxPro adds to fill each field to its specified size. These spaces are called *padded spaces*. You can easily remove them by using Visual FoxPro's trim( ) function, which removes padded spaces before displaying the field. Press ESCAPE to return to the Report Designer, move the cursor over the Lastname field, and click the right mouse button (a right click). Click Properties, and the Properties dialog for the Lastname field appears. For now, disregard all but the text box labeled Expression and click the small button to the right of this box. You just launched Visual FoxPro's Expression Builder. For now, disregard all but the text box labeled Expression for Field on Report. This box allows you to construct an expression using the Visual FoxPro language to manipulate data in the Lastname field control on your report. Type the following expression in this text box: **trim(lastname)+', '+trim(firstname)**

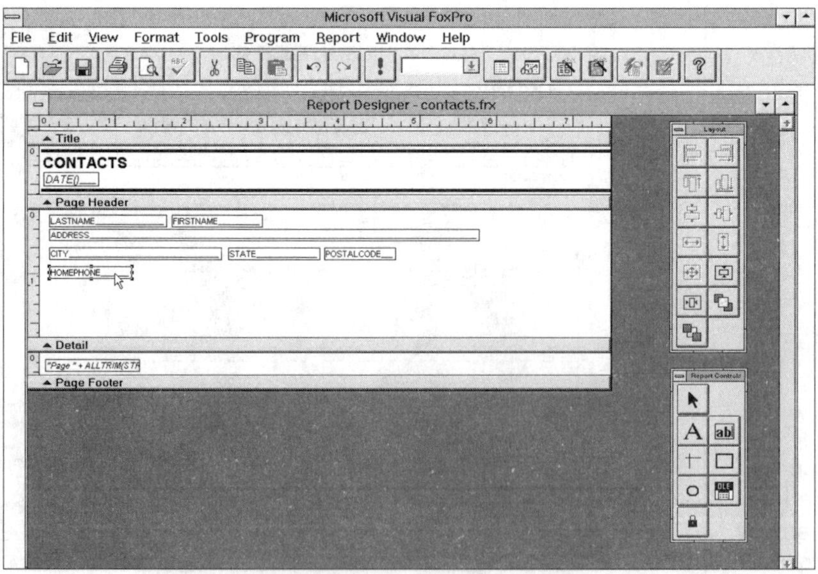

The Report Designer screen with the fields rearranged

Figure 9-8.

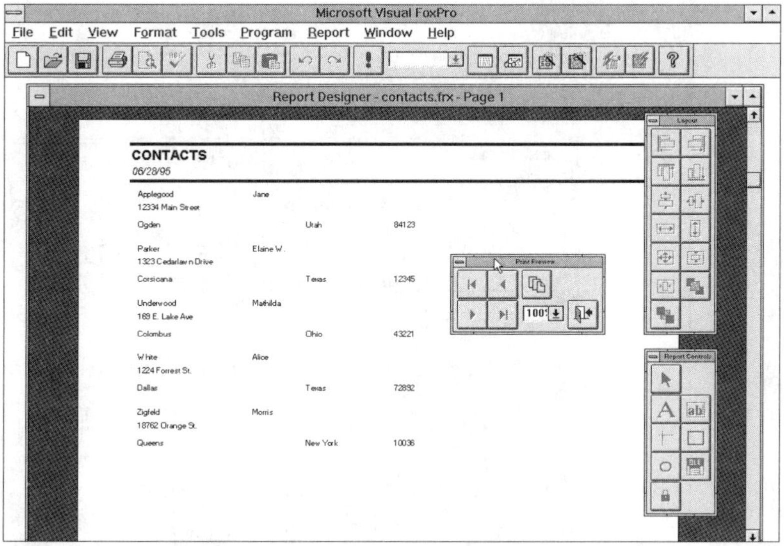

The Print Preview screen for *contacts.frx*

Figure 9-9.

Tip: What you have just done is called concatenating a string. This simply means you constructed a string of text characters by tying together two character fields from your data table, stripped of their padded spaces, and adding a comma and two spaces. You will learn more about strings in Parts 3 and 4.

Your screen should now look like Figure 9-10.

Click OK, and you will see that your expression now appears in the Expression text box of the Report Expression dialog box. Click OK again, and your new expression appears in the field control that previously held only the Lastname field. You can now delete the Firstname field control because you concatenated Firstname with Lastname in the first box on the line. Just select the Firstname field control and press DELETE.

You now need to stretch the modified control to accommodate the new expression you just inserted in it. Select the control and drag its right side about three quarters of the way across the band so it looks as shown in Figure 9-11.

Click the Print Preview button again and see the results of your handiwork. The Lastname and Firstname fields look better without the extraneous spaces between them. The comma and the spaces your expression placed in the

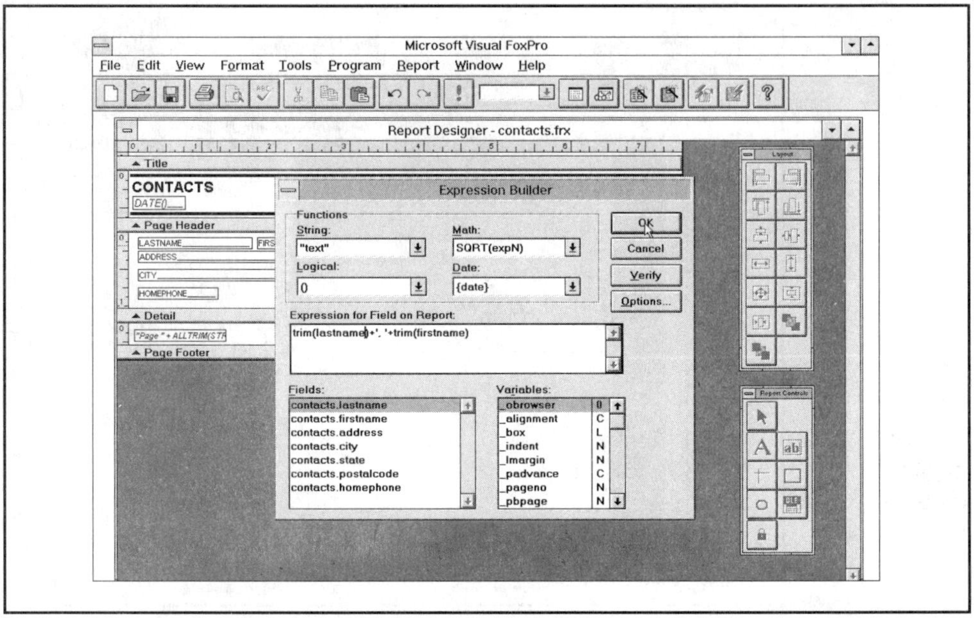

Entering an expression to remove padding characters
Figure 9-10.

control appear just as they should. Now do the same with City, State, and Postalcode fields. Select the City field control and add the appropriate

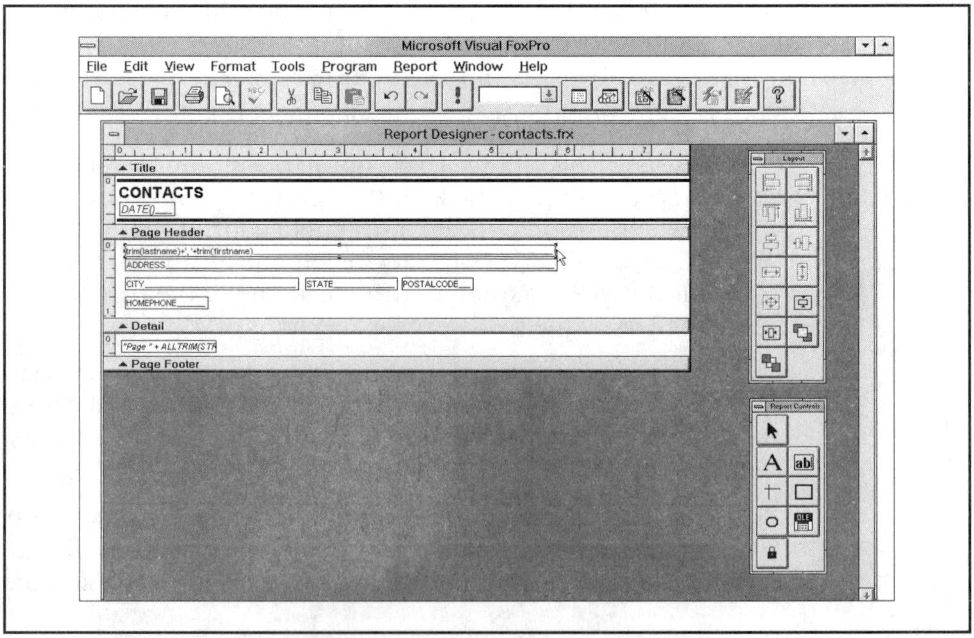

The modified control in the Report Designer
Figure 9-11.

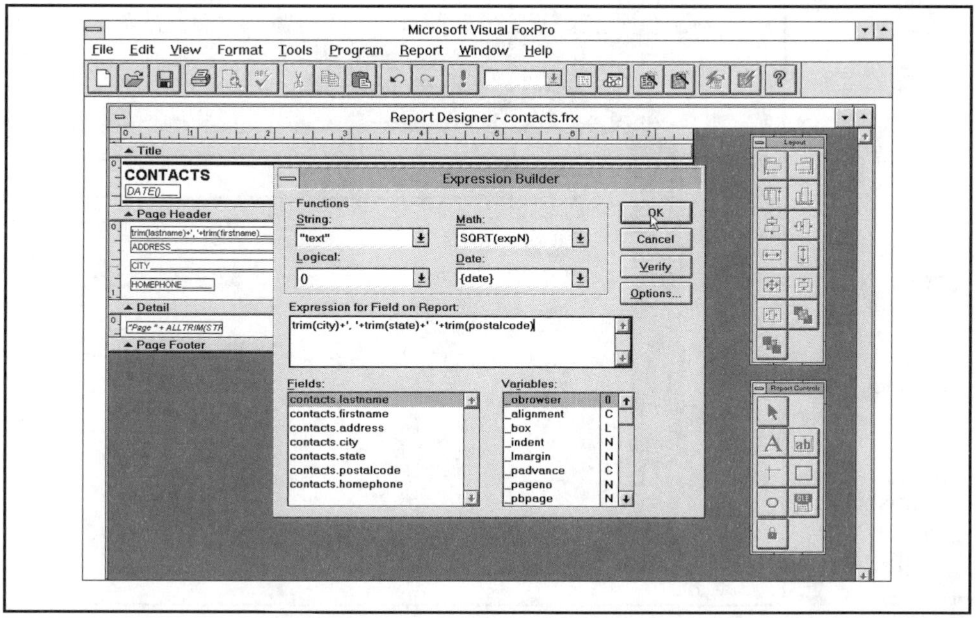

The Expression Builder with another expression entered

Figure 9-12.

expression as you did before. When you finish entering the expression into the Expression Builder dialog box, your screen should look like Figure 9-12.

Click OK in the Expression Builder dialog box. Then click OK in the Report Expression dialog box to return to the Report Designer. Delete the State and Postalcode field controls and again stretch the remaining control on the line to hold the longer expression you just inserted into it. Click Print Preview one more time to see your finished form. It should look like Figure 9-13.

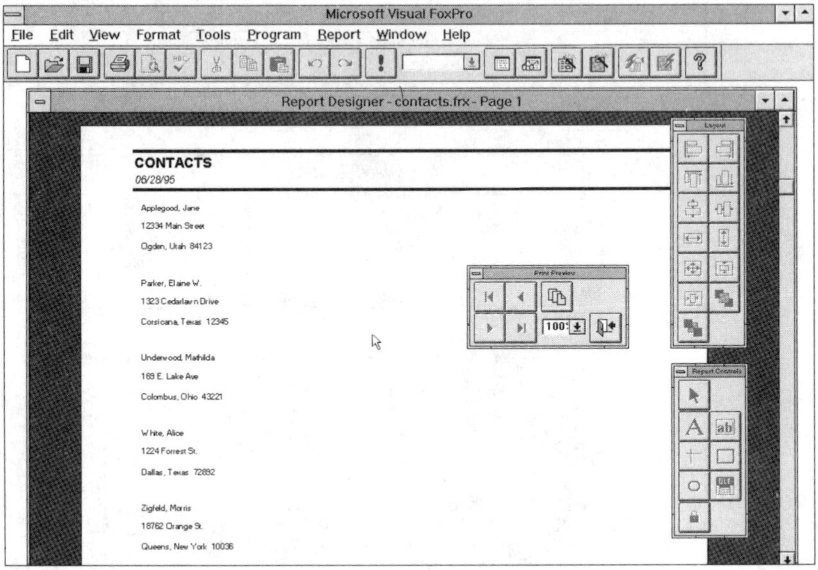

The finished form
Figure 9-13.

part 3

Building Useable Applications

10

Relating Data Tables

This chapter lays the foundation for your understanding of relational databases, which is the topic of Part 3. In this part, you will build a multi-table database and use it to explore some of the issues involved in relating data. Chapter 10 starts with a discussion of the whys and hows of relating tables and ends with the construction of a four-table database you will use in the rest of the section. Chapter 11 discusses some of the methods for displaying related data. Chapter 12 explores some of the advanced controls for handling related data. Finally, Chapter 13 shows you how to print reports using the sample data you developed in this section.

Relating Data: The Power Behind Visual FoxPro

Chapter 3 touched on the relational database model. In that chapter you learned that a relational database calls for data to be stored in tables that are related to one another by common values. For instance, if you have a table of order information, you can relate this information to a customer table by the customer number—that is, both the customer table and the order file can have a field called CustNo, and when you enter a new order, you can enter the customer's number, from the customer table, in the order table's CustNo field. The beauty of this concept is that you do not need to store customer information such as name, address, and terms, with each order. You simply relate the order to the customer table by storing the customer number in the order table.

Relational databases store information in related tables. To better understand this rather dry definition, consider the following example.

Adding to CONTACTS

In Part 2, you created a name and address table, CONTACTS. In it, you put a home phone number field, HomePhone. This phone number field is likely to be sufficient for many of your contacts, but in this age of communication overload it may not be enough for some. You may also want to include numbers for a work phone, fax, cellular phone, or pager. So now you need to expand *contacts.*

You set out to expand your table, adding fields for each of these types of numbers. What about 800 numbers? Or direct numbers that bypass the receptionist? Or voice mailbox numbers? So you add more fields. Then you run into someone who has multiple work numbers because the person has offices at both corporate headquarters and a regional sales office. You add more fields. Some companies run computer bulletin board systems that provide support and sales information. You add still more fields.

As you can see, you are very quickly up to ten or more numbers—and as soon as you get these fields settled, someone will surely come up with a number that does not fit neatly into your plan. You end up with a data table that looks something like this:

Field Name	Type	Length
LastName	Character	20
FirstName	Character	15
Address	Character	80
City	Character	30
State	Character	15
PostalCode	Character	10
HomePhone	Character	14
WorkPhone	Character	14
FaxPhone	Character	14
Cellular	Character	14
Pager	Character	14
TollFree	Character	14
DirectLine	Character	14
VoiceMail	Character	14
BBS	Character	14
WorkPhone2	Character	14

As you can see, the table contains considerable repetitive information, with all those character-type fields 14 bytes long. (The table uses 14-byte fields to allow for numbers in the format (999) 999-9999.) At 14 bytes each, the ten phone numbers take up a total of 140 bytes in each record. If your table contains 100,000 records, these phone numbers will take up about 14 megabytes of space. You may not have that many names in your table, but remember that every extra field takes up space on each and every record. This will become an important point as you consider storing other types of data.

More vexing in this example is the inflexibility of this approach. All phone numbers must fit into one of the fixed categories. If you discover a new need, you must modify the structure to reflect this need or settle for a poor fit. And you're pulling all this baggage along for people who have only one number.

A Better Way: Relating Data

The approach you just used has several problems: There are too many different numbers for most of your records, there are not enough numbers for a few of your records, and the categories are fixed and not always useful. For instance, you have a TollFree field and a BBS field, but suppose you belong to CompuServe. You might put the toll-free customer service number in TollFree and the local access number in BBS. But CompuServe also has an 800 number for accessing its service. This number is convenient for out-of-town trips, because it saves you the trouble of finding the local access number for your destination. But what category would you put it in? TollFree is already taken, as is BBS.

The idea of relating data rescues you from this situation. You can create a second table with two fields of information: PhoneDesc and Phone. You can also have an ID field for relating the record back to CONTACTS. Then you can delete all the phone fields from CONTACTS and add an ID field.

Note: For convenience, this example uses the simple field name ID in both tables. As you develop more complicated tables, you'll see that more descriptive field names are better. Also note that, although recommended, the fields do not have to have the same name.

The new CONTACTS table looks like this:

Field Name	Type	Length
LastName	Character	20
FirstName	Character	15
Address	Character	80
City	Character	30
State	Character	15
PostalCode	Character	10
ID	Numeric	5 (0 decimals)

The new PHONES table looks like this:

Field Name	Type	Length
PhoneDesc	Character	20
Phone	Character	14
ID	Numeric	5 (0 decimals)

These changes cover both ends of the spectrum, from people with only one number to the rare exception who has ten numbers or more. Because you store the description in the PhoneDesc field, you also avoid the limitations of fixed categories; for instance, you can store "California office" instead of the vague WorkPhone2.

You've also optimized storage of the data because space is used only when there is a number to store.

Types of Relationships

There are four types of possible relationships between two tables: one-to-one, one-to-many, many-to-one, and many-to-many.

One-to-Many

In the example, you created a type of relationship known as one-to-many; that is, each record in CONTACTS can have one or more related records in PHONES. Figure 10-1 shows this type of relationship.

One-to-many relationships are the backbone of database work. Almost all useful relationships, as with the CONTACTS/PHONES example previously discussed, are one-to-many.

Many-to-One

The complement of one-to-many is many-to-one. A relationship in which many records in one file relate to one record in another file is a one-to-one relationship; that is, each record in the first file relates to a single record in the second file. For instance, you may have an orders table and a customer

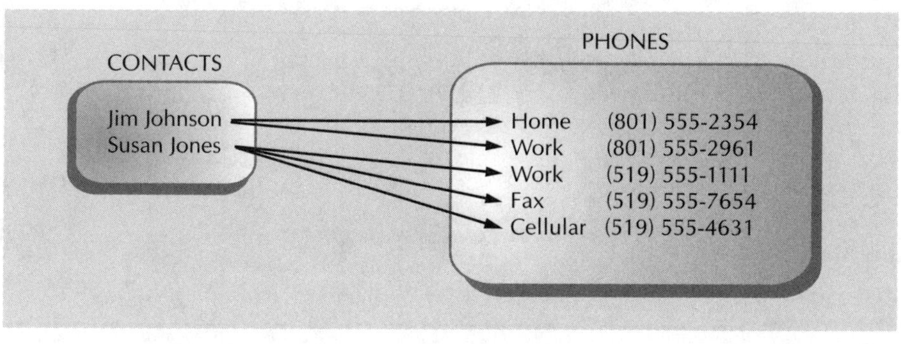

One-to-many relationships
Figure 10-1.

table. Each order would relate to one, and only one, entry in the customer table. Because each customer can have several orders, the relationship is many orders to one customer. Figure 10-2 illustrates this type of relationship.

Although the distinction of many-to-one is important to remember—that one or more records are related to a single record in the other file—you will mainly work with a many-to-one as a one-to-one. For instance, you may have an orders table and a customer table. Each order would relate to one, and only one, entry in the customer table. Because each customer can have several orders, the relationship is many orders to one customer.

One-to-One

One-to-one relationships, where only one record in the first table relates to only one record in the second table, usually indicate a poor design or a relic. Earlier dBASE incarnations were limited to 64 fields and a maximum field length of 255 bytes. These limitations led to the development of parallel files. A programmer could overcome these limitations by creating a second table that had a record for each record in the first table—in effect stretching one record over two or more tables. In early versions of dBASE, one-to-one relationships were standard. However, with all of the current Xbase products, including Visual FoxPro, overcoming this limitation, true one-to-one relationships are rarely seen anymore.

Many-to-Many

Many-to-many relationships have no apparent redeeming value. Consider the following: Jane Smith has an entry in your CONTACTS table and several

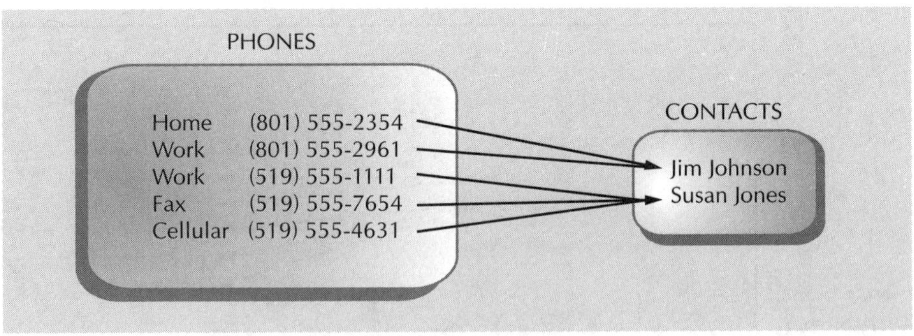

Many-to-one relationships
Figure 10-2.

phone numbers in PHONES. If you wish to add her husband, John, you can add another record in CONTACTS and copy Jane's numbers from PHONES, giving John, and the copied numbers, a new ID. This might be a useful feature for the contacts program.

The wrong thing to do would be to create a new record in CONTACTS and give it the same ID as Jane. If you look at the relationship from the CONTACTS side, both Jane and John *seem* to have their own numbers, but from the PHONES side, which one is it related to? Jane or John? If you change Jane's cellular phone number, you also change John's.

Although in this example you save a little space by having two people share a set of phone numbers, such a beneficial result is an exception when you use a many-to-many relationship. Usually, you end up with a many-to-many relationship by accident—by failing to *normalize* your tables. (Normalization is the process of structuring your database for minimal duplication of information. You will learn about normalization in Part 4.)

Setting Up the Sample Database

In the remainder of Part 3, you will work with an example of a database for a fictitious company, HiPrice Snacks, a supplier of snack bar supplies to movie theaters. HiPrice wants to automate its ordering. The company wants to be able to find out: Which customers order which items? What items are the best sellers in the different seasons? Do the dollar theaters sell more expensive candy or less than the full-price theaters?

The First Cut

You meet with HiPrice's president, and he shows you the standard sales order pad. Sales representatives, he tells you, go to each theater once a week and take orders. The order form has a box at the top for the customer name and address and a band of boxes in the middle for terms, order date, and so forth. The body of the form has space for the name of each item ordered, the quantity ordered, and the price. The bottom of the form provides a total box and an area for the customer signature. Figure 10-3 shows this form.

"This is the center of our business," the president tells you. "Everything we need to know is on this form. Computerize it for us."

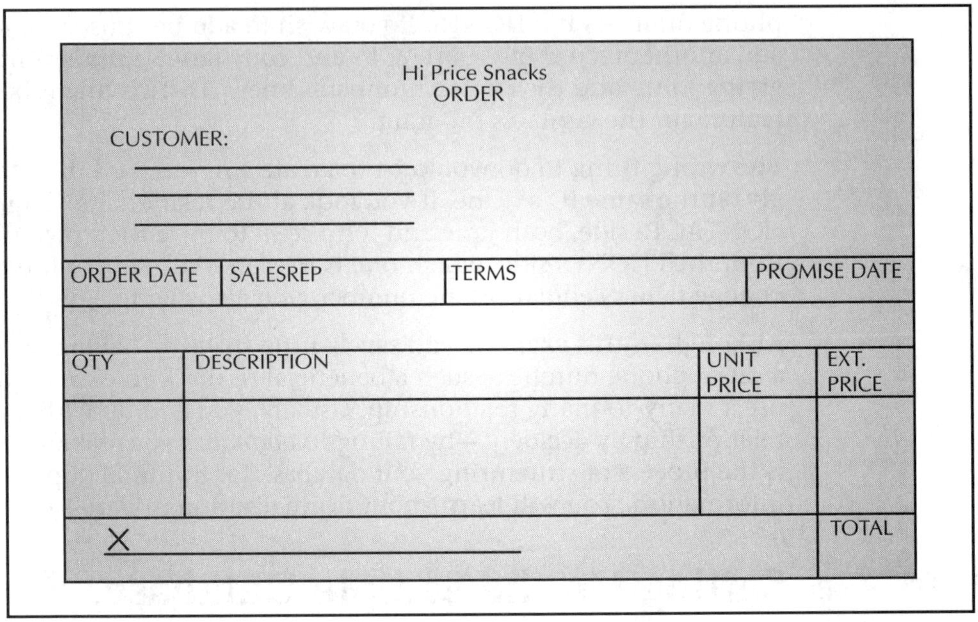

Figure 10-3. Sample of HiPrice's sales order form

The job is easy; you already have the model, so you create a table, ORDERS. After a quick look at the form, you create the structure shown in the following table.

Field Name	Field Type	Field Length
CustomerName	Character	30
Address	Character	30
CityState	Character	30
Phone	Character	14
OrderDate	Date	
PromiseDate	Date	
Terms	Character	20
SalesRep	Character	20
Item	Character	40
Quantity	Numeric	4
UnitPrice	Numeric	7 (2 decimals)
OrderTotal	Numeric	9 (2 decimals)

This structure has a problem though: It provides only one space for items, and most orders contain several items. If you put each item in its own record, you will be wasting a huge amount of space and duplicating information grossly.

However, it is a starting point, so create an ORDERS table. From the Visual FoxPro menu, select File, then select New, and then press the Database radio button as shown here:

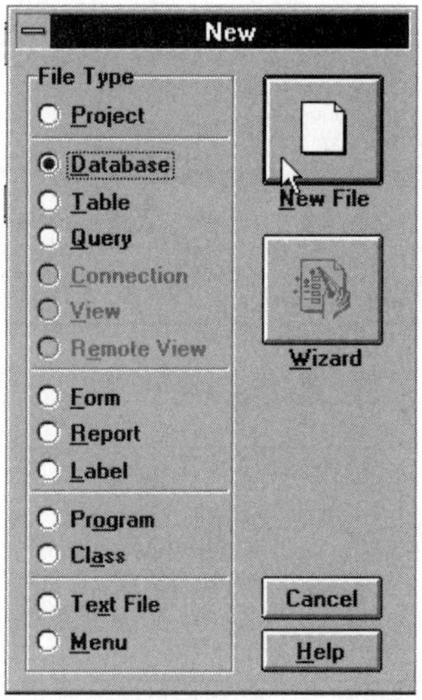

Note: You have selected Database, not Table, because you will be adding more tables, and they will have persistent relationships.

The standard File dialog box appears. Name the database HiPrice by entering **hiprice** as shown in Figure 10-4.

After you have named the database, select Create. The Database Design screen appears. Select New Table on the database toolbar and name the new table **ORDERS**. This brings you to the Table Designer shown in Figure 10-5.

Enter the structure for ORDERS as shown earlier in the table. When you are finished, select the OK button. You are returned to the Database Designer, and ORDERS is now displayed as in Figure 10-6.

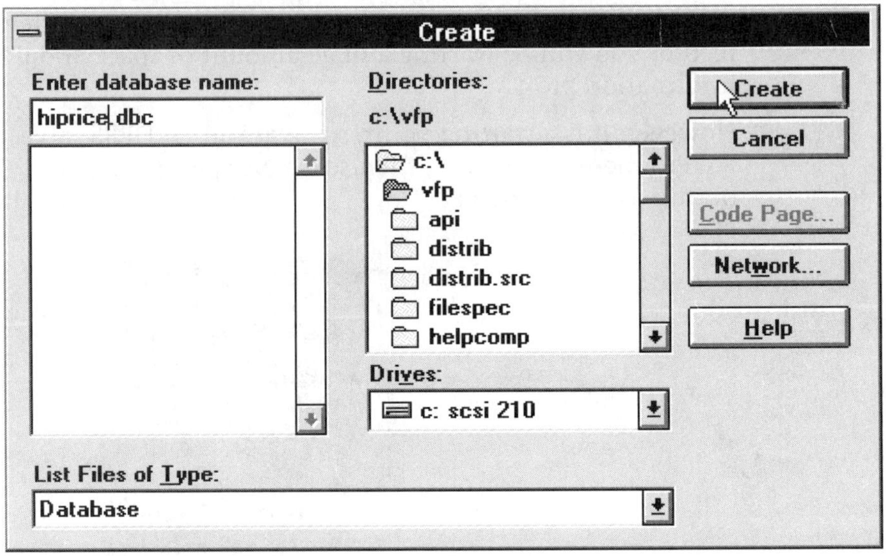

Naming the new database
Figure 10-4.

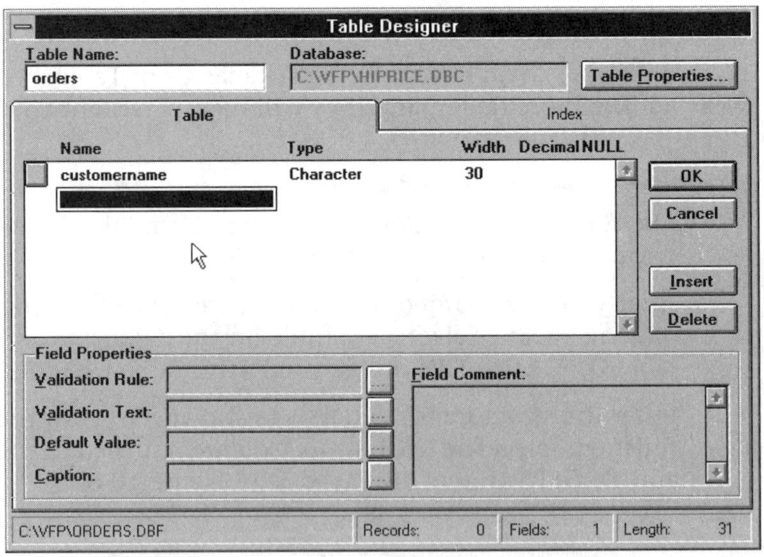

Table Designer for the ORDERS table
Figure 10-5.

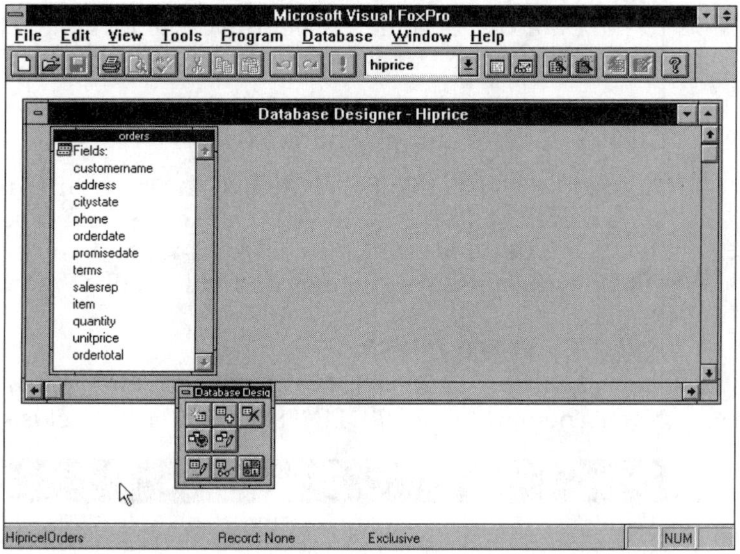

The ORDERS fields in the Database Designer
Figure 10-6.

Splitting Up the Table

As you saw in the CONTACTS example, you need to split up the ORDERS table. First add a new field to ORDERS: OrderNo. This field will contain an individual order number for each order. You can then create a new table, ORDLINES, that will also have the OrderNo field. Each line item on the order will be a record in ORDLINES.

Your modified ORDERS table will now look like the following table.

Field Name	Field Type	Field Length
OrderNo	Numeric	6 (0 decimals)
CustomerName	Character	30
Address	Character	30
CityState	Character	30
Phone	Character	14
OrderDate	Date	
PromiseDate	Date	
Terms	Character	20
SalesRep	Character	20
OrderTotal	Numeric	9 (2 decimals)

Modifying ORDERS

In the Database Designer, select the ORDERS table. Then click the Modify Table icon on the Database toolbar as shown in Figure 10-6.

Select the field to be deleted. Select the Item field as shown in Figure 10-7. Click the Delete button, and the field is removed.

Now add the OrderNo field. Click in the space after the last field, OrderTotal. Type **orderno** in the name field. Make the field type Numeric with a width of 6 and 0 decimals. Click the OK button, and you are finished modifying ORDERS for now. Your screen should look like Figure 10-8.

Creating ORDLINES

Now create a new table; select the New Table icon from the database toolbar. Name the new table ORDLINES and enter the fields shown here.

Field Name	Field Type	Field Length
OrderNo	Numeric	6 (0 decimals)
ItemDesc	Character	40
QtyOrdered	Numeric	5 (0 decimals)
UnitPrice	Numeric	6 (2 decimals)

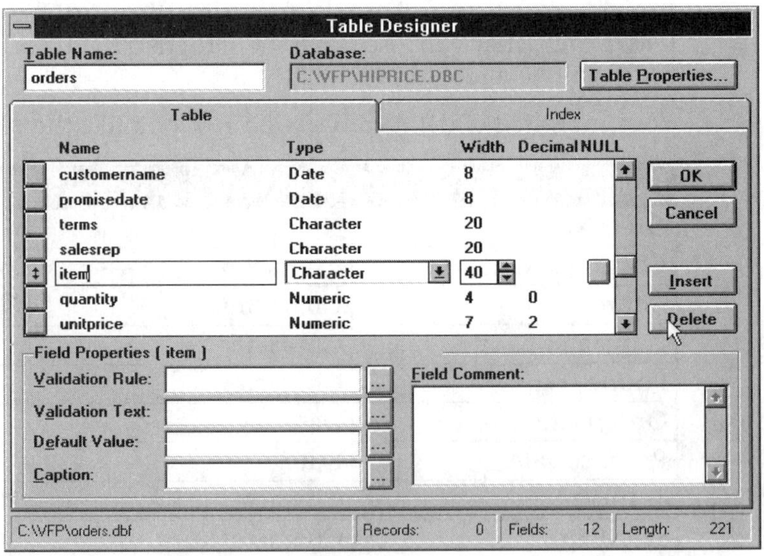

Modifying the ORDERS table
Figure 10-7.

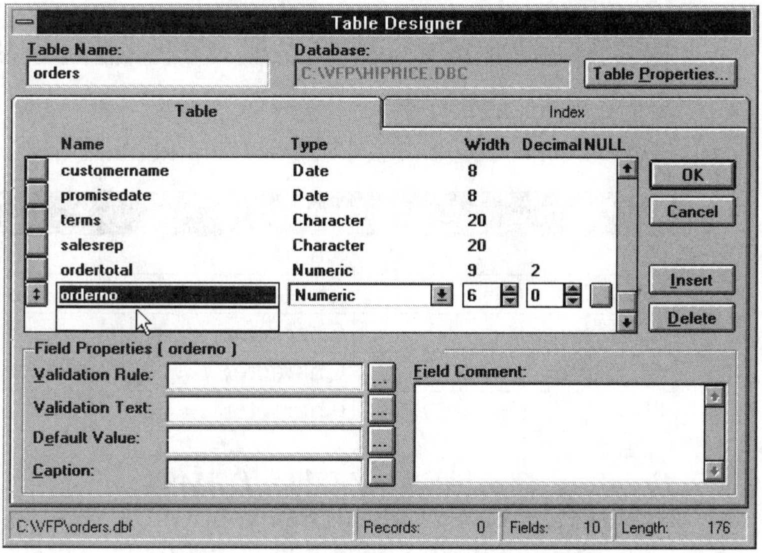

Adding the OrderNo field

Figure 10-8.

Creating the CUSTOMER Table

Turning your attention to ORDERS again, you can see that each order includes the customer information name, address, citystate, and phone. Again, including all this information is wasteful; with this arrangement, every time a new order is entered, the user needs to type all the customer information. It also leads to errors because on one order the user may, for example, enter the name Bijou 6-plex and on another just Bijou, or perhaps the misspelling Beejoo. When the sales information is reported, the system will not be able to tell that these customers are the same. Instead, it will see each as a separate customer.

As you have probably guessed, you are going to take the customer information from ORDERS, add a customer number field, and create a new CUSTOMER table.

Delete the following fields from the ORDERS table:

Field Name	Field Type	Field Length
CustomerName	Character	30
Address	Character	30
CityState	Character	30
Phone	Character	14

Then add the CustNo field as shown here:

Field Name	Field Type	Field Length
CustNo	Numeric	6 (0 decimals)

Create a new table called CUSTOMER and place the following fields in it:

Field Name	Field Type	Field Length
CustNo	Numeric	6 (0 decimals)
Name	Character	30
Address	Character	30
CityState	Character	30
Phone	Character	14

Creating Another New Table: ITEMS

Further examination reveals that your ORDLINES table has a field for the item description. This is another wasteful item because a Hershey bar is not likely to change its name. So as a final trick you will create one more table: ITEMS. As before, you will need a code to identify the item. This time ORDLINES gets the new field ItemNo, and ItemDesc is deleted.

Since you are deleting one field and adding one field, you can simply replace ItemDesc in ORDLINES with ItemNo. Type **itemno**. Also change the field type to Numeric. Here is the new structure of ORDLINES:

Field Name	Field Type	Field Length
OrderNo	Numeric	6 (0 decimals)
ItemNo	Numeric	6 (0 decimals)
QtyOrdered	Numeric	5 (0 decimals)
UnitPrice	Numeric	6 (2 decimals)

Now create the final table for the example: ITEMS. Here are the fields for this table:

Field Name	Field Type	Field Length
ItemNo	Numeric	6 (0 decimals)
ItemDesc	Character	40
UnitPrice	Numeric	6 (2 decimals)

Notice that both ORDLINES and ITEMS have a field called UnitPrice. Why the duplication? Because UnitPrice is applicable to both files but in different ways. The price may fluctuate, and you will need to keep it up-to-date in the ITEMS file. But an order is an agreement to sell goods at a particular price. If you look into ITEMS for the unit price, then the order will change each time the price changes. Besides, HiPrice might want to give a good customer a special price.

A Word about Naming Fields

You have given all the fields in this example useful titles. Every once in a while you may set up a new scheme in which you give the fields generic labels, such as Field1. Then the table can be generic, and you can reuse a lot of code simply by naming all fields serially: that is, as Field1 through Fieldxx.

We don't find this a good practice, nor do we recommend using short field names to save typing. ItemNo is much more understandable than ino or i_no.

We also strongly recommend naming related fields in different tables with similar names. CustNo and ItemNo are examples. Though you do not need to do this to set up relationships, this practice results in a table that is much simpler to maintain.

Indexing: The Key to Relationships

Visual FoxPro uses indexes to relate data. In the ORDERS-CUSTOMER relationship discussed earlier, the customer table needs to be indexed by the related field, CustNo.

Indexes Revisited

Part 2 discussed indexes in relation to the single table CONTACTS. Because indexes are so central to relationships, they are addressed again here.

Indexes are the way that you order your data. For instance, in some cases you want your CUSTOMER table organized in order of the customer names so you can quickly look up a customer.

In the case of the relationship with ORDERS, you want CUSTOMER organized in order of the customer numbers because these are what ORDERS uses to identify customers. What you will do is create two indexes and maintain them both. However, only one index can be in control of the order at a time. In other words, you will see the file either by customer name or by customer number (you can also see it in raw order—that is, with no index in control). Visual FoxPro can maintain more than one index at a time so that both indexes are updated when you add a new customer.

Indexes and Actual Data Organization

Indexes give the impression that data is stored in the order displayed by the index. However, the data need not be so ordered. Consider the index of a book: Key words are alphabetized in the index, and page numbers are listed. To find a topic, you look in the index for the key word and then turn to the page shown.

The book analogy fails, though, because a table can have several indexes: organized by name, by customer number, and by annual sales, to name a few. Only one index has control of the order at a time, but all open indexes are updated so that no matter which index is in control when you change the key value, all indexes will be updated to place the new value properly.

Using Key Expressions

Every index has a *key expression* that determines the order for that index. For instance, in your CUSTOMER table, you will want alphabetical ordering by customer name. The key expression will be from the Name field.

Calculated Expressions Name is a character-type field, so the data will be sorted by the ASCII sequence for characters.

Note: ASCII is the standard character assignment for PC computers. Each character, and several nonprintable elements, is assigned a number from 0 to 255. For example, the lowercase letter a is 97 in ASCII, and uppercase A is 65.

This plan seems okay until you realize that if you enter Carmike Cinema and CINEPLEX, when you look at CUSTOMER by name, CINEPLEX will come before Carmike since a capital *I* precedes a lowercase *a*.

Not surprisingly, Visual FoxPro has a solution for this problem. The function UPPER will turn a mixed-case character expression into all capital letters. You can then use the expression UPPER(*name*) for your index. This expression does not change the actual values—only the order in which they appear.

Caution: You can use any Visual FoxPro function in an index key, as well as functions you write. Care must be exercised, though, not to change the length of the expression. For instance, the length of the Name field is 30 characters. UPPER does not change this length. However, another common function, TRIM, does. TRIM removes the trailing spaces from an expression, thus changing its length. You can get around this problem, but you need to be aware of it. If you do fall into this trap, you may not even realize it until later when odd things happen to your data.

Combination Expressions A key expression can also be a combination of fields. As with the CONTACTS table, you will want to index by LastName and then FirstName. To create an index, you put the two fields together (concatenate them) like this: LastName + FirstName. Then you sort on the resulting value.

Using Index Types

You've seen, ever so briefly, the index types that Visual FoxPro offers. Here's what they do and why you need several types.

Primary A primary index is used for referential integrity. There can be only one primary index, and it must contain no duplicates; that is, its value or expression must be *unique*.

Note: Unique has another meaning in the Xbase world, as you will see shortly, but for now unique means that the field or fields of the primary index must not contain duplicates. For example, in ORDLINES you could not use OrderNo as a primary index key because ORDLINES may contain several records for a single order, and therefore several records would have the same OrderNo value. You could, however, use OrderNo in ORDERS since each order should have a unique order number.

Candidate A candidate index is like a primary index in that it does not allow duplicates. However, each table can have more than one candidate index. Again, the main use of this type of index is to maintain referential integrity.

Regular A regular index is the standard Xbase type of index. It can contain duplicates and is used normally for the actual ordering of data; that is, you use it for SEEK and BROWSE operations. It is also the type of index to use for the "many" side of a one-to-many relationship.

Unique A unique index is just a regular index that will not show more than one record for each value.

Note: Unlike primary and candidate indexes, a unique index does not enforce uniqueness. You can enter a record with a duplicate value. The difference between regular and unique indexes is that only the first record with a value will show up in a unique index. For instance, in the ORDLINES and ORDERS example, a unique index using OrderNo in ORDLINES would show only the first line item for each order.

Storing Indexes

Visual FoxPro offers three different index storage formats, which affect the way the index is stored and used:

- Structural CDX
- Nonstructural CDX
- Stand-alone IDX

Structural CDX An index stored as a structural CDX is given the same name as the table—for instance, *orders.cdx*—and is opened whenever the table is opened. Primary and candidate indexes must be stored in structural CDX format to ensure that they will be open when the table is modified. Because primary and candidate indexes require unique values, they must be open whenever their values can be changed. Primary and candidate indexes also must be opened along with the table because they are used to maintain referential integrity.

Structural CDXs can contain many indexes stored as *tags*. A tag is a name for an index and is used when you want to change the index that controls the order of your data.

Nonstructural CDX A nonstructural CDX differs from a structural CDX only in that it is not opened automatically when the table is opened. You will use nonstructural CDXs mainly when you need a particular ordering but do not want the burden of updating the index in normal use.

Like structural CDXs, nonstructural CDXs can contain many indexes stored as *tags*.

Stand-Alone IDX A stand-alone IDX is a file that contains only one index key. Prior to version 2 of FoxPro, this was the standard index format for FoxPro and its predecessor, Foxbase. Like a nonstructural CDX, a stand-alone IDX must be opened manually.

You will use stand-alone IDXs mainly for ad hoc index work such as one off reports. This storage type is also used in an environment where some programs written in Foxbase or FoxPro version 1 may be accessing the data.

Index Overhead

All indexes of any type that are open for a table are updated whenever the table is updated. As a general rule, this overhead is not a large performance burden and, if you need these indexes in normal use, you really don't have a choice. But if a complex index is only rarely used, you should consider its effect on your system. The more complex the key expression, the more time consuming the maintenance and the greater the impact on performance.

For instance, for a monthly report of sales by customers you may want an unusual ordering—say, year-to-date sales by sales representative. Because this is a rather complex index, and because you run the report only once a month, you can put this index in a nonstructural CDX and open it and update it only once a month.

Setting Up the Indexes

Now it's time to create the index keys you will be using. Start with ORDERS since it is the center of the HiPrice system.

Indexing ORDERS

In the Database Designer, select the ORDERS table and click the Modify Table button on the toolbar. The familiar Table Designer appears. Click the Index tab, as shown in Figure 10-9.

Click the blank box in the Name field. Type **orderno**. Press the TAB key to move to Type and click the arrow. You will see the choices for the index type, as shown in Figure 10-10. Select Primary.

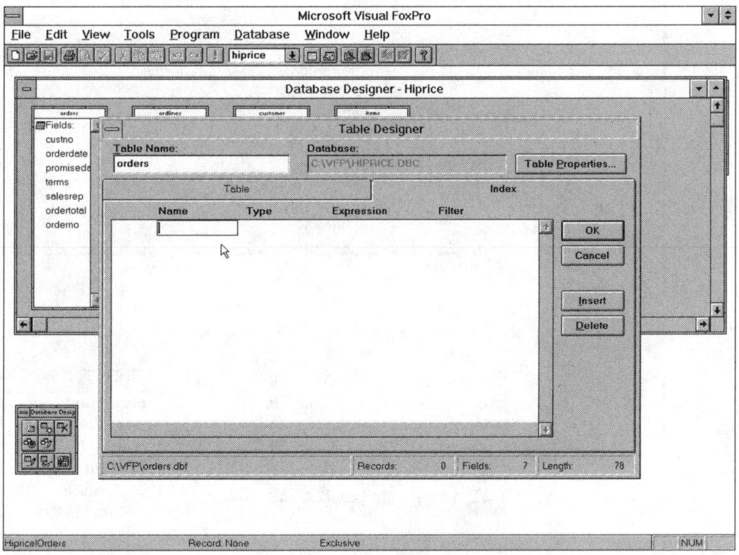

Adding indexes to ORDERS
Figure 10-9.

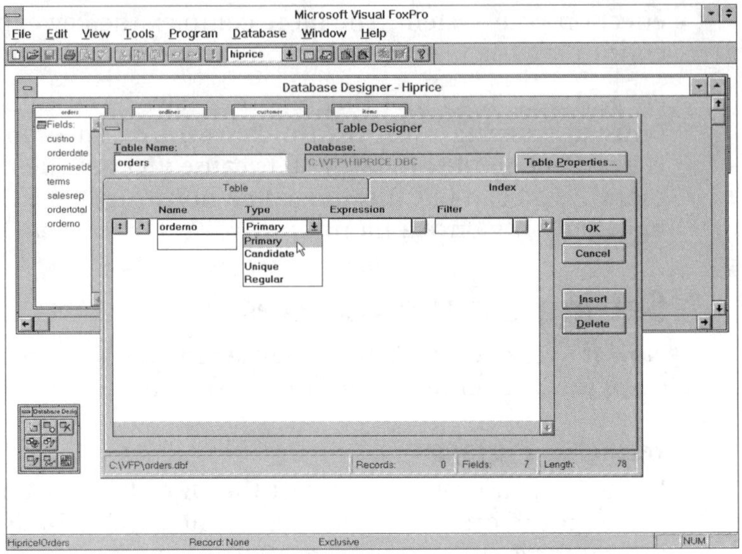

Selecting an index type
Figure 10-10.

Press TAB to move to Expression and press the button at the right. This brings you to the Expression Builder, shown in Figure 10-11. You can use this visual tool to build the key expression. Here, just double-click the field OrderNo.

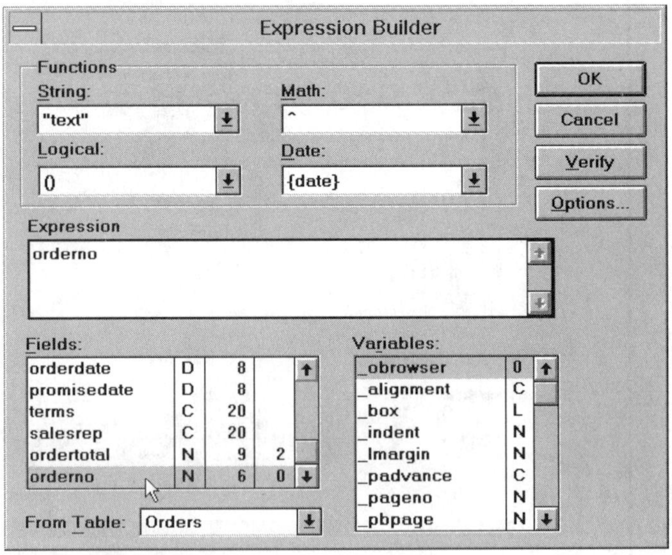

The Expression Builder
Figure 10-11.

You will also need indexes based on CustNo and OrderDate to sort orders for two reports. Add these indexes as shown in Figure 10-12.

Press the OK button and verify that you want to make the structure changes permanent. The ORDERS table in the Database Designer has an entry for indexes with each of the three you created. OrderNo has a key symbol next to it signifying that it is a primary key.

Indexing CUSTOMERS

For the CUSTOMER table, you will need a primary key on CustNo since you need to enforce uniqueness on this value. This key will allow you to look up the customer information from the ORDERS table.

You also want an alphabetical index by name. As discussed previously, you will want to use the expression UPPER(*name*). Figure 10-13 shows the two indexes for CUSTOMERS.

Indexing ORDLINES

ORDLINES needs to be indexed on OrderNo because of its relationship with ORDERS and on ItemNo because of its relationship with ITEMS. Both of these keys will, and should, contain duplicates, so use regular types for both. Figure 10-14 shows the keys for ORDLINES.

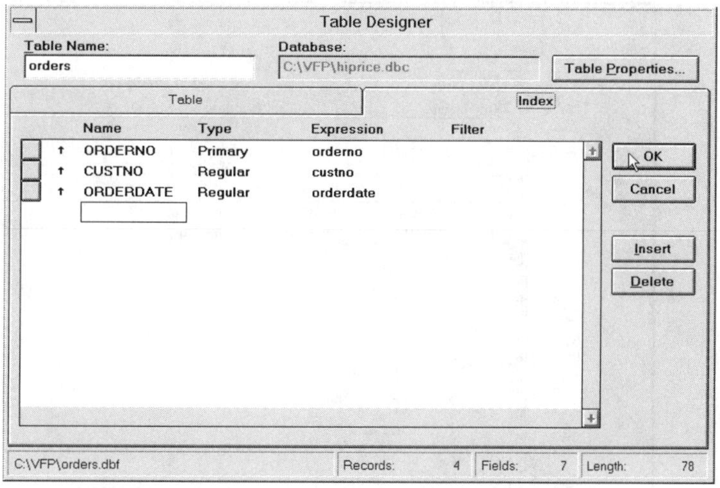

The rest of the ORDERS indexes

Figure 10-12.

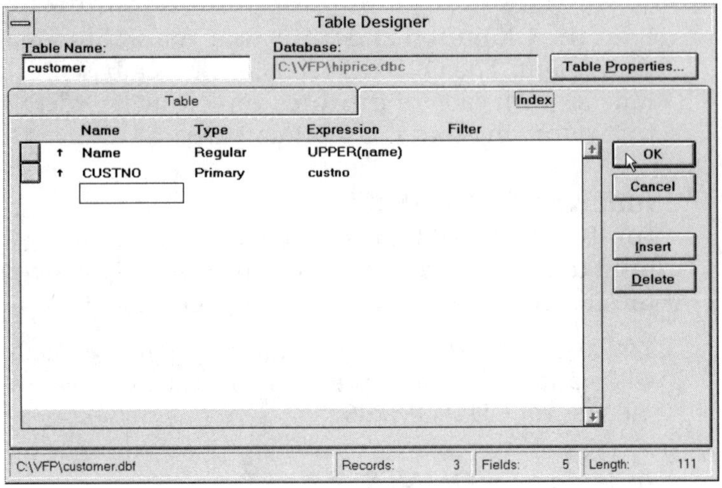

Indexes for CUSTOMER
Figure 10-13.

Indexing Items

ItemNo will be a primary key for Items. You will also have an index by ItemDesc for alphabetical lookup. Again, you will use the UPPER function for this key. Figure 10-15 shows these keys.

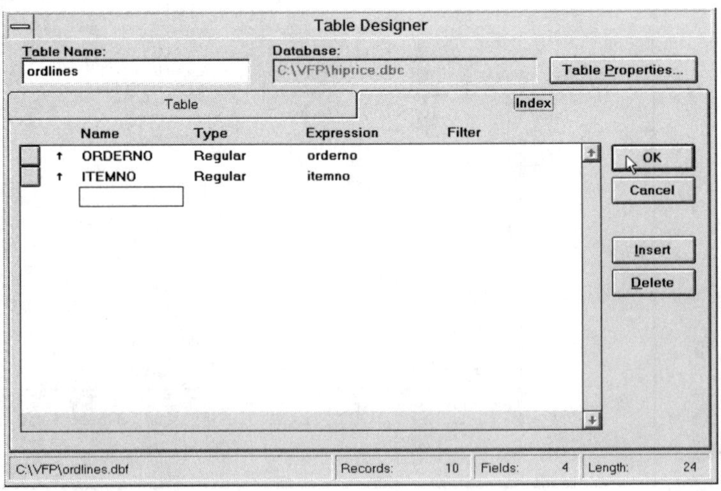

Indexes for ORDLINES
Figure 10-14.

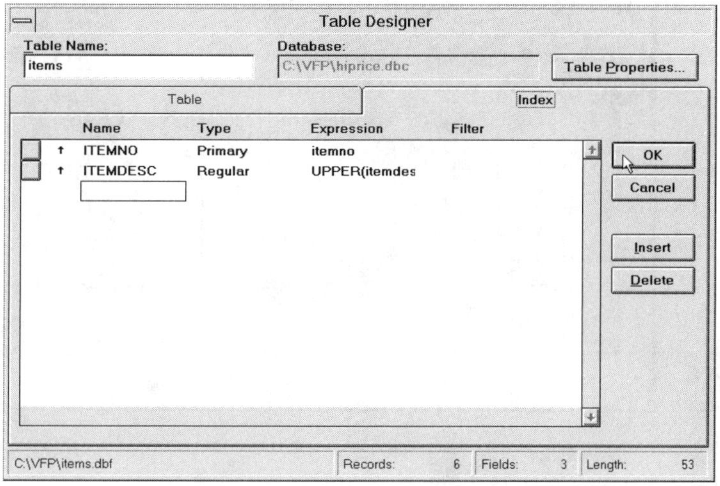

Indexes for ITEMS
Figure 10-15.

Relating the Tables

Now is the moment you've been waiting for: It's time to relate your tables together in a database. Here's a first look at the terminology used to talk about relationships.

Parents and Children

The most common way of referring to relationships is with the terms *parent* and *child*. Master and slave are also sometimes used, but this metaphor has a gruesome legacy, so we will not use it.

The parent is the controlling table; that is, it is the one you manipulate directly. The child or children are tables that are manipulated via their relationship to the parent. Figure 10-16 shows an example right from your tables. ORDERS is open as the parent, and CUSTOMER is open as a child. When you move to the next record in ORDERS, CUSTOMER automatically moves to the corresponding record for the new customer in ORDERS.

Relating CUSTOMER to ORDERS

Since ORDERS is central to this example and customer information is central to ORDERS, relate CUSTOMER to ORDERS. To do this, simply point the mouse at the index key in CUSTOMER (CustNo), hold down the right mouse button, and drag to the related key in ORDERS (also called CustNo—giving

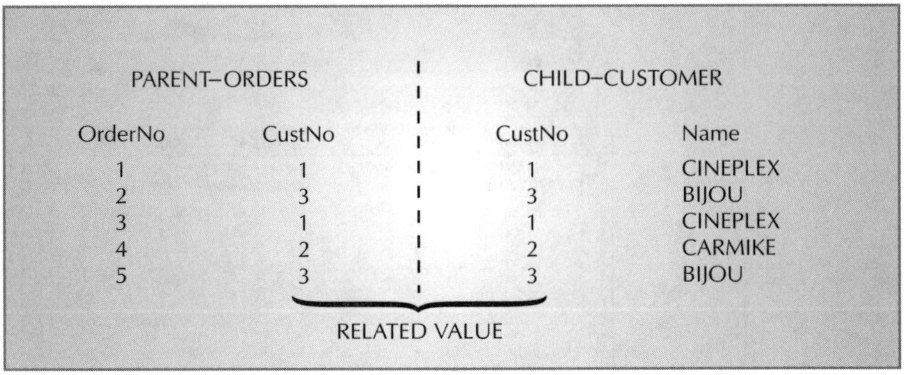

Parent and child relationship
Figure 10-16.

related keys common names is very helpful). This procedure draws a line between the two as shown in Figure 10-17 and brings up a dialog box verifying the relationship.

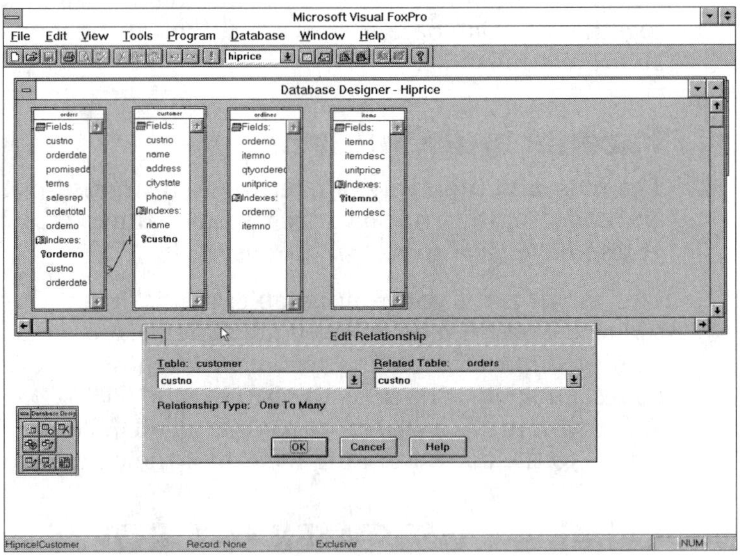

Relating CUSTOMER to ORDERS
Figure 10-17.

10

Tip: You can create a persistent relationship only if one of the keys is a primary or candidate key. You must start the drag operation from this key. The other key can be of any type but will normally be a regular or unique key.

Relating ORDLINES and ITEMS

Next, you'll build the relationship between ORDLINES and ORDERS. Drag OrderNo from ORDERS to ORDLINES. Do the same for ItemNo in ITEMS and ItemNo in ORDLINES. Figure 10-18 shows the completed relationships.

Entering Some Sample Data

You'll want to put some data in your tables so you will have something to look at when you get to the next chapter. Start by double-clicking the name of the ITEMS table in the Database Designer. This brings up a blank grid showing the field names across the top. Pressing CTRL-Y will allow you to append a new record. You can also access the appropriate screen from the Table menu bar. Enter the information as shown in Figure 10-19, appending records as you go. Then double-click the menu bar icon to close the table.

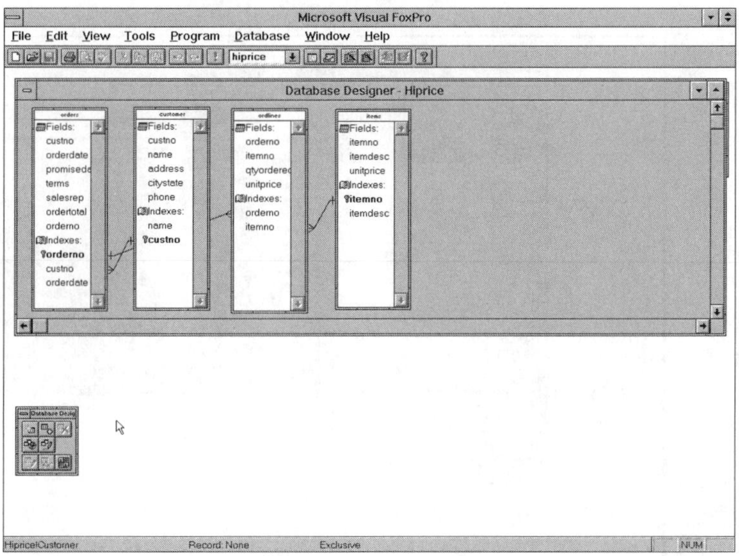

Data relationships for HiPrice Snacks
Figure 10-18.

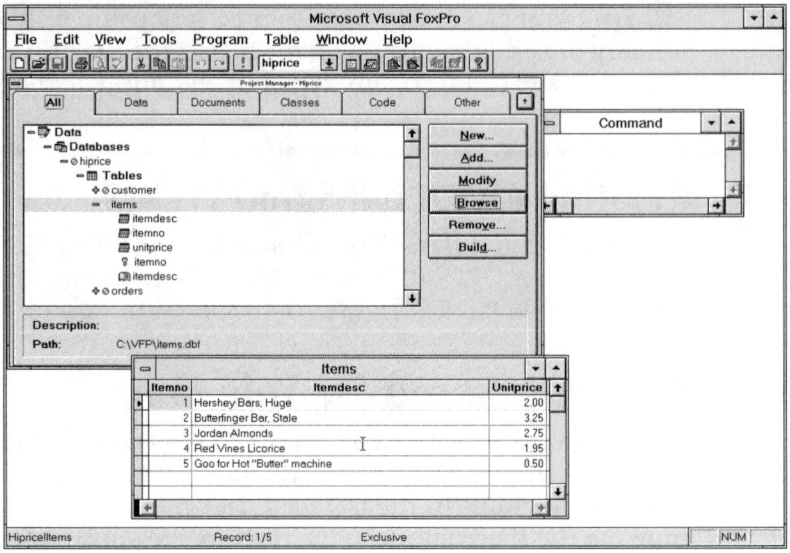

Adding records to ITEMS
Figure 10-19.

Now enter records for ORDLINES as shown in Figure 10-20.

Repeat the same procedure for ORDERS as shown in Figure 10-21.

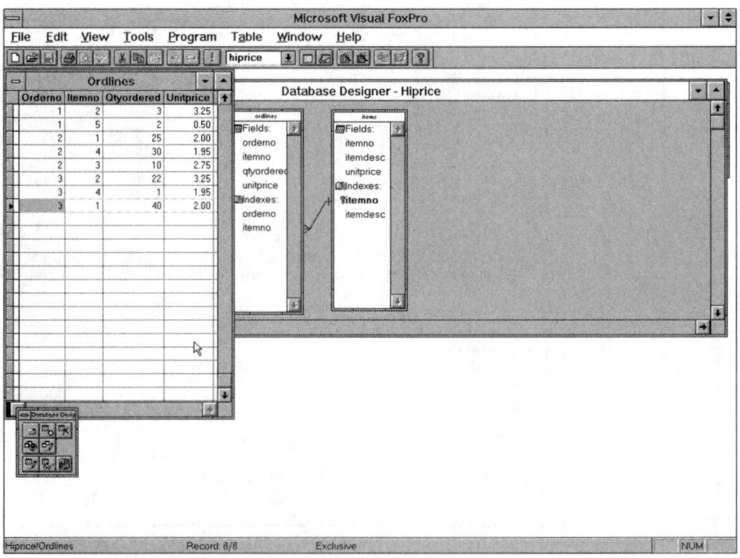

Records in ORDLINES
Figure 10-20.

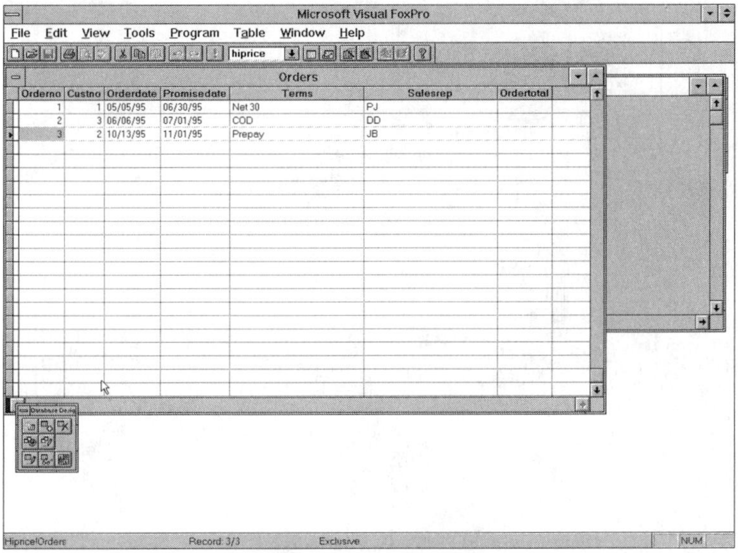

Records in ORDERS
Figure 10-21.

Finally, enter the CUSTOMER data shown in Figure 10-22.

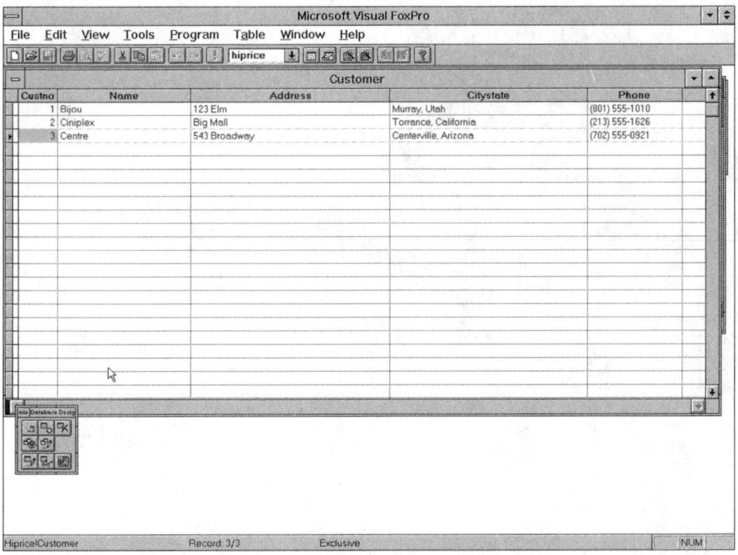

Records in CUSTOMER
Figure 10-22.

11

Displaying Data from Multiple Tables

In this chapter you will take the data you created in Chapter 10 and create a screen form to display it. You will examine in a little more detail Visual FoxPro's Properties window and how to use it. You will start by putting your data in a project using the Project Manager.

Putting Your Data in a Project

Visual FoxPro's Project Manager lets you bring all of the elements of a system together. Code, data, screens, objects, and so forth are all accessible through the Project Manager.

Creating the HiPrice Project

Creating a new project is simple. Select File and New from the menu bar. Make certain the Project radio button is selected and click the New File picture button as shown here:

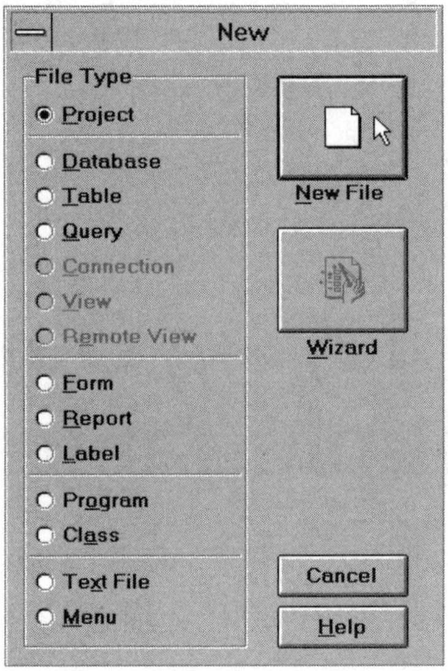

This brings up the standard Windows File dialog box. Replace the default name (proj1, or something similar) with **HiPrice** as shown here:

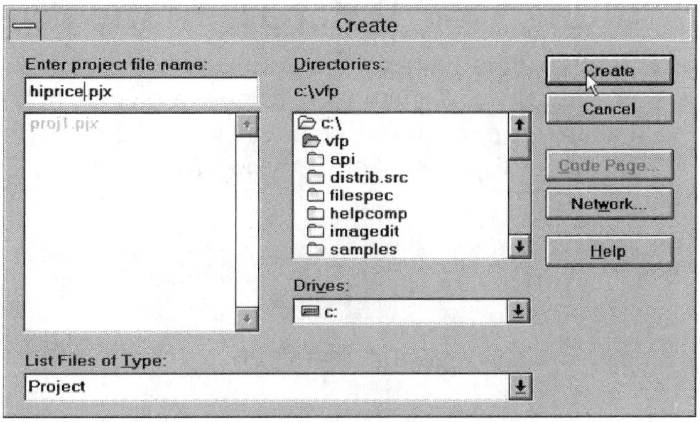

Visual FoxPro creates a new project window with tabs for All, Data, Documents, Classes, Code, and Other. The default tab is All, which shows all the project elements. Figure 11-1 illustrates your new project.

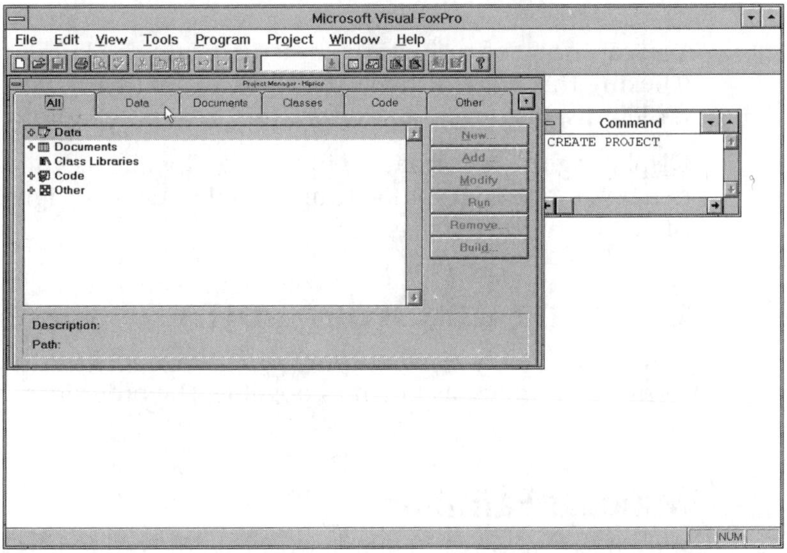

The new HiPrice project
Figure 11-1.

Putting Your Database in the Project

You have already created a database with tables, indexes, and relationships. You will now add them to your new project. Click the Data tab or highlight the Database entry on the All tab. Click the Add button, and the File dialog box is once again displayed. Select the *hiprice.dbc* file as shown here and click OK.

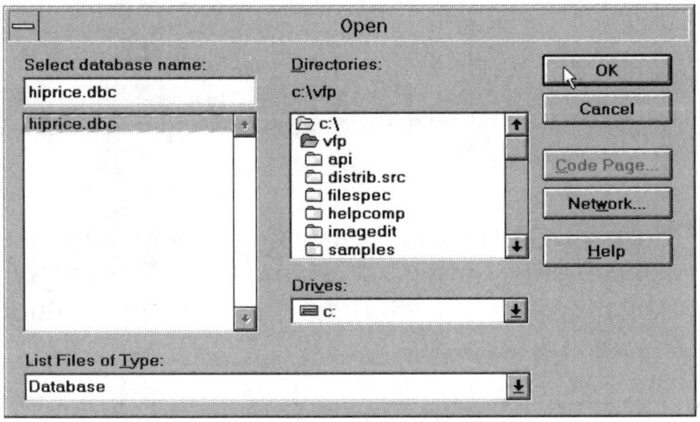

You can now see a + mark immediately to the left of the Database entry. Clicking this mark displays the HiPrice database. Clicking the = mark at the far left displays your tables from the previous chapter.

Displaying this information in a hierarchy allows you to view the level of detail you need without getting buried in details. Figure 11-2 shows the full hierarchy of the database.

Creating an Order Form

Now you're ready to create your order form for HiPrice. You will create a form that mimics, as much as possible, the order form introduced in the last chapter.

Make It Familiar

It might strike you as odd that we are going to mimic the order form on the screen when the last chapter spent time tearing down the idea of mimicking the order form in a table. Here is an important rule, one of the most important in database programming: *The representation of the data is* not *the data.*

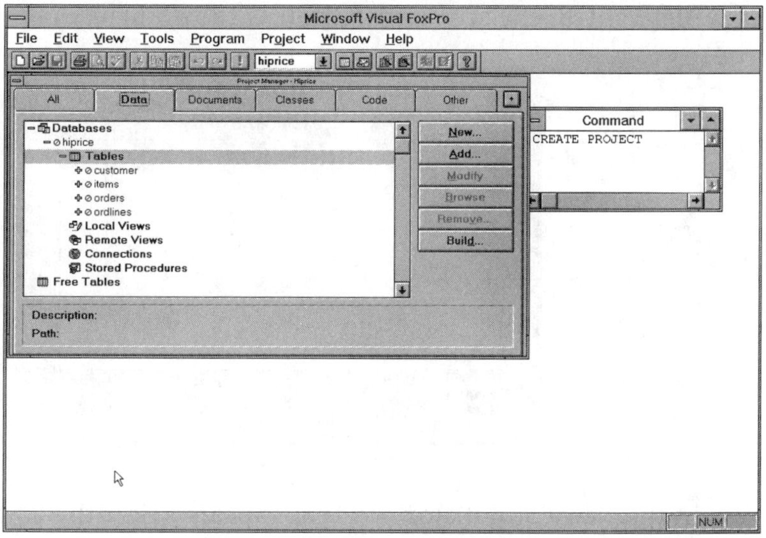

Hierarchical view of HiPrice's database
Figure 11-2.

Put another way, what the end-user sees and how the data is actually stored are two different things.

You could make a table that is a duplicate of the order form. In Chapter 10 you learned why this isn't a good idea, and in the next section you will revisit the subject in a discussion of normalization. For now, remember that the road map is not the road.

What you want is a system that the user is comfortable with. This is why your order form will look like, or something like, the paper form.

The Strategy for the Order Form

What you need to do then is to link data from four tables—ORDERS, ORDLINES, ITEMS, and CUSTOMER—into a single representation. You will let a Visual FoxPro Wizard start you off and go from there.

Starting Off: Using the One-to-Many Wizard

Since orders are the key element in the HiPrice project, you will start by using the Forms Wizard to create a one-to-many form from ORDERS and ORDLINES. After you have made this form, you will add information from CUSTOMER and ITEMS.

Click the Documents tab of the HiPrice project window. With Forms highlighted, click the New button as shown here:

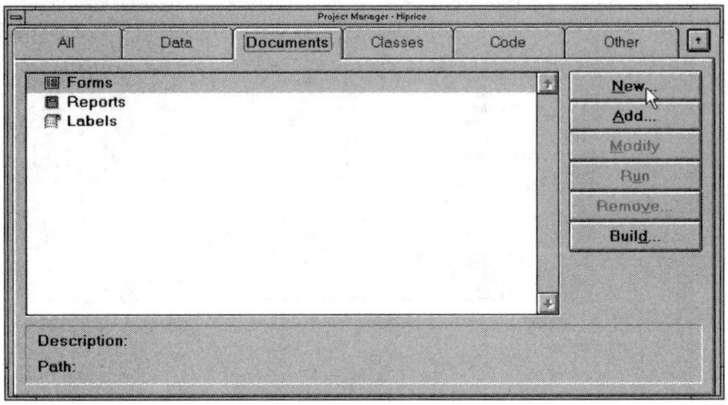

In the New Form dialog box that appears, select the Form Wizard button:

You are presented a choice of the Form Wizard or the One-to-Many Form Wizard. Choose the One-to-Many Form Wizard and click OK, as shown here:

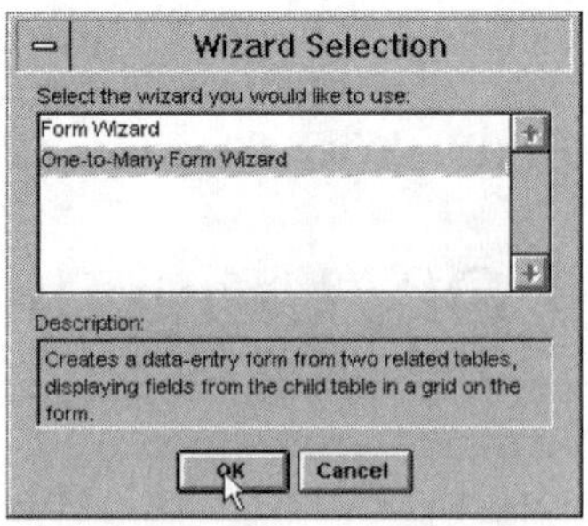

The One-to-Many Form Wizard, shown in Figure 11-3, appears.

The top half of the wizard screen indicates that your first step is to select the parent data. HiPrice is already selected in the Databases/Tables field on the lower-left side of the screen. If the HiPrice database is not selected, you can select it by clicking the ellipses button to the right of the entry field. This will bring up the standard Windows File dialog box. Select Database from the List Files of Type box or just type **hiprice.dbc**.

Below the Database/Tables field are the tables that make up the HiPrice database. Select the ORDERS table, as shown in Figure 11-3, since it is the parent of this form.

Your next action is to select the fields from ORDERS that you want this form to display. In the middle of the bottom half of the wizard screen you will see a list of the fields. To the right of this are several buttons. Your action will be a standard Windows select/deselect operation. You can select fields, that is, move them to the right-hand box, by highlighting the field and clicking the right arrow button. You can also double-click the field to move it. Clicking the right double arrow button selects all fields. You perform deselection in a similar manner using the left arrow and left double arrow buttons.

Click the right double arrow button to move all the fields to the Selected Fields box. Then deselect Orderno, Custno, and Ordertotal. You do not want Orderno and Custno displayed since they are linking fields; that is, their purpose is to link information for other tables. When you are done, your wizard dialog box should look like Figure 11-4.

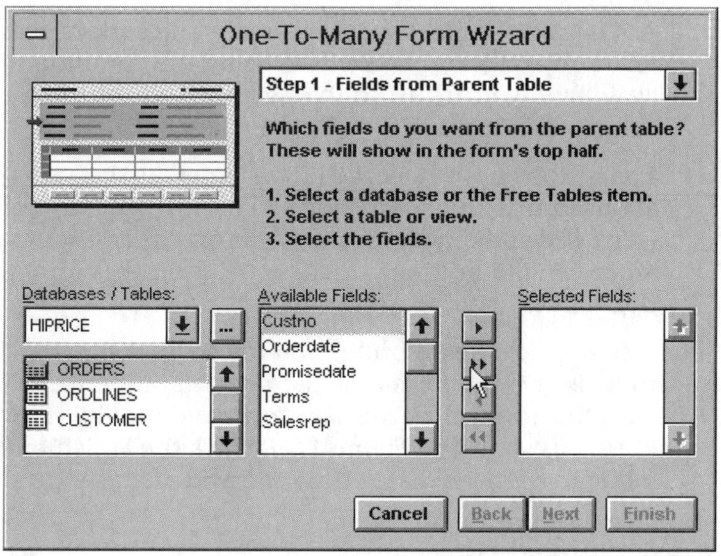

Step 1 of the One-to-Many Form Wizard
Figure 11-3.

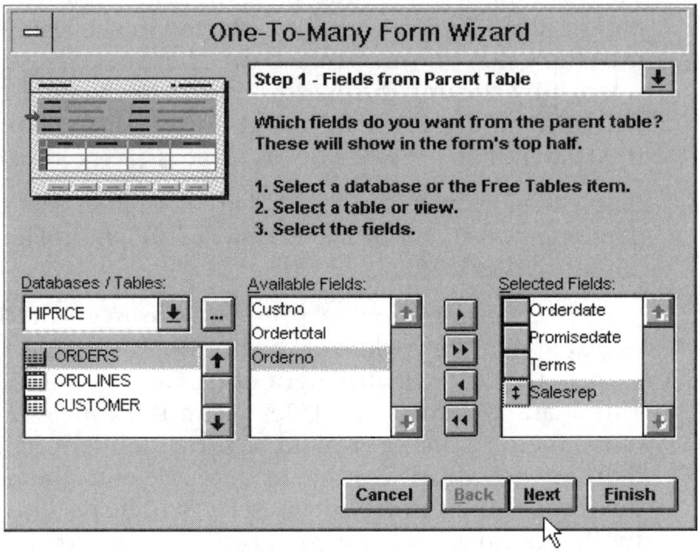

Step 1 of the One-to-Many Form Wizard completed

Figure 11-4.

Press the Next button to go to Step 2 of this One-to-Many Form Wizard. Figure 10-5 shows all the fields in ORDLINES selected except for Orderno.

Step 2 proceeds just like Step 1, but this time you are selecting fields from the child, or many, side of the relationship. Click the Next button to continue to Step 3, shown in Figure 10-6.

As you can see, the wizard has made the correct guess: that you want to relate ORDERS and ORDLINES using the common field Orderno. Press Next again, and you are asked to select the style of the form. Figure 11-7 shows this screen. Accept the default settings, and press Next again.

The next step is to select the sort order, as shown in Figure 11-8. You learn about sorting this form shortly. For now, you do not want to sort this form. If you did, you would sort it on either Custno or, more likely, Orderno. Since you did not include these fields on the form, they are not available in the wizard.

Pressing Next again brings you to the final step for this wizard. All you need to do is give the form a name. The default name, ORDERS, is fine. To go on with this form, click the Save form and modify it in the Form Designer radio button as shown in Figure 11-9. Click the Finish button and give the form a name in the Save dialog box, and you are taken to the Form Designer.

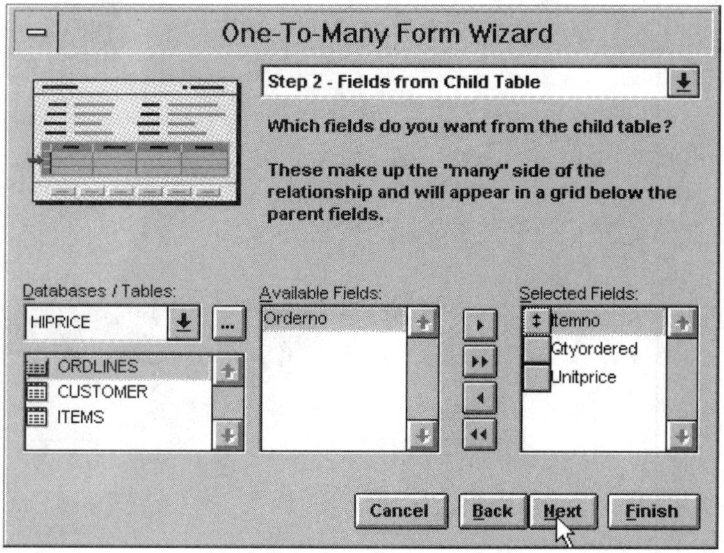

Step 2 of the One-to-Many Form Wizard
Figure 11-5.

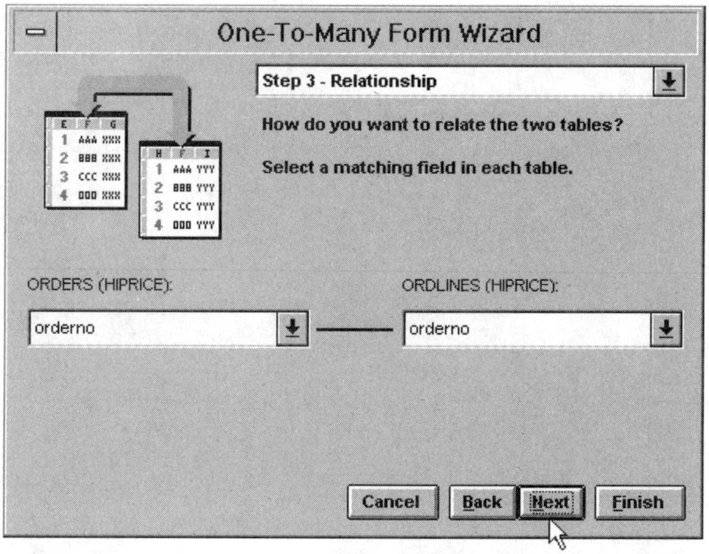

Deciding how to relate ORDERS and ORDLINES
Figure 11-6.

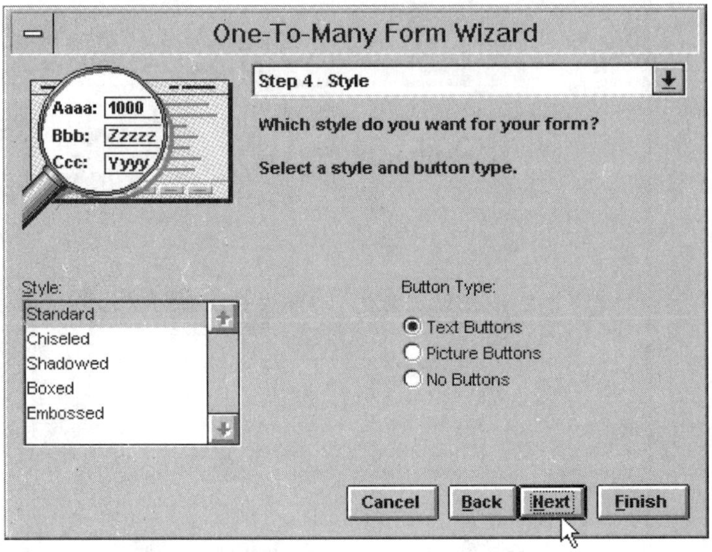

Setting the form styles
Figure 11-7.

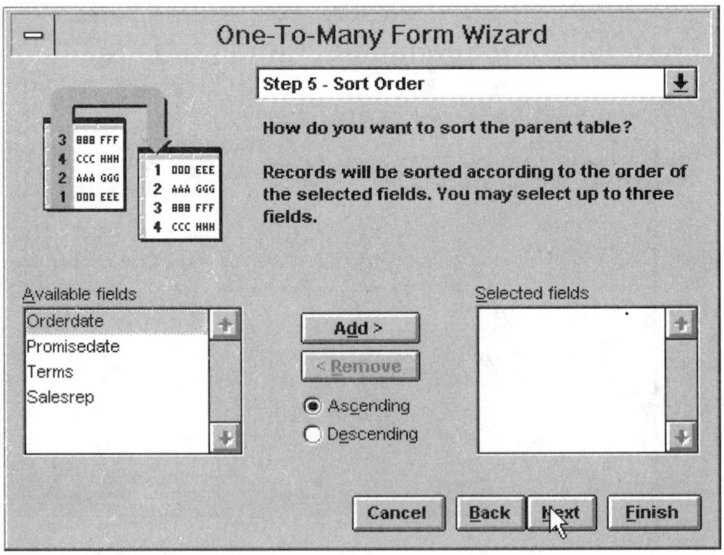

The sort order screen
Figure 11-8.

Step 6 - Finish
Figure 11-9.

Modifying the Default Form

The Form Designer is a graphical tool for creating and modifying screen forms. You just created a one-to-many form using the Form Wizard. Now you will start to modify the form to suit your needs. Before starting, you may find it helpful to arrange your screen as shown in Figure 11-10.

A Quick Tour of Visual FoxPro's Form Designer

The left side of the screen shown in Figure 11-10 contains the Form Designer. This is the work area where you draw your screens. To its right is the Properties window. This window is where you set all the properties and methods for an object—in this case, the Orders form.

Centered near the bottom is the Form Controls toolbar, which gives you quick access to many common Form tools.

Changing Properties

In Chapter 2 you learned that objects, in object-oriented work, have properties and events. These are controlled using the Properties window. For instance, you can see that the AutoCenter property is set to True—but what does this mean?

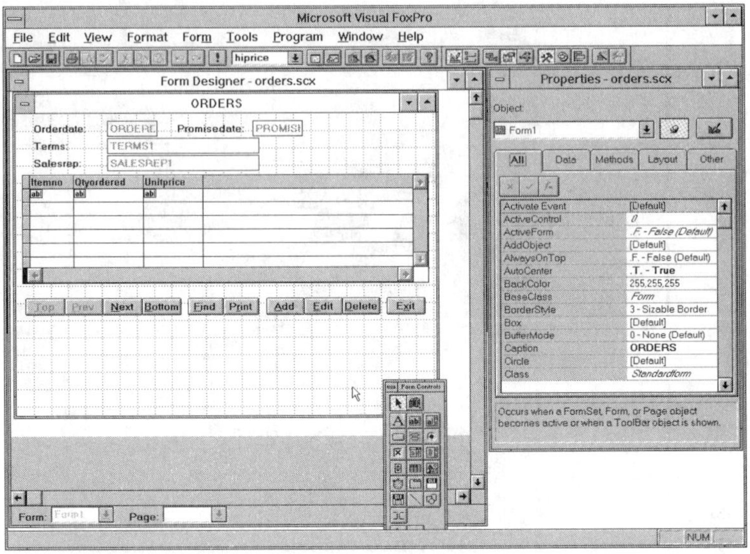

Arranging the screen

Figure 11-10.

Highlighting the AutoCenter box of the Properties window and pressing F1 for help displays a description of the property and its settings. In this case, you can see that AutoCenter means that the form will put itself in the center of the Visual FoxPro screen when the form is invoked. If AutoCenter is set to False, the form will be placed according to the Top and Left properties. A brief description of the property also appears at the bottom of the Property window.

If you want change value shown—in this case, to change True to False—you have several options. You can click the AutoCenter property so that it is highlighted. This brings the value into a window just below the page tabs. You can then click the drop-down button to see the possible values of True and False. Clicking False changes the value. Figure 11-11 shows this change.

You can also cycle through the choices by double-clicking the property. Double-click AutoCenter again, and its setting will return to False.

Some values do not lend themselves to a limited set choices and so are not set in either of these ways. For example, look at the Caption property. This sets the name displayed in the title bar of your form. The default name, ORDERS, is not too descriptive. Here's how to change it.

Click the Caption property to display the default caption, ORDERS, in the value window below the page tabs as shown in Figure 11-12.

Move the mouse cursor over the value window, and it changes to an I-beam, or text cursor. Click the text ORDERS and change it to **HiPrice Snacks —**

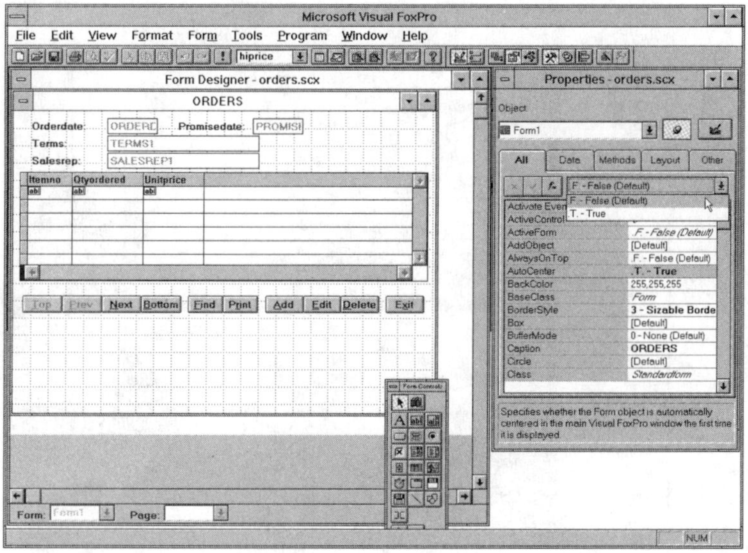

Setting the AutoCenter property

Figure 11-11.

Order Form. Then press the ENTER key. You will notice that the title bar of your form has changed to reflect the new name, as shown in Figure 11-13.

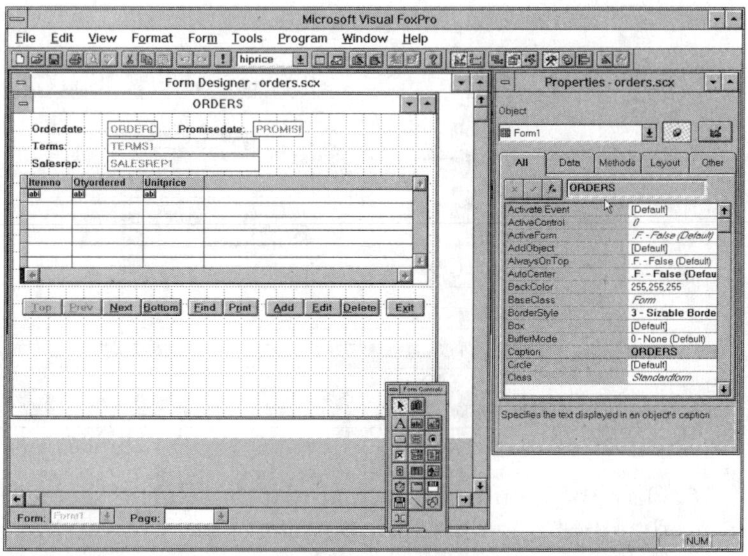

Setting the Caption property

Figure 11-12.

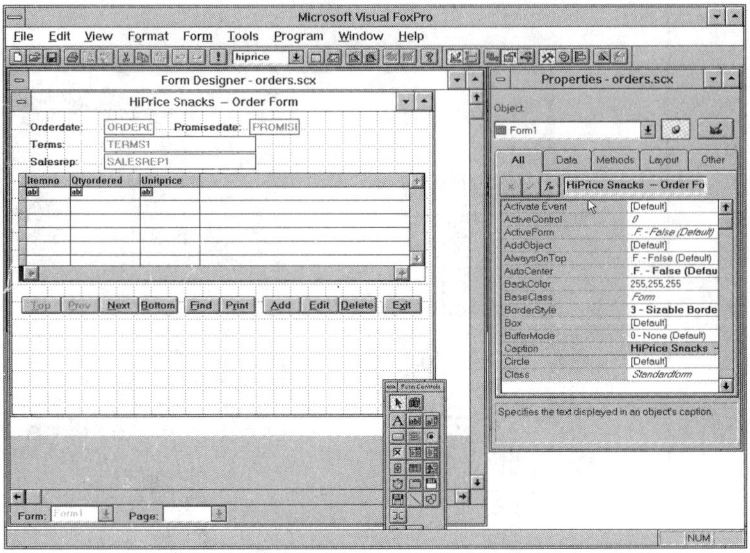

Changing the caption of your form

Figure 11-13.

Moving Screen Elements

You need to make room on your form for customer information. From the Edit menu, choose Select All or press CTRL-A. Your screen will look something like this:

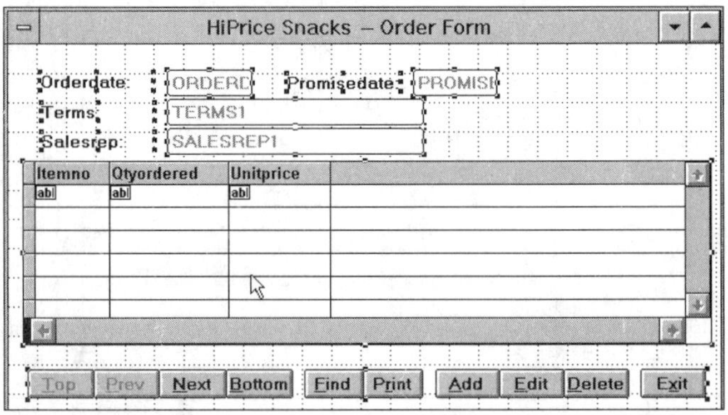

Place the mouse cursor in any of the selected elements and drag the block so that the bottom is at the bottom of the screen. Then release the mouse button. Figure 11-14 shows the approximate layout you want.

11

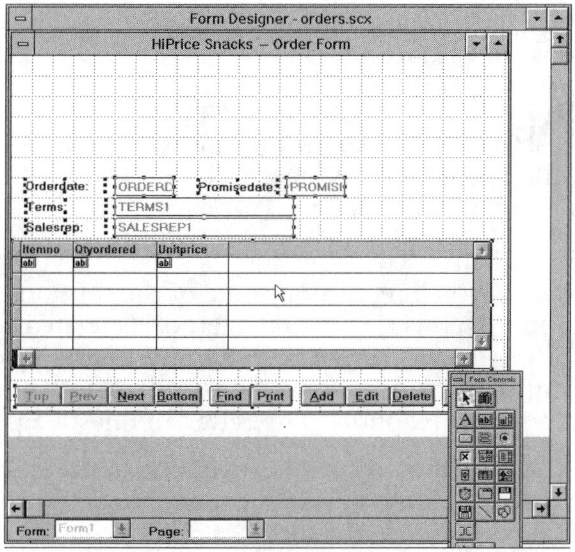

Moving screen elements down
Figure 11-14.

Before you begin adding other information, make this form a little more attractive and informative. First you'll change the captions. Notice that the wizard has used the field names as the captions for the various fields. You will change Orderdate to Order Date and Promisedate to Promised.

Click your mouse on the caption Promisedate in the Screen Designer. Now highlight Caption in the Properties window. The current caption is Promisedate. Move up to the entry box and change Promisedate to **Promised** as shown here.

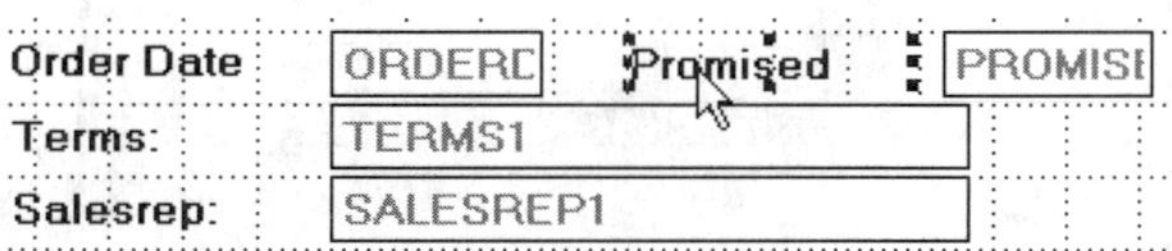

Similarly change Orderdate to **Order Date**.

Now to move the controls around a little. To select a control and its caption, you select one using the mouse button and then select the other while holding down the SHIFT button. Click the mouse on the caption Terms. Move to the right and while the mouse cursor is in the Terms control, hold down the SHIFT button and click the mouse button again. The control bars should now be visible for both items.

Holding down the mouse button, move the set of items to the right and release the mouse button. Likewise, move the other items so that your screen looks like Figure 11-15.

Note: You can get fine control of positioning by using the cursor keys while the item is selected.

Finally, you'll reposition some of the captions. Notice, for instance, that the caption Terms is well to the left of its related control. Clicking the caption shows that its size is larger than necessary. By clicking the left-side sizing control (shown in Figure 11-16 with the mouse cursor pointing to it), you can size the caption to fit better and nestle up to its control.

When the mouse cursor is over one of the sizing handles, it changes to a cursor that looks like a + sign, as shown here. This symbol lets you know that you can size the item.

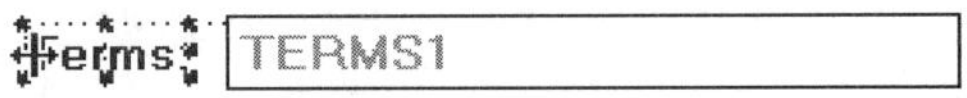

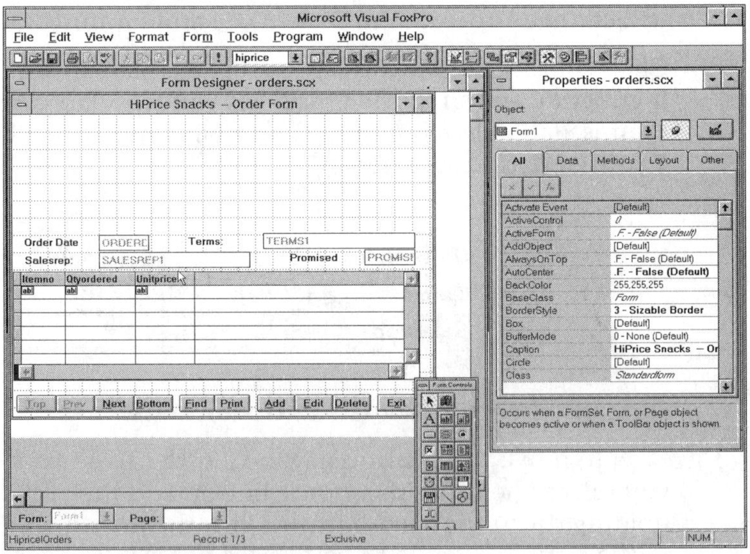

Changing the layout

Figure 11-15.

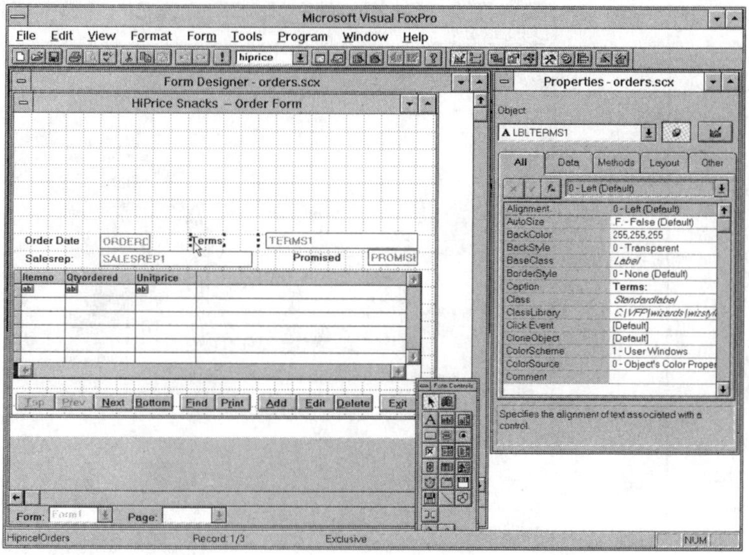

Sizing control blocks
Figure 11-16.

11

Saving and Running Your Form

It's time to take a look at your handiwork. First save your work. Then run the form as an executable program.

Note: This is the first time that you will save your work. This should not be an indication of the importance of saving your work. Save as often as possible and never do a lot of work between save operations. Windows, and programs running under Windows, can crash unpredictably.

You can save your work in several ways: Select Save from the File menu, click the floppy disk icon on the toolbar, or use the CTRL-S shortcut key.

To run your form, select the ! icon from the toolbar. In a moment you will see your screen form with real data in it. It should look like Figure 11-17.

Click the Exit button to close the form. When Visual FoxPro runs the form, it closes the Screen Designer so double-click the orders form in the Project window.

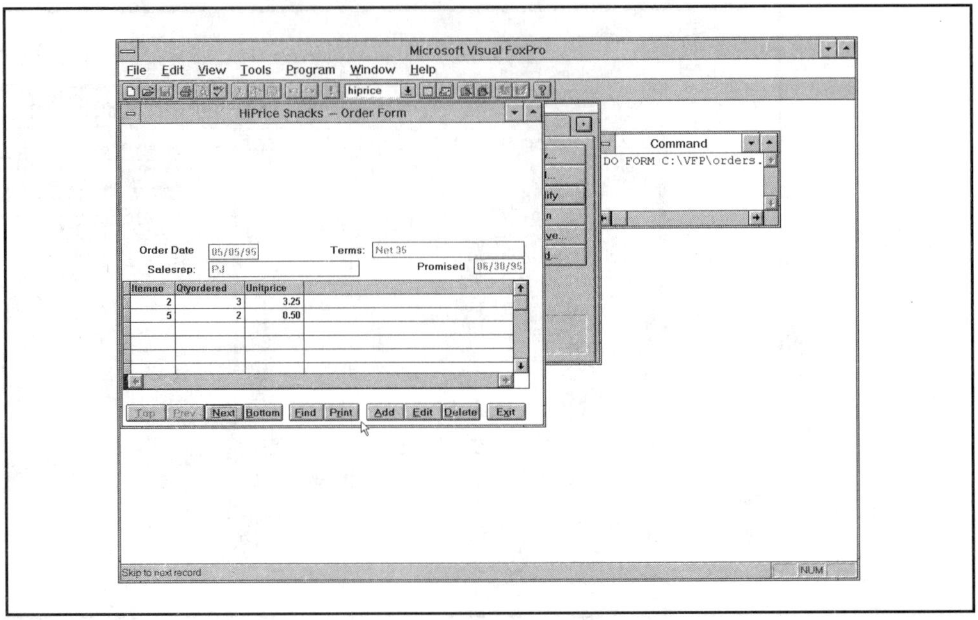

Running your screen form
Figure 11-17.

Adding Customer Information

The next trick is adding customer information from the CUSTOMER table. In the previous chapter, you built your database around the ORDERS table. You related customer information to the CUSTOMER table using the Custno field in ORDERS.

First open the CUSTOMER table. In the View menu, select Data Environment. A window opens with the tables related to this form. Right-click a blank area of this window and select Add. This brings up a File dialog box. Select the CUSTOMER table. Then select the ITEMS table. Figure 11-18 shows this process.

Relating the Data

Now you need to relate CUSTOMER and ITEMS to the existing ORDERS-ORDLINES relationship. You did create relationships in the previous chapter, but these were persistent relationships; these don't come into play until you examine advanced data handling in Part 5.

In the meantime, you still need to relate this data. You can do so from the Data Environment just as you did previously in the Database Designer, by dragging and dropping. The key difference is that the parent table does not need to be a primary or candidate key on the related field.

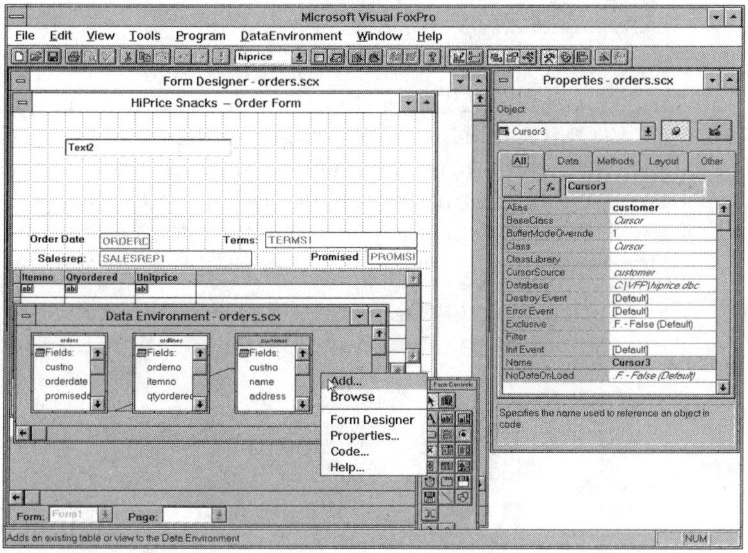

Adding tables to the form

Figure 11-18.

Recall that to define a persistent relationship, you needed a unique key, in the form of a primary or candidate index, in the parent table. For example, you created a primary key in CUSTOMER on the Custno field and used it to create a relationship with ORDERS. In that case, CUSTOMER was the parent, and ORDERS was the child.

However, you can see that in the current form, ORDERS is the parent and CUSTOMER the child; that is, you select an order and then want to see the related customer. Likewise, in your persistent relationship between ITEMS and ORDLINES, ITEMS is the parent and ORDLINES the child. But in this form, ORDLINES is the parent and ITEMS the child.

Note: ORDLINES is both a child, to ORDERS, and a parent, to ITEMS. This stringing together of relationships is a necessary part of using relational databases effectively.

The point is that here a parent need not be controlled by, or even have, a unique key. The child does have to be indexed on the related field or fields.

Creating the Relationship

Now create a relationship.

From the Data Environment window, select the ORDERS table and highlight the Custno field. Using the left mouse button, drag the field to the CUSTOMER table. When you get to the child table, CUSTOMER in this case, you will see that the table window scrolls down to the indexes for that table. Drop the field onto the custno index. You will then see a line from ORDERS to CUSTOMER, just as you saw when you created the persistent relations in the previous chapter. Figure 11-19 shows the relationship line.

Similarly, relate ORDLINES to ITEMS so you can show the item description instead of just the item number. The relationship is shown here:

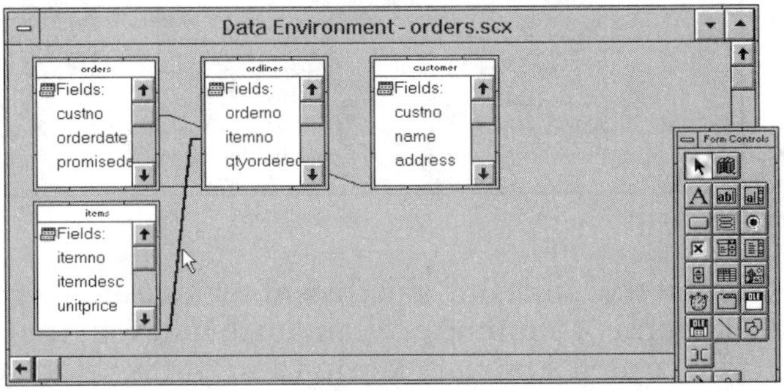

You are finished with the Data Environment for now, so close it.

Putting the Customer Data on the Form

Now to add a control for the customer's name. Click the Text Box icon, shown here, on the Form Controls toolbar.

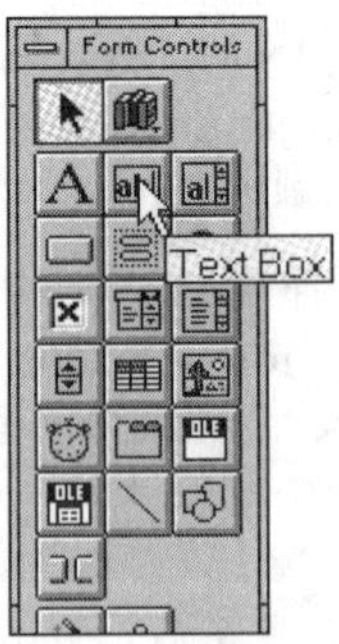

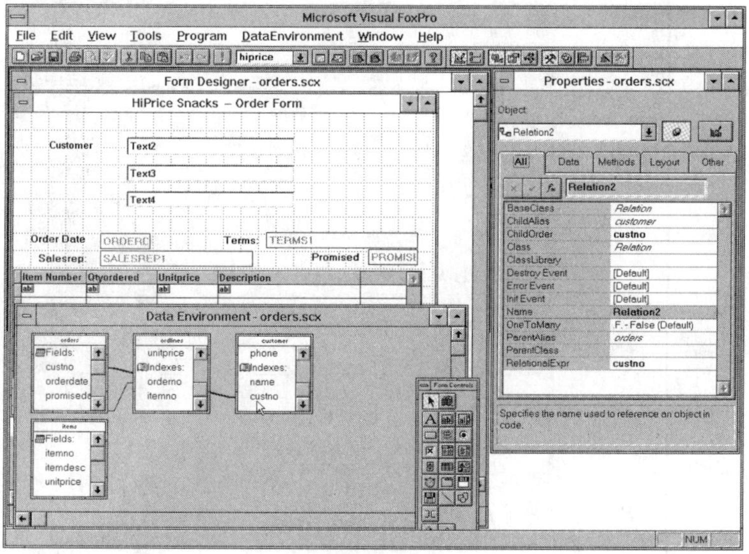

Relating ORDERS to CUSTOMER

Figure 11-19.

Move the mouse cursor into the top part of the Screen Designer and click the mouse button again. Exact placement is not necessary. You can use the handles to size the text box as needed. Alternatively, when you drop the text box on the form with the second mouse click, you can hold down the mouse button and drag the box to the shape you want.

Now you want to associate the text box with the CUSTOMER table. Select the Data tab in the Properties window. Highlight the ControlSource property and, in the entry box, type **customer.name**. Figure 11-20 shows the screen.

Save the screen and run the form again. Note that the text box you just created shows the customer's name.

Finishing Up CUSTOMER Data

Add controls for the customer's address and a caption identifying the information. Drop two more text boxes onto the screen and associate them, in the Properties window, with customer.address and customer.citystate fields.

After you've added the controls, add a label to identify these boxes as customer information. Select Label from the Screen toolbar. Drop the label to the left of the name Text Box, making room as necessary. Size the label to fit nicely, and in the Caption entry box in the Properties window, type **Customer**.

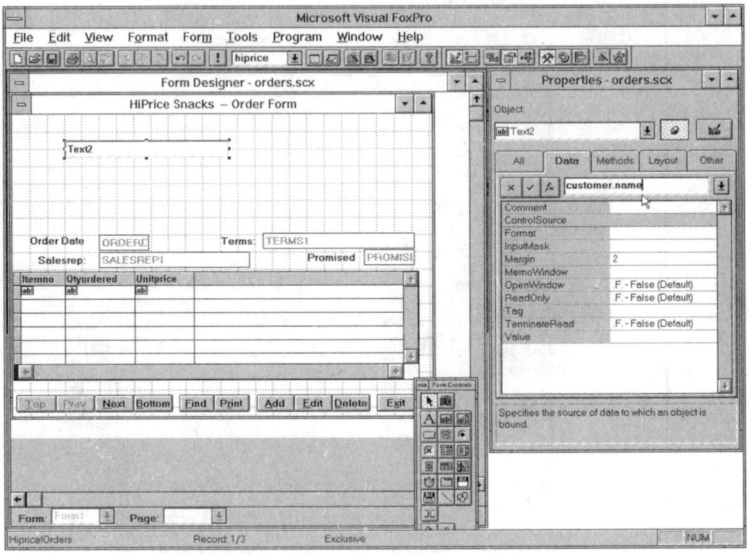

Binding the text box to the customer name field in CUSTOMER

Figure 11-20.

Save your work and run the form again.

Adding Item Order Information

You've neglected the box on your form that looks like a spreadsheet. This is a grid, and it allows you to display data in a tabular manner. This format is useful here because it lets you see the multiple order items on a single form.

You will do three things to this area: First, you will make the labels a little more sensible. Next, you will add the description from the ITEMS file to supplement the item code. Finally, you will add an extended price column that contains the calculation of the quantity ordered times the unit price. This is a calculated item, and there is no reason to store it in your table since you can do the arithmetic any time you want.

Changing the Captions

To change the caption of the first column from Itemno to Item Number, click the drop-down button in the Properties window just below the word "Object." Scroll down to Header1, which you can see is a subclass of Grid1. Figure 11-21 shows the Header1 object highlighted and the mouse cursor pointing to the parent object, Grid1.

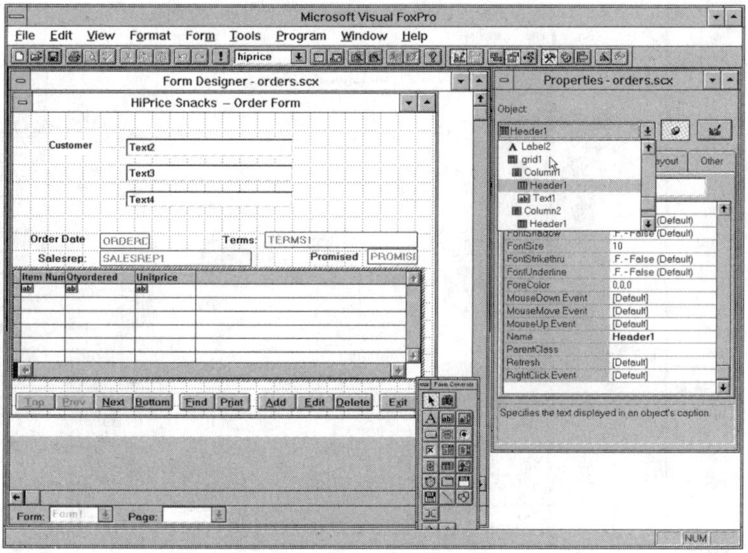

Selecting the column header

Figure 11-21.

Once you have selected the header, select the Caption property, just as you did previously, and change it to **Item Number**. After you have done this, you will see that the header in the grid does not have enough room to spell out Item Number; it shows just Item Num.

Looking through the properties for this header, you will not see a width setting. So how do you change the width to accommodate your caption?

Other Grid Objects

When you selected the Header1 object in the Properties window, you may have noticed that there were other subobjects below Grid1— that is, objects that are related to Grid1. These are indicated by an additional indent level under Grid1. One of these is Column1. Selecting this object does display a Width property.

A width of 86 seems to work well on the display. Why 86 instead of 85 or 90? Here's another trick for you to use. Place the mouse cursor between the columns, as shown on Figure 11-22, and the sizing cursor again appears. Now you can simply drag the column as you wish.

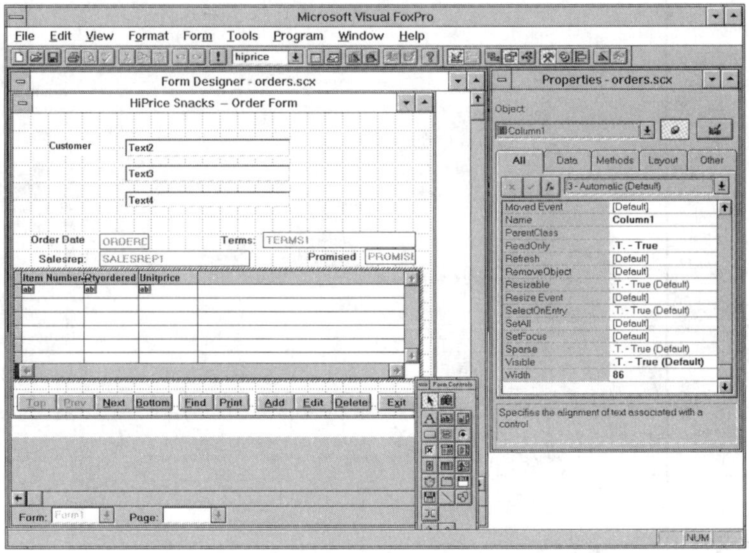

Increasing the width of a column using the mouse

Figure 11-22.

Adding a Description Column

Next add a new column to contain the description from ITEMS. An easy way to do this is to select the grid object, GRID1 in the example, and then select the Layout tab. On this page you will see the property ColumnCount. Highlight ColumnCount and change it from 3 to **5**. You want 5 because you will be adding your calculated column. Figure 11-23 shows ColumnCount set to 5.

Now select the Heading1 object under Column4. Change the caption to **Description**. Now select the Column4 object, select the ControlSource property, and enter **items.description**. Size the column to make a little room for a real description.

Adding a Calculated Column

Finally, add a column that lists the extended price. The extended price is simply the quantity ordered times the unit price.

Change the heading as you just did for the previous column, and in ControlSource enter **ordlines.qtyordered * ordlines.unitprice**. Figure 11-24 shows the completed form.

11

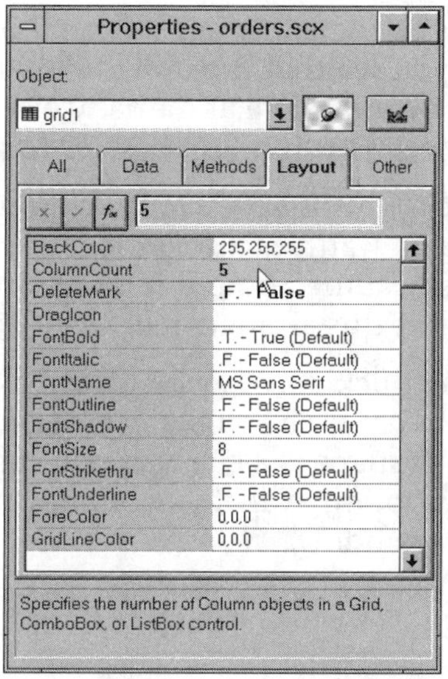

Setting the ColumnCount property to add two new columns
Figure 11-23.

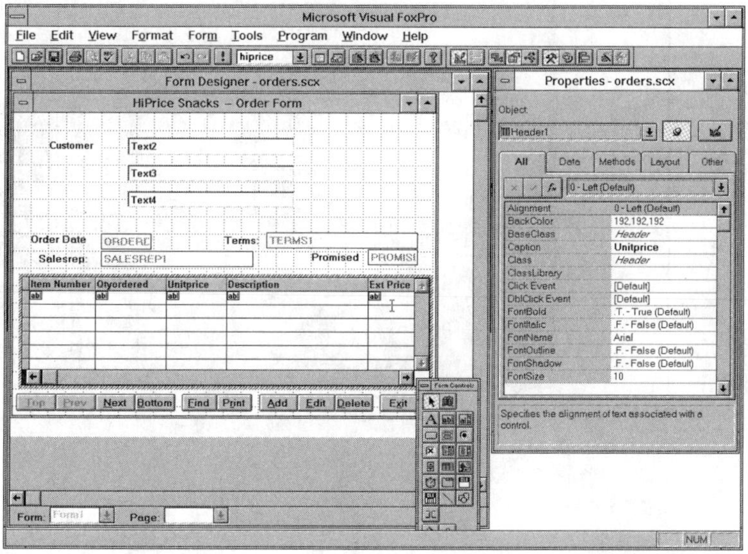

Added columns
Figure 11-24.

Making the Form a Little More Orderly

Returning to the paper order form that HiPrice showed you in the previous chapter, you see that the order body has quantity first, then description, followed by unit price and finally extended price. The order form is coming together well, but it might be nice to order it more like the original.

Fortunately, this is easy. Grab a column heading with the mouse and move it where you want it to go. Probably the simplest procedure is to grab the Unitprice heading and put it between Description and Ext Price. Figure 11-25 shows this arrangement.

Notice the thick down-arrow shape of the mouse cursor when it is in a position to drag. The cursor can be seen in the heading Unitprice in the figure. This shape is a cue that you can perform a drag operation here. To make this option available, you may need to select the column object in the Properties window.

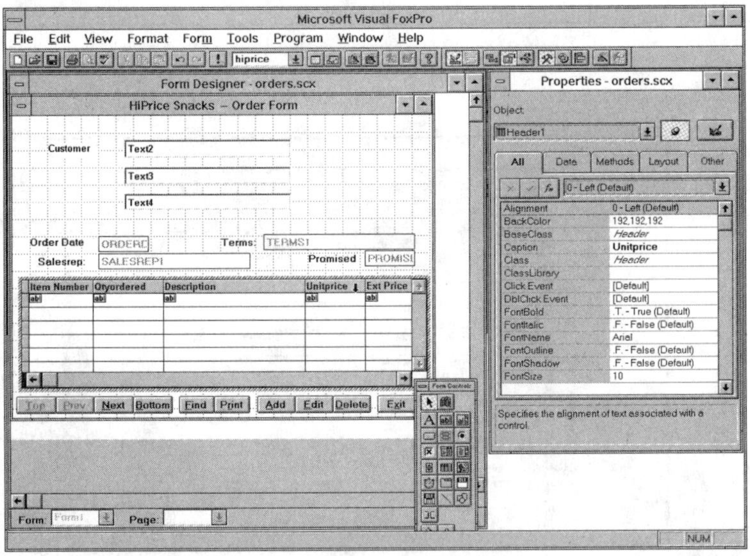

Final arrangement
Figure 11-25.

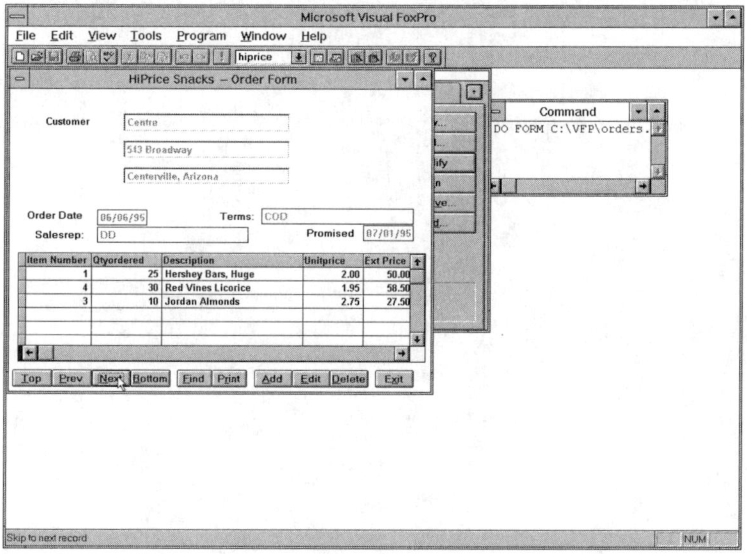

Running the finished form

Figure 11-26.

Save your work and run the form. It should look like Figure 11-26.

12

Adding Screen Controls

In the previous chapter you created a screen form with the data from the HiPrice example. In doing so, you placed elements, called controls, on the form. It may seem odd to refer to the more mundane items as controls.

For instance, this is a label control:

It seems perhaps pretentious to call this—just a little bit of text that says "Customer"—a control. Pretentious or not, it is a control, and its simplicity provided a simple way for you to learn about controls.

After describing the simple label control, this chapter discusses some more "control-like" controls: drop-down combo boxes and spin buttons. All of the examples in this chapter are built on the screen form you designed in Chapter 11 and the database you designed in Chapter 10.

Working with a Label Control

The humble label control puts a bit of text on your screen form. You created a label control with the text "Customer" in the previous chapter. Why think of this simple element as a control? This label is a control because, though simple, it hides a fair amount of complexity, and this is what controls, or objects, do.

For instance, in the earlier versions of the Xbase dialects, you might accomplish what this label control does by writing a line of code like this:

```
@10,2 say "Customer"
```

Note: The @ signifies that what comes next, 10 and 2, are the screen coordinates at which the SAY command displays the text "Customer"; that is, the text is displayed on row 10 starting at column 2.

With this entry, the task was complete. What often went unnoticed is that a lot of assumptions are made in this simple command. For instance, it assumes that the current default color is used. The programmer could add a COLOR clause to set the color specifically but most often did not. The programmer also could add a PICTURE clause to control other aspects of the displayed value such as capitalization, numeric formatting, and template characters.

Controls Encapsulate Information

A look at the Properties window in Figure 12-1 shows that a label has more than 50 properties. These range from Alignment and AutoSize to WordWrap and ZOrder.

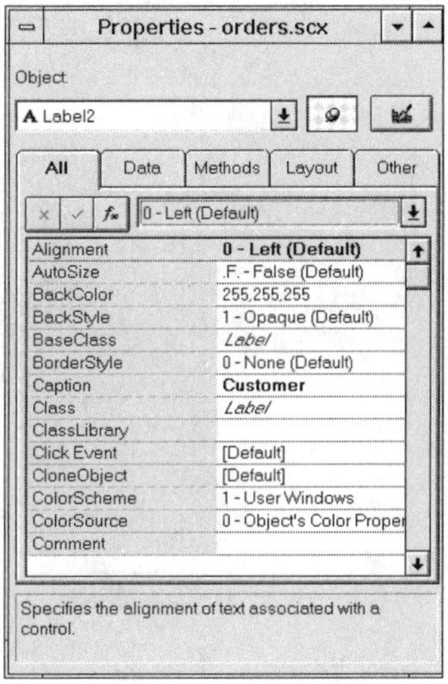

Some of the properties of a label control
Figure 12-1.

Note: Alignment, AutoSize, and WordWrap should not be too foreign, but what is ZOrder? ZOrder lets you work in a third dimension on your screens. Suppose you want to say where a particular word in a book is located. You could say, "Page 23, fourth line, third word." In this example, "fourth line, third word" are the traditional screen dimensions of X and Y: that is, width and height. Page 23 is the Z dimension and is likely new to the Xbase programmer. It is required because graphical user interfaces offer the possibility of two or more screens lying on top of one another. ZOrder tells you what place each overlapping piece occupies.

Some of these properties, such as foreground and background color (ForeColor and BackColor) are familiar. Others—FontName and FontSize, for instance—are provided because of the new power of the graphical user interface. Still others set how the control responds to certain actions. The gathering of all this information on your control is called encapsulation; everything about the piece of text is encapsulated in the label control.

Changing the Method for a Control

Properties that control responses are the methods for an object. Generally, methods control events. For example, there is a ClickEvent method. Figure 12-2 shows the Properties window with ClickEvent highlighted.

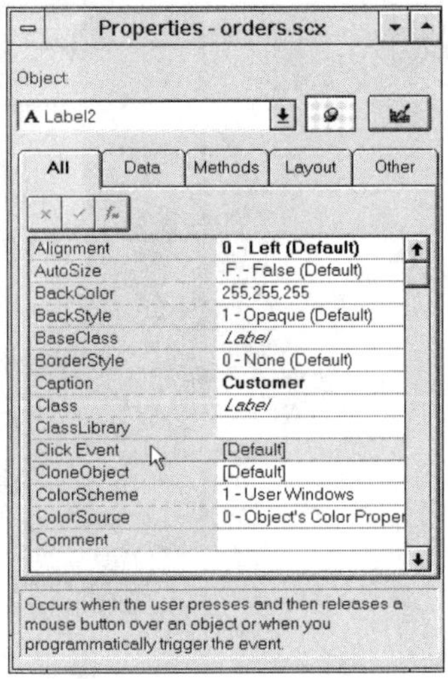

Properties window for a label control with ClickEvent highlighted

Figure 12-2.

Looking at the bottom of the Properties window, you see the Help hint for this event. It tells you that this event is triggered whenever the user clicks the mouse over this label.

Note that the current status for this method is [Default]. This means that you have not specified an action. To examine how events are handled, you can add some code to this event. What you will do is ring the system bell when the mouse is clicked on this label.

Adding Code to a Method

To ring the system bell when the mouse is clicked on the Customer label, do the following:

1. Double-click the ClickEvent line in the Properties window, and you are taken to the code editor for the label's click event. Enter the command

   ```
   ?? chr(7)
   ```

   as shown in Figure 12-3.

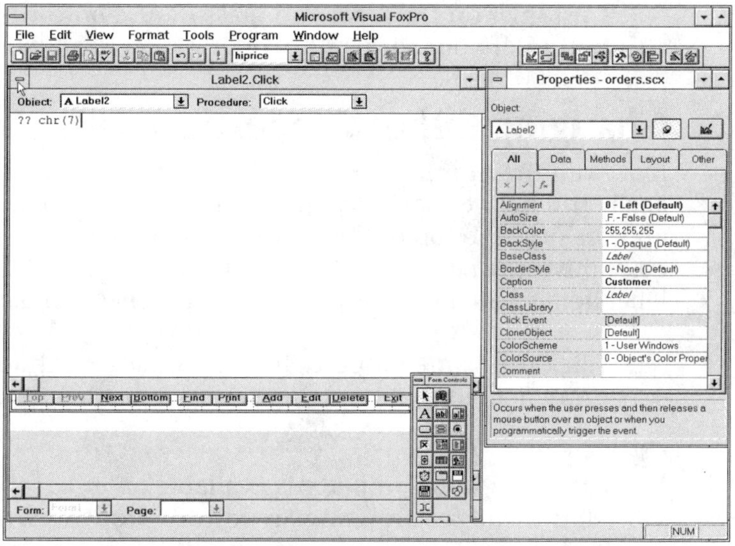

Adding code to the ClickEvent
Figure 12-3.

Note: This command is a moldy-oldy from way back. The ?? is a command to output what comes next to the standard output device, normally the screen. The chr( ) function converts a decimal number to its ASCII value, and 7 is the ASCII value for BEL, a command to issue a warning sound. In short, what this command does is beep the speaker or, if you have a sound card, make it go "bing." This command was an indispensable aid in debugging since you could add it to your program code and hear when it was executed. It is still handy since it is a simple command with a noticeable result.

2. Double-click the title bar icon to close the code editor. The ClickEvent entry in the Properties window should now look like this:

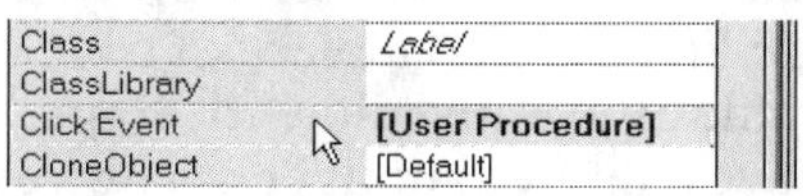

The User Procedure is the simple ring-the-bell command.

3. Save your work and run the form. Place the mouse cursor on the word Customer on the form and press mouse button 1, normally the left button. If your speaker is working, you should hear a beep.

Changing Other Properties

Exit from the running form and return to the Form Designer. Click the label again and notice that the name for this label, Label2 or something similar, appears near the top of the Properties window. This name is not very descriptive; the name Label2, for instance, simply tells you that it is the second label item created on this form. Give it a new, more descriptive, name.

1. Click the Name property in the Properties window. This action puts an entry field in the Properties window just below the tabs.

Tip: The Name property is available on either the All tab or the Other tab. All is useful for browsing an object's properties, but the specific tab, such as Other, is usually easier to use since it has fewer choices.

2. Click your mouse in this field, type **Customer_label**, and press ENTER. Your screen should look like this:

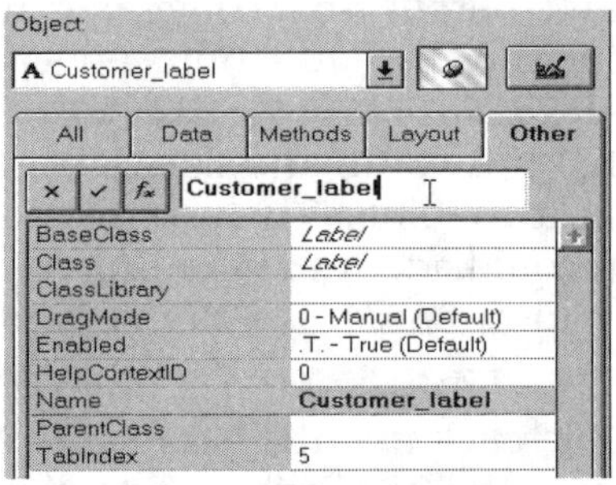

You've now seen two different ways to change properties associated with a control: You can add a piece of code as you did with ClickEvent, or enter a new value as you just did with Name. A third method exists for properties that have a limited number of choices such as true or false or 1, 2, or 3, as with the Alignment property, shown here:

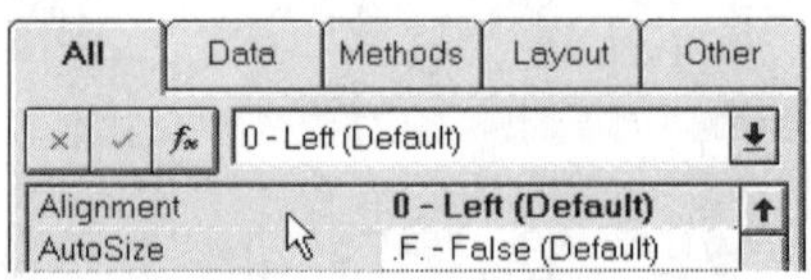

The cue that this property has a set of choices is the 0 part of 0 - Left (default). In addition, when Alignment is highlighted, the value entry field has a drop-down down arrow button to its right. Click this button, and your choices will appear like this:

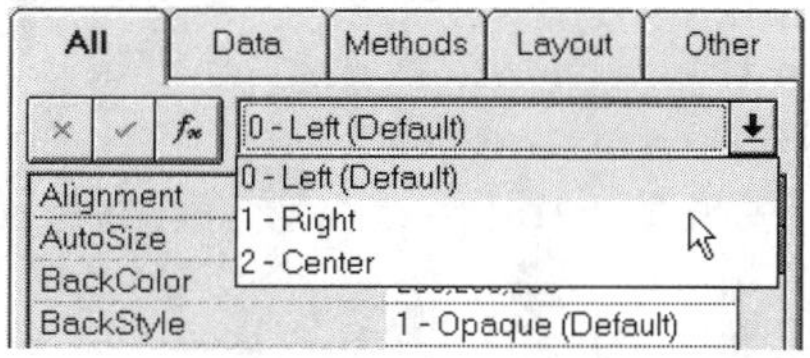

Selecting 1 - Right will make the caption, Customer, move to the right edge of the label field. You can also cycle through the possible choices by double-clicking the property. Move your mouse cursor to the Alignment entry and double-click it. This causes the next choice to be selected. If you were at Right, the selected choice will now be Center. Double-clicking again takes you back to Left, the default selection.

Using double-clicks to cycle through the choices is an easy way to work if you are familiar with the choices. Using the drop-down menu is convenient for seeing the choices in list form.

Controlling Default Behavior

One of the advantages of the Windows environment is predictability. For instance, it is standard to invoke Help by pressing the F1 key. It is also standard to move to a given entry field by moving the mouse cursor to the location and clicking the mouse button.

Visual FoxPro uses these standard behaviors to lift a great burden from your shoulders. For instance, clicking the mouse button in an entry field moves you to that location without your having to do anything else. This kind of power leads to the "no programming required" claims examined in Part I. However, suppose you want to change the default behavior. Do you need to reinvent the whole action? For example, suppose you want to issue a beep whenever a user clicks the Terms entry field, a text box. You want to do this to provide an aural warning to the user that this field should usually be left alone. Since you do want users to be able to edit the Terms value, you can't just make the field unavailable. Thus, you want to beep the speaker and then allow the default action: editing the field.

Changing the ClickEvent for a Control

To change the default ClickEvent value for the Terms1 control by sounding a beep when the user clicks the Terms field, do the following:

1. Select the text box labeled TERMS1 as shown here:

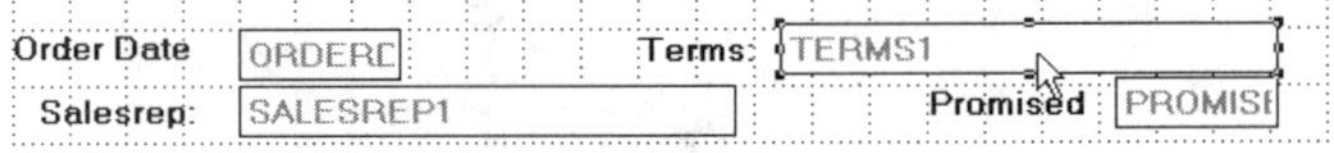

Note: Select the text box Terms1, not the label Terms.

2. As you did before, double-click ClickEvent in the Properties window to bring up the code editor for this event. Add the line

   ```
   ?? chr(7)
   ```

   as you did previously. Your screen should look like Figure 12-4.

Tip: Note that the title bar in the code window says "Terms1.Click". This is the actual code name for the method you are modifying. Click is the method name, and Terms1 identifies the object, or control, to which it applies. This referencing allows you more specifically to control objects.

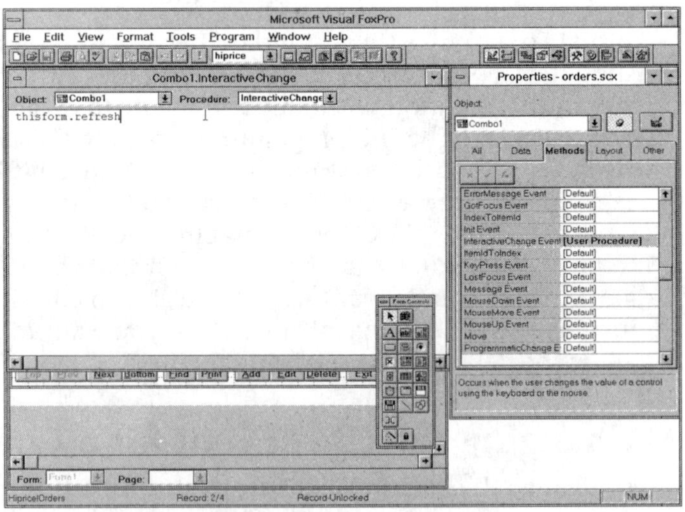

Adding code to ClickEvent
Figure 12-4.

Adding Comments to Your Code

You have now twice used the ?? chr(7) trick in code. Will you remember what this means later? Will others understand it? It is an old trick, some may not have used it before, and it is more than a little cryptic. This is a good place to add a comment to your code. If you "comment your code," then sections that may be obvious when you write can be understood later when the code is less obvious.

Visual FoxPro recognizes two types of comments: inline and line. An inline comment is one that appears after some code and continues to the end of the line. Two ampersands (&&) signal the beginning of an inline comment. Here you see them used to mark a comment that tells you what the ?? chr(7) does:

```
?? chr(7)  && ring the bell
```


A line comment is marked by an asterisk (*). If an asterisk is the first nonspace character on a line, then the entire line is treated as a comment. Here you see this style of comment used to add a comment line above the code line:

```
* ring the bell
?? chr(7)
```

Tip: You can use comments to make code inactive. Suppose you want your finished form to use the bell ring you added earlier but are tired of hearing it while you are testing and developing. You can put an asterisk in front of the ?? chr(7), and the command will be treated as a comment; that is, it will not ring the bell. You can then remove the comment character before finalizing the program.

Testing Your Changes

It's time to test your form with your changes in place.

1. Double-click the title bar icon in the code editor to close the editor. Save your changes and click the Run [!] button. Your screen should look something like Figure 12-5.

   Clicking on the text box for Terms produces an eerie silence. You need to put the form in edit mode.

2. Click the Edit button. Now click the Terms text box, and you will hear a satisfying beep.

   Note that the behavior, once the beep has sounded, is standard; the mouse cursor is placed in the field for editing.

3. When you are finished testing, press the Save or Revert button, close the form, and return to the Form Designer.

Adding a Drop-Down Combo Box

Drop-down combo boxes are the work horses of data display. They look like a text box except for the drop-down button on the right. Clicking this button allows you to scroll through a list of choices. The combo box is a compact tool that still allows a nice visual display. You saw a combo box when you modified the Alignment property of the label control. It looks like this when not dropped down:

When you need to scroll through the possibilities, you press the button and it looks like this:

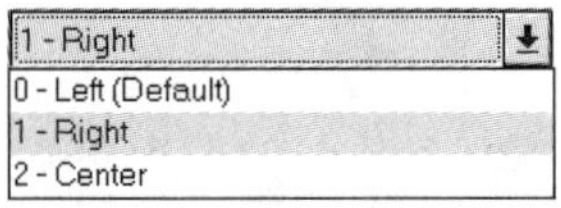

Note: A combo box allows manual entry. A list box is similar, but it allows you to choose only from the defined items. The terms "combo box" and "list box" are used interchangeably most of the time. Here, the term "combo box" is used.

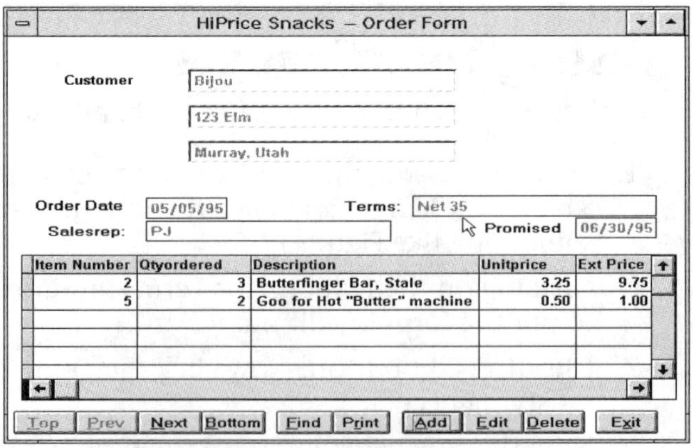

Running the modified form
Figure 12-5.

For this screen form you will add a drop-down combo box to allow the user to select the order number to be displayed. This feature will allow your users to scroll through the orders by number, and it will add the order number, which is not now displayed, to the screen.

1. Click the Combo Box button on the Form toolbar.

Note: If you cannot select anything from the Form toolbar, you need to select the form first by clicking the mouse anywhere on the screen form.

The following illustration shows the Form toolbar with the mouse cursor on the Combo Box button.

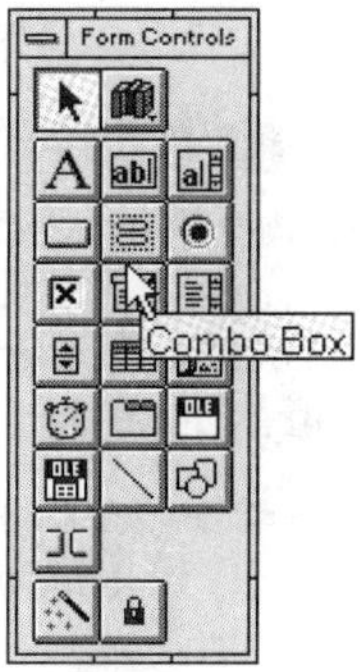

2. Move the mouse cursor to the right of the Customer information and click again. This places a combo box on the form, as shown in Figure 12-6.

Tying Your Control to Data

You have placed the control on the form. Now you need to associate it with the order number. The Combo Box Builder makes this easy.

1. Click the right mouse button on the new combo box and select Builder as shown here:

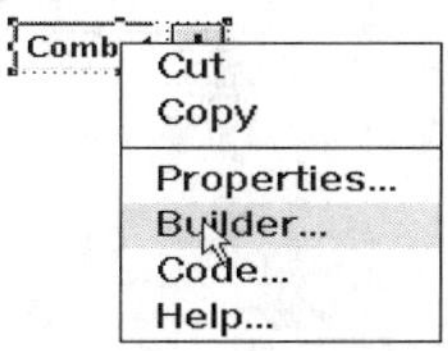

The builder lets you define the behavior of your combo box. Just above the middle of the builder window is a combo box for selecting the possible sources for your combo box. It looks like this:

The choice you want, to fill in the values from a table or view, is already displayed. You can also fill in values by hand or from an array.

2. Select the Orderno field from the ORDERS table as shown in Figure 12-7.
3. The default values on the other tabs are fine, so click the OK button, and you are returned to the Form Designer.
4. Save your work and click the Run [!] button. Your screen should look like Figure 12-8.

Correcting the Refresh Method Bug

Using the form you just modified, click the drop-down button and select another order. When you do this, the grid showing the order items changes to reflect the new order. However, the customer and order information may not be similarly refreshed. Why is this so?

There appears to be a bug in version 3.0. This bug may be fixed in your version, but even if it is, you may find it useful to see how to solve this problem.

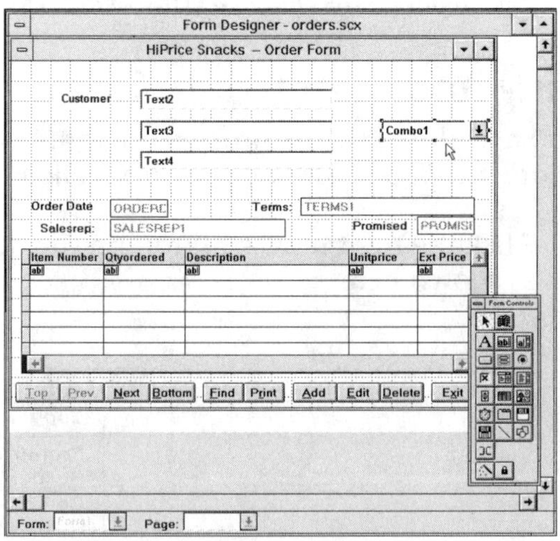

Combo box on the screen form

Figure 12-6.

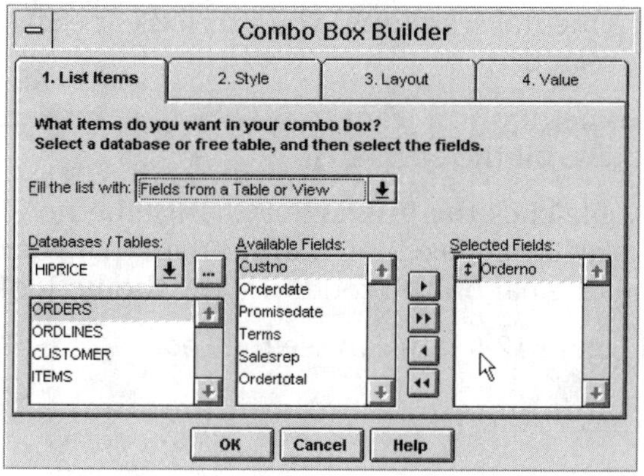

Selecting the Orderno field for the combo box

Figure 12-7.

What should be happening is that when the combo box value is changed, the form on which the combo box resides—that is, the parent form for the control—should be refreshed. However, only the grid items are being refreshed and not the others.

The solution is to hook your own code, calling the form's refresh method, to an event that signals that the combo box has changed its value. Perusing the list of methods associated with your combo box locates a possibility: InteractiveChange. This method is called every time the combo box's value changes: for example, by typing a letter or number in it. Thus, if you are using a character value and enter "Joe," the method will be called three

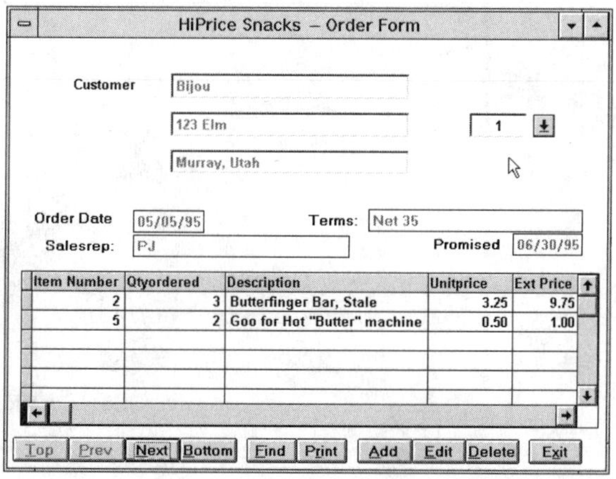

Running the form with a combo box

Figure 12-8.

times: once each after "J," "o," and "e." This method can be useful for incremental searching; you can look at each keystroke and try to refine the search.

The method you want to invoke to refresh the form is Refresh. This method redraws all the elements.

Double-click the InteractiveChange method in the Properties window to display the code editor. Make certain that your combo box is the selected item. The title bar on the code window should look like the one in Figure 12-9.

In Figure 12-9 you can see the code

```
thisform.refresh
```

Here's what it means.

Using the Reserved Names This, Parent, and ThisForm

Recall that earlier in this chapter you learned that a property is associated with an object. You modified the click event of the object, or control, Terms1. Terms1.Click was how that property was referenced.

Now you want to modify your main screen form, Form1, but how do you refer to it from inside another control? You know the name, so you might try entering Form1.refresh. However, when you do so, an error message

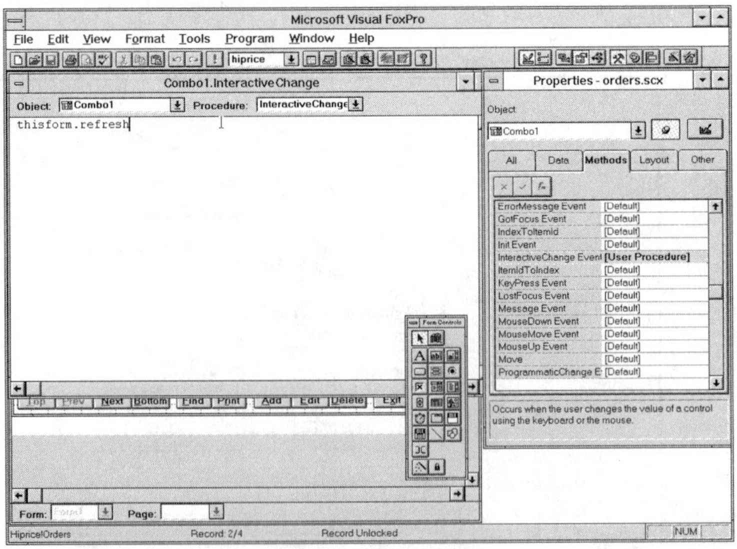

Making the form refresh
Figure 12-9.

appears saying that the system doesn't recognize Form1. The reason the system doesn't recognize Form1 has to do with visibility. Combo1, your combo box, cannot "see" its parent, Form1, directly; thus, it cannot invoke any of its parent's methods.

The answer to this dilemma lies in several reserved names: This, Parent, and ThisForm. These are special names. The name This refers to the current object. For example, to invoke the refresh method for the combo box itself, you would use the following code:

```
this.refresh
```

ThisForm refers to the operating form—in this case, Form1. To invoke the form's refresh method, you would enter the following:


```
thisform.refresh
```

This is just what you need to do.

Tip: Remember that Visual FoxPro is not case-sensitive; ThisForm and thisform are equivalent.

The name Parent refers to the parent of the object. Because you may need to refer to another object's parent, you need to be unambiguous in naming the parent. Enter the following:

```
this.parent.refresh
```

In this case, the parent is Form1, so this code is the same as thisform.refresh. Note that this line contains two periods. These are referred to as member-of operators, or dot operators. It is not uncommon to use more than one of these operators as you have done here. "This.parent" serves the same function—to provide unambiguous identification—as "thisform" did in the previous example.

Double-click the title bar icon in the code editor to close the editor. Save your work and click the Run button. Your form should now refresh the customer information when you select a different order number.

Finishing the Combo Box

You'll want to add a label to identify the new combo box. Click the Label button on the Forms toolbar. Drop it on the form near the combo box.

Change the Caption property to **Order** # and move it and the combo box to a convenient spot as shown here:

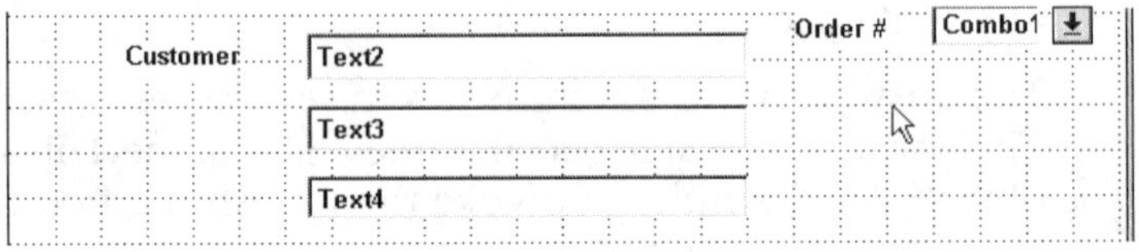

Adding Spin Buttons

Spin buttons, or spinners as Visual FoxPro calls them, provide a convenient method for setting numeric values. Here is a standard spinner:

The small arrows on the right side of this spinner let you raise or lower the value by clicking them.

You can use a spinner for any numeric value. Here you will put one on the grid of order line information.

1. Select the grid by clicking it.
2. Select the column for your spinner by selecting the column—for example, Column2—from the Properties window as shown here:

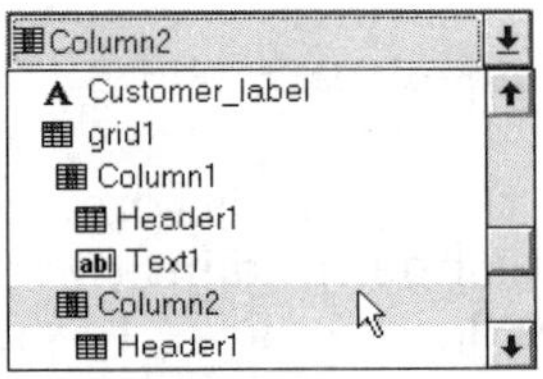

3. Click the Spinner button on the Form toolbar. Move the mouse cursor to the body of Column2 and click again to put a spinner in this column.

   Notice that this column already contains a text box icon. The text box is the default means of presenting information in a grid. You don't need this text box anymore since you will be using your spinner, so delete it. Again, the easiest way to select a column item is through the Properties window.
4. In the Properties window, choose Text1 as shown here:

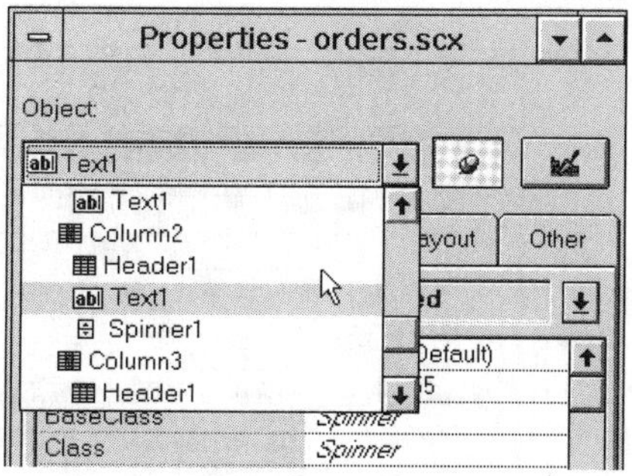

Then delete it by pressing the DELETE key.

5. Again select the Column2 control in the Properties window. To edit the ControlSource property, click ControlSource and then click the drop-down button beside the value window. Select orders.ordquantity as the control source.
6. You want to prevent entry of a negative quantity or zero, so change the KeyBoardLowValue and SpinnerLowValue properties to **1**. Figure 12-10 shows these settings.
7. Save your work and then click the Run button. Click the Edit button and then click the qtyordered column. Note that you can either use the up and down spin buttons or enter a value from the keyboard.

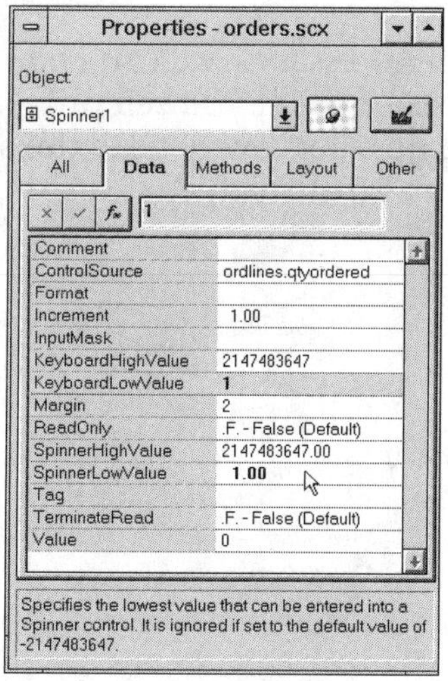

Setting low values

Figure 12-10.

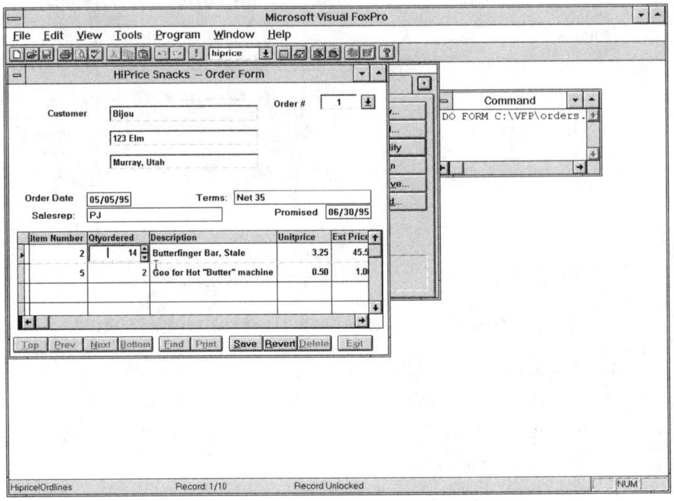

Grid with taller rows

Figure 12-11.

As you can see, or not see, as the case is here, the height of the rows is too small. You cannot see the whole number, and the spin buttons are almost impossibly small.

8. Select the grid and change the RowHeight property to **30**. Now the rows are taller. Again save your work and run the form. It should look like Figure 12-11.

Note that, if necessary, you can change the increment of your spinner's values. For example, if you sell only by the dozen, you can set the increment to move 12 numbers every time the spin button is pressed.

13

Reporting Data from Multiple Tables

Now we will turn our attention to reporting data from the HiPrice database. Reporting information from multiple data tables has always be a chore in the Xbase environment. The early tools were not up to the task, and Xbase developers usually resorted to writing program code to print reports. They got away with this because the reports were based on the 66 row, 80 column page; there was little room for enhancing reports in that limited format. Just as graphical user interfaces drove programmers to rapid application development, detailed in Chapter 4, sophisticated printer control languages such as Adobe's PostScript and Hewlett Packard's PCL are driving programmers to visual reporting tools.

Visual FoxPro's report generator is up to the task. With it, the great majority of reporting needs can be met. In this chapter, you will examine a standard type of report: a listing of order information. This report uses the data that you defined in Chapter 10.

Starting with the Report Wizard

The strategy again will be to use the Report Wizard to get going and then modify the report to suit your needs. Highlight Reports on the HiPrice Documents page. Select New to display the dialog box where you can choose between the Report Wizard and Report Designer. Select Report Wizard as shown in Figure 13-1.

Just as with most other wizards, you are given a choice of several options. Choose the One-to-Many Report Wizard, as shown here, to take advantage of the natural relationship between ORDERS and ORDLINES.

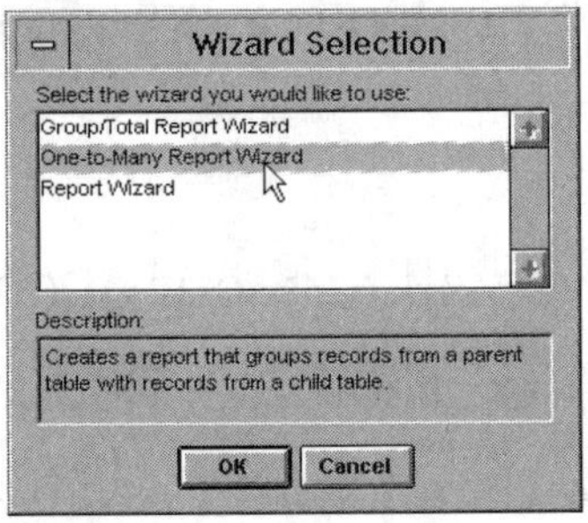

You are now asked to choose the parent table and fields from it. Select ORDERS as the parent and select the fields shown in Figure 13-2.

Click the Next button. You will be asked to select the child table and fields. Select only the Qtyordered and Unitprice fields since Orderno and Itemno are keys linking other information. As you did in Chapter 11, you will be linking the description from ITEMS later in the report process. Figure 13-3 shows the child table page of the wizard.

The next question to address is the relationship between ORDERS and ORDLINES. Again, the wizard has correctly deduced that the relationship is on Orderno in each table. Click Next again to address the question of order.

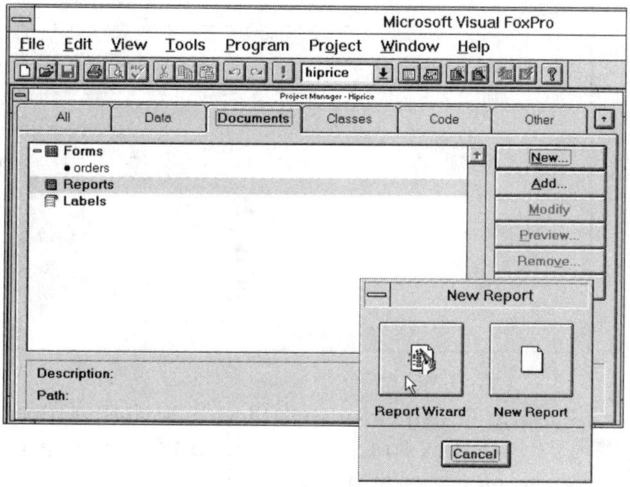

Choosing Report Wizard
Figure 13-1.

Since the field you want to use to order this report, customer.name, has not yet been acknowledged, skip this step for now and click Next again.

The next choice is the report style. Accept the default settings by clicking the Next button. This brings you to the last step. Click the Save report and modify it in the Report Designer radio button, then click the Finish button. Figure 13-4 shows the Finish screen.

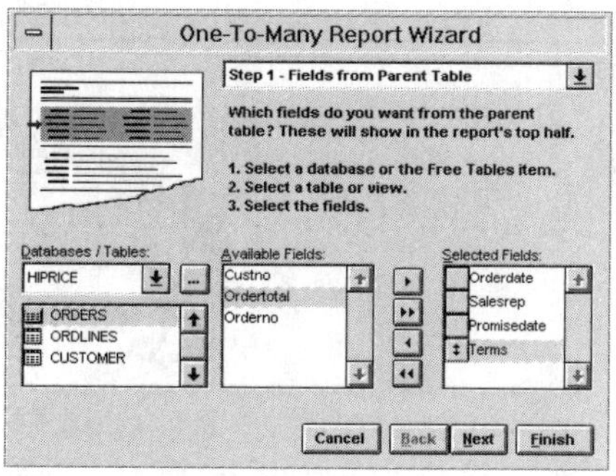

Selecting fields from the parent table, ORDERS
Figure 13-2.

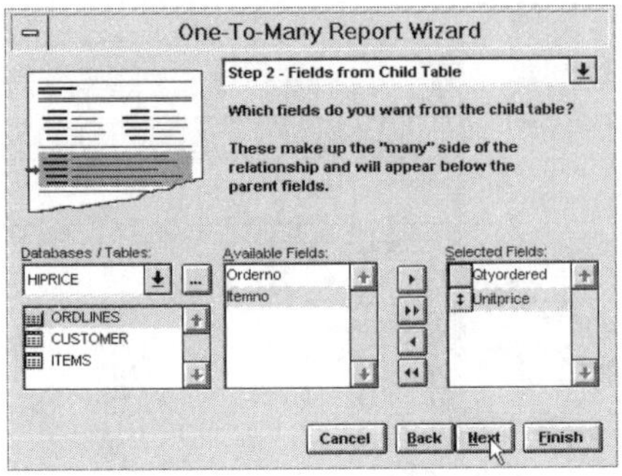

Selecting fields from the child table, ORDLINES
Figure 13-3.

Clicking Finish brings you to a File dialog box. The default name, orders.frx, is fine so click the Save button, and you are finished with the wizard. The Report Designer appears.

Using the Report Designer

In this section you will be adding data from CUSTOMER and ITEMS, creating groups and subgroups, and ordering the information in the report. First size the Report Designer window so you can see all the bands. Figure 13-5 shows the window sized and the Report toolbar move to the side.

Note: Report bands are discussed in Chapter 9.

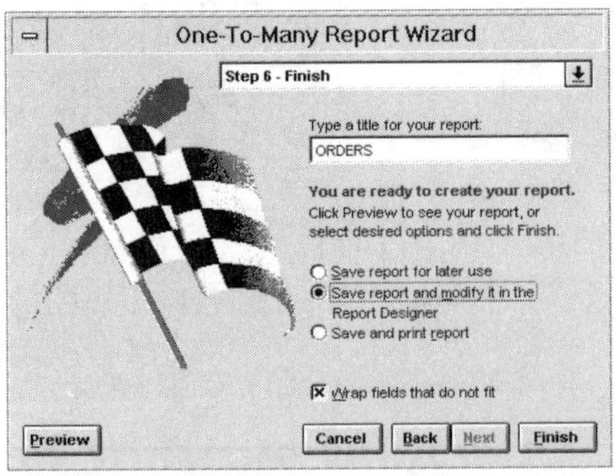

The Finish screen
Figure 13-4.

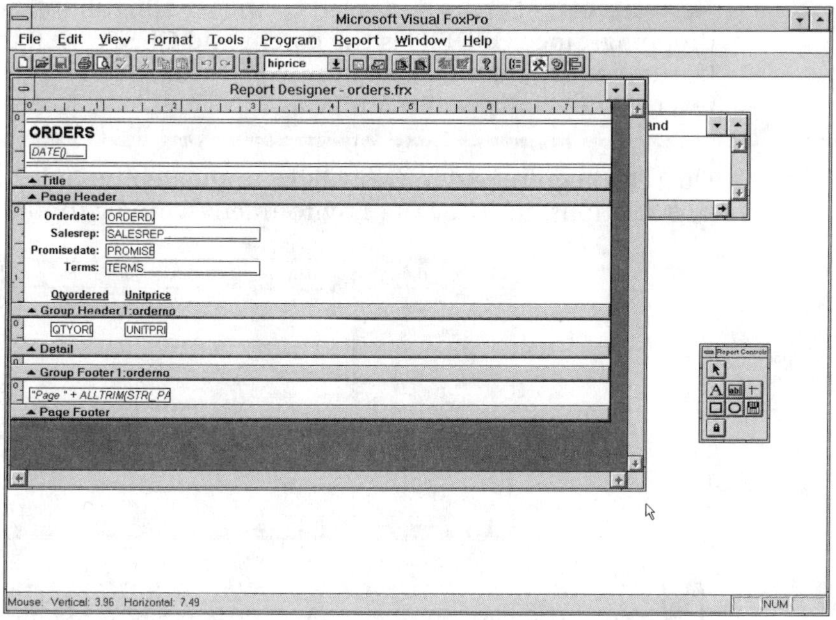

Sizing the Report Designer window

Figure 13-5.

13

Adding Data Tables

As in Chapter 11, the method for adding data tables to the report is to use the Data Environment window. Select it from the View menu as shown here:

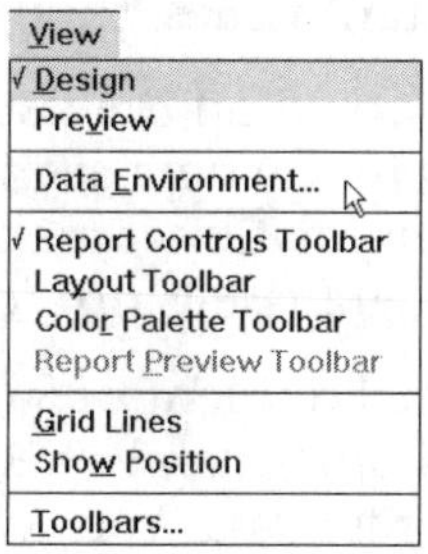

Clicking the right mouse button on an empty space in this window brings a pop-up menu. Select Add. Then in the File dialog box, select ITEMS. Repeat the process to add CUSTOMER.

Setting Relations

Drag the custno field in ORDERS to the custno index in CUSTOMER to create that link.

Caution: Do not be fooled by the seeming simplicity of dragging and dropping. Since ORDERS is the parent and CUSTOMER the child, you must be sure to drag from ORDERS to CUSTOMER. Even though you can do the reverse, the results would not be as expected.

Drag the itemno field in ORDLINES to the itemno index in ITEMS to create that relationship. The Data Environment window should look like this:

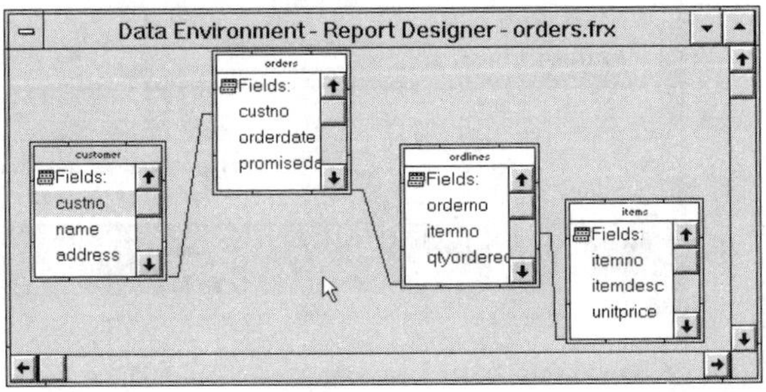

Note: The vertical placement of the tables is for illustrative purposes only, to show the parent-child relations. Also, the wizard created the link between ORDERS and ORDLINES.

Setting the Report Order

In designing reports, you generally think of layout and such issues. One of the most important issues, though, is the order in which the data appears.

This book has harped on the issue of properly defining your databases and will do so again in the next section. In understanding the importance of building a proper relational model, you cannot lose sight of the fact that the data in the database is not "data" as the customer sees it.

Sally Smith, Vice President of Sales for HiPrice, wants the orders report in order of the customer names because that is the most convenient way for her to look up order data. You could try to convince her that customer number ordering makes more sense, but this would be just a good way to lose the account or your job.

Alternatively, you could concoct a numbering scheme in which you take part of the name, say the first four letters, and add a digit or two at the end to account for duplicates. Carmike might then be CARM01 in such a scheme. The problem is that Carmel Theater would be CARM02 and would come after Carmike—which is not alphabetical order, though sometimes such a sequence is good enough.

In earlier, text-mode days, this method was often the best compromise since the elegant list boxes and drop-down combo boxes of modern graphical user interfaces were not available or were too cumbersome. This limitation meant that you had to ask the user for a customer number. Since the user was going to have to know customer numbers, it made some sense to use a scheme that made them easier to remember. However, the "visual" part of Visual FoxPro gives you powerful tools to use, so it is time to discard this practice. There is no longer a good reason for the user to even know that the customer number exists. It is just a key for you to use to relate information and should now be considered *for internal use only.*

ORDERS, the master table of this report, doesn't include the customer name as a field. How do you make the report come out right? It is now time to pull a rabbit out of the relational magic hat. The relationship between the master tables, ORDERS, and CUSTOMER, where the name is stored, is a many-to-one. Recall that in Chapter 10 you learned that a many-to-one relationship could be seen as a one-to-one relationship because, seen individually, each record on the "many" side relates to only one record on the "one" side. Here is where you will put that concept to work.

Having set up the relationship between ORDERS and CUSTOMER, you can now treat each record in ORDERS as though it had a name, address, citystate, and phone field. It gets this information from CUSTOMER. How do you access it?

Magic tricks use the technique of *misdirection;* database work uses *indirection.* Indirection is like dialing the area code before dialing the phone number. If you just dial the phone number without the area code, the phone company assumes you want the phone number in your local area code. By dialing an area code, you are saying "get me this phone number but in a different area." Indirection in database work is like saying "get me this piece of information from there," or "get me this name; it is stored in the CUSTOMER table."

Using the New . Operator in Place of the -> Operator

Xbase used -> as the indirection operator. The first release of FoxPro heralded the **.** (or dot) operator as a replacement. Initially only a typing aid, it has dovetailed nicely with Visual FoxPro's object-oriented nature. In object orientation, the dot operator is also known as the member-of operator. For example, if you want to call the refresh function of a list box, List1, you can specify List1.refresh, which calls the refresh function that is a *member of* List1.

Likewise, you can specify the name field that is a *member of* the customer table like this: **customer.name**. In Chapter 11 you used this form to add a grid column from ITEMS.

Indexing Using Indirection

The goal then is to have the ORDERS table sorted by the name field in CUSTOMER. You will do this by attaching some program code to the initialization event for the data environment.

Click the right mouse button in a blank area of the Data Environment window and select Properties. Be sure that the object selected in the Properties window is Dataenvironment.

Double-click the InitEvent item in the Properties window. This brings up the code editor window. Enter the code shown in Figure 13-6. The first line is a belt-and-suspenders verification that you are indexing the proper table. You want to index the ORDERS table on customer.name, so you need to be sure that ORDERS is the selected table. The second line creates a compact index, c:\ordname.idx—you can name it whatever you want and put it wherever you want—on customer.name.

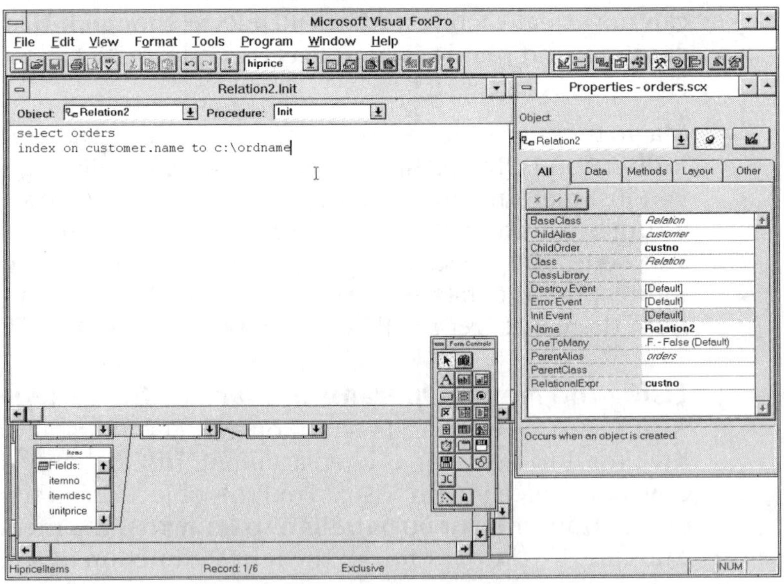

Adding index code

Figure 13-6.

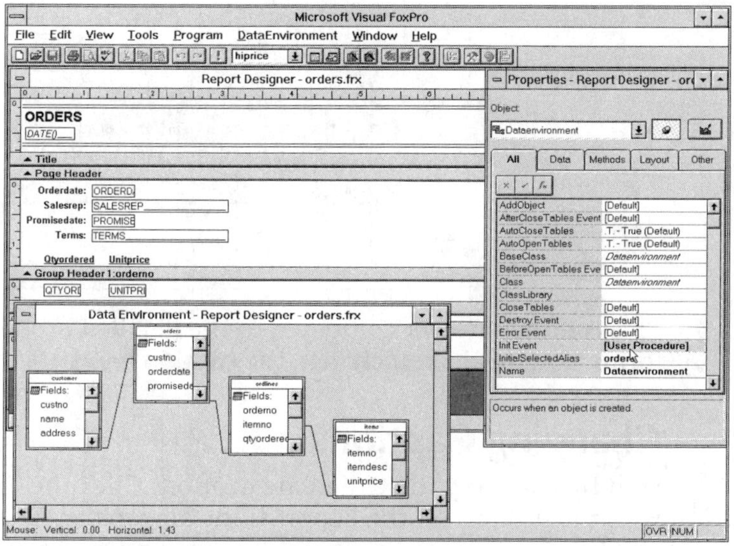

User procedure attached to InitEvent

Figure 13-7.

13

Note: The Xbase language, including Visual FoxPro, is case-insensitive; that is, it treats ORDERS, orders, and OrDeRs as the same input. You should use mixed-case names for readability. For example, customer.CityState is usually easier to read than either customer.citystate or CUSTOMER.CITYSTATE.

Close the code editor by either double-clicking the title bar icon or pressing ALT-F4. The InitEvent item in the Properties window should now show [User Procedure] instead of the default value [Default]. Figure 13-7 shows the changed event.

Now is a good time to save your work. Select Save from the File menu. If Save is dimmed, then click in the Report Designer window and select File again.

Modifying the Report

In Chapter 11 you modified the captions and added data from the CUSTOMER and ITEMS tables for your screen form. Now you will modify these items again for your report. Modifying a report is different, though. For instance, double-clicking a caption displays the following properties screen:

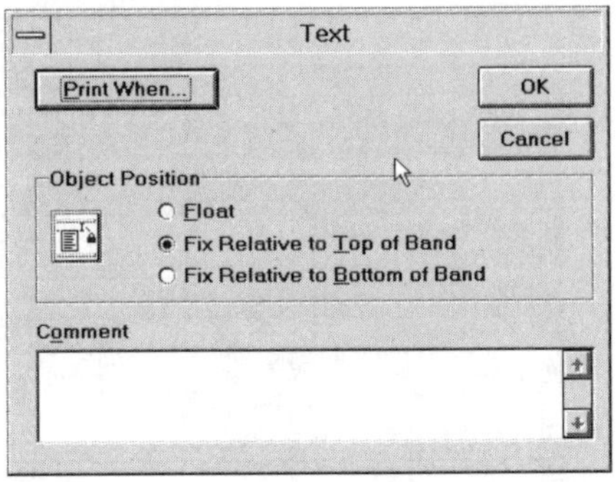

This is rather meager compared to the detailed properties available for screen forms. So how do you change the caption?

Changing Captions

Start by changing the Orderdate caption. Click the Text button (the button with the A on it) on the Report Controls toolbar. The cursor should now be an I-beam. Move the cursor to the caption Orderdate and click. Change the caption to Order Date. Then click the arrow button on the toolbar, or move the cursor away from the caption and click the mouse.

Now change the other captions as shown in Figure 13-8.

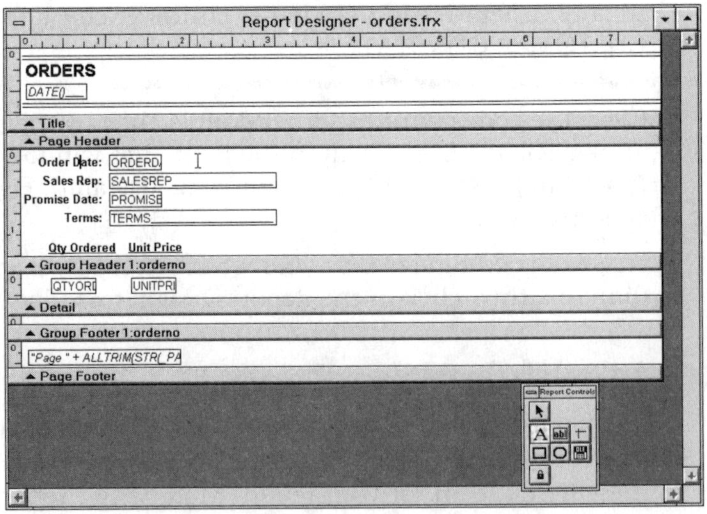

Changing a caption
Figure 13-8.

Adding Customer Grouping

To add the grouping for customers, in the Report menu, select Data Grouping. Press the Insert button and enter **customer.name** as shown in Figure 13-9. This will group all the orders for a customer and allow you to subtotal by customer.

Click the OK button, and your Report Designer should look like Figure 13-10.

Drag the header labeled Group Header 1:name down to make room for the customer name. Click the Label button on the toolbar and then click again in the area above Group Header 1. Type **Customer** as shown in Figure 13-11.

You've gone to a lot of trouble to place the customer's name on this report, so why not make it stand out? With the customer label selected, go the Format menu and select Font. Click Bold Italic and select 14-point type. Now the label stands out.

Click the Field button of the toolbar (the button to the right of the Label button). Move the cursor to the right of the new customer label and click again. This brings up the Report Expression dialog box. Enter **customer.name** in the Expression field as shown here: 13

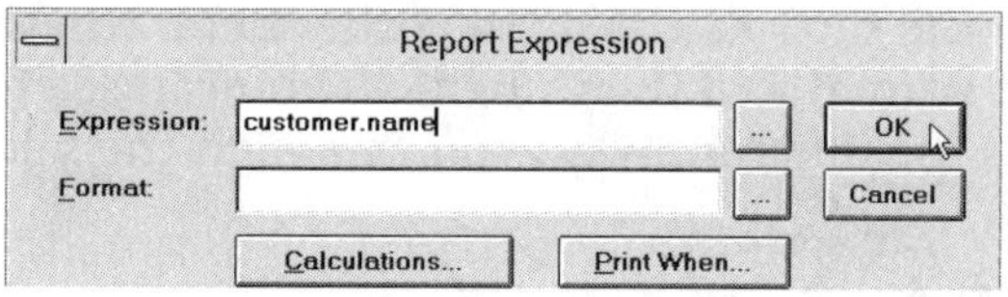

Click the OK button, and you see the name field on the report. The name field is rather small. Click the field so that the handles are visible and drag the field to a more appropriate width, like this:

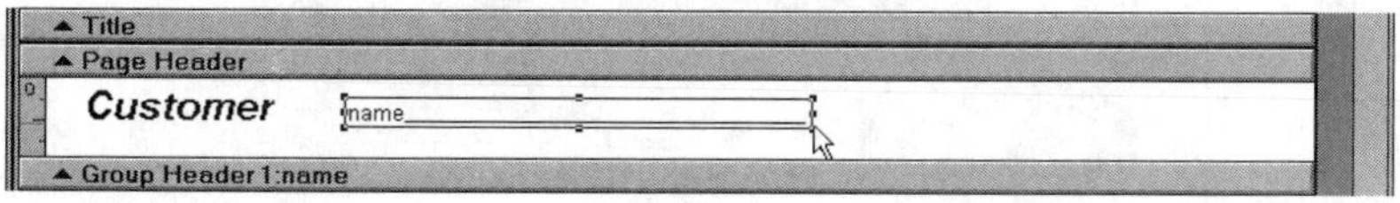

Note: The handles are the little boxes that appear around a selected element. They are visible in the illustration at each corner and in the center of each line.

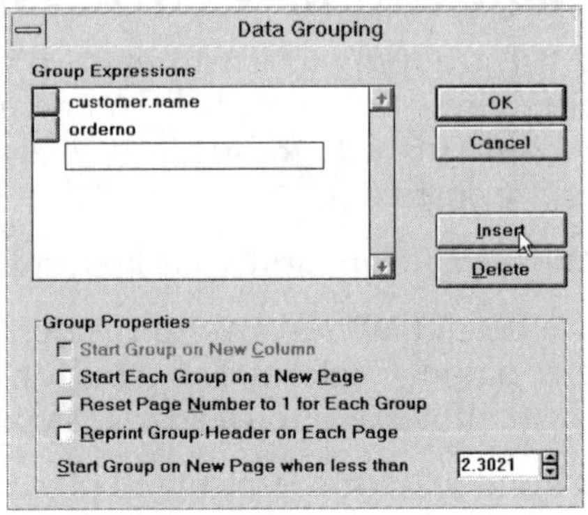

Adding grouping by customer
Figure 13-9.

You made the Customer label stand out. Now do the same for the field. Select Format and then Font. This time select Italic and, again, select 14-point type.

Before you leave the customer information, make sure that the label and the field line up. Select either the field or the label and then, while holding down the SHIFT key, click the other field. Now both fields should be selected. Select Format and then Align. As you can see in Figure 13-12, the side menu shows the different ways you can align the select elements.

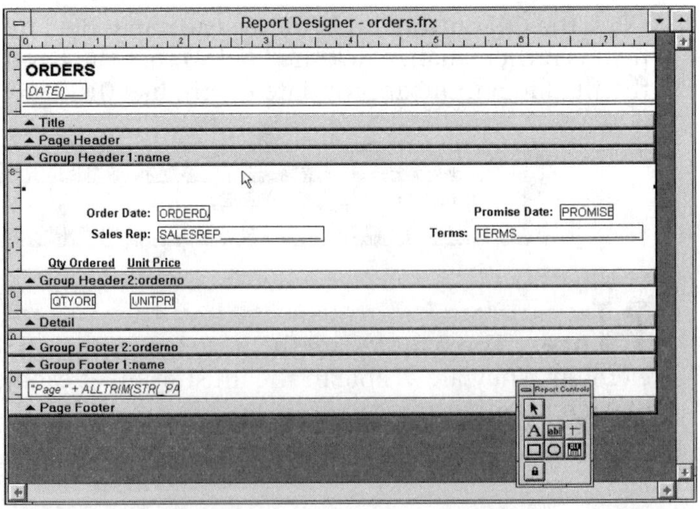

Group header for customer.name
Figure 13-10.

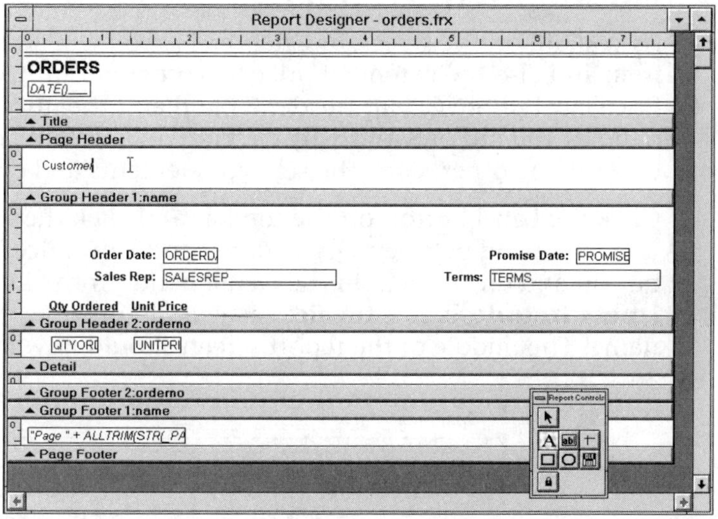

Adding the Customer label

Figure 13-11.

Select Align Bottom Edges. While you have the two elements selected, you can also move them about as a pair. You do this with the mouse to make gross adjustments or the cursor arrows to make fine adjustments.

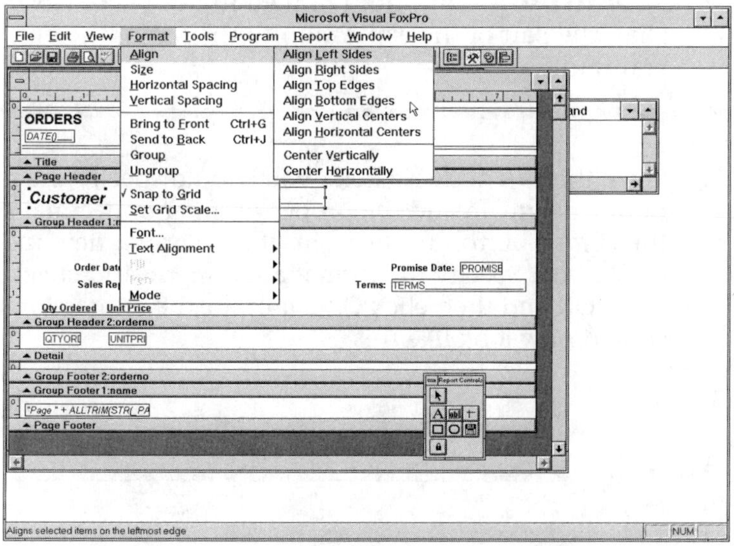

The Align menu

Figure 13-12.

Adding Item Details

As you did on the screen in Chapter 11, you will add a description for each item and also the extended price (qtyordered * unitprice). Select the Unit Price label in the Group Header 2 band and the unitprice field in the Detail band as you did previously by clicking one, holding down the SHIFT key, and clicking the other. Grab the selected elements and drag them to the right.

Click the Label button on the toolbar and click the mouse in the Group Header 2 band between Qty Ordered and Unit Price. Click the Field button and drop a field in the Detail band. In the Expression box, enter **items.itemdesc**. Size the field as you did previously for the customer name. The middle of the report screen should now look like this:

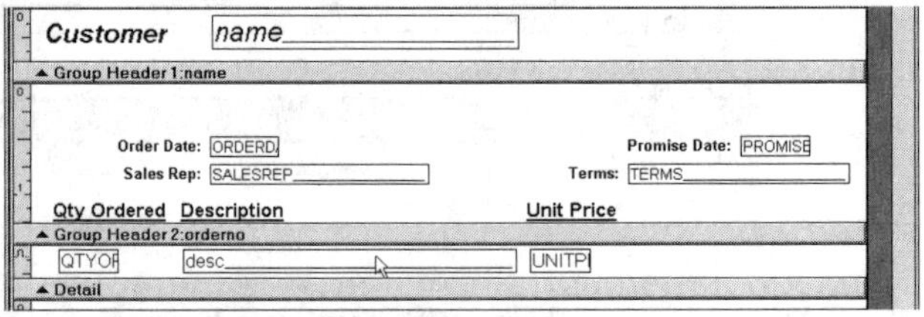

Now add a field for the extended price. In the Expression box, enter **ordlines.qtyordered * ordlines.unitprice**.

Caution: Unitprice is a field in both ORDLINES and ITEMS. Using the alias, the part of the expression to the left of the dot, makes clear which field you want.

Since this is a numeric field, you should specify the formatting so that the numbers line up and the proper number of decimal places is shown. Click the ellipsis button to the right of the Format field in the Report Expression dialog box. Specify the format as Numeric and check the Currency box. Click OK and then click OK again for the Expression dialog box. Your screen should now look like this:

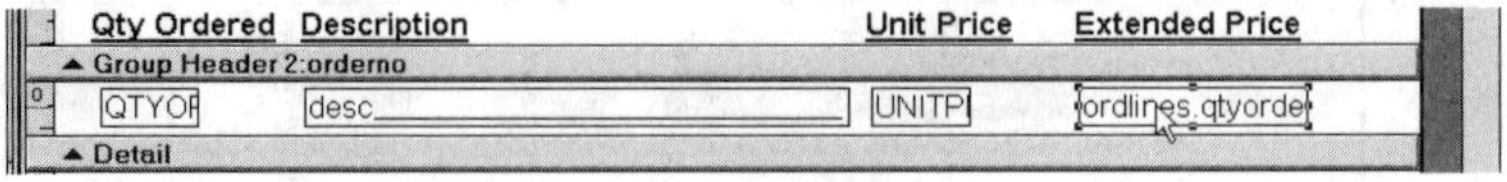

Adding Subtotals

You are going to want subtotals and grand totals. To subtotal each order, you need to drop a field on the Group Footer 2 band.

Note: You may need to expand this band, which you can do by clicking within the band and dragging the band downward.

Click the Field button on the Report Controls toolbar. Drop it on the Group Footer 2 band below the Extended Price field, which is in the Detail band.

This brings you to the Report Expression dialog box. In the Expression field, enter **ordlines.qtyordered*ordlines.unitprice** like this:

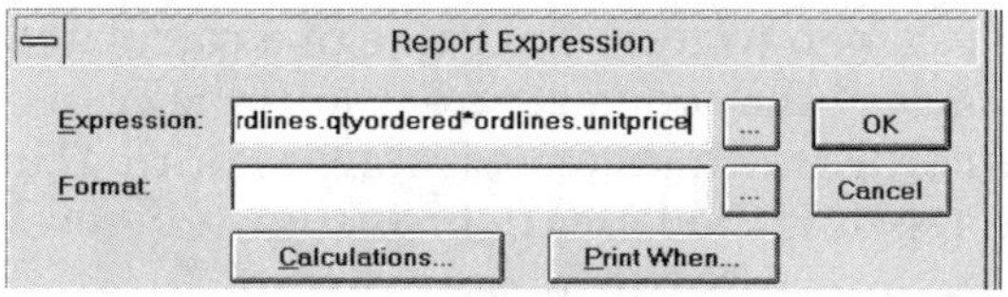

Click the ellipsis button to the right of the Format field. This brings up the Format dialog box. Check the Currency box and enter **999,999.99** in the Format field as shown here:

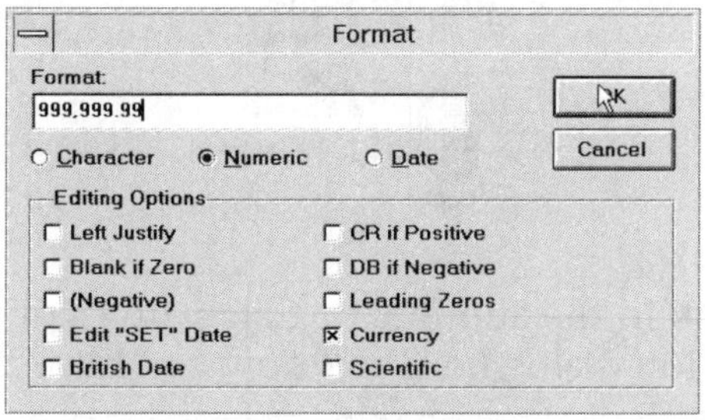

Note: The 999,999.99 tells Visual FoxPro how to format a numeric field. In this case, it uses two decimals (.99) and up to six digits with a comma between the hundreds and thousands. The comma will appear only if the value is greater than 999.99.

Click the OK button in the Format dialog box.

Caution: Version 3.0 of Visual FoxPro sometimes enters an erroneous value in the Format field if you use the Format dialog box to create it. The finished format should be as follows: @$ 999,999.99

The left-hand side (@$) tells Visual FoxPro to precede the value with a dollar sign. This is a template in Xbase parlance; it applies to the whole field. The rest is a picture clause; it tells Visual FoxPro how to format the actual value. In this case, Visual FoxPro uses standard American format.

Now click the Calculations button below Format in the Report Expression dialog box. This brings up the Subtotal or Calculate Field dialog box. The Reset field should already have the correct value, orderno. This tells Visual FoxPro when to reset the value of a calculated field. In this case, you are subtotaling the order, so orderno is the correct reset value. In other words, when orderno changes, it is time to print a subtotal. Click the Sum radio button below the Reset field as shown here:

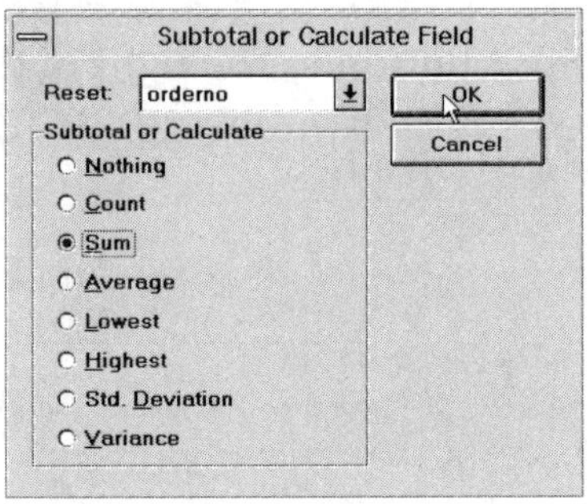

Click OK in the Subtotal or Calculate Field dialog box and OK in the Report Expression dialog box, and now you have a subtotal for each order.

You can also calculate a subtotal for each customer in the same manner. However, this time the field goes in the Group Footer 1 band, and the reset value in the Subtotal or Calculate Field dialog box is customer.name. The expression is the same as for the order subtotal.

Add a label for each subtotal using the Label button on the toolbar, and your report design should look like Figure 13-13.

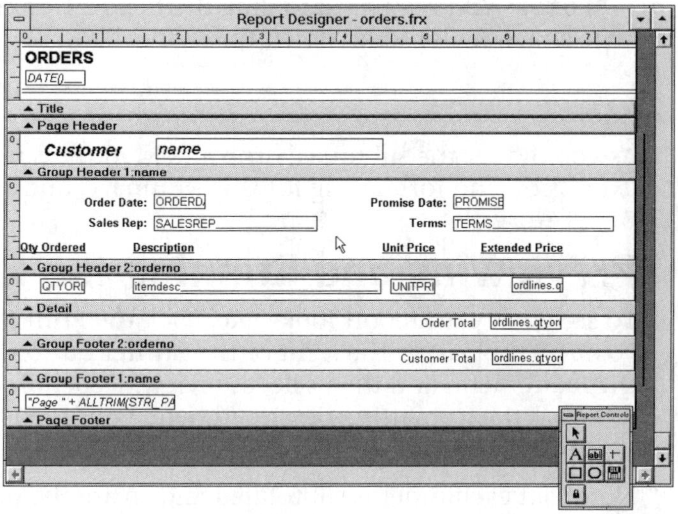

The report with subtotals
Figure 13-13.

13

Note: This book has already addressed formatting, sizing, and other appearance issues. We have made some formatting changes to the report as seen in Figure 13-13, but to avoid repetition, these changes are not detailed in the text.

Adding Summary Totals

The last task is to add a grand total to this report. In the Report menu, select Title/Summary. This brings up the Title/Summary dialog box. Click the check box for Summary Band, like this:

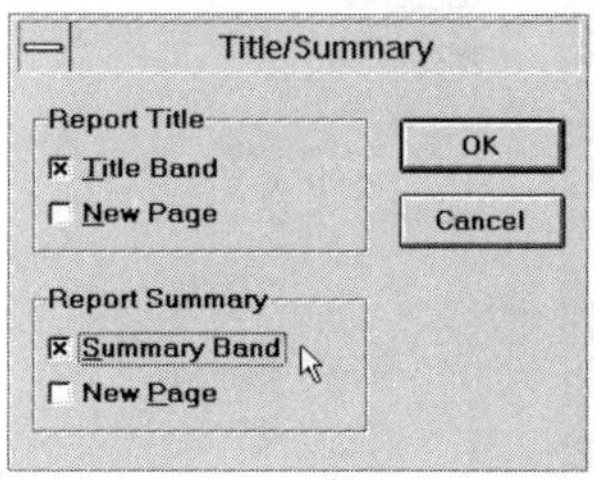

Click the OK button, and a Summary Band is added to the Report Designer.

Note: You may need to drag the Report Designer window to make it a little larger or else scroll down to see this band.

As you did for the subtotals, drop a field in the Summary band, enter the expression and formatting for this summary, and add a label.

Previewing and Running the Report

To see what your report looks like, click the Print Preview button on Visual FoxPro's toolbar, to the right of the printer button, or select View from the main menu and then select Preview. Depending on how closely you followed the formatting described here, your report should look similar to Figure 13-14.

Note that each order is subtotaled and so are the orders for each customer.

Printing the Report

To print this report, click the Print button on the Visual FoxPro toolbar. A standard Print dialog box appears so you can control the printing of the report. Make changes as necessary and click OK.

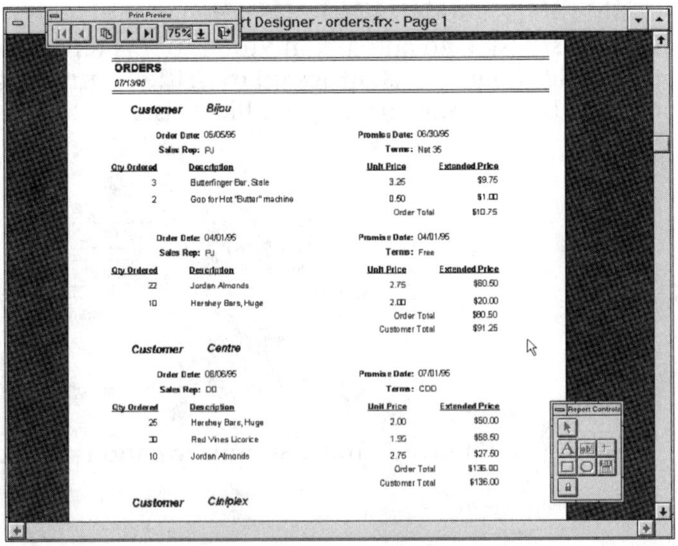

Previewing the report

Figure 13-14.

Index Exists, Overwrite It?

The second time you preview or print this report, you might see a warning dialog box like this:

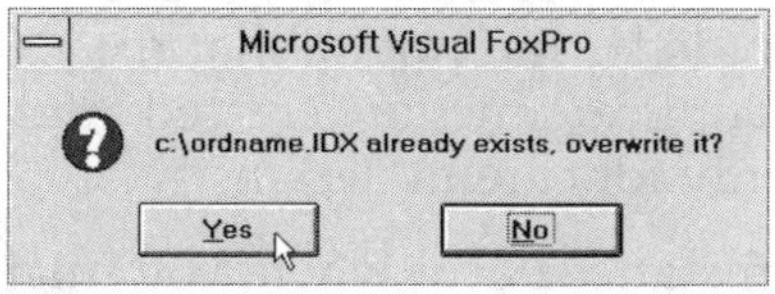

Because you created a stand-alone index for this report, the second time you create the report, the index will already be there. This dialog box verifies that it is okay to overwrite the existing index. Click Yes.

You are not going to want such an ominous message displayed when a person at HiPrice runs this report. Recall that you added initialization code to Dataenvironment for this report; that is what creates the index. Adding another command, set safety off, will prevent this message from appearing.

Bring up the Properties window by clicking mouse button 2 in a clear area of the Data Environment screen. If the Data Environment is not visible, you can open it by clicking View in the main menu and then Data Environment.

In the Properties window, double-click on the InitEvent line. This brings you back to the code editor. Create a new line above select orders and enter **set safety off** as shown in Figure 13-15.

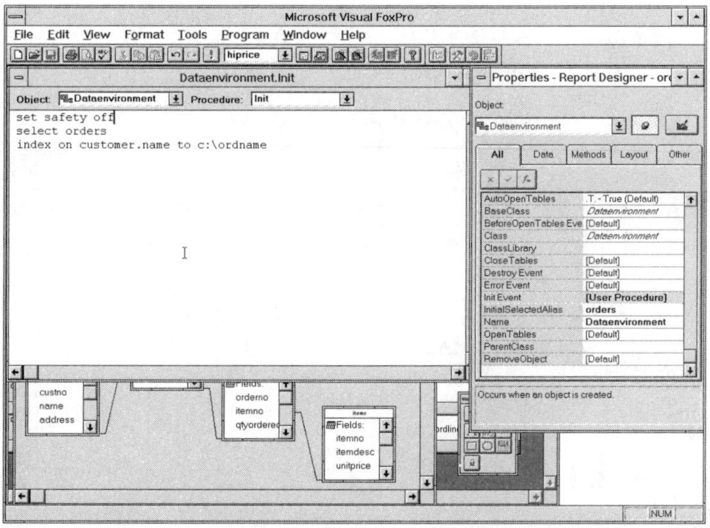

Adding a line to InitEvent
Figure 13-15.

Close the code editor window. Now when you run the report, the warning dialog box will not appear.

Safety or Not?

To turn off safety may seem a risky move. For programmatic operations, it is standard to do so and not all that risky. The logic of your programs will control when duplicate files are created, and since you are creating them, there is need only for careful design.

Should a circumstance occur where you might want to prevent overwriting, you can create your own dialog box with a more informative message, such as "You are about to overwrite last month's sales totals. Are you sure that you want to do this?"

part 4

The Polished Application

14

Normalizing Visual FoxPro Data

When you design or modify a database structure, you should always normalize the data. Normalization requires planning, thoughtful design, and discipline—all of which are hard work. However, your efforts will yield a big payoff: stable, reliable data structures that can be expanded with minimal risk.

What If You Don't Plan Ahead and Normalize?

Most programmers have designed at least one small application that, over time, became unexpectedly successful—growing, enhancement by enhancement, frill by frill, into an unmanageable patchwork of redundant tables and data fields. Such programmers know the torment of unplanned success: By the time they realize their data structure is in trouble, they already have a large investment in development, and the application has become essential to the everyday routine of doing profitable business. Restructuring a database under such circumstances is expensive, dangerous, and disruptive to its users. When databases become disjointed and redundant, every programmatic change is like rolling loaded dice. However, failure to restructure prevents essential program growth and invites disastrous data corruption.

Fortunately, this familiar scenario is absolutely avoidable!

What Is Database Normalization?

Normalization minimizes data redundancy and greatly increases the reliability and stability of the databases you design. Although normalization theory is founded in precise, rigorous mathematical terms, it is easily understood by learning a few systematic rules and procedures, governed by common sense. The goals of normalization are to accomplish the following:

- Arrange data in a structure of tables that have no repeating records, as shown in Figure 14-1.
- Ensure that related data items in different tables are associated by the correct index keys to minimize redundancy.

Normalization usually comes late in the database design process. It is only after you have a firm understanding of what types of information will

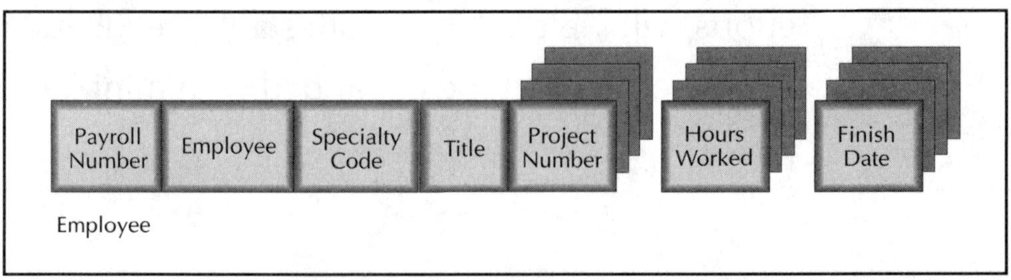

Data table with no repeating records
Figure 14-1.

populate the database and how the database needs to be organized that you can begin the normalization process to prevent unnecessary redundancy.

Why Avoid Redundancy?

Redundancy creates several different kinds of difficulties that consume valuable system resources such as memory, disk space, and computing cycles:

- **Storing the same information in more than one place is an invitation to database corruption.** You can get away with this common mistake—for a while. When you update redundant data, you have to be extremely careful to update *every* occurrence of that data. Failure to do so can and *probably will* result eventually in a hopelessly corrupt database. For example, if you can retrieve or reference a customer number from more than one record field, then you have created a trap that allows different numbers to exist for the same customer in different records. This type of corruption is usually very difficult to find and correct.
- **Repetitive information cannot be stored efficiently in a record that also contains nonrepetitive information.** This issue is particularly relevant in the common case where a programmer cannot predict how many data repetitions may occur. In such cases, you have no choice but to include enough fields in each record to accommodate the maximum possible number of fields you may need. For example: Line items on an invoice. You may have to provide 100 fields to accommodate the maximum case, when the average invoice may have only three line items. This month's invoice for client Jones may contain one line item, while client Smith's may contain 95 line items—and every month's invoices are different. In a large database, such inefficiency can waste tens of megabytes of disk space and slow program operation precipitously.
- **Redundancy unnecessarily consumes processing time, slowing program execution.** The computer has to process every extra field each time you index or otherwise manipulate and access the data table. This problem is exacerbated by the fact that extra data fields tie up system memory and processor registers, reducing the amount of resources the computer needs to perform the necessary work.

Don't be misled by testing the performance of your program with small databases. The problems discussed here will not become obvious until the data table grows very large, which is a very bad time to try and fix them.

The Normalization Process

The objective of normalization is twofold:

- To organize the data so that each type of item, such as *name* or *customer number,* in a data table is represented by only one field. No groups of repeating items such as *line item* are allowed. Such repeating groups are moved to their own table (or tables), which is linked to the parent table through a common key field.
- To associate data items with index keys to ensure minimal data field redundancy.

Note: Normalization does not totally eliminate data redundancy. This is not possible because, for example, common key fields are necessary for normalization. Normalization does minimize redundancy, and it minimizes or eliminates data corruption resulting from redundant data fields.

What Is a Normal Form?

A normal form is simply one of the five formal phases of normalization; thus there are five normal forms:

- **First normal form** removes repeating groups.
- **Second normal form** removes functional dependence.
- **Third normal form** removes conditional or transitive dependence.
- **Fourth normal form** removes multivalued dependencies.
- **Fifth normal form** involves, in some cases, *de*normalization of fourth normal form.

You will seldom, perhaps never, need to go beyond the third normal form. Therefore, this chapter discusses only the first three normal forms.

First Normal Form

The first step in normalizing any database is to remove repeating groups simply by creating a separate record for each element in the repeating group. To understand this step, assume that you need to design an employee database for a small company. The owner needs a program that can track the number of hours each employee works on each of the company's various active projects. The program also needs to track completion dates for each project. Your first layout of the employee data fields might look something like this:

Payroll Number	Employee	Specialty Code	Title	Project Number	Hours Worked	Finish Date

Remember: The one objective of the first normal form is to remove repeating groups by creating a separate record for each element in the repeating groups. You determine that this requires creating a separate record for each project. A sample of the database in first normal form then looks like this:

Record Number	Payroll Code	Employee	Specialty Code	Title	Project Number	Hours Worked	Finish Date
1	22548	Brown, Cynthia	4451	Executive	026	709.6	12/31/96
2	22548	Brown, Cynthia	4451	Executive	149	9.6	08/11/96
3	22548	Brown, Cynthia	4451	Executive	268	121.7	02/29/96
4	53905	Henderson, Herman	9326	Sr. Engineer	026	298.2	12/31/96
5	53905	Henderson, Herman	9326	Sr. Engineer	268	29.4	02/29/96
6	73090	Stilwell, Hildegarde	9855	Programmer	026	208.9	12/31/96
7	73090	Stilwell, Hildegarde	9855	Programmer	149	182.3	08/11/96
8	73090	Stilwell, Hildegarde	9855	Programmer	268	23.5	02/29/96

If a major objective of normalization is to reduce redundancy, what happened here? It looks like you accomplished just the opposite by positioning the data in first normal form! This dramatic *increase* in data redundancy is a common artifact of the first normal form.

First normal form is not a stand-alone procedure. The unexpected redundancy you observe occurs because the first normal form is only one step of the normalization process; by design, it leaves loose ends that have to be fixed later in the process. Normalization beyond the first normal form is always required. Depending upon the data involved and the complexity of your design, the first normal form can produce a variety of undesirable attributes, of which redundancy is only one. Fortunately, one additional normalization step removes this artificial redundancy and greatly improves both the structure and reliability of your database.

Second Normal Form

Positioning records in the second normal form requires an understanding of the concept of *functional data dependence*. Functional data dependence refers to a field that is uniquely identified by a key field in the same record. For example, in the table using the first normal form, it is clear that the field Payroll Code uniquely identifies the fields Employee, Specialty Code, and Title. For a given payroll code, there can be only one employee, who can have only one specialty code and one title. These three fields are, therefore, functionally dependent on the key Payroll Code field, which must be unique.

Placing a database in the second normal form necessitates identifying all groups with functional dependencies and then creating separate data tables for each group. The functionally dependent group just identified will then be used to create the new EMPLOYEE data table containing the fields shown here:

Payroll Code	Name	Specialty Code	Title
22548	Brown, Cynthia	4451	Executive
53905	Henderson, Herman	9326	Sr. Engineer
73090	Stilwell, Hildegarde	9855	Programmer

Two more dependent records, Project Number and Finish Date, are used to create a second new table, FINISH. This table consists of the two fields keyed on Project Number, as shown here:

Project Number	Finish Date
268	02/29/96
026	12/31/96
149	08/11/96
268	02/29/96

The remaining field, Hours, is functionally dependent on two fields: Payroll Code and Project Number. This relationship is established by concatenating these two fields in a single sort key. The third and final new table, HOURS, looks like this:

Payroll Code	Project Number	Hours
22548	026	709.6
22548	149	9.6
22548	268	121.7
53905	026	298.2
53905	268	29.4
73090	026	208.9
73090	149	182.3
73090	268	23.5

Your hypothetical database is now in second normal form. In each of the three new tables you created, every record, except the *necessarily* redundant key record, is now functionally dependent on that table's key record. There still seems to be some redundancy, however. The Payroll Code field appears in two tables, and the Project Number field appears in two records. The remaining redundancy is not as serious as the redundancy that existed before or after first normal form. This current level of redundancy, albeit minimal, is not an uncommon result after you position data in the second normal form. The second normal form can be, and often is, the simplest and most satisfactory way to organize your data. Often, you can consider the second normal form sufficient and stop there.

Caution: When any database has redundant fields, it is absolutely essential that you include programmatic safeguards to protect each redundant field against accidental corruption. It has to be the *program's* responsibility to ensure accurate updating of redundant fields, independent of any possible direct user action.

Third Normal Form

The third normal form introduces the concept of derivative dependence, sometimes called *transitive dependence.* This is one of those concepts that is much easier to understand than it is to describe succinctly. First look at a formal definition. Then look at an example to clarify the words.

Derivative dependence is defined as follows: If record B is dependent on record A, and record C is dependent on record B, then by derivation, record

C is dependent on record A. For example, Mary's baby (A) is dependent on Mary (C) for financial support. Mary, who works for Acme Engineering Company (B), is dependent on Acme for her income. Therefore, Mary's baby is dependent, by derivation, on Acme. Figure 14-2 shows this concept.

The hypothetical employee database you have been designing now contains one case of derivative dependence: If you assume that each Specialty Code has only one associated Title, then Title is functionally dependent on Specialty Code. Because more than one employee can have the same specialty code, Payroll Code is *not* functionally dependent on Specialty Code. This means, as shown in Figure 14-2, that Title is relatively dependent on Payroll Code, just as Mary's baby is conditionally dependent on Acme.

Since your objective is to position the database in the third normal form, the conditional relationship just described must, by definition, be removed. You can do this by removing the Title field from your EMPLOYEE table and creating a new table containing two fields: Specialty Code and Title. The new table has to be keyed on the Specialty Code field.

Your database, now in the third normal order, consists of four related tables and looks like Figure 14-3.

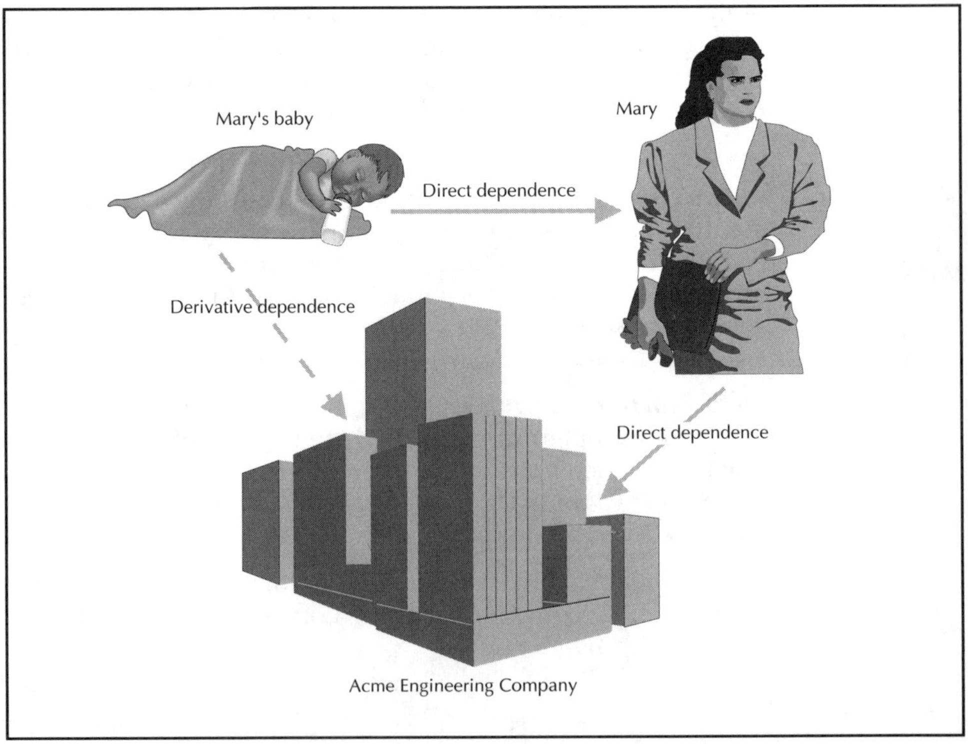

Derivative dependence
Figure 14-2.

Specialty Code	Title
4451	Executive
9326	Sr. Engineer
9855	Programmer

Specialty

Project Number	Finish Date
268	2/29/96
26	12/31/96
149	8/11/96
268	2/29/96

Project

Payroll Code	Project Number	Hours
22548	26	709.6
22548	149	9.6
22548	268	121.7
53905	26	298.2
53905	268	29.4
73090	26	208.9
73090	149	182.3
73090	268	23.5

Hours

Payroll Code	Name	Specialty Code
22548	Brown, Cynthia	4451
53905	Henderson, Herman	9326
73090	Stilwell, Hildegarde	9855

Employee

Four data tables In third normal form

Figure 14-3.

Tip: A data table is in the third normal form *only* if it first qualifies as being in the second normal form *and* if it contains no fields that are conditionally dependent on the primary key.

With few exceptions, positioning data in the third normal form is as far as you need to go. Although higher forms are possible, they are beyond the scope of this book and exceed most database design requirements.

15

Data-Driven Controls and Displays

In Chapters 8 and 12 you learned how to design forms and create and manipulate controls using Visual FoxPro's Form Designer. In this chapter you will learn how to design forms that can modify controls and the data they contain while your application is running. This process is called dynamic control manipulation. To dynamically manipulate controls, you must first learn how to reference objects within the Visual FoxPro container hierarchy.

Referencing Visual FoxPro Controls

To dynamically manipulate a control, you have to identify it in relation to its location in the container hierarchy. For example, to manipulate a control located on a form that is part of a form set, you need to reference the form set, the form, and the control.

Note: In Visual FoxPro, a form set is one or more forms grouped as a named set. Forms do not have to be grouped into form sets; however, a form set must contain at least one form.

Think of referencing controls in the same way you think of providing an address. Referencing simply tells Visual FoxPro where to find the control you want to manipulate. For example, if you give a friend in Paris only your street number without including the street name, city, and state, your friend will have difficulty locating you.

Absolute Referencing

Absolute referencing is a procedure that allows you programmatically to identify any specific control as well as any of its available properties, so you can change them with program code, such as event code. Absolute referencing specifies an object's full container hierarchy by using a command like this:

```
FormSet1.Form3.Button2.BackColor=255
```

This command references a control, Button2, located on Form3, which is a part of FormSet1. The command also modifies the command's BackColor property by specifying a new value.

Building a Form with Dynamic Controls

The best way to understand Visual FoxPro's data-driven controls is to work with them. Therefore, you will spend the remainder of this chapter building a form that demonstrates many of the dynamic features of Visual FoxPro controls.

Creating a Very Basic Form

Either manually, using the Form Designer, or automatically, using the Form Wizard, create a new form named *Demo1.scx*. Place one timer control (Timer1) and one text box control (Text1) on the form and arrange them to look approximately as shown in Figure 15-1. (Functionally, the arrangement is unimportant; however, to better follow the examples in this chapter, you should arrange the form as shown in the figure.)

You first need to modify the controls you placed on the new form, using the Properties window, as follows:

1. Click the All tab in the Properties window and set the Timer1 Interval property to **1,000** milliseconds (1 second).
2. Click the Layout tab and set the Text1 BackColor property to **192,192,192**. The best way to change color is, while BackColor is highlighted, to click the ellipsis button to the right of the Properties window text box and launch the Color dialog box.
3. Set the Text1 FontSize property to **24** and FontBold to **.T**.
4. Set the Text1 ControlSource property to **mtime**. This action binds the Text1 control to the data contained in a variable named *mtime*.

Tip: Using the ControlSource setting to bind controls to their data was discussed in Chapter 8. You may want to refresh your memory regarding this important Visual FoxPro concept.

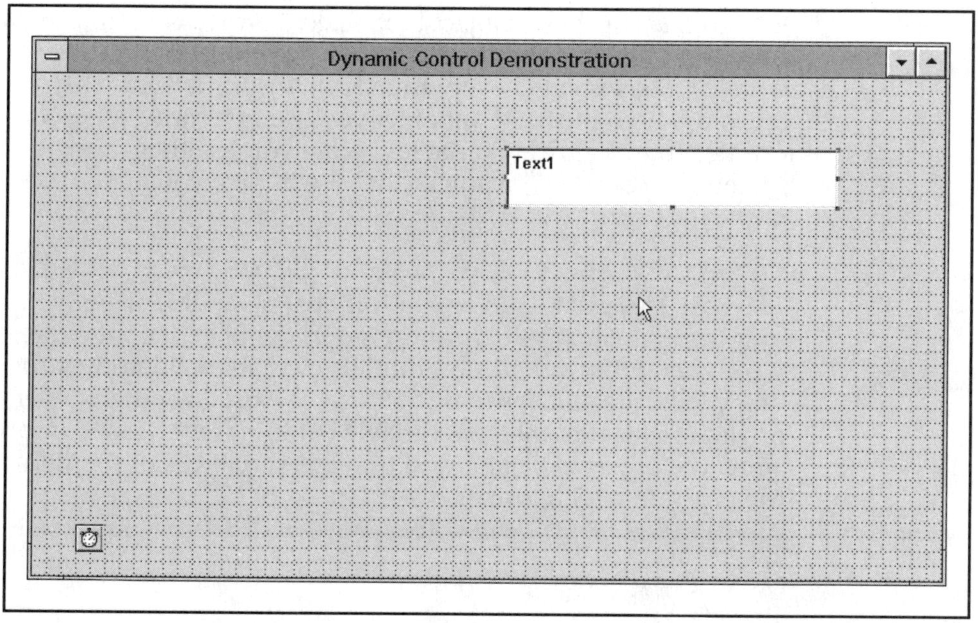

A simple form with a text box and timer
Figure 15-1.

Making a Simple Clock

You can easily modify these two simple controls you created to work together and display the current system time. Timer1 triggers an event every 1,000 milliseconds (1 second). Therefore, you can easily assign event code to this event and place the current time in Text1 once (or as many times as you wish) every second. The following paragraphs describe one simple way to do this.

Creating a Variable Using Form Event Code

First you need to create a variable, *mtime*, to contain the system time. One way to do this using Visual FoxPro event code is to initialize the variable when the form is initialized. Double-click anywhere on the form to launch the Form Designer's code window for your form. The code window has two combo boxes along the top: one labeled Object and the other labeled Procedure.

Tip: The box labeled Procedure can be misleading. Rather than procedures, it displays the standard events for a selected object. For example, the Init selection in this window is actually an event that is triggered every time a form is initialized. The label Procedure probably means that the code you write in this window becomes a procedure to be executed every time the form's init event is triggered.

In the code window's Object box, select Form1. Then in the Procedure box, select Init. These selections tell Visual FoxPro that the code you are about to write is to be executed every time Form1 is initialized. This is usually a good, reliable way to initialize variables you use in a form. It is good programming practice to initialize all variables before you use them. Doing so may sometimes seem inconvenient, but it will save you a lot of debugging work in the long run.

Tip: In Visual FoxPro, you initialize a variable when you first store a number in it. Such initialization has many benefits; therefore, we strongly recommend that you always initialize variables when the program starts. This procedure ensures that the variable exists when you refer to it programmatically, that the variable contains any needed information when the program begins, and that the variable is of the right type when the program tries to use it.

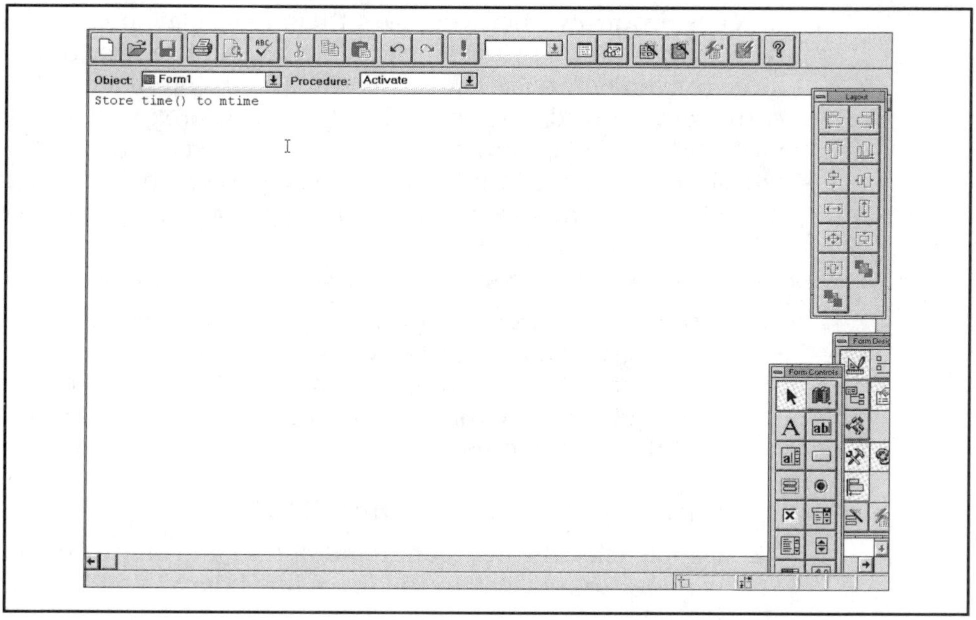

The code window for the clock
Figure 15-2.

Adding Event Code

In the code window, type **Store time( ) to mtime** to initialize the variable *mtime* with the current system time. The code window should now look like Figure 15-2.

In the event code Object box, select Timer1, and in the Procedure box select Timer. In the code window, type the following two lines of code, which will be executed at each 1-second timer event:


```
Store time() to mtime
ThisForm.Refresh
```

The first line of code stores the current time to the variable named *mtime*. The second line refreshes all of the form's controls. In this case, the reason you refresh the form is to display, in Text1, the newly stored contents of the variable *mtime*.

Tip: Most containers, including text boxes, are not updated automatically on the form when a change occurs in the data to which they are bound. It is usually necessary (and almost always a wise procedure) to write event code to refresh controls when you want them to display updated information. In this demonstration program, because it uses only a few controls, it might be more convenient to use the ThisForm.Refresh command, which refreshes the entire form instead of refreshing only the text box. When designing complex programs and larger forms, especially when execution speed is a factor, refreshing the entire form to update a single control is not as efficient as using the ThisForm.Text1.Refresh command or an equivalent command appropriate for that control.

The two simple lines of event code you just typed are all Visual FoxPro needs to convert your text box into a versatile system clock. Before running the form to see how it works, you need to add one more control to allow you a graceful way to exit the form: Place a command button on the lower-left corner of the form and modify it in the Properties window as follows:

1. Change the Caption property to **EXIT**.
2. Double-click the new command button and launch the button's code window; select Click in the Procedure box, and add the following line of event code:

   ```
   Release ThisForm
   ```

   This command gracefully exits the running form and returns you to the Visual FoxPro main window.

At this point, your screen should look like Figure 15-3.

Examining Your Work

Now run your form and observe how the time in your text box is updated every second. The timer control you placed in the lower-left corner of the form is not visible when the form is running. The control exists on your form; however; its functionality does not require that it be visible at run time because no visible properties were designed into it.

You have successfully demonstrated how easily you can bind a control to data, create a specific event, write event code, and refresh forms. You accomplished these tasks using two simple Visual FoxPro controls. You can now build on this simple design, adding features to the clock to demonstrate most of the basics of programmatic control manipulation and event handling.

Dynamically Modifying Your Controls

You can *dynamically* modify virtually all control properties as easily as you can change them in the Properties window. For example, to change the

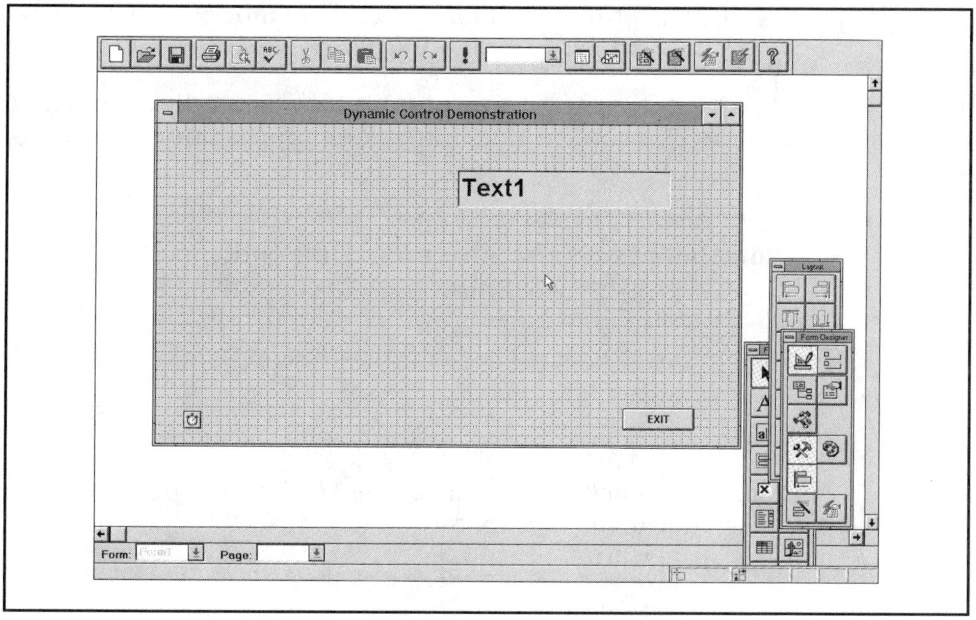

A form with command button added
Figure 15-3.

timer control to trigger its timer event twice per second instead of once per second as you configured it in the Properties window, you need only change its Interval property using the following command:

```
ThisForm.Timer1.Interval=500
```


Manipulating Dynamic Features

You can quickly add a control that toggles the timer interval between 1,000 milliseconds and 500 milliseconds using the Visual FoxPro option group available on the Control toolbar. Here's how you do so:

Place a two-button option group to the left of the text box and change the following properties using the Properties window:

1. Change the top button's Caption property to **1 Second** and the bottom button's Caption property to **1/2 Second**.
2. Using the Control Edit feature, adjust the size of the option group elements to accommodate the new captions. Invoke the Edit feature by right-clicking the control and then clicking Edit.
3. Change the BackColor property of both option group buttons to **192,192,192.**

4. Change the BackColor property of OptionGroup1 to **192,192,192.**

Note: Changing the control's color properties serves no functional purpose; however, it does improve the appearance of your form.

Now all that's necessary to enable these option buttons to modify the timer's Interval property is one line of event code added to each option button's click event.

5. In the click event code for the 1 Second option button, insert the following line of code:

```
ThisForm.Timer1.Interval=1000
```

6. In the click event code for the 1/2 Second option button, insert the following line of code:

```
ThisForm.Timer1.Interval=500
```

Changing the State of a Control

The new feature you've added creates one small problem: Because the box refreshes faster than the system's time( ) function updates, you can't confirm whether the option buttons are working properly. In other words, you will see no effects on your form. You can easily solve this problem by programming a short beep at each timer event. In case you don't want to listen to the beep all the time, you can also create a check box to turn the beep on and off. Here's how:

1. Go back to the Form Init code screen and add a line of code to initialize a logic variable called *mbeep* by entering the following:

```
Store .f. to mbeep
```

2. Place a new check box control on the form, under the lower-left corner of the text box. Bind the control to a variable named *mbeep* by entering **mbeep** as the control's ControlSource property.
3. Change the control's Label property to **Beep**.
4. Return to the timer's Click event code window. After the existing code, add the following three lines:

```
if mbeep
    ?? chr(7)
endif
```

Your form should look like Figure 15-4.

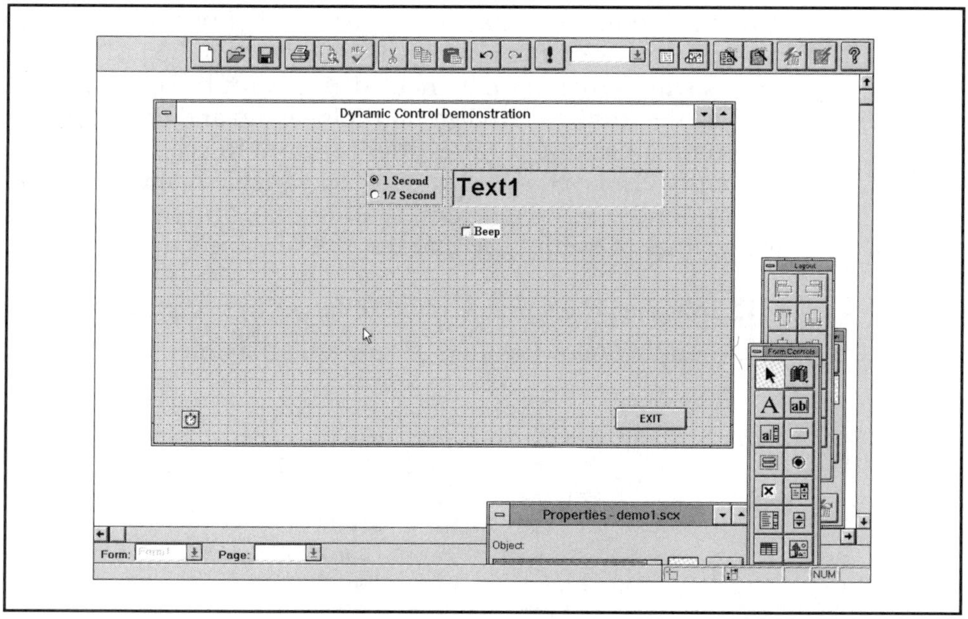

Text box added to turn beep on and off

Figure 15-4.

If necessary, adjust the control positions and sizes to conform to the figure. Then run the form.

Logically Testing and Dynamically Changing a Control's State

Note that the check box's BackColor property is still set to its default value of white. Color is a matter of preference, so you can change it or not. A powerful feature of Visual FoxPro is that it allows you to modify a control's colors, fonts, or sizes based on dynamic data, on events, or on both. Here's an example of how easy it is to modify a control's BackColor property on your form to flash, in tempo with your timer. You can do this by adding a check box and a few simple lines of event code:

1. Initialize a new logical variable named mflash to true (.t.) using the form's init event code.
2. Place a new check box on your form and change its Label property to **Flash**.
3. Type the variable name **mflash** in the control's ControlSource property field to bind this control to the data in the *mflash* variable.

Up to this point, you haven't done anything new to create this particular control. However, the next event code needs to be just a little more complex. Here's why: When flash is enabled, you want the program to alternately display the text box's background color as red and then its normal color. This alternating flashing requires your program to keep track of which color is currently displayed by using a logical variable named *mred*. When the background is set to red, *mred* is set to true; otherwise, it is set to false. A few lines of event code that test the variable's state do the rest.

1. Initialize the variable mred to false (.f.) using the form's init event code.
2. Add the following lines of code after the timer's existing timer event code:

```
Do Case
   case ! mflash .and. mred
         ThisForm.Text1.BackColor=12632256
         store .f. to mred
   case mflash .and. ! mred
         ThisForm.Text1.BackColor=255
         store .t. to mred
   case mflash .and. mred
         ThisForm.Text1.BackColor=12632256
         store .f. to mred
endcase
```

Note: The Do Case statement is simply a series of logical tests followed by code to be executed if the tests evaluate to true. The program steps through the cases, executes the first one that evaluates to true, and then skips to the statement after the End Case statement. Also, the Do Case series does not include one possible case: mflash .and. ! mred. This case is omitted because it requires no programmatic action.

At this point, your Form Designer screen should look like Figure 15-5.

Examining the Event Code

This is a good time to examine the event code you have written and be sure you understand it before you proceed to the next step. The timer control's timer event code should look like this:

```
Store time() to mtime

if mbeep
    ?? chr(7)
endif
```

```
Do Case
    case ! mflash .and. mred
        ThisForm.Text1.BackColor=12632256
        store .f. to mred
    case mflash .and. ! mred
        ThisForm.Text1.BackColor=255
        store .t. to mred
    case mflash .and. mred
        ThisForm.Text1.BackColor=12632256
        store .f. to mred
endcase
ThisForm.Text1.refresh
```

The form's init code should look like this:

```
Store time() to mtime
store .f. to mred
store .f. to mbeep
store .f. to mflash
```


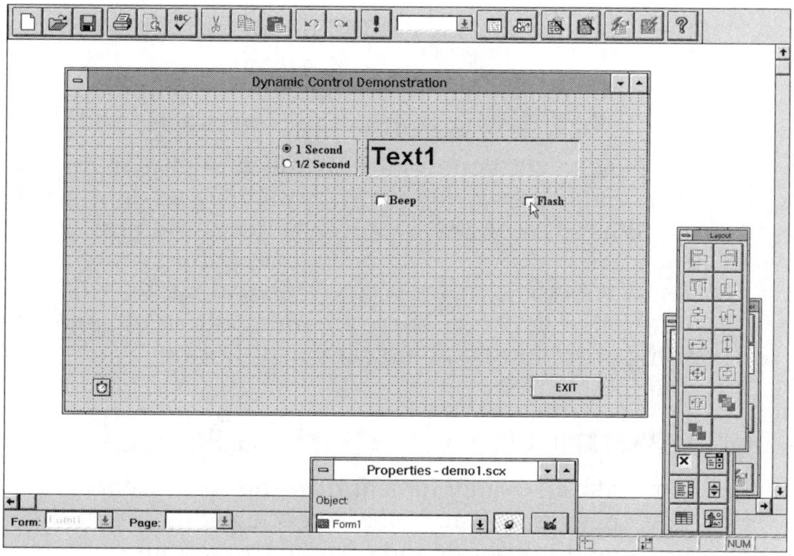

Check box added to modify a property
Figure 15-5.

You might also look at the single lines of event code for OptionButton1 and OptionButton2 to be sure you understand how they fit into the functionality of your form.

Changing the Time Format

Visual FoxPro makes it easy to change, under program control, the way your form displays almost any information. For example, you can set the way your clock displays time. Some people and organizations like 12-hour time, and others prefer 24-hour time. Now you will see how a simple control can be used to manipulate data formatting and display. An easy way to accomplish your goal is with a two-button option group that allows selection of either the 12-hour or 24-hour time format.

1. Create a two-button option button group between the two check boxes below your text box.
2. Change the Label property of the top button to **12 Hour Time** and the bottom button to **24 Hour Time**.
3. In the top button's click event code, add the following statement:

   ```
   Set Hours to 12
   ```

4. In the top button's click event code, add the following statement:

   ```
   Set Hours to 24
   ```

That's all there is to it! Your form should now look like Figure 15-6.

Here are two practical control problems to think about:

- How would you modify this form to automatically shift to and from Daylight Saving Time at the correct dates and times?
- How might you modify the form to display time in different cities around the world simply by clicking an appropriate option button? What data, if any, would you need, and how would you store it?

These are problems for you to think about; we will not answer them or illustrate them here. There are many different approaches to these problems using procedures you have learned thus far.

Testing the Control's Operation

Now take an overall look at how the controls on your form function and how they respond to and affect one another. Run the form and while it's running think about and operate the various options and functions.

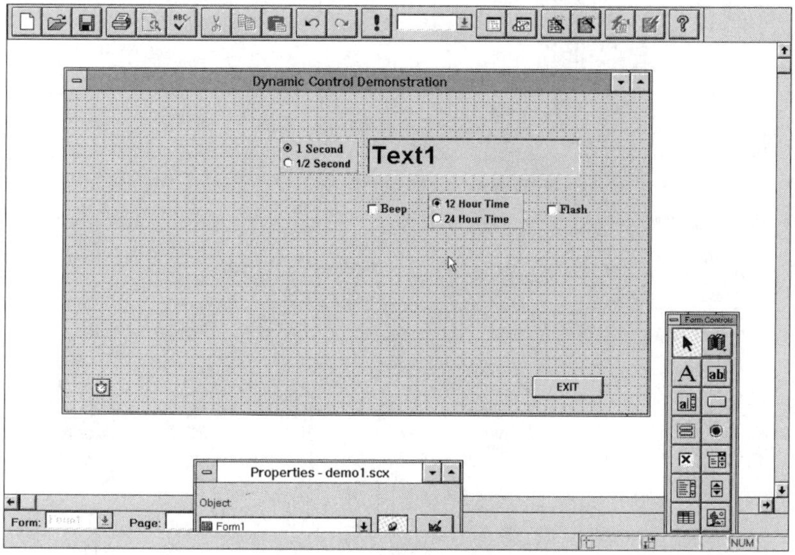

Option group added to modify time format

Figure 15-6.

The form was initialized with the 1 Second and 12 Hour options selected and the two check boxes deselected. Begin by clicking the 1/2 Second option button. Nothing seems to have happened, right? Wrong. Something did happen; you just can't see it because of the way the system dates the Time ( ) function. You can demonstrate the interrupt interval change in two different ways with controls on the form. First, click the Beep check box. The form should now beep twice per second, indicating that the timer interrupt is being triggered every one-half second. Click the 1 Second option button and notice that the beep changes to once per second. Click the Beep check box again, and the beep is silenced. Now click the Flash check box, and the text box background alternately flashes red and gray once per second. Click the 1/2 Second option button, and the flash rate changes to every one-half second.

Because this form is initialized in 12-hour time, it displays time in hours, minutes, and seconds followed by AM or PM, as appropriate. Click the 24 Hour Time option button, and the display changes from 12-hour format to 24-hour format.

This form with its few simple controls and a little event code demonstrates the essential elements of form design, control manipulation, and event handling. With the tools and techniques you used in this chapter, you can design forms that provide virtually any Visual FoxPro functionality.

16

Designing Visual FoxPro Menus

The menu bar is often the *first* place users look for information on how to use a program. What they find in your menu system will influence, perhaps determine, their first impression of your work. The Visual FoxPro Menu Designer organizes tasks and operations into logical menu groupings.

Each element of a Visual FoxPro application can have its own menu system. However, unlike other features we have described thus far, you must *compile* the application to incorporate its menu system. The Menu Designer is a little more awkward and less visual than the other Visual FoxPro designers; however, it is still easy to master and *well* worth the effort.

Planning Menu Systems

Well-designed menu systems enhance both the power and the convenience of Visual FoxPro applications. You need to plan an application's menus to ensure that users will accept them and be able to use the application more quickly and easily.

Basic Principles

Organize your menus according to how users work—not according to the relationships of the programs in the application's structure. Menus should map the application's *functional* organization, and invite users to see what the program does by examining the application's menus and menu items. Consider how users need to think about and perform their work.

Here are some simple guidelines:

- Each menu title should convey a maximum of information. For example, use commonly understood, succinct terms that the user should be familiar with.
- Organize your menu's structure according to anticipated frequency of use, logical order of use, or alphabetical order. For example, if you can predict the frequency of use, this is usually best. If you cannot, then consider, in each instance, whether logical or alphabetical order will best serve the user.
- Where you cannot predict the above information, it makes sense to organize your menu items alphabetically. Alphabetical order is usually effective when a menu comprises more than eight or ten items because alphabetical arrangement usually simplifies and expedites scanning and locating items.
- Insert separators, such as spaces or separator bars, between logical groups of menu items.
- Limit the list of items on a menu to *no more* than the screen's vertical capacity. If the required number of items exceeds this capacity, then create submenus as appropriate.
- Choose access keys and keyboard shortcuts for menus and menu items where it makes sense. For example, ALT+D might be an appropriate shortcut to access a Data table menu.

- Select menu titles that unambiguously describe their associated menu items. Use common terms that describe items rather than using computer jargon. Simple active verbs best indicate actions that result when choosing menu items. Avoid nouns as verbs. It is generally most effective to use the same part of speech to describe each item in a group. Your Visual FoxPro menu bar is an excellent example of how to implement this strategy's straightforward simplicity.
- Use mixed upper and lowercase in your general descriptions. Use uppercase *only* for emphasis and use it sparingly. For example, it is usually better to use Invoices rather than INVOICES.

The Visual FoxPro Menu Designer

You should use the Menu Designer to create Visual FoxPro menus, menu items, submenus for menu items, and the lines that separate groups of related menu items. The Menu Designer also allows you to customize your Visual FoxPro menu, if you should find that necessary. However, you will usually use the Menu Designer to add menus to applications of your own design. This convenient tool provides all the features you need to design custom menus for Visual FoxPro or applications you create within the Visual FoxPro integrated development environment.

Note: The Menu Designer does not follow Visual FoxPro's *visual* paradigm as closely or with as much refinement as most of the other designers we have studied thus far. Even though this tool is less "object-oriented" it is just as powerful and almost as easy to use as the other designers.

Launch the Menu Designer by selecting New from the File menu. This launches the New dialog box. Click the Menu button at the bottom of the dialog box, then click the New command button. This action launches the Visual FoxPro Menu Designer, which should look like Figure 16-1.

Exploring the Menu Designer's Features

The Menu Designer comprises the following features:

- **Prompt**: Specifies menu titles and menu items in your menu system.
- **Mover Control**: A double-headed arrow button to the left of the Prompt column that facilitates visual arrangement of menu items.
- **Result** : Specifies what action occurs when users choose a menu title or a menu item (for example, executing a command, opening a submenu, or running a procedure).

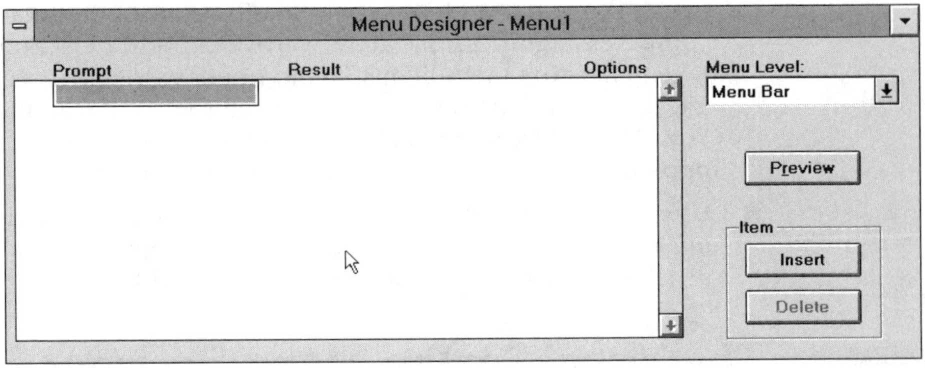

Visual FoxPro Menu Designer
Figure 16-1.

- **Create**: Specifies a submenu or a procedure to be associated with a menu title or a menu item.
- **Edit**: Changes a submenu or a procedure associated with a menu title or a menu item.
- **Options**: Opens the Prompt Options dialog box, which defines keyboard shortcuts and menu options.
- **Menu Level**: Selects the menu or submenu with which you will work.
- **Preview**: Displays information on the menu you are creating.
- **Insert**: Inserts a new row in the Menu Designer window.
- **Delete**: Deletes the current row from the Menu Designer window.

Creating a Visual FoxPro Quick Menu

The best way to learn Visual FoxPro's Menu Designer is to begin by examining and customizing your existing Visual FoxPro menu system. Microsoft made this easy by providing the Quick Menu feature which automatically places the entire Visual FoxPro menu system in the Designer for you to modify and manipulate.

With the Menu Designer running, as shown in Figure 16-1, click the Menu menu on the Visual FoxPro Main menu bar and select Quick Menu. This action places your Visual FoxPro menu system in the Menu Designer, which appears as shown in Figure 16-2.

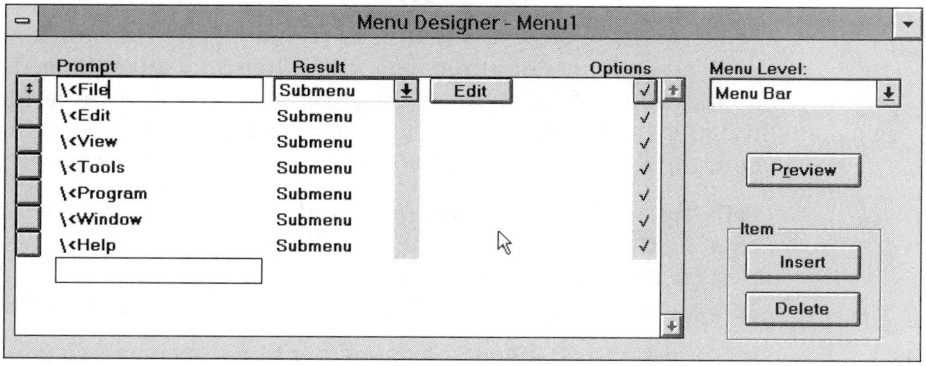

Menu Designer after selecting Quick Menu

Figure 16-2.

Customizing the Quick Menu

By installing the Visual FoxPro Main menu complete with all its features in the Menu Designer, Quick Menu gives your application a colossal jump-start in several ways: First, Visual FoxPro's menu features are already implemented, debugged, and ready to use in your application. This eliminates a great deal of design, coding, and debugging effort. This menu system also provides a standard Windows interface that is already familiar to most users. Finally, you are free to select, modify, and expand this set to suit your needs, using the standard menu system as a model for your custom changes. Here's how to use the Menu Designer.

Inserting a New Menu Item

You can insert a new item anywhere in this menu system. Your application may use several different Visual FoxPro forms which users can easily access from the menu. For example, if your application has a hierarchy of forms to examine invoices, you might insert an Invoice menu item just before the Help menu.

Tip: Experienced users expect to find application-specific menu items *after* standard Windows menu items and before Help, which is usually last. Most Microsoft applications, and those of other major suppliers, follow this familiar convention.

Creating Menu Items

After you have created a menu, as you did using the Quick Menu feature, you can easily insert and delete menu items to suit the needs of your applications. Menu items represent Visual FoxPro commands or procedures the user can execute from the menu. Both menus and menu items may contain submenu items to provide additional, associated functionality.

Let's pursue the Invoice example and insert just such a menu item by clicking the Mover button next to the Help menu entry, clicking the Menu Designer's Insert button, then typing **Invoice** in the Prompt column. Figure 16-3 shows how your screen should look after you have added the menu.

If you need to change the arrangement of your menu to conform to Figure 16-3, do so by dragging the mover bar to reposition menu items.

Adding Submenu Items

Submenu items are like menu items; however, they are accessed through higher level menu items, such as Invoices. For example, under Invoices you might want the ability to choose current or delinquent invoices by adding submenus. Here's how you create Visual FoxPro submenus and add submenu items to Invoice:

1. Add a menu item by clicking the menu title, in the Menu Designer Prompt column, to which you want to add an item. For this example, click the Invoice item you just inserted to add a submenu item.
2. Select Submenu in the Result box and a Create button appears at the right of the list.

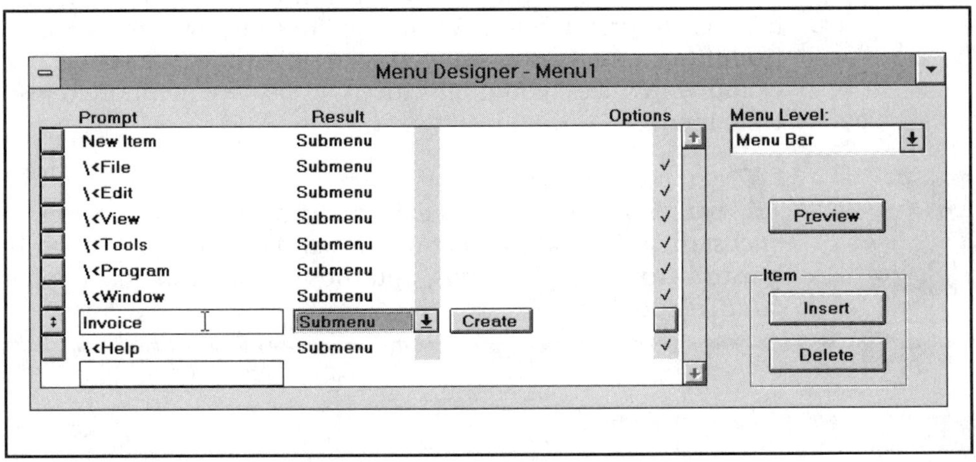

Menu Designer showing new menu item

Figure 16-3.

3. Click the Create button and an empty Menu Designer window appears.
4. Type the names of your new submenu items in the Prompt column of this new window. For example, you may wish to examine either current or delinquent invoices. To implement the choices, type **Current** in one menu and **Delinquent** in another as shown in Figure 16-4.

Multiple Levels of Submenus

You may also want to examine aging of delinquent invoices by adding two submenus under the Delinquent submenu to display delinquent invoices over 30 days or over 60 days. Here's how to do it.

1. Click the menu item under which you wish to add a submenu. For this example, click the Delinquent menu item you just created.
2. Select Submenu in the Result box and a Create button appears to the right of the box, unless a submenu already exists. If one does, an Edit button appears instead; however, in this case the Create button will appear.
3. Click the Create button and a new Menu Designer window appears, as it did in the previous examples.
4. Type the names of your new menu items in the Prompt column, as you did before; only in this case, type **Over 30 Days** for one item and **Over 60 Days** for the other item.

At this point, your Menu Designer window should look like the one shown in Figure 16-5.

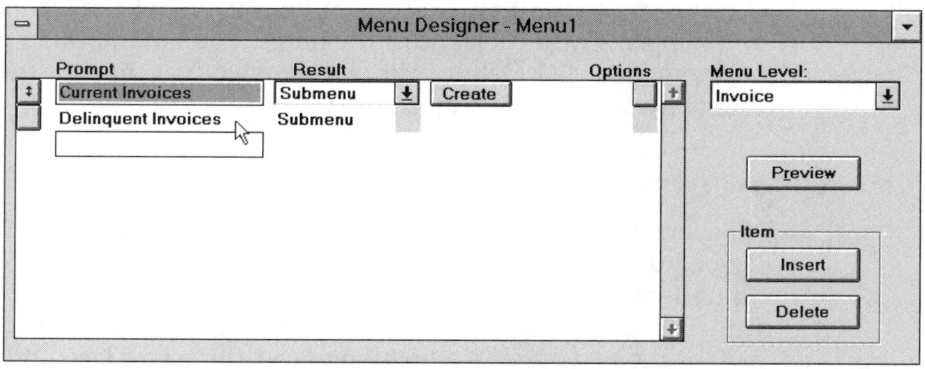

Menu Designer showing added submenus
Figure 16-4.

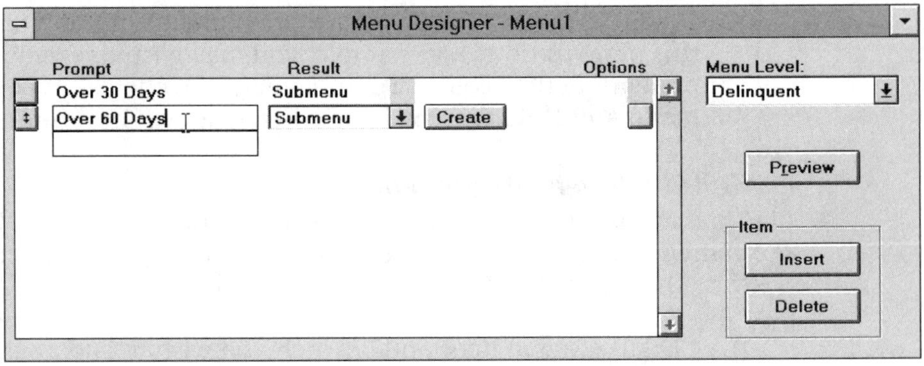

Menu Designer showing added layer of submenus
Figure 16-5.

Previewing Your New Menu

Now is a good time to preview how this new menu will appear in your application, or in any application to which you apply it. In the Menu Layout box on your current Menu Designer dialog, click Menu Bar to return to the top level in Menu Designer. Click Preview and two things happen.

1. A Preview dialog box appears, showing the menu's filename, the assigned prompt, and the assigned command.
2. Your new menu *temporarily* appears in the Visual FoxPro menu bar.

As long as the Preview dialog is showing, you can test the functionality of your new menu. Click your new Invoice menu item and the next level of submenus appears.

Because you haven't assigned procedures to any of the menu items, nothing will happen if you click one of the items. You have another level of submenus, so click Delinquent to display your entire new Invoice menu hierarchy, as shown in Figure 16-6.

Access Keys

Your menus should also provide access, or shortcut, keys to facilitate quick keyboard access to menu functions. Access key assignment is represented by an underlined letter in the menu title or in the menu item. For Example, "T" is the Visual FoxPro Tools menu access key. Visual FoxPro automatically assigns the first letter of a menu name as the access key, unless you specifically assign an access key to a menu item or title. You did not assign

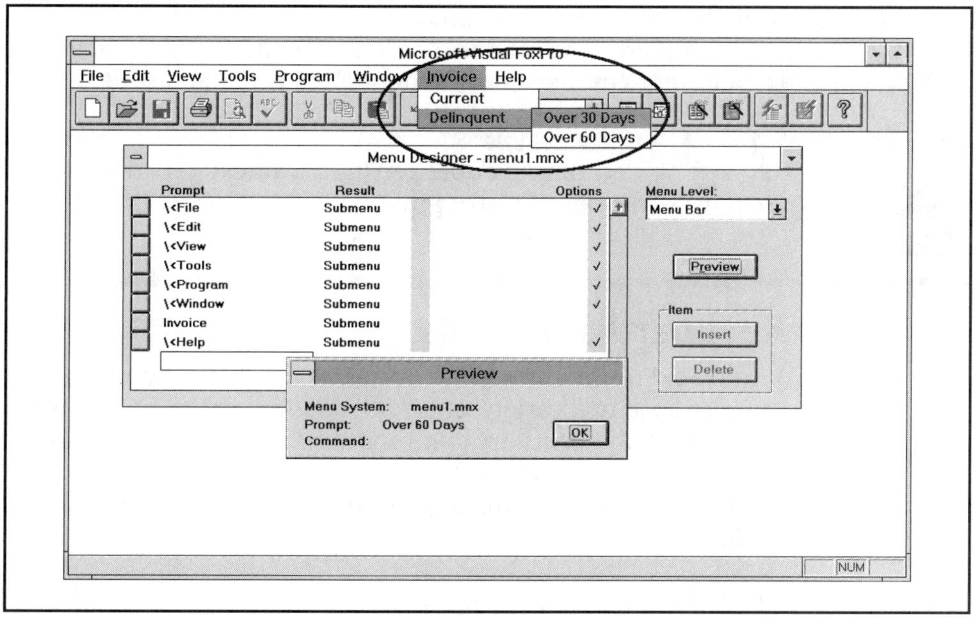

Menu hierarchy
Figure 16-6.

an access key to the Invoice menu item you created earlier; therefore, Visual FoxPro assigns the first letter "I" as the access key.

You can assign an access key to any menu or menu item by typing \< to the left of the letter you want to assign as its access key. For example, you can easily assign the letter "I" to the Invoice menu item you created earlier. Simply replace **Invoice** with **\<Invoice** as shown in Figure 16-7.

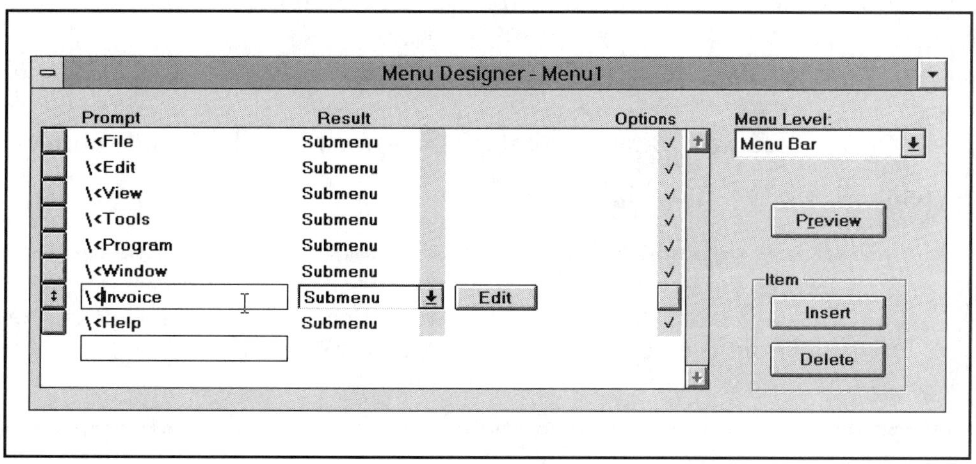

Menu Designer showing access key assignment
Figure 16-7.

If the letter "I" should be unavailable because it is used by another item at that menu level, select another letter, such "v," by replacing **Invoice** with **In\<voice**. You have now assigned "v" as the access key.

Tip: If you have trouble getting an access key to work correctly, it may already be in use by another menu item at the same level.

Keyboard Shortcuts

Visual FoxPro provides more options than just assigning access keys. You can also specify a variety of keyboard shortcuts to access menus and menu items. Such shortcuts are combinations of the CTRL key and another key. Keyboard shortcuts are different from access keys in that they allow you to access menu items by displaying the menu. Here's how you specify a keyboard shortcut.

1. Click the desired menu title or menu item appearing in the Prompt column. For example, click the Invoice menu title.
2. Click the small button in the Options column to launch Prompt Options dialog.
3. Click the Shortcut check box to launch the Key Definition dialog.
4. Enter your preferred key shortcut combination in the Key Label box. For example, enter CTRL+I.

Note: If a keyboard shortcut hasn't been assigned to a menu item, Visual FoxPro enters "(press the key)" in the Key Label box to prompt you to press the keys you want to assign.

Tip: Be aware that CTRL+J is not a valid keyboard shortcut combination.

Note: Visual FoxPro automatically inserts the shortcut key combination from the Key Label box into the Key Text box.

5. Type into the Key Text box the text you wish to appear beside the selected menu item. For example: Type **^I**, which is the common notation indicating CTRL+I, and your screen should look like the one shown in Figure 16-8.

Dynamically Controlling Visual FoxPro Menus

You can easily enable and disable menus and menu items dynamically, during program execution, based upon changing logical conditions within the program.

Enable or disable menus and menu items in the following manner.

1. Click an appropriate menu title or menu item in the Menu Designer Prompt column.
2. Choose the button in the Options column to display the Prompt Options dialog.
3. Click the Skip For check box to launch the Visual FoxPro Expression builder, which looks like the one shown in Figure 16-9.
4. Type into the Expression Builder's Skip For box an expression, function, or procedure that will determine the enabled or disabled state of the menu or menu item.

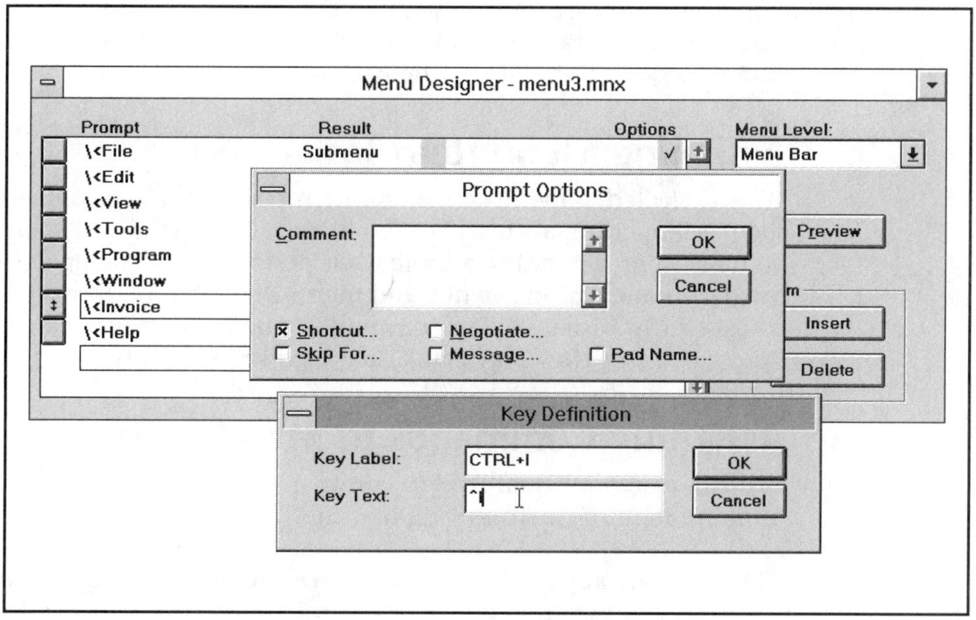

Key Definition box

Figure 16-8.

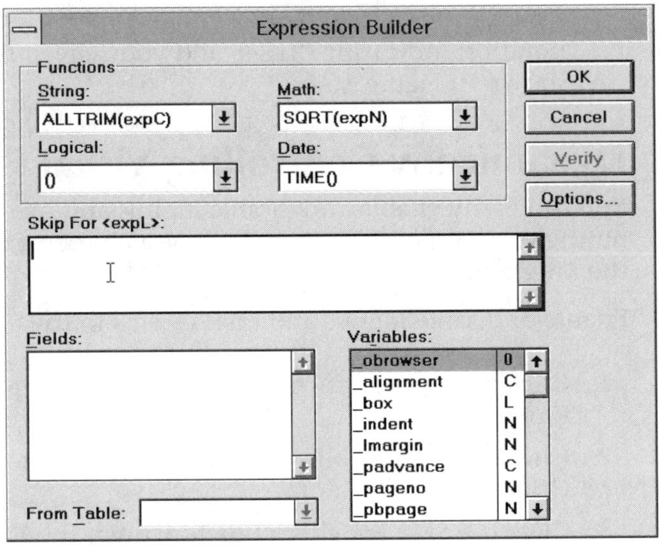

Visual FoxPro Expression Builder
Figure 16-9.

When this expression in the Skip For box evaluates to false (.F.), the menu or menu item is enabled. If the expression evaluates to true (.T.), the menu or menu item is disabled and is unavailable to the user. When a menu system is displayed, you can control whether the menu or menu item is enabled or disabled by programmatically invoking the SET SKIP OFF command. For details, see SET SKIP OFF in the Appendix.

Assigning Menu Item Tasks

When selected, a menu or a menu item performs a preassigned operation, such as launching a Visual FoxPro form, opening a file, displaying another menu system, activating a toolbar, or performing some predefined programmatic action. Menus and menu items can perform their tasks only by executing Visual FoxPro commands. Such commands can comprise one line of code, or they may call Visual FoxPro procedures.

Assigning Commands to Menu Items

You can assign a Visual FoxPro command, function, or procedure to a menu or menu item in the following manner.

1. Click the appropriate menu title or menu item in the Prompt column of the Menu Designer.

2. Click Command in the Result box and the Menu Designer looks like that shown in Figure 16-10.

3. Type the required command into the small box to the right of the Menu Designer's Result box.

Note: If the command you entered executes a procedure in the menu's cleanup code, you should invoke the following syntax: DO *procname* IN *menuname*. Using this procedure, menuname indicates the location of the cleanup code procedure. Because menuname is the filename of the menu file, it must include the .MPR extension. If you don't include the path to menuname, you will have to point to it with SET PROCEDURE TO menuname.MPR.

Assigning Procedures to Menu Items

You can also assign procedures to your menus or menu items. The method for assigning procedures depends upon whether the menu or menu item contains submenus.

You can assign a procedure to a menu or menu item *without* submenus in the following manner.

1. Click the appropriate menu title or menu item appearing in the Prompt column.
2. Click Procedure in the Result box.
3. Click the Create or Edit button.
4. Type the appropriate code in the window.

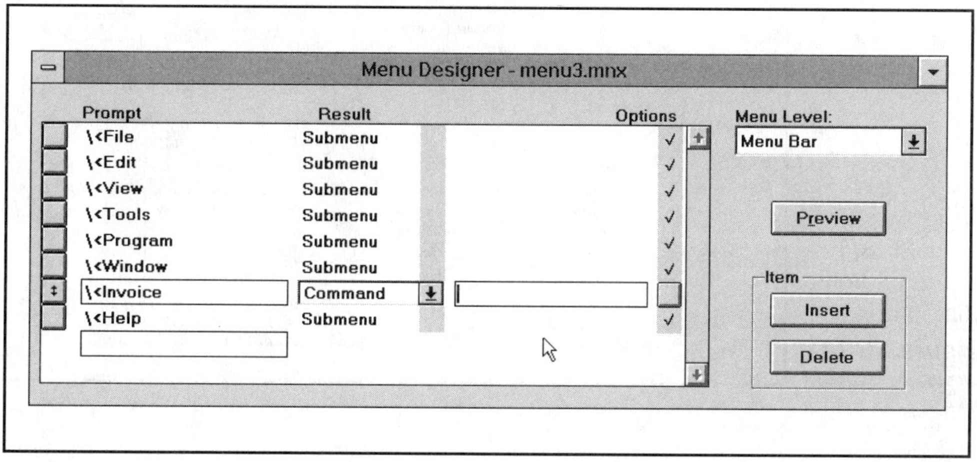

Menu Designer command assignment
Figure 16-10.

You can assign a procedure to a menu or menu item *with* submenus in the following manner.

1. Select the menu level in the Menu Level box to display the menu or menu item you want to modify. For example, select the Invoice menu item you created earlier.
2. From the Visual FoxPro Main menu's View menu, click Menu Options and launch the Menu Options dialog, as shown in Figure 16-11.
3. Specify the procedure you want this menu item to execute, by doing one of the following:
   - Coding or calling the procedure in the Menu Options Procedure box
   - Clicking the Edit button, then the OK button to launch a separate edit window, then writing or calling the procedure you require

Customizing Menus

After creating a basic menu system, you can customize it. For example, you can create status bar messages, define menu locations, or define default procedures.

Displaying Status Bar Messages

You can design your menu system to display status bar messages describing each menu item any time that item is active. For example: If the cursor is placed over the Invoice menu item, the status bar message might display "Select Among Invoice Types." These messages assist the user in quickly and

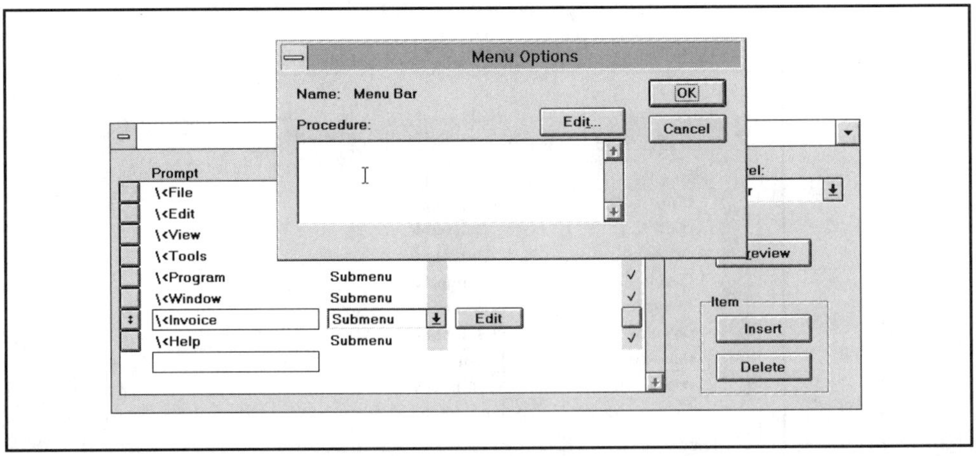

Visual FoxPro Menu Options dialog box

Figure 16-11.

easily selecting an appropriate menu choice. Here's how you can display informative messages when a user selects one of your menus or menu items.

1. Click a menu title or menu item in the Prompt column. For this example, use the Invoice item you have been working with.
2. Click the small button in the Options column and launch the Prompt Options dialog.
3. Click the Message check box.
4. Type the message you want to display in the Prompt Options dialog Message box. For this example, type "**View Active Invoices**", as shown in Figure 16-12.

Tip: Remember always to enclose character strings, such as "View Active Invoices", inside either single quotes or double quotes.

Using the Preview key, you can examine your new message. Click Preview, then click and hold your Invoice menu item. Notice that your message now appears in the status bar, as shown in Figure 16-13.

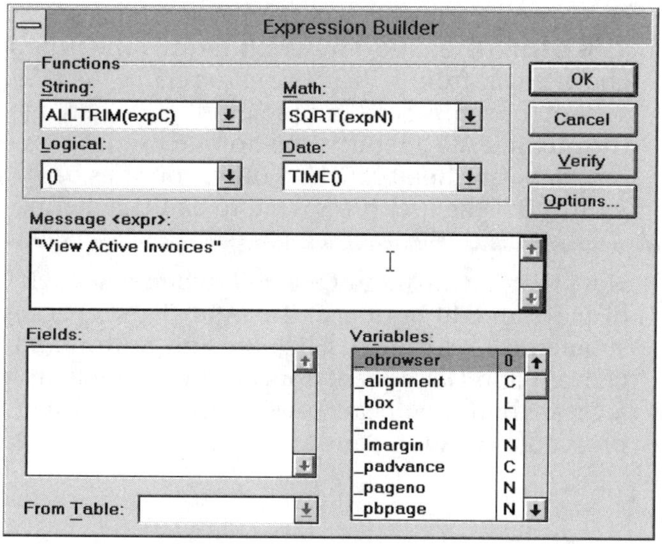

Expression Builder showing expression

Figure 16-12.

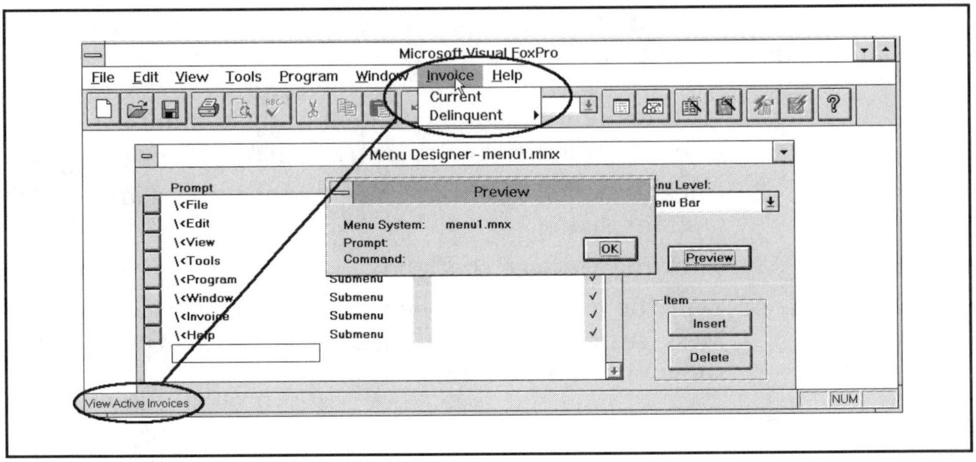

Visual FoxPro menu showing new items
Figure 16-13.

Defining Menu Procedures

You may assign either a submenu, a command, a procedure, or a Bar # to a menu item.

- Command is any valid Visual FoxPro command
- Procedure is the name of any valid Visual FoxPro procedure
- Bar # returns the Visual FoxPro Bar() function.

Note: The BAR( ) function returns the number of the most recently chosen item from a Visual FoxPro menu. Visual FoxPro assigns each item on a menu or submenu a unique number. When a menu item is chosen from the menu, BAR( ) returns the unique number assigned to that item. Your program can then branch to other routines based on the BAR( ) value. BAR( ) returns 0 if the user presses ESC to exit the menu.

Note that in the Menu Designer, when you click your Invoice menu item, it displays an Edit button to the right. This is because you have assigned submenus to this item. Click the Edit button and your two submenu items. Current and Delinquent appear in their separate window. Click Current and a Create button appears because the Current menu item does not have any procedures or submenus assigned.

When the Create button is present, its presence indicates that no items have been defined below the selected item. Click Delinquent and an Edit button appears telling you that more defined items appear below. Click Edit and both your Over 30 Days and Over 60 Days menu items appear. Go up one layer to Invoice and click Current. The Create button appears, inviting you to enter a procedure by selecting Procedure in the Results box. Click Procedure and the Create Procedure box appears, as shown in Figure 16-14.

You can now write the code for any valid Visual FoxPro procedure in this box and it will execute when you click the Current menu item. Double-click the upper-left corner of this box to exit and click Command in the Current Results box. A dialog box will appear asking if you want to delete the procedure. Click Yes, then click Command in the Results box. An outline appears in place of the Create box, as shown in Figure 16-15.

Any valid Visual FoxPro command you type into this box will automatically execute when you click the Current menu item.

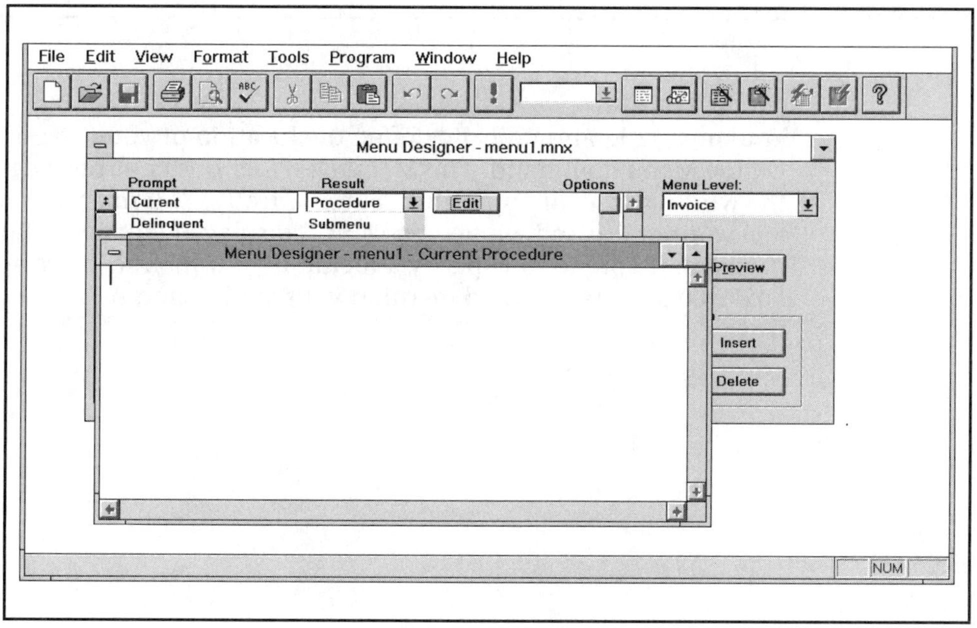

Visual FoxPro Create Procedure box
Figure 16-14.

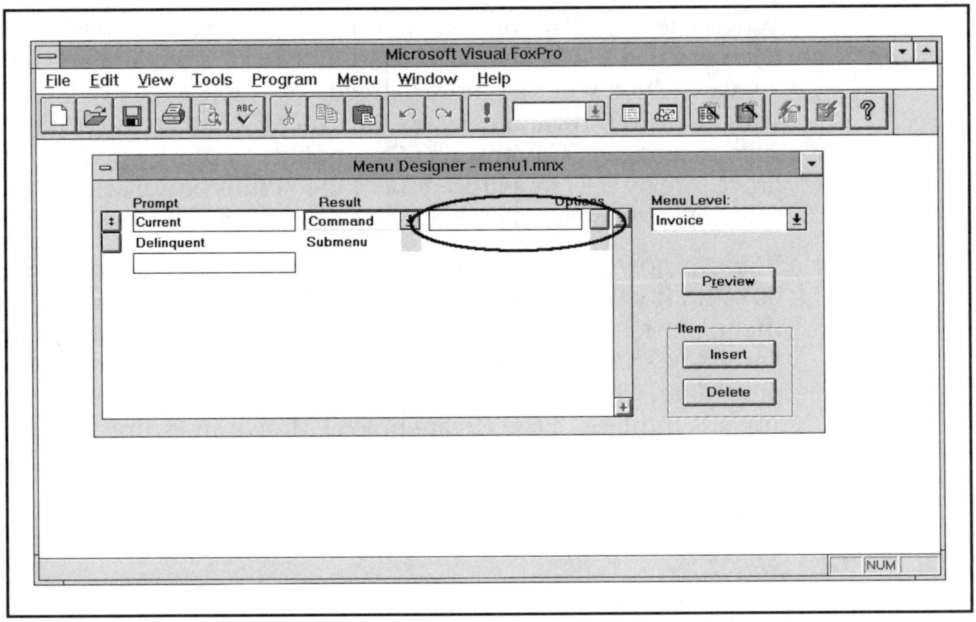

Menu Designer command entry
Figure 16-15.

Menu Location

You must programmatically define the location of your menu using the Define Menu command. The Menu Designer does not provide for placing the window in your application automatically. You must specify the menu you want to use and where you want it displayed when you build your program. If you do not specify a menu in your main code window, Visual FoxPro places its standard menu in your application by default.

17

Building and Distributing Visual FoxPro Applications

Whether you create Visual FoxPro applications for your own use, for internal use in your organization, or for distribution, the process is very similar. You work in the Visual FoxPro integrated development environment building and integrating objects, forms, reports, and all the other elements that comprise a finished application.

However, when you plan to distribute the application, you are obligated to go one step further and test it in the run-time environment. Such testing, which is essential to the integrity of your product, has come to be known as Beta testing. Beta testing is a final step in the development cycle, where applications are tested in the "real world" by having actual users exercise the product in their own run-time environment before production and sale.

This chapter addresses two similar and related aspects of application building: those steps essential to building any application and some additional steps that are essential if you plan to distribute it. Our treatment of this subject is not intended to be comprehensive; instead, our objective is to give you a basic overview of the required procedures. This is by no means a difficult process if you have developed a strategically sound, well-designed, and well-implemented application up to this point.

Application Structure

Visual FoxPro applications are usually structured, as a minimum, to provide users with a database, tables, a menu, and a set of one or more forms for manipulating and displaying the data. Beyond creating the necessary functional components of your application, you also need to:

1. Establish a project's main program
2. Manage your application's environment
3. Control your application's response to events
4. Ensure the integrity of data
5. Return the environment to its initial condition as it existed before your application

The Application's Starting Point

Your application's Main program file is the functional starting point for your application every time it is launched in the run-time environment. The Main program can be any program, form, or query you include in the project. Generally, larger applications have as their main program a specific program designed for that purpose; however, as you shall see, other Visual FoxPro elements can be made to serve as the main program.

Structuring the Main Program

Your main program's code should be structured to call the essential functional components of your application. Those components then reference the other key elements of your application. To build a main program, you need to include (depending on the application) some or all of the following elements:

1. Set up the application's environment.
2. Launch the initial user interface.
3. Establish the event loop.
4. Restore the environment upon exiting the application.

Here is an example of what a typical simple main program for a small, uncomplicated application might look like:

```
DO setenv.prg     & Code that sets up your program's environment
DO mainmenu.mpr   & Main menu screen
READ EVENTS       & See online help for detailed explanation
DO restore.prg    & Code that restores the environment upon exiting
```

Set the starting point of your Visual FoxPro application by launching the Project Manager and doing the following:

1. Select the file you have created or modified to serve as the application's Main program.
2. Select Set Main on the Project menu

This procedure tells the Program Manager which file is your Main program and ensures that its code is executed first every time the application starts.

Structuring a Main Form

It is possible, and often desirable in small simple applications, to use a form as the main program. Bear in mind, however, that the best programming strategy is usually to specify a *separate* main program in your application that issues the READ EVENTS command, as shown above. Having said that, you *can* combine the functionality of a main program and the initial user interface, such as a form, by designating the form as the application's main program. Create a Main form by:

1. Selecting the method associated with the form's Load event and adding the following code to preserve the system's initial environment: 17

   ```
   DO setenv.prg
   ```

2. Establishing the data environment for the form or form set by opening the necessary databases, tables, views, relationships, and indexes.

3. Selecting the method associated with the form's Unload event and adding code, as above—only this time to restore the initial environment when exiting the program:

```
DO restore.prg
```

Setting Up an Application's Environment

Sound programming practice suggests that it is prudent to save initial environment settings, then set up an appropriate environment for your application in the Main program's setup code. You will usually need to include code to:

- Initialize variables.
- Set the default path.
- Reference external resources such as libraries and procedure files, using the SET LIBRARY command.

For example, you might need to test the default value of the SET NEAR command, store the value, and SET NEAR OFF for your application. To accomplish this, you might insert this code in your setup procedure:

```
IF SET('NEAR') = "ON"
    SET NEAR OFF
    cNearVal = "ON"
ELSE
    cNearVal = "OFF"
ENDIF
```

The reason you store the value in cNearVal is to facilitate restoring the environment when you exit.

The Event Loop

After you set up the environment and you have displayed the application's initial user interface, you may need to establish an event loop, which will wait for user interaction. To control the event loop you need to:

1. Issue the READ EVENTS command. After this command is in effect, Visual FoxPro starts processing events.
2. Issue a CLEAR EVENTS command to stop processing events.

Tip: You need to provide a path to exit the event loop before you start it. Make sure your code includes a mechanism—for example, an Exit button or menu command—that can issue the CLEAR EVENTS command. If you fail to do this, your application may collapse into an unending loop that you can only recover from by pressing the ESC key or rebooting your computer. This is *not* considered good programming practice.

Building A Project

When you build your project, Visual FoxPro automatically creates a project table with a .PJX file extent by opening and processing the program files that you specify, such as menus, reports, labels, forms, and library files. Using this project file, you can create one of the two possible program types: an application file with a .APP extent or an executable file with a .EXE extent. The Visual FoxPro project table keeps track of all files necessary to create your application, plus any dependencies, references, and connections that may exist between the files. After you specify the components that comprise your project, Visual FoxPro ensures that your application is built from the most recent source files.

The Build Options Dialog Box

The Build Options dialog box is where you tell the Project Manager how you want it to build your project, using the following options:

- **Rebuild Project:** Creates, if necessary, and builds a Visual FoxPro project file. This option is equivalent to the BUILD PROJECT command.
- **Build Application:** Builds your project, compiles any project files that are out of date, and creates a project file with the .APP file extent. This option is equivalent to the BUILD APP command.
- **Build Executable:** Creates a Visual FoxPro executable file from your project. This option is equivalent to the BUILD EXE command, which is available only in the Visual FoxPro Professional Edition.
- **Recompile All Files:** Recompiles all your project files and creates, if necessary, a Visual FoxPro object file for each source file in your project.
- **Display Errors:** Displays compile errors in an edit window after Visual FoxPro has completed the build. Figure 17-1 shows the Build Options dialog box.

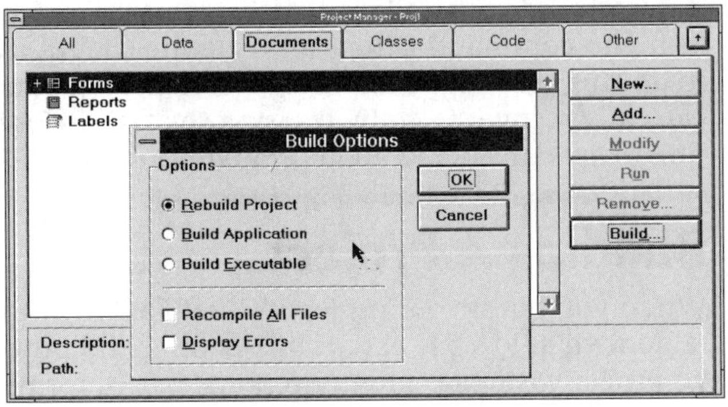

Build Options dialog box
Figure 17-1.

Building the Application

Before you can build an application you need to verify references within the project and regenerate any elements that may have changed or been updated since the last build. Here's how you build a project from within the Project Manager:

1. Choose Build.
2. Select Rebuild Project in the Build Options dialog box.
3. Select any other needed options and click OK.

As an alternative, you can also type the BUILD PROJECT command into the Visual FoxPro Command window. For example, if you want to build a project named *PROJ1.PJX*, type **BUILD PROJECT proj1** into the Command window.

Building a project, either from the Project Manager or by using the BUILD PROJECT command, automatically creates a project table with a *.PJX* extent. Visual FoxPro accomplishes this by opening and processing your project's programs, menus, reports, labels, forms, and specified library files. You can then use the project file to create either of two program types: an application file with a *.APP* extent or an executable file with a *.EXE* extent. Your project table keeps track of and manages all the files required to create the application, plus any dependencies, references, and connections that you may have created among the files. After you specify all the elements in your project, Visual FoxPro ensures that it compiles the application using your latest source files.

If Visual FoxPro finds a program, menu, or form file while creating a project file, it also finds its compiled counterpart and compares the time and date stamp of the two related files. If the time and date stamp of the source is later than that of the compiled version, Visual FoxPro then recompiles the source file. All project files contain time and date stamps to facilitate refreshing the project file when you make changes or when dependencies change. This precaution helps to ensure that applications created from your project files always use the most recent source file's code.

To refresh your project file at any time, just click Build while in the Project Manager and Visual FoxPro will automatically update the project. When you build your project, unresolved references and other errors are reported but they do not prevent creation of the project file. This enables you to build and test a partial project even though all the necessary elements may not have been created.

Building The Application

When you can successfully build your project without errors, you are ready to take the next step and build the application. To build an application from the Project Manager:

1. Click Build.
2. Click Build Application in the Build Options dialog box.
3. Select any other needed options and click OK.

As an alternative, you can also type the BUILD APP command into the Visual FoxPro Command window. For example, if you want to build an application called *APP1.APP* from a project named *PROJ1.PJX*, type: BUILD APP app1 FROM proj1. Whether you use the Build option in Project Manager or the BUILD APP command, the result is an application file with an *.APP* extent.

Before building an application be sure the project file contains all the files needed in your application. If any required files are missing or not found during the build, Visual FoxPro generates an error. Compile errors are written into an error file with an *.ERR* file extent. The first eight characters of this error filename are the first eight characters of your project file's name.

Running Your Application

If Visual FoxPro finds no compilation errors during the build, you are now ready to run your application and see how it performs in the run-time environment. You have two options for running an application:

1. Click Do from the Program menu and select your application file like this:

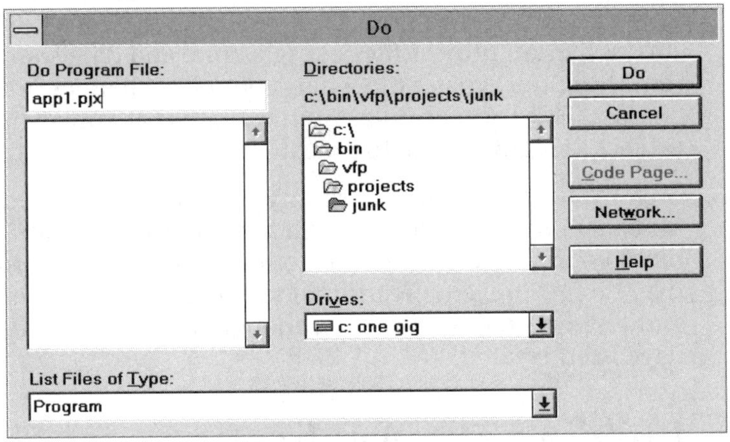

2. Type DO and the name of your application file into the Command window.

For example: if you want to run an application called APP1, type **DO *<path>app>*** into the Command window like this:

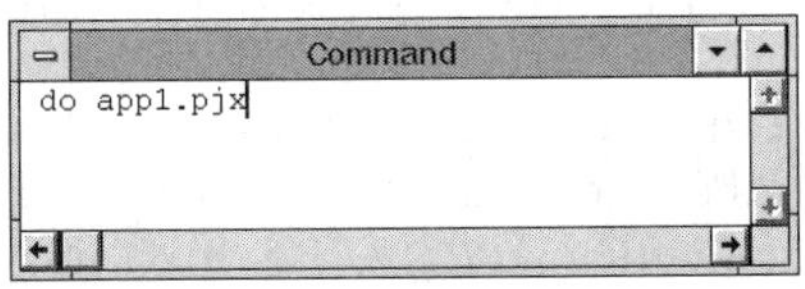

Distributing Visual FoxPro Applications

Before you can distribute a Visual FoxPro application you have to create an application file with either a *.app* extent, or an executable application file with a *.exe* extent. However, the option of creating executable Visual FoxPro applications is available only in the Visual FoxPro Professional Edition.

Caution! Restricted Files

Visual FoxPro contains many files that are licensed for *your use only* for design, development, and testing purposes. See LICENSE.TXT, located in your Visual FoxPro directory, for a list of restricted files.

If your application contains any of the files in the restricted list referenced above, remove them. Your license agreement with Microsoft does not permit you to ship these files in your application or on your disks—*doing so is a violation of your agreement.* The Setup Wizard checks for these files and will exclude them from distributable disk sets. Do not assign these filenames to any files you will distribute.

Distributable Files

If you are a registered owner of Visual FoxPro you may distribute any Visual FoxPro file that is *not restricted.* Visual FoxPro files must be distributed only in conjunction with a legitimate Visual FoxPro application. The following Microsoft guidelines apply to distributable Visual FoxPro files.

Note: It is your responsibility to check your license agreement and ensure that any Visual FoxPro files you distribute fully comply with the law and with your contractual agreement with Microsoft. The information furnished here is only to alert you of your obligation. The responsibility is yours alone.

Setup Wizard

Any files in the Visual FoxPro DISTRIB.SRC and SETUP directories that are required to support a corresponding application may be distributed. When you use the Setup Wizard to create distribution disks, it automatically places the required files from these directories on the distributable disks in a compressed format. Upon installation, these file are decompressed and are installed by name in the appropriate directories on the user's machine. It is not necessary to copy these files to your distribution tree.

Samples

Files in the Visual FoxPro SAMPLES and API\SAMPLE directories are provided for you to learn from and build upon. Although you may not distribute unmodified Visual FoxPro sample applications, you may refer to portions of sample application code as examples for building your own application. If you use any files in the Visual FoxPro SAMPLES or API\SAMPLE directories (including all .BMP, .ICO, and .CUR files), these files must be included in your project and in the application build. They must not appear by name on the distributable disks and may not be distributed independently of your applications.

Class Libraries
You can use any .VCX file without modification in your applications. The libraries must be included in your project and in your application build.

ODBC Files
Refer to the Microsoft License Agreement you received with Visual FoxPro for specific restrictions with respect to your redistribution of ODBC files.

part 5

The Finished Product

18

Structured Query Language Fundamentals

In this part you will learn about connecting to database servers. These servers usually run a form of structured query language, or SQL, so you will first take a quick look at the basics of SQL. Chapter 19 steps you through the procedures for connecting to Microsoft's SQL Server program. Microsoft's product has the advantage of being from the same company as Visual

FoxPro. For instance, the Upsizing Wizard that comes with Visual FoxPro makes the task of moving from the Xbase data format to the server-based data manager much easier. Chapter 20 discusses views, both remote and local, and queries. Chapter 21 discusses the database topics of referential integrity, triggers, and validation. Though Visual FoxPro extends these capabilities beyond SQL it is easiest to view them from the SQL perspective in which they were created.

Note: You will be using the data from the HiPrice Snacks example developed in Chapter 10.

In this chapter we will examine the basics of SQL. Using the example developed in Chapter 10 we will cover querying and modifying data using the Visual FoxPro SQL commands.

For additional information on SQL, see the *LAN Times Guide to SQL* by James R. Groff and Paul N. Weinberg (Osborne/McGraw-Hill, 1994). You will find this guide is invaluable if you plan on doing work using SQL.

A Brief Overview of SQL

Structured query language, often referred to by its pronounced acronym (SQL) as "sequel," is an outgrowth of research at IBM and elsewhere into the relational database model. Dr. E. F. Codd proposed this model in a paper published in the *Communications of the Association for Computing Machinery* in June 1970.

SQL, with its powerful query language, took off and soon became a standard in databases. SQL has largely been used for so-called decision-support systems. These are applications that mainly report data: for example, a sales report. The other branch of database use is online transaction processing (OLTP). OLTP applications use databases for processing data: for example, an order entry and inventory system.

Decision-support applications are rarely performance centered. It is not unreasonable for a sales report to take 10 or 15 minutes or more to run. If such an application takes a long time to run, the user may start it before going home at night so that it will be ready in the morning. OLTP has no such luxury. An OLTP-based system typically needs a response time in the 1-second range. It is a common experience to call an order number and have the person taking your order say something like "wait a minute while your account comes up." This lag is evidence of a poorly designed OLTP system or one that is overloaded.

There are now database servers that range from running on a DOS machine to running on an IBM mainframe. You can start with IBM's DB2/2 running on an OS/2 database server and, as your needs grow, go all the way to the biggest of the big iron. Oracle, Sybase, and other vendors of large database servers have products that span a wide range of hardware platforms. This scalability lets you choose a server and hardware platform that meet your needs now and be assured there is room for future growth.

Standard Is Not Too Standard

The SQL standard, codified by the American National Standards Institute (ANSI) most recently in 1992, is called SQL-92. In fact, however, it is a little misleading to call it a standard at all. This committee product leaves a lot of freedom for vendor implementations. The effect is that different vendor's products can be incompatible in major areas and still all be SQL-92 compliant.

You can apply one of two strategies, or a combination of both, when you use SQL. You can avoid using any features or capabilities that are not part of the standard. The problem with this approach is that it will lock you out of innovations made since the standard was adopted; plus, the standard leaves many useful features vendor dependent. Alternatively, you can try to plan for future growth and use a vendor that can supply you as your needs grow. This approach lets you use vendor-specific features while still allowing for future growth since most vendors have the same set of features available within the whole product line.

Choose Carefully

There's an old carpenters' saying: "measure twice, cut once." You should use this same level of care in choosing a database server. The products available are excellent, but this is not a one-size-fits-all choice. You will need to investigate carefully to find the best fit for your application.

Xbase versus SQL

The biggest difference between Xbase and SQL is a vision. Xbase is based on records and assumes that users and their programs know what they are doing. SQL is based on sets of records and allows the database administrator to control the actions that users and programs can take.

For example, suppose you have a table of orders, and that table contains a customer key so you can relate the order to the customer table. There is nothing in Xbase that prevents you from deleting a customer who has orders. When you report the orders, you'll simply have orders with a blank for the customer name.

SQL features referential integrity as a solution to this potential problem. The database administrator can specify as a part of the database itself an action that occurs whenever a customer with orders is deleted. The action might be to delete the orders or to deny the deletion of the customer record.

Chapter 21 describes referential integrity in much greater detail. The point here is that, in SQL, the database server protects the integrity of the database. In Xbase, each user is a world unto himself or herself and can do whatever he or she wishes.

Language versus Query Language

SQL is a query language. Unlike Xbase, it has no commands for displaying or manipulating information. Xbase is a high-level programming language. Although it would be silly, you could write a word processor or spreadsheet program in Xbase. SQL lacks most programming language features and is suited mainly to storing and retrieving data. These are not trivial tasks, as the multibillion dollar market for database servers demonstrates. The point is simply that you can't move a program from Xbase to SQL or write a program in SQL. If you use SQL you need another language or platform to implement all the mundane display features and so forth.

Database Servers

In the next several chapters, you are going to hear a lot about database servers. The term "server," however, can be confusing. Servers in the sense that many users know them are *file servers*, as in Novell networks. Also, Microsoft has a product called SQL Server, which we will be exploring. To avoid confusion between SQL servers and the SQL Server program, this book refers to servers generically as *database servers*. The database server is the out-of-sight part of database work that does the data crunching. Clients, such as your programs, connect to it, and they do the interface work.

Visual FoxPro is a client tool in that it can issue requests to database servers instead of processing the data itself. Visual FoxPro can also process data in its native file format, but that is not important to this discussion.

SQL: A Query Language

Structural query language is, of course, a query language. It supports the approach in which users, at least experienced users, issue queries to the database and examine the results. Most SQL database servers offer an interactive SQL tool. With it, you can issue a query and see the results in a spreadsheet format. This tool is much like the Command window in FoxPro. The results are displayed as for a browse operation.

In fact, you can enter SQL commands from the Visual FoxPro Command window, and that is how you will be experimenting with SQL. You can also use embedded SQL, in which your source code contains actual SQL statements that are translated and run from within your program.

The Power of a Query

As when you use the command line in Xbase, interactive SQL, whether through Visual FoxPro or an independent SQL product, can produce powerful results. Unlike the Xbase command line, however, it can do everything in one statement. Tables can be joined and related, subqueries can be issued, summary information can be reported—all in a single SQL command. This task is not necessarily easy—the process can be tangled and intricate—but it is possible.

The result of a query is a *flat file*: that is, a file with rows representing records and columns representing fields. The number of rows depends on your query conditions. In Xbase, a record is selected and processed. In SQL, a set of records is selected and processed. The results of a SEEK operation in Xbase would be a set with a single record in SQL.

You will sometimes hear the Xbase standard *.dbf* file referred to as a flat file, but it is not. A flat file contains only records; its first byte is the first byte of the first record. Xbase uses a header at the beginning of the *.dbf* file to store information such as field names and lengths and whether a memo file is associated with the file.

Using SELECT Statements

The SELECT statement is the workhorse of SQL. Note that SELECT is also a command in Xbase; however, the SELECT statement and command do not do the same thing. Visual FoxPro detects which SELECT you mean by examining the remainder of the entry. If it is followed by a numeric value or the alias of an open table, Visual FoxPro issues the Xbase command. Otherwise, it executes a SQL SELECT statement.

Running a SELECT Statement

The Visual FoxPro desktop has a window that you have not used until now. It is the Command window, and it looks like Figure 18-1.

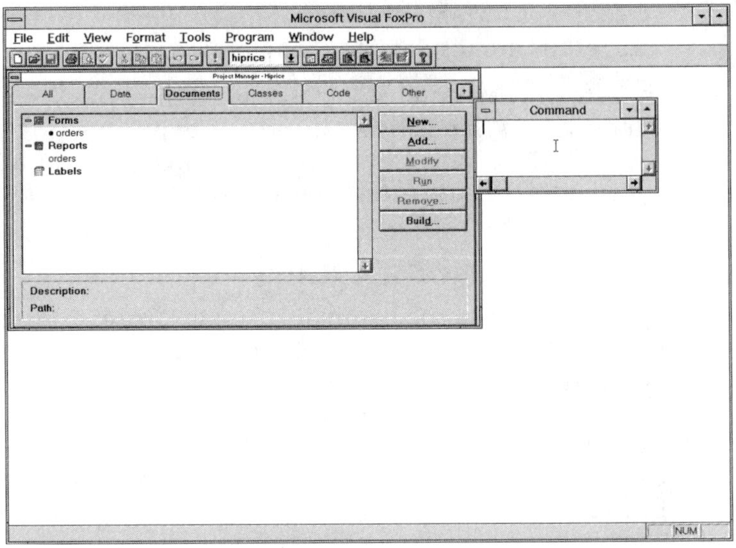

The Command window
Figure 18-1.

You will be entering some long commands, so move the Command window to the bottom of the screen and stretch it to the full width of your screen as shown in Figure 18-2.

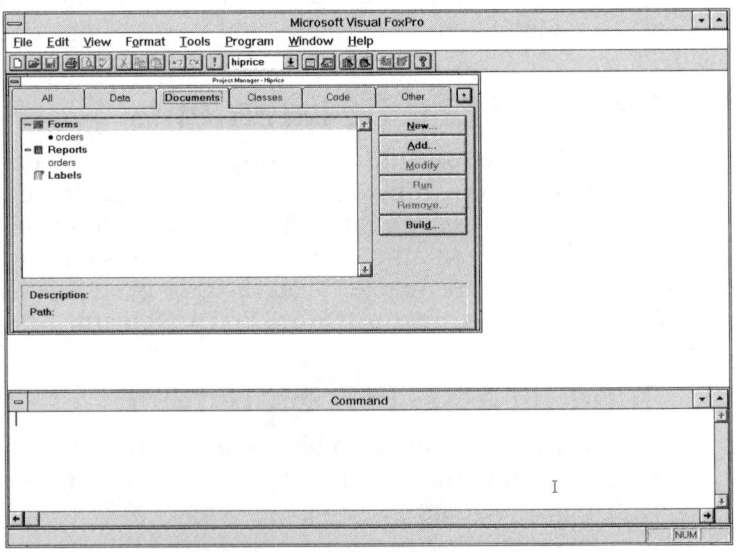

Stretching the Command window
Figure 18-2.

Now it's time to run your first SQL query. Type this command in the Command window:

```
select * from customer
```

The command "select *" tells Visual FoxPro to select all fields, and "from customer" tells it where to find the data. Press the ENTER key, and your screen should look like Figure 18-3.

Now enter another query:

```
select custno, name from customer
```

The resulting set will contain only the Custno and Name fields for the three records in customer. You can enter an asterisk (*) as in the previous query to select all fields, or you can choose the fields and their order by naming them specifically in the select clause as in this query.

Moving to the ORDLINES file allows you to examine some other tricks. For instance, to display all the line items with their extended prices, enter this command:

```
select orderno, qtyordered, unitprice,;
unitprice*qtyordered from ordlines
```

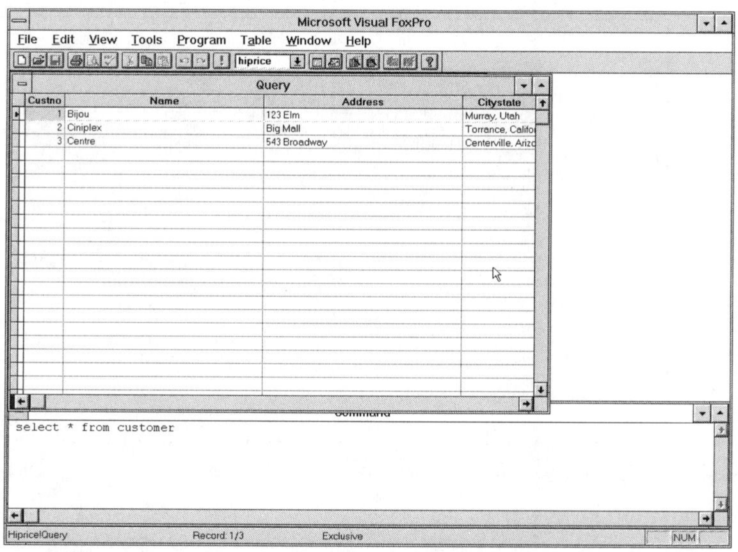

Results of the SQL query **Figure 18-3.**

As you will see, SQL queries can get very long and complex. To promote clarity, you can break up the command over several lines. Most interactive SQL tools have an Execute command—Watcom's is F9, for instance—that runs the command when you type it. Here you see a command broken into two lines with the semicolon signaling the break. Visual FoxPro recognizes the semicolon as an indication of line continuation and will not execute the command until you have finished it.

Figure 18-4 shows the result of this query.

Filtering Queries with the WHERE Clause

Now you'll examine how to limit the number of records displayed. For instance, suppose you want to see only the records for a particular customer.

The WHERE clause is the most common restrictive clause. It takes a logical statement, one that is either true or false, and only displays the records that are true.

Here are three samples of the WHERE clause:

```
select * from orders where custno = 1
select * from ordlines where qtyordered > 5
select orderno, qtyordered,;
unitprice, qtyordered*unitprice;
from ordlines;
where qtyordered*unitprice >= 10
```

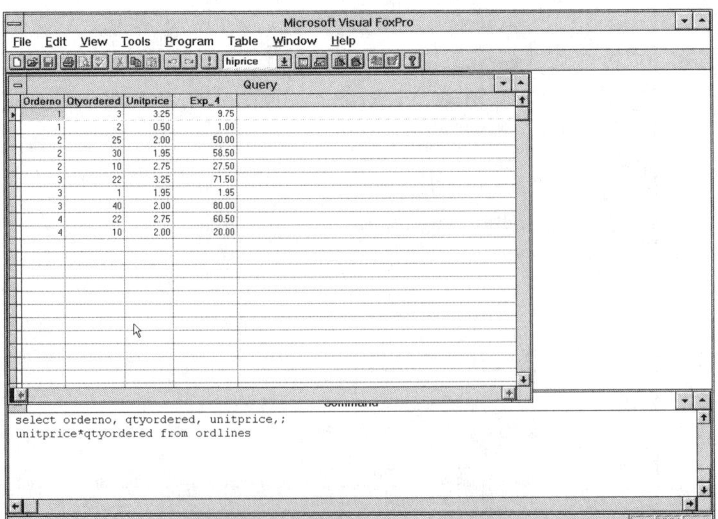

A calculated column

Figure 18-4.

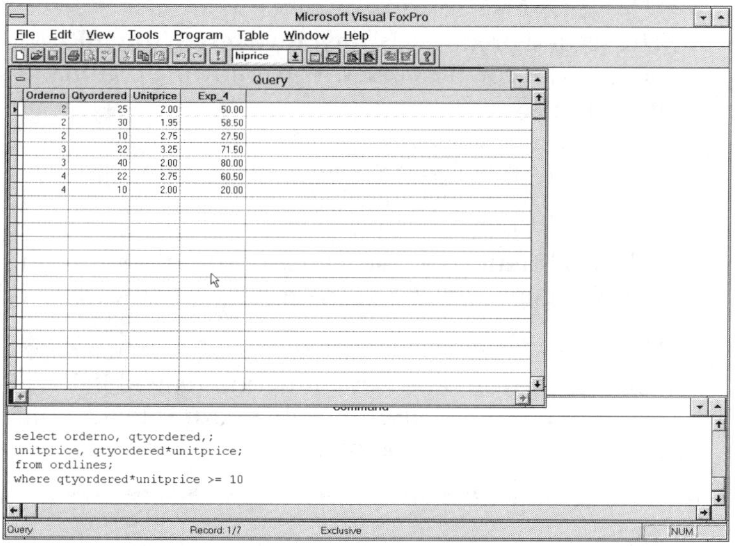

Using the WHERE clause
Figure 18-5.

Figure 18-5 shows the results of the last command, which is four lines long. ANSI SQL recognizes five search predicates for use in the WHERE clause:

```
Comparison operators (see table 1)
Range -- BETWEEN
Membership -- IN
Pattern matching -- LIKE
Null value -- IS NULL
```

Comparison Operators

Comparison operators, listed in the following table, are the same as in Xbase.

Operator	Left Value Compared to Right Value
>	Left value greater than right value
<	Left value less than right value
>=	Left value greater than or equal to right value
<=	Left value less than or equal to right value
=	Left value equal to right value
<>	Left value not equal to right value

BETWEEN

The second predicate is the range test. Using BETWEEN, you can specify a range of acceptable values. The following command shows orders in the first half of 1995:

```
select * from orders where orderdate;
between {01/01/95} and {07/01/95}
```

BETWEEN returns a true value for the endpoints: in this case, January 1 and July 1. Figure 18-6 shows the results of this command.

Tip: FoxPro also has a function named BETWEEN. You can use it with the SQL WHERE clause since its return is logical—just as you can any function that returns a logical value.

IN

IN is the member predicate. If you supply a list of values, IN will tell you if a specified value is in that list. For instance, suppose item numbers 1, 2, and 5 come from a particular distributor, and you want to see how those are selling. This command will show you:

```
select * from ordlines where itemno in (1,2,5)
```

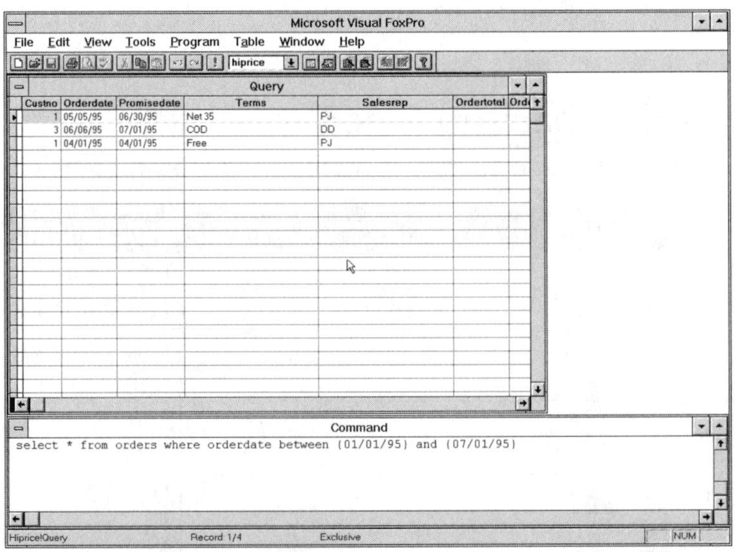

Using BETWEEN
Figure 18-6.

You will return to this command when you use ordering queries.

LIKE

LIKE performs pattern matching. Like DOS, LIKE has a single-character wildcard, _ (DOS uses ?), and a multiple-character wildcard, % (DOS uses *). The following command shows all customers whose names start with the letter C.

```
Select * from customer where name like "C%"
```

IS NULL

IS NULL checks for null values. Remember that a null value is a nonvalue. Empty character strings, zeros, and empty dates are not null; null is no value.

Suppose that you had a counter that counted cars on a road. Once an hour, it dumps this count into your table and starts again at zero. Then someone crashes into your counter, and it takes you three hours to get it back on line. For those three hours, no cars are counted, so the value should be null, not zero. Zero, by contrast, would mean there were no cars on the road during the period.

A null value often means that there is a problem with a record or that the data should be discarded. Usually, you will want to exclude rows with null values, and you will use IS NULL and the NOT operator, discussed next.

Compound Predicates

As you've probably noticed, the WHERE clause requires a logical true or false value. IS NULL, IN, LIKE, BETWEEN, and the comparison operators all return a logical value. Sometimes you will need to massage those logical returns, either by combining them or negating them, or both.

NOT

NOT performs logical negation; that is, it takes a true value and makes it false, and vice-versa. For example, you could add a logical value, called SHIPPED, to your orders table. This flag would be set to true when an order was shipped. If you wanted to see the orders that are not yet shipped, you could use the NOT operator by specifying WHERE NOT shipped.

When comparing numbers or character strings or other nonlogical values you can use the <> operator. In fact, this operator is the equivalent of a NOT and an equal (=) operator.

Truth Table for NOT
Table 18-1.

Value	Result
True	False
False	True

When working with logical operators, it is often helpful to use a truth table. Table 18-1 is the truth table for the NOT operator.

AND

Sometimes you need to check several conditions. For example, suppose you want to see how many times you sold more than a dozen of item number 1. You would enter this command:

```
Select * from ordlines where;
qtyordered > 12 and;
itemno = 1
```

The AND condition will be true if *both* its values—in this case, qtyordered > 12, and itemno = 1—are true. If one or both are false, then false is returned. Table 18-2 is a truth table for AND.

OR

Using the OR operator, you can specify two tests for which, if either one of them is true, the result will be true. Table 18-3 is a truth table for OR.

Grouping Compound Predicates

It won't be long before you'll need to group two or more compound predicates. For example, if you are a basketball coach looking for a trade you might specify the following:

```
Select * from players_on_block where;
points_per_game >= 20 and not trouble_maker;
or points_per_game >= 35
```

Truth Table for AND
Table 18-2.

Left Value	Right Value	Result
True	True	True
True	False	False
False	True	False
False	False	False

Left Value	Right Value	Result
True	True	True
True	False	True
False	True	True
False	False	False

Truth Table for OR
Table 18-3.

In other words, you don't want anyone who can't score at least 20 points per game, and you don't care if a player who can score at least 35 points per game is a troublemaker, but a player who scores between 20 and 35 points had better not be a troublemaker. However, you could also be saying that you don't want a troublemaker or a player who scores 35 or more points per game played.

To understand this, say the previous command out loud. When you stress the AND it comes out wrong, but if you stress the OR it will be correct.

Order of Precedence

The ANSI SQL standard says that logical operators are processed in this order: NOT, AND, OR. It is not handy to have to remember this order, so there is another operator that relates only to precedence: parentheses. If you put parentheses around groups of combination operators, that group is processed first.

For instance, parentheses can be added in the basketball example as follows:

```
(points_per_game >= 20 and not trouble_maker);
or points_per_game >= 35
```

ANSI SQL processes this command to achieve the following results: It selects players who either score 20 or more points per game and are not troublemakers or score 35 or more points per game.

Tip: We strongly urge you to use parentheses liberally. Even if you can cite the orders of precedence in your sleep, parentheses will make your code clearer and less troublesome.

Adding the ORDER BY Clause

Having your results in some order is useful. You can order your results by using the ORDER BY clause. ANSI SQL specifically does not guarantee that the data in a table will be in any order. ORDER BY allows you to add order to a SELECT statement.

Recall previously that you issued the following command:

```
select * from ordlines where itemno in (1,2,5)
```

The resulting data set looks like this:

Orderno	Itemno	Qtyordered	Unitprice
1	2	3	3.25
1	5	2	0.50
2	1	25	2.00
3	2	22	3.25
3	1	40	2.00
4	1	10	2.00

Notice that the data is in Orderno order. This is how you entered the records, so this display is not surprising, but remember that SQL does not guarantee that the data will be, or remain, in that order. Anyway, you want to see it in Itemno order, so you will use the ORDER BY clause:

```
select * from ordlines where itemno in (1,2,5);
order by itemno
```

Here are the results:

Orderno	Itemno	Qtyordered	Unitprice
2	1	25	2.00
3	1	40	2.00
4	1	10	2.00
1	2	3	3.25
3	2	22	3.25
1	5	2	0.50

Performing Join Operations

SQL uses join operations to relate data tables. For instance, if you want to link the ORDLINES table to the ITEMS table and show the description of the item instead of the item number, you would use a join operation.

Using Inner Joins

An inner join is the standard type of join operation. Here is an example:

```
select * from ordlines, items;
where itemno = itemno
```

When you execute this command, an error message appears saying that Itemno is not unique and must be qualified. This means that in the expression itemno = itemno, Visual FoxPro can't tell which item number you mean. This problem can be solved by following the advice given earlier to use aliases to keep commands unambiguous. Change the command as follows:

```
select * from ordlines, items;
where ordlines.itemno = items.itemno
```

The result looks like this:

Query

Orderno	Itemno_a	Qtyordered	Unitprice_a	Itemno_b	Itemdesc	Unitprice_b
1	2	3	3.25	2	Butterfinger Bar, Stale	3.25
1	5	2	0.50	5	Goo for Hot "Butter" machine	0.50
2	1	25	2.00	1	Hershey Bars, Huge	2.00
2	4	30	1.95	4	Red Vines Licorice	1.95
2	3	10	2.75	3	Jordan Almonds	2.75
3	2	22	3.25	2	Butterfinger Bar, Stale	3.25
3	4	1	1.95	4	Red Vines Licorice	1.95
3	1	40	2.00	1	Hershey Bars, Huge	2.00
4	3	22	2.75	3	Jordan Almonds	2.75
4	1	10	2.00	1	Hershey Bars, Huge	2.00

This is a poor display. It has duplicate columns: Itemno and Unitprice, the sequence of columns is not conducive to understanding, and the records are not logically ordered. You can fix these flaws with the following entry:

```
select ordlines.orderno, ordlines.qtyordered,;
items.itemdesc,;
ordlines.unitprice,;
ordlines.qtyordered*ordlines.unitprice from;
ordlines, items;
where ordlines.itemno = items.itemno
```

Now you have eliminated duplicate fields and, in the case of Unitprice, eliminated ambiguity. The result looks like this:

Query

Orderno	Qtyordered	Itemdesc	Unitprice	Exp_5
1	3	Butterfinger Bar, Stale	3.25	9.75
1	2	Goo for Hot "Butter" machine	0.50	1.00
2	25	Hershey Bars, Huge	2.00	50.00
2	30	Red Vines Licorice	1.95	58.50
2	10	Jordan Almonds	2.75	27.50
3	22	Butterfinger Bar, Stale	3.25	71.50
3	1	Red Vines Licorice	1.95	1.95
3	40	Hershey Bars, Huge	2.00	80.00
4	22	Jordan Almonds	2.75	60.50
4	10	Hershey Bars, Huge	2.00	20.00

This entry involves a lot of typing, which can lead to aggravating typos. However, just as Xbase uses alias, so can SQL. You specify an alias by including it after the table name. Here, you'll call ORDLINES "o" and ITEMS "i":

```
select o.orderno, o.qtyordered,;
i.itemdesc,;
o.unitprice,;
o.qtyordered*o.unitprice from;
ordlines o, items i ;
where o.itemno = i.itemno
```

That entry is much easier on the fingers, and with thought about choosing aliases, your goal is no less clear.

Note that you used the WHERE clause to specify the related fields. You can use that same WHERE to filter records, like this:

```
select o.orderno, o.qtyordered,;
i.itemdesc,;
o.unitprice,;
o.qtyordered*o.unitprice from;
ordlines o, items i ;
where o.itemno = i.itemno;
and o.qtyordered > 10
```

Last, you can join other tables like this:

```
c.name, o.orderno, o.qtyordered,;
i.itemdesc,;
o.unitprice,;
o.qtyordered*o.unitprice from;
ordlines o, items i, ;
customer c, orders r;
where o.itemno = i.itemno;
and o.orderno = r.orderno;
and r.custno = c.custno
```

The result, with the fields sized to fit, looks like this:

Query

Name	Orderno	Qtyordered	Itemdesc	Unitprice	Exp_6
Bijou	1	3	Butterfinger Bar, Stale	3.25	9.75
Bijou	1	2	Goo for Hot "Butter" machine	0.50	1.00
Centre	2	25	Hershey Bars, Huge	2.00	50.00
Centre	2	30	Red Vines Licorice	1.95	58.50
Centre	2	10	Jordan Almonds	2.75	27.50
Ciniplex	3	22	Butterfinger Bar, Stale	3.25	71.50
Ciniplex	3	1	Red Vines Licorice	1.95	1.95
Ciniplex	3	40	Hershey Bars, Huge	2.00	80.00
Bijou	4	22	Jordan Almonds	2.75	60.50
Bijou	4	10	Hershey Bars, Huge	2.00	20.00

Note that you used the orders table to get to the customer name, but you did not display any information from that table.

Using Outer Joins

Outer joins are a fairly new tool in SQL. When you use the WHERE clause to control the relationship between two or more tables, SQL discards any records that do not have a matching record. Recall that in the previous discussion of inner joins, you used this line:

```
where o.itemno = i.itemno;
```

If ITEMS did not contain a matching record for a line item in ORDLINES—perhaps the record was accidentally deleted—the record would not be displayed because this is also a logical statement, and it is false. In other words, since there are no records in ORDLINES that match the record in ITEMS, no record will appear for that item in the query.

Outer joins are rarely used in a properly designed database.

Performing Insert, Update, and Delete Operations

You need to be able to insert new records and rows in a database and to modify them or delete them.

Inserting Records

To insert a new record, use the INSERT statement to insert a row, like this:

```
insert into items;
(itemno, itemdesc, unitprice);
values (6,'Raisinettes',1.75)
```

Caution: Visual FoxPro requires the use of single quotation marks (') around character strings in this command. Using double quotation marks (") causes an error.

Note that the second line of this statement is a list of the fields in ITEMS. The SQL standard allows you to omit this list, but we do not recommend doing so. By specifying the fields, you are adding clarity.

Now issue a SELECT statement like this:

```
select * from items
```

The new item, Raisinettes, will appear.

Note that most database servers enforce security and require users to have permission from the database administrator to insert records into a table.

Updating Records

Updating is how you modify existing records. The syntax of the UPDATE statement is a little different from that of the INSERT statement in that you must specify a column name and its value, like this:

```
update items;
set unitprice = 1.1 * unitprice
```

This statement raises all prices by 10 percent. Issuing another SELECT command yields this result:

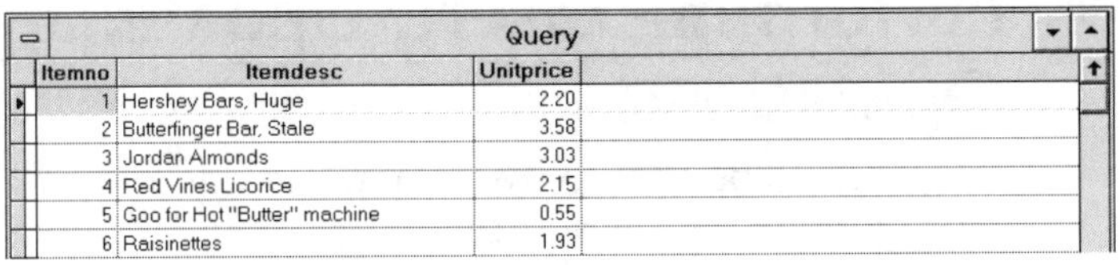

Itemno	Itemdesc	Unitprice
1	Hershey Bars, Huge	2.20
2	Butterfinger Bar, Stale	3.58
3	Jordan Almonds	3.03
4	Red Vines Licorice	2.15
5	Goo for Hot "Butter" machine	0.55
6	Raisinettes	1.93

Again, you will need the proper permissions from the database administrator to run these commands on a database server.

Deleting Records

Finally, you need to be able to delete records. Here, you will delete the Raisinettes entry you just added. You can use a WHERE clause to control which records to delete, using the LIKE predicate, as follows:

```
delete from items where;
itemdesc like 'Raisine%'
```

Enter a SELECT statement, and the ITEMS table looks like this:

Query

Itemno	Itemdesc	Unitprice
1	Hershey Bars, Huge	2.20
2	Butterfinger Bar, Stale	3.58
3	Jordan Almonds	3.03
4	Red Vines Licorice	2.15
5	Goo for Hot "Butter" machine	0.55
6	Raisinettes	1.93

Note that there is a black mark to the left of the Itemno. This indicates that the record has been deleted.

Caution: Xbase marks records for deletion as shown here. The record is not actually removed, it is marked as deleted but not actually removed from the table until a PACK command is issued. SQL does not work this way; do not count on it. Most database servers will actually remove the record when it is deleted.

19

Attaching Visual FoxPro to Database Servers

In Chapter 3 we talked about the advantages of data independence; now we will put the idea to work. Unfortunately, as we write this, the only 32-bit ODBC drivers are from Microsoft for its SQL Server version 6. Watcom and Oracle will be providing drivers soon, and other database server companies should be as well.

Since SQL is a sort-of standard, we can use the SQL Server as an example. We will try to maintain a high level of compatibility with other SQL database servers. In this chapter, we will discuss getting onto the database server, including both server permissions and database permissions.

Microsoft's SQL Server version 6

In the second quarter of 1995, Microsoft released version 6 of its SQL Server product. No, you didn't miss version 5, version 6 is an upgrade from version 4.21. It offers a number of enhancements and new features. Most important of these for this discussion are the Open Database Connectivity (ODBC) version 2.5 32-bit drivers.

ODBC, along with the new drivers, will be discussed with connecting Visual FoxPro. Before you can connect, you need to be set up to talk with the SQL Server and have the proper permissions.

Preparing Your Server

SQL Server runs on Microsoft's Windows NT server operating system. Microsoft recommends that the SQL Server machine be running version 3.51 of NT. We concur. Despite its fractional upgrade number, 3.51 is much improved over 3.50.

Getting Permissions on the NT Server

It is not necessary to have a user account on the NT server that is running SQL Server. One of the advantages to SQL is that it administers its own security. Since the SQL Server is using the services of its NT server, and you are not, you only require permissions for SQL Server.

This is a critical distinction for security reasons, so here's an example. Our NT server is called the workbench, and on it we are running an SQL server, also called the workbench. SQL Server names its process the same name as the computer name. On the workbench (the SQL Server), there is a database, which we create soon, called HiPriceSnacks.

Note: Remember that in SQL and Visual FoxPro parlance, a database is a collection of data tables.

The database or network administrator gets the workbench (the NT server) running and starts the SQL Server process (also called workbench). You have an account on workbench (the SQL Server) that lets you make changes to HiPriceSnacks. Even though these actions take place on the NT server, they are performed by the SQL Server. You are making requests to it and it is doing the actual reading and writing.

So, unless you—or your users—need access to the NT server workbench for some other purpose, such as file or print services, you should not have an account on it.

Getting Permissions on the SQL Server

Note: This discussion is for database administrators. If you are not an administrator for your SQL Server, you can skip it. You just need to ask your database administrator to give you the proper permissions.

All users who will be accessing data on the SQL Server need an account on it. The SQL Server will default to creating a system administrator account for all NT users who have Administrator permissions on that server. You should revoke these privileges; a system administrator can do virtually anything to your data and good security requires that only a limited number of users should have this power. You need at least one administrator and perhaps more, but the default of all server administrators can cause trouble.

Tip: Network and data security is far too big an issue to be addressed in this book, but we urge (if you are in a position of administering a network) that you work out a solid plan and review it frequently.

In Figure 19-1, you see the SQL Enterprise Manager. Enterprise Manager lets system administrators manage SQL Servers. With it you can add, delete, and configure users. You can also start and stop SQL Server processes, including ones on other NT Servers. In fact, you do not even need to run it on an NT Server; it can be run from a Windows 95 or Windows NT workstation. Since it is a 32-bit program, you cannot run it under Windows 3*x*.

Note: For the rest of this chapter when we refer to workbench we will mean the SQL Server, not the NT server. When we need to refer to the NT server we will say so specifically. Also, note that your SQL Server will be unlikely to be called the workbench. Where we refer to an action on workbench, substitute your SQL Server name.

Adding a User To add a user, click on the + sign next to WORKBENCH. Then click on the + next to Logins. Now press the right mouse button and select New Login. This takes you to the Manage Logins window. You can also access this using the Manage Logins icon button on the menu bar, third from the left next to the traffic light button. This is shown in Figure 19-1.

Enter the user name **john_doe** in the example. Tab down to the password field and enter a password; the password is not displayed.

Note: Each user should have a password.

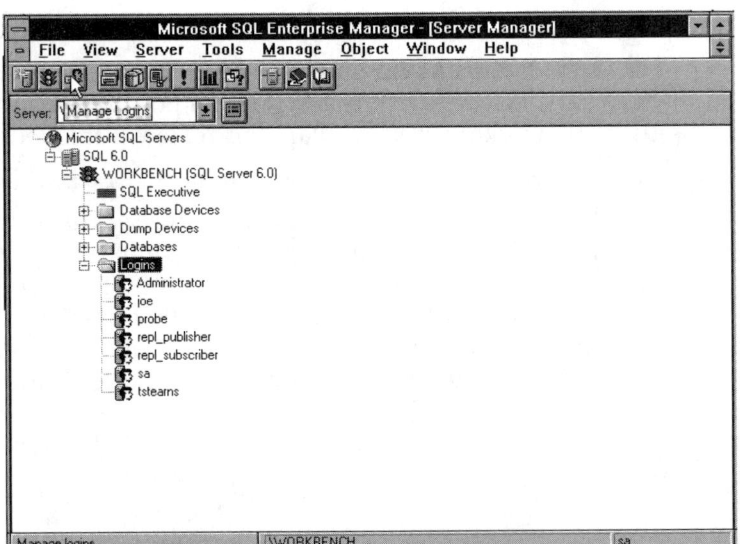

SQL Server Enterprise Manager
Figure 19-1.

In the Database access, click the permit column for the table "pubs." This is shown in Figure 19-2. Click on the Group column and select Users. Click the Modify button, then click the Close button.

On the Enterprise Manager screen you should now see john_doe under users.

Adding Users to a Group Each user on the SQL Server is a member of the Public group. It is wise then not to grant that group wide powers. What you should do is make different groups, each with the proper permissions for their tasks.

In the previous section, you put john_doe in the group Users for the database "pubs"—or you thought you did. Click the + next to Databases on the Enterprise Manager screen. Then click + next to pubs, click + next to Groups/Users, and, finally, click + next to Users.

Note: This is the group called "users." Not all users are members of the users group.

When you've done all this, you will not see john_doe, but you know you added him. This may be a small bug, but, in any case, you need to click the

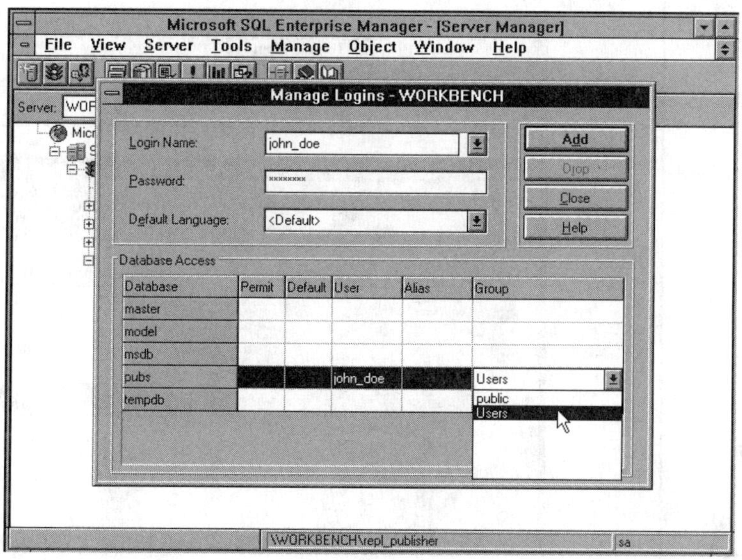

Adding john_doe
Figure 19-2.

right mouse button on Users and select Edit from the pop-up. When you do, you'll see a screen something like Figure 19-3.

Note that john_doe is already in the right column. To make this permanent, just click the Modify button, then click Close.

Tip: You must press the Modify button or the changes will not take place.

Underneath Users, you will now see john_doe.

Adding Permissions to a Group Now you need to give the group Users permission to access a table.

Note: We will be creating a database when we examine the Upsizing Wizard shortly. Since that table does not yet exist, we will be using the pubs database, a sample database included with SQL Server 6. We will show you how to grant permissions on this database, but we will only grant Select permission on one table.

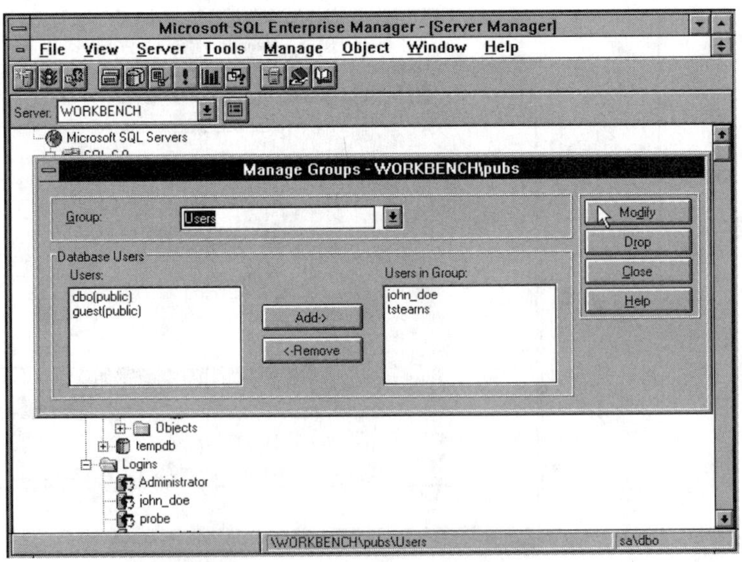

Managing group membership
Figure 19-3.

Highlight Users, that is, the group Users, right below Public. Click the right mouse button and select Permissions from the pop-up menu. From Groups/Users select the group Users.

From the grid below Users, click the Select check box for the table Authors. Click the Grant button.

Note: Of the other permissions, some should be familiar: Insert, Update, and Delete. These are commands that act on table rows. Execute is for stored procedures and DRI is Declarative Referential Integrity.

Click the Close button to finish this task.

Preparing Your Workstation

This consists of little more than making sure that your workstation can talk to the NT server that is running the SQL Server and making sure that your workstation has the latest network upgrades.

Important Note to Windows for Workgroups Users

A word of warning: If you are using Microsoft Windows for Workgroups version 3.11 on your workstation, or your users are, you need to upgrade some files. Your NT server CD should have a directory called clients. Under it is a subdirectory called wfw. Here, there are several files. These files need to go into the windows subdirectory and the system subdirectory. Here are the files from our Windows NT 3.51 server disk and where they need to go:

In your windows directory (typically c:\windows):

```
NET.EXE
NET.MSG
```

In your system subdirectory (typically c:\windows\system):

```
NDIS.386
NETAPI.DLL
NWNBLINK.386
VNETSUP.386
VREDIR.386
VSERVER.386
```

Our system includes a Novell Netware server, and we were unable to get a successful connection from SQL Server to our NT Server until we upgraded these files.

Connecting Visual FoxPro to Your Server

The remainder of this chapter will deal with connecting to the SQL Server using ODBC drivers and running the Upsizing Wizard that Visual FoxPro Professional Edition comes with.

Installing Client Utilities and ODBC Drivers

If you want to be able to use the interactive SQL program that comes with the SQL Server, you need to install the client utilities.

16-Bit

If you are running 16-bit Windows, version 3.*x*, then you install the utilities from the SQL Server CD in the clients directory, win16 subdirectory. Run the setup program located here.

To install the ODBC drivers, descend into the ODBC directory and run the setup program there.

32-Bit

Windows NT or Windows 95 users run the setup program located in the i386 directory of the SQL Server CD. When you get to the screen that lets you choose what to do, select Install Utilities Only.

When you have done that, you can install the ODBC drivers by going into the ODBC subdirectory and running setup there.

Open Database Connectivity

Open Database Connectivity is Microsoft's standard to allow programs to write to disparate database servers while using a common interface. Visual FoxPro uses ODBC version 2.5 32-bit drivers. To configure the SQL Server ODBC driver, select the ODBC Administrator icon. There is one in the Visual FoxPro folder. The following illustration shows approximately what you'll see (some drivers may be different).

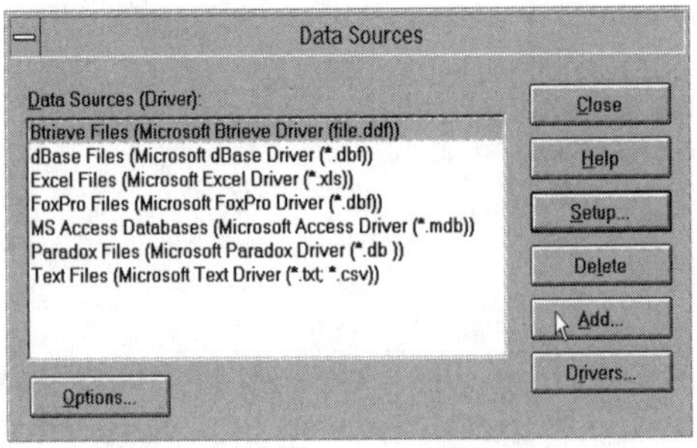

Select the Add button. This brings up a list of installed drivers. At, or near, the bottom should be SQL Server, as seen here:

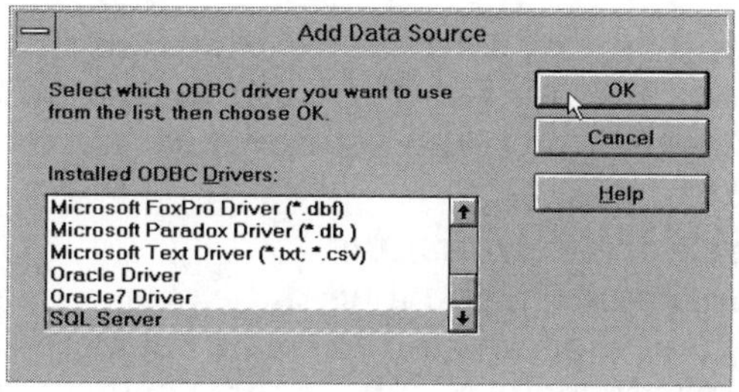

Select it and click the OK button and the Configuration dialog box comes up. Give the data source a name; we've called ours SQL6. Enter a description of this source in the description box.

In the Server field you may not be able to see your server, depending on the security setup. If you cannot, just type in the name here. Figure 19-4 shows what our filled-in dialog box looks like.

Click OK and that will complete your ODBC setup.

SQL Server Upsizing Wizard

The Professional Edition of Visual FoxPro comes with a wizard to make converting FoxPro format data to SQL Server fairly easy. This process is called upsizing. The term originates with downsizing, which is the process of moving data off of mainframes and bigger minis to small minis or PCs. The anti-downsizing crowd coined upsizing to mean moving data to more powerful platforms.

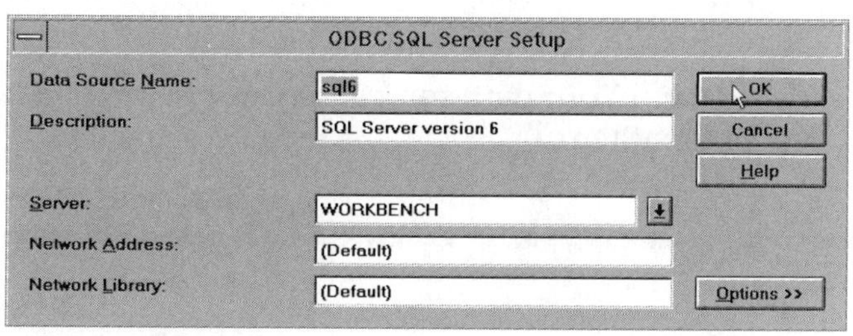

Naming the data source
Figure 19-4.

The jargoneers then coined right-sizing, which is the process of figuring whether the future is up or down. All of this terminology can be safely ignored; just remember that upsizing is what Microsoft calls their wizard.

We will use the database we created in Chapter 10, HiPrice. If you haven't created this, it is OK. The Upsizing Wizard makes it easy enough that you can follow along with your own database.

Necessary Permissions

Before you start, you'll need the proper permissions on your SQL Server. You'll need permission to create databases. Normally, this permission rests with the sa login. You have three choices. First, you can get the system administrator to run the Upsizing Wizard for you. Second, you can get your system administrator to give you, however temporarily, create database permission. Lastly, if you are a system administrator, you can log in under that username and run the wizard.

Running the Upsizing Wizard

From the menu bar select Tools. Click on Wizards and select Upsizing, near the bottom. The opening screen looks like this:

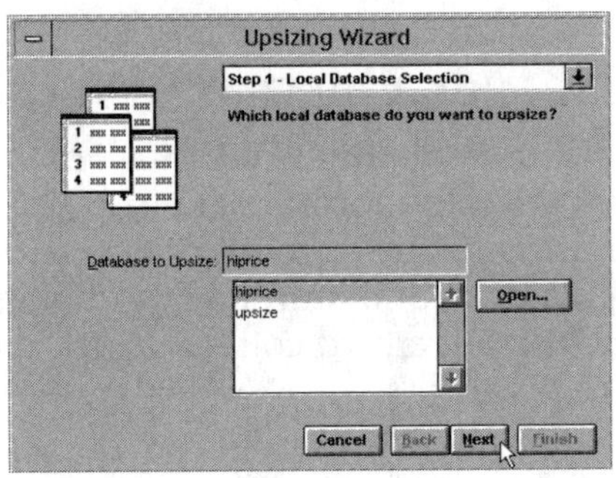

If HiPrice is not selected, select it and click Next. The second step asks for the data source. Select ODBC data sources and SQL6.

Note: Your data source may not be named SQL6; use whatever name is on your system.

The screen looks like this:

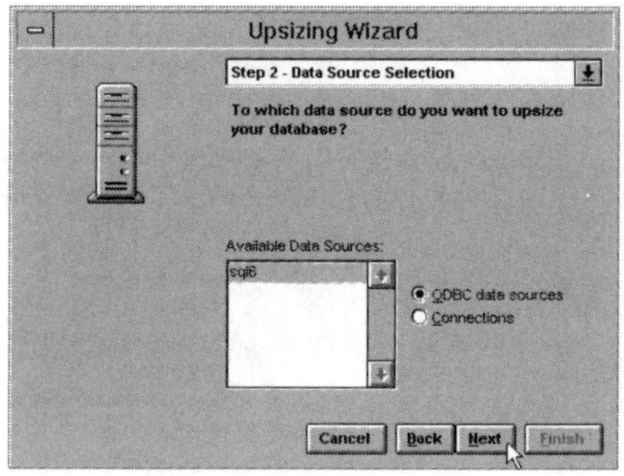

Select Next and you see Step three. Here you are asked for login information. Here is where you need a user with the proper permissions. Use sa, or a login that has administrator privileges, as shown here:

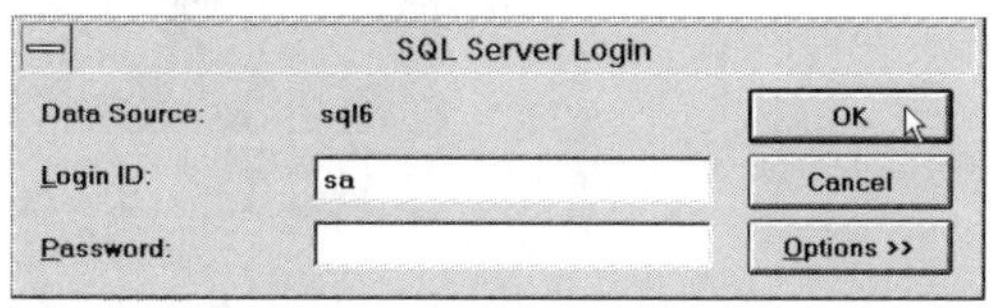

Step three asks you to name the database; we have elected to create a new database. You do this by selecting the New button and entering the new name, as shown here:

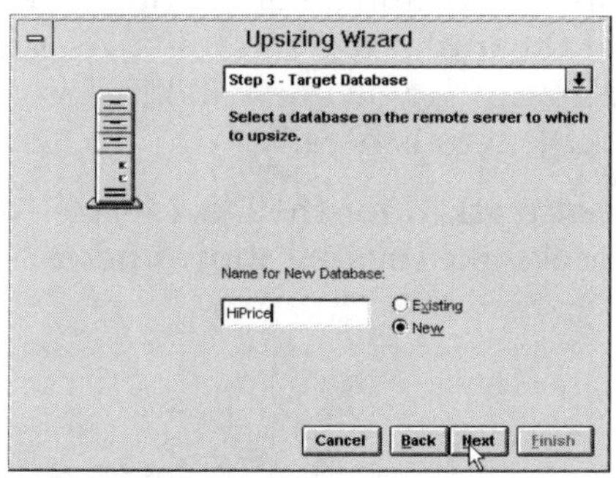

You can also choose to add the tables to the existing Master database or another existing database. Selecting Next again takes you to the Database Device step. You will be putting the HiPrice database on its own device.

Hitting the drop-down button on Database Device lets you choose <Create New Device>, as shown here:

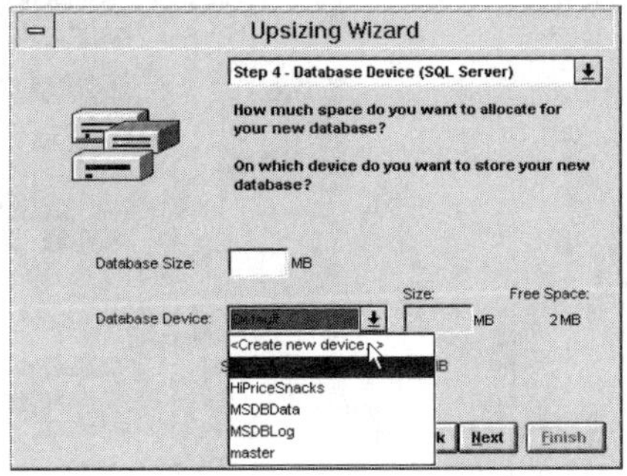

Once you've selected the new device option, the Upsizing Wizard prompts you for the new device name. Enter **HiPriceSnacks**, as shown here:

Now you need to specify the Database Size and the Device Size. SQL Server allocates space for a database in advance. This is partly for speed and partly to make sure that your database has the size it will need by taking it now.

You can resize a database once it has been created, but this is time-consuming and a perfect opportunity for data corruption. You should consider the initial size carefully. We selected 25 megabytes for the Database Size arbitrarily. If you are installing on a working SQL Server, you will want to be less generous here.

You are also asked for the Device Size. We chose 50 megabytes, and our screen looks like the one shown here:

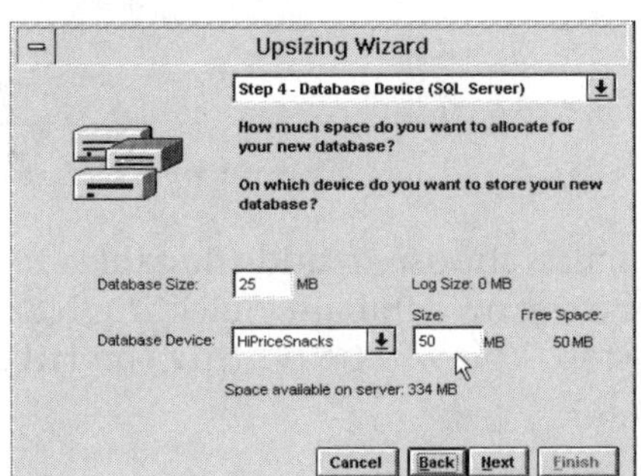

Step five asks for the size and location of the transaction log. This log is used to recover from incomplete updates and as a method to update external backups. Be generous; select 10 megabytes, and select the newly created HiPriceSnacks device to store it on, as shown here:

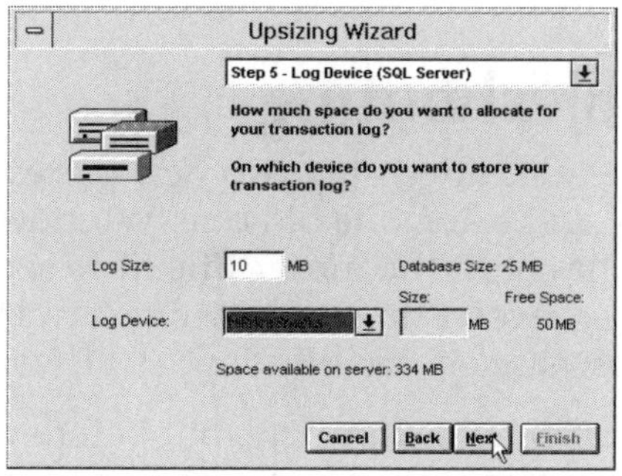

Step six asks for the tables to include in this upsizing. Select them all by clicking the double right arrow button.

Step seven shows you how the Wizard is going to convert your FoxPro data to SQL data. Field types and lengths are shown in Figure 19-5.

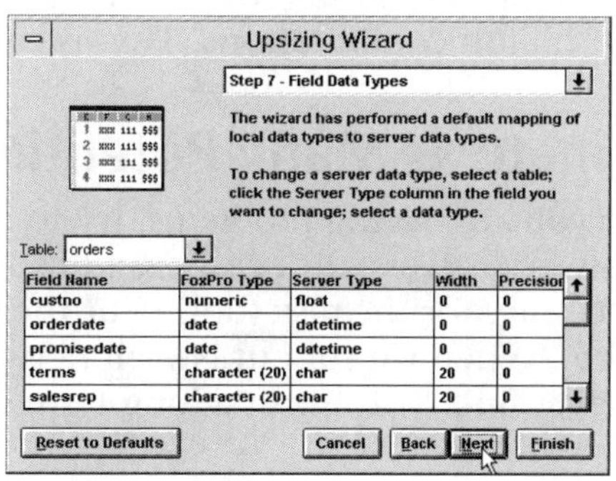

Converting field types

Figure 19-5.

Of particular interest is the Reset to Defaults button in the lower left corner. If you get to changing them around, this can be a real help.

Step eight selects the upsizing options. Accept the defaults and hit the Next button. You are now at the finish. Hit the Finish button and the Upsizing Wizard will complete its work (it may take a few minutes).

Troubleshooting

We have been discussing two new pieces of software, Visual FoxPro and SQL Server 6, and using one old one, Windows for Workgroups version 3.11. This chapter has been the most difficult to set up of all. In our case the problems seemed to revolve around having Netware client and Windows network client software on our Windows 3.11 workstation.

We will offer a few tips here, but before we do, a word about problems. It is easy and tempting to blame someone for our troubles. Since Microsoft made all the software here, maybe we should blame them. There are two problems with this. First, it is only cathartic; that is, you may feel better, but you are no closer to the solution. And second, they probably don't deserve it.

Today's computers are hugely complex. We have networks, operating systems, protocols, transports, and so on. Each of these adds complexity geometrically. For example, we were installing Quarterdeck's QEMM on our Windows for Workgroups machine a few days ago. QEMM has an Optimize feature that will take all of your DOS drivers, such as networks and disk caches, and try to fit them in high memory for maximum DOS memory. It will try all of the possible ways to load these drivers. On our machine there were 41 billion combinations. That is complex.

Eliminate as Many Potential Conflicts as Possible

First, if you are having problems, try to get a minimum configuration going. Cut network drivers, disk caches, and so forth. Obviously, only cut the ones not necessary for the task (don't cut the connection to your NT server, for instance). When we cut out Novell network drivers, we could connect to SQL Server fine. This is not a long-term solution, but it may help point the way to a solution.

Roll the Dice

Think back to the 41 billion and try loading drivers in a different order. Also, load just the Windows software necessary, Visual FoxPro and Windows network software. We were able to get a session to work by reloading Windows and reopening programs in a different order.

If you've cut the fat and are now loading drivers and find one that seems to cause a problem, but doesn't seem related to the problem, try loading it in a different place. If it is a Windows program, try loading it after you've got the Visual FoxPro connection up and running.

Call for Help

Microsoft support is expensive for the SQL Server, $150 per call as this is written. It may seem unwise to go to your manager and tell her or him you need to make a $150 phone call, but we urge you to. These sorts of troubles are often seen as you get close to completion; you think that with one more try, it will work. This idea is a black hole for time. You can easily spend 2-3 days working on a problem that is "almost fixed." We did.

Also, these problems are often common. That $150 call may present you with a quick solution like the one mentioned in "Important Note to Windows for Workgroups Users." The support person at Microsoft had this problem in the tech support database and was able to give us a quick answer.

There is also free, or almost free, help available on CompuServe and other online services. SQL Server comes with a nice collection of online books, as does Windows NT. These come with a search engine to let you look for a word, or set of words, in the entire manual set.

20

Views, Queries, and Cursors

In this chapter, you will examine alternative ways of handling data in Visual FoxPro. Queries allow you to see only the data that is relevant. You might, for example, want to send a mailing to all your customers in Kansas. You already have a label form created that reads customer data and prints labels. You can use a query to treat the customer data as if only customers in Kansas existed; thus labels for only them are printed.

Views are like queries except that where queries are read-only, a view can update data. A cursor is a tool to make disparate data appear as a single table. This allows processing a cursor in a row-by-row manner.

We will again be using the data in the HiPrice Snacks example first discussed in Chapter 10.

Views

A view is an SQL statement that you give a name and can reuse. Views can be local or remote. A local view is one using data in Visual FoxPro database, or DBF format, even if the file is located on a server. A remote view is from an ODBC data source such as the SQL Server discussed in Chapter 19.

Note: Xbase has a view as well, so in Visual FoxPro you will use SQL View to specify that you want the kind of view discussed here. In Xbase, a view is a way to store the data environment for reuse.

The result of a view is like any Visual FoxPro table; you can SKIP, INDEX ON, or BROWSE just as if it were a DBF file. These views allow you to use Xbase commands to manipulate data on database servers that do not support Xbase commands. This may not be good for performance reasons, and we will not be emphasizing this trick.

Single Table (Local) View

Caution: If you ran the Upsizing Wizard from the previous chapter, you need to be sure to reselect the HiPrice project and the HiPrice database.

The simplest view is one from local data that only uses one table. In Chapter 18 you used this simple command

```
select * from customer
```

to see all of the fields of the Customer table. To make this into a view, your command will be

```
create SQL view cust1 as select * from customer
```

Note that the part after "as" is the same as the previous command. cust1 is the name of your view and "create SQL view" is the Visual FoxPro command. Type this command in the Command window.

The first thing you are likely to notice is that no window pops up with the results as it does with the plain select command. What you have created is a definition; to put it to work, type this command:

```
use cust1
```


Still no display, but this looks suspiciously like an Xbase command. It is. The USE command opens a table, and a view is, in a sense, a table. You can do the standard Xbase things; give it an alias, index it, replace field values.

To see your view, type

```
browse
```

This is again an Xbase command; it displays the view in tabular format. Figure 20-1 shows this display.

Browsing the cust1 view
Figure 20-1.

A view is simply another way of organizing your data. In this single-table form, it is often a waste of energy, but next you will examine multitable views and these can be powerful and make your work easier.

Multitable Views

A single-table view such as the one you just did is a bit of overkill, but when you start relating data and filtering it, this is when the value of views begins to be realized. An SQL statement can do a lot of work in a single command. With Visual FoxPro, you can work up the statement from the Command window and then put it into a view when you have perfected it. By storing statements into a view, you can avoid the tedium of typing them out, not to mention the possibility of typos.

There is another, powerful, reason to use views. Recall that in Chapter 3 you read that Visual FoxPro would let you prototype your application on local data and translate it easily to a database server. Here is where you get to do it.

Recall also that in Chapter 18 we said that the result of a SQL statement is a flat file—that is, rows and columns. Even when you have a multitable statement such as

```
select o.orderdate, l.itemno, l.qtyordered;
from orders o, ordlines l;
where o.orderno = l.orderno
```

what you get back is a table with three columns and several rows. Since orderdate applies to a whole order, each line item of an order has the same date, like this:

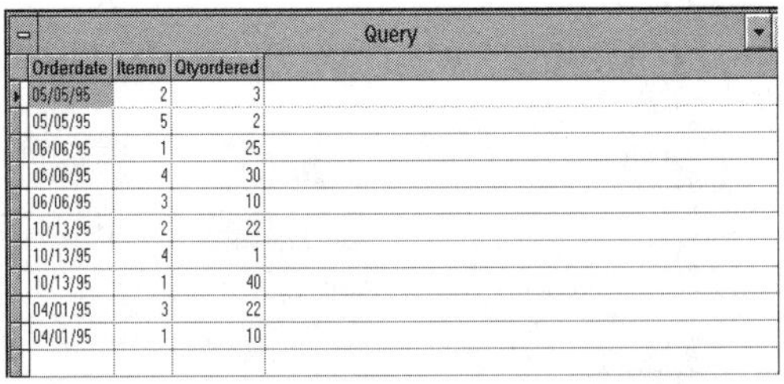

Query

Orderdate	Itemno	Qtyordered
05/05/95	2	3
05/05/95	5	2
06/06/95	1	25
06/06/95	4	30
06/06/95	3	10
10/13/95	2	22
10/13/95	4	1
10/13/95	1	40
04/01/95	3	22
04/01/95	1	10

You don't want to design a table this way, with duplicated information, as discussed in Chapter 14. The reason that a discussion of normalization has to take place, though, is that it is a natural way to think. Multitable SQL statements let you see data in the more natural, unnormalized, form without sacrificing the advantages that the relational model offers.

Multitable views allow you to work with data from a collection of sources, even other views, as if it were all one. To illustrate this combination, you will use the view you just created, cust1, and the SQL statement in the previous example to create a new view, combo1.

1. To be sure you are working with the proper data, enter these two commands:

   ```
   close database
   open database hiprice
   ```

   This ensures that no previous experiments will foul the results.
2. Enter this statement in the Command window:

   ```
   create SQL view combo1 as select c.name,;
   o.orderdate, l.itemno, l.qtyordered;
   from cust1 c, orders o, ordlines l;
   where o.orderno = l.orderno and;
   c.custno = o.custno
   ```
3. Use the view:

   ```
   use combo1
   ```
4. Display the result by typing

   ```
   browse
   ```

The resulting screen looks like this:

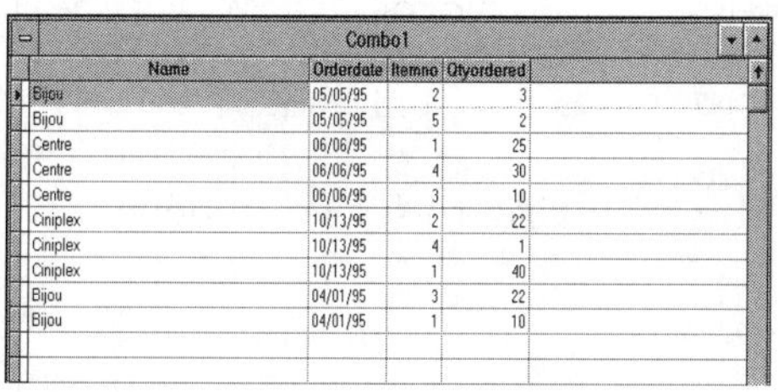

Combo1

Name	Orderdate	Itemno	Qtyordered
Bijou	05/05/95	2	3
Bijou	05/05/95	5	2
Centre	06/06/95	1	25
Centre	06/06/95	4	30
Centre	06/06/95	3	10
Ciniplex	10/13/95	2	22
Ciniplex	10/13/95	4	1
Ciniplex	10/13/95	1	40
Bijou	04/01/95	3	22
Bijou	04/01/95	1	10

It bears repeated emphasis that a view is its own creature, it is not the same as a bunch of relationships in Xbase. When you used the cust1 view in combo1 you saw the customer name appear in the new view. This was perhaps uninspiring. After all, cust1 was just a view of the Customer table. You could just as easily have gone to the Customer table in combo1 directly.

You notice that, uh-oh, you forgot to add the item description. Using an SQL select statement, this will get big. It will look like this:

Note: you do not need to type the following; it is merely a demonstration of the power views offer.

```
select c.name, o.orderdate,;
l.itemno, l.qtyordered, i.itemdesc;
from cust1 c, orders o, ordlines l,
items i;
where o.orderno = l.orderno and;
c.custno = o.custno and;
i.itemno = l.itemno
```

If you wanted to make it a view, and that is the point, you'd add

```
create SQL view uhoh as
```

to the front of the statement.

This statement looks a lot like the one you used to create combo1. This is where views become very handy. Instead of having to type the ungainly statement above, you can use a shortcut. Type this command in the Command window:

```
create SQL view combo2 as;
select c1.name, c1.orderdate,;
c1.itemno, c1.qtyordered, i.itemdesc;
from combo1 c1, items i;
where c1.itemno = i.itemno
```

Type the following to see your view:

```
use combo2
browse
```

The result looks like that shown in Figure 20-2.

Still a bit of typing, but a lot easier and less prone to error since the logic of 3/4ths of it has already been tested.

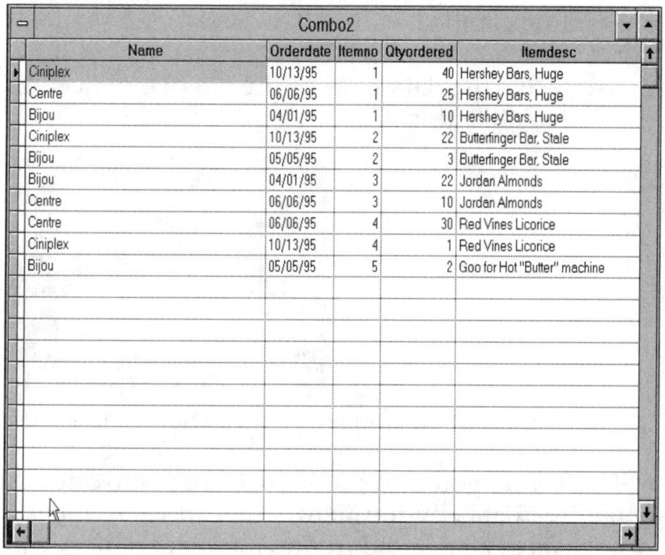

Combo2

Name	Orderdate	Itemno	Qtyordered	Itemdesc
Ciniplex	10/13/95	1	40	Hershey Bars, Huge
Centre	06/06/95	1	25	Hershey Bars, Huge
Bijou	04/01/95	1	10	Hershey Bars, Huge
Ciniplex	10/13/95	2	22	Butterfinger Bar, Stale
Bijou	05/05/95	2	3	Butterfinger Bar, Stale
Bijou	04/01/95	3	22	Jordan Almonds
Centre	06/06/95	3	10	Jordan Almonds
Centre	06/06/95	4	30	Red Vines Licorice
Ciniplex	10/13/95	4	1	Red Vines Licorice
Bijou	05/05/95	5	2	Goo for Hot "Butter" machine

View using another view
Figure 20-2.

Note: The combo1 view is expressed as c1 in this view. You can use c for this, but doing so will cause trouble when you get to the View Designer next.

View Designer

Note: We've broken from our pattern in this chapter. Previously, we have used a wizard first and modified its result to suit. In this chapter, you will go from the most manual, the commands you have entered, through the builder/designer to the wizard. We take this approach because SQL is such a powerful and useful tool and Visual FoxPro hides it too well. Using Visual FoxPro's visual tools, you can almost entirely avoid any SQL. This is powerful and we do not mean to imply anything like "real programmers work from the command line." Rather, we are just trying to demystify SQL by showing a little of it at work.

View Designer gives you a graphical way to design and maintain views. First, examine combo2 in the View Designer.

1. Select the data page of the HiPrice project. Expand as needed to make it look like this:

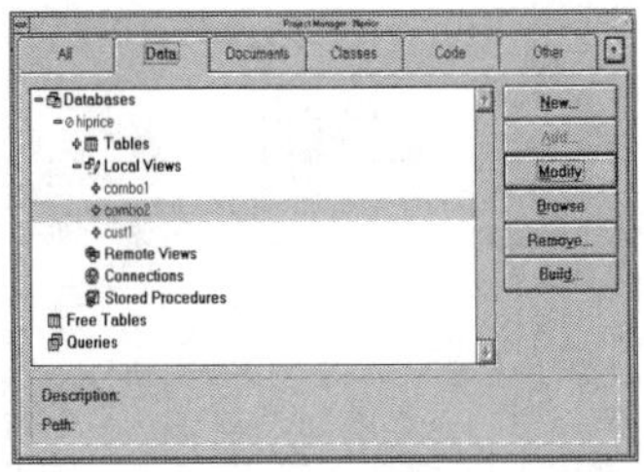

2. Highlight combo2 and click the Modify button.

This brings you into the View Designer. Notice that on top you see the familiar data environment. You can see that cust1, your first combo view, appears as a table did in previous experiences with tool. So here it is again—a view is a table from Visual FoxPro's perspective.

Notice that, even though c1 is a compilation of data from two tables and another view, c1 is treated as a unit and only the fields specified in the creation of the current view, combo2, are shown. For instance, CustNo is not a choice; it wasn't included in the view, even though you use it to relate the order information with the customer information.

In the lower half of the View Designer, shown in Figure 20-3, you see that the only relation that combo2 seems to know about is the one that relates c1 into the items table.

On this Selection Criteria page you can set the rules that join the tables and views. The join criteria can be any of the logical operators discussed in Chapter 18. In the previous example, the code that did this was

```
where c1.itemno = i.itemno
```

This is translated almost exactly in the Selection Criteria as c1.itemno equals i.itemno. Visual FoxPro's Designer lets you create this in a more forgiving environment.

Turning now to the Fields page of View Designer, you can see the fields available to your view. Notice again that only the fields in c1 are available, not the fields of its constituent tables. In Figure 20-4, you can see the dropped-down menu for Functions and Expressions.

SQL has a rich set of functions for analyzing data. Some of them are shown here.

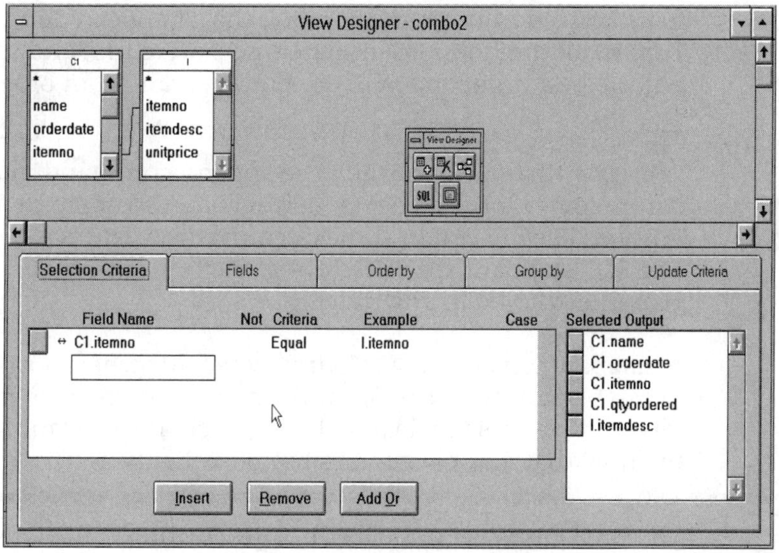

View Designer for combo2
Figure 20-3.

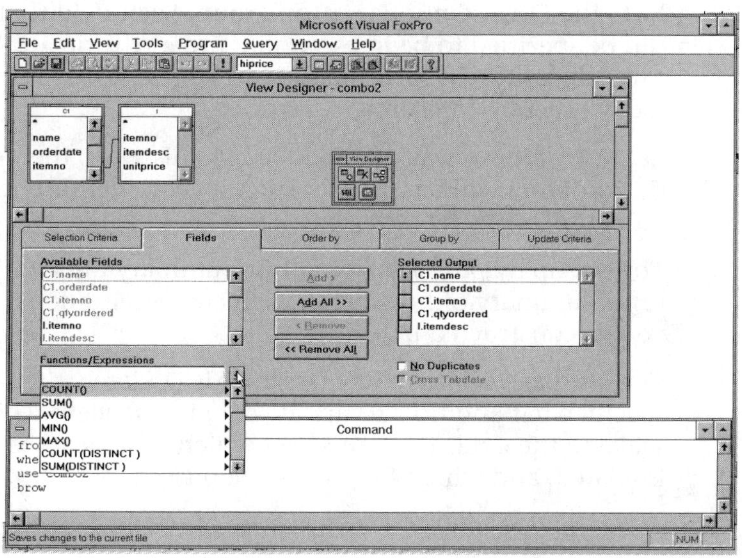

Fields page showing Functions/ Expressions menu
Figure 20-4.

The Order by page is where you can set how the data will appear. You might have noticed in browsing combo2 that it appeared in the order of itemno. That is, all the lines ordering itemno 1 were first and so on. This is probably not the best order and SQL does not guarantee an order on unordered data.

Tip: Xbase, when using the append command, puts records in chronological order. That is, new records are appended to the end of the file. This has been useful in some circumstances and has become relied upon. The SQL standard specifically says that the "raw order" of the data is not guaranteed to be in any order.

A database server is free to put new records wherever. There may be space in the beginning of the file and a new record may go there. Most database servers have tools to deal with this, such as timestamp fields, but you need to know that you have to use them explicitly.

You probably want this data displayed by order, all items in an order together. You could use orderno for this, except that orderno was not included in the view c1. Even though it is used to join the orders and ordlines tables in the view, it is not included in the fields and so you can't use it.

Here, you will select c1.name and c1.orderdate to order by. Select c1.name and click the Add button. Then select c1.orderdate and do the same, as shown in Figure 20-5.

Note the Order Options button group. Each field that you choose to order by can be specified to be in ascending order (the default) or descending order. Ascending order is from smallest to largest; for example, 1 is before 2 and today is before tomorrow.

Because orderno was not included in this view, there is no guarantee that this ordering will be by order since a customer might have placed two or more orders on the same day.

The Group by page lets you set up summary queries. You might want to see just a summary of how much each customer ordered rather than the detail you've constructed here.

The last page on this View Designer is Update Criteria. Here is where you can specify what and how to update data in the view. This is for changes you make to the data. You can select which tables can be updated, how the data is related, and which fields can be updated.

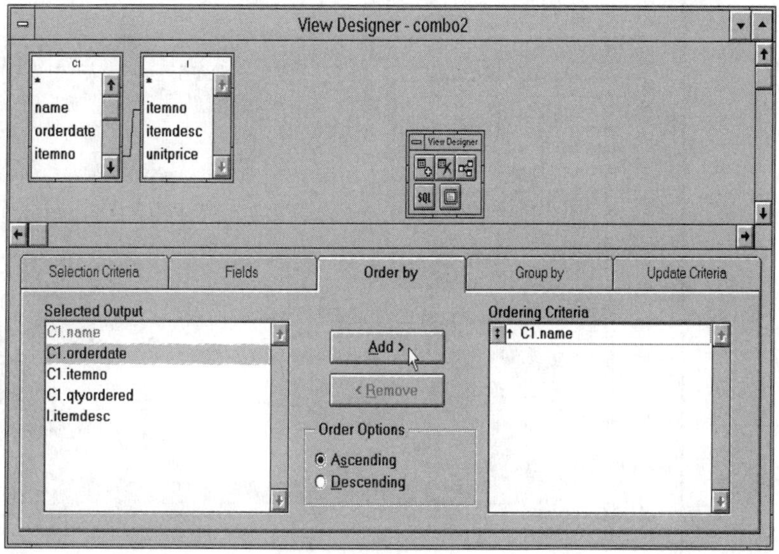

Ordering the view
Figure 20-5.

Note that since most of this view consists of another view, combo1, you will need to modify combo1 as well for updating its fields.

The last sight on this tour of View Designer is Update using, seen in Figure 20-6. Here is where you tell Visual FoxPro how to update the data. You can choose to delete the record that has been changed and then create a new record with the changed data. The default, using the SQL update command, is the recommended normal way, but on some servers you may need to use the delete and insert combination.

Using SELECT on a View

A view is a table, in most ways. You can issue SQL commands against it as though it were a defined table. To demonstrate this do the following.

1. Close the View Designer if it is still open.
2. From the Command window, type the following:

```
select * from combo2;
where qtyordered > 10
```

This will produce a Query window, just as the SQL statements in Chapter 18 did.

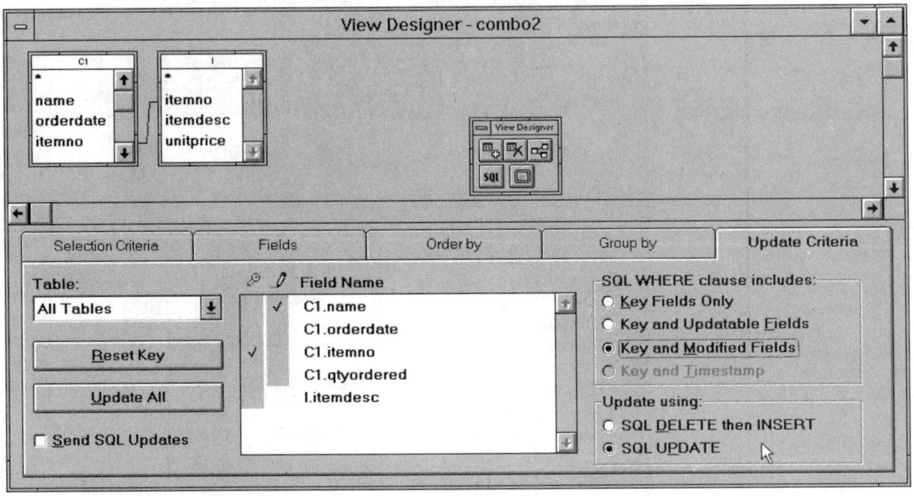

Controlling updates
Figure 20-6.

Tip: We had a problem after exiting the View Designer. We found it necessary to remake the view before the previous command worked properly. If you created the view in your current Visual FoxPro session, you can scroll up to where you made it first and hit the ENTER key.

Using Xbase Commands on a View

Standard Xbase data manipulation language commands will work on a view. Skip, index on, go top, and so forth all do the expected things. Beware the performance penalties that may accrue to using these though. It is easy to fall into the trap, when using local data and/or small sets of data, of using low performance commands.

Before you release a program for general use, you should always test its performance under realistic circumstances—that is, across the network and using a representative number of records.

Remote Views

A remote view is one that uses data from an ODBC data source, like the SQL Server you used in Chapter 19. If you are not going to be running a database server, you can safely skip this section. Here, you will use the Remote View

Wizard. Since, at this writing, SQL Server has the only ODBC 2.5 driver, we will again be using it as an example. The example is applicable to all database servers.

1. Select Tools from Visual FoxPro's menu bar.
2. Select Wizards from this menu.
3. You will not see a View Wizard listed, so click on the All menu selection. This brings up a dialog box with all the wizards listed.
4. Scroll down to Remote View Wizard as seen here:

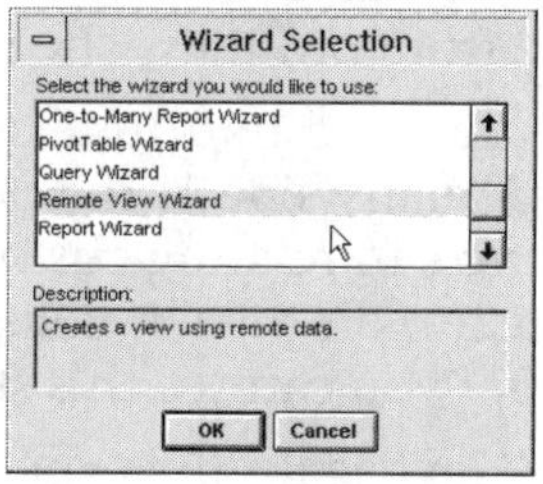

   Click the OK button.

5. The first step in this wizard is selecting your data source. Here, you select the name you gave your SQL Server in the ODBC Administrator. We called ours SQL6, and selecting it looks like the screen shown in Figure 20-7.

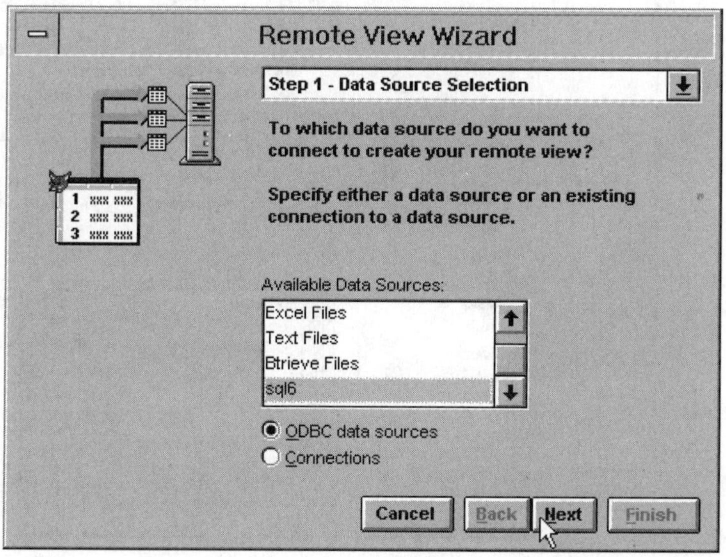

Selecting the remote data source

Figure 20-7.

Note: Your choice of data sources may not be the same as ours, depending on what drivers you have previously installed.

You are asked to give a login name for SQL Server. Enter a valid name and password.

6. Click the Next button and you see the field choice screen. You can select fields from more than one table. Select the name field from customer, itemdesc from items, orderdate from orders, qtyordered and unitprice from ordlines. The finished screen is shown in Figure 20-8.
7. Clicking the Next button takes you into the Relationship step. You have to put the many side of the one-to-many relationship on the left side. For instance, in relating customer and orders, you would put orders.custno on the left column and customer.custno on the right. In Figure 20-9 you can see this step completed.
8. Clicking Next again puts you into the Order by step. For this sample, you will just order by customer.name. Highlight this entry and click the Add button.
9. The next step is to select filter conditions. This lets you see only a subset of records. There is no need to select a filter so click Next again.

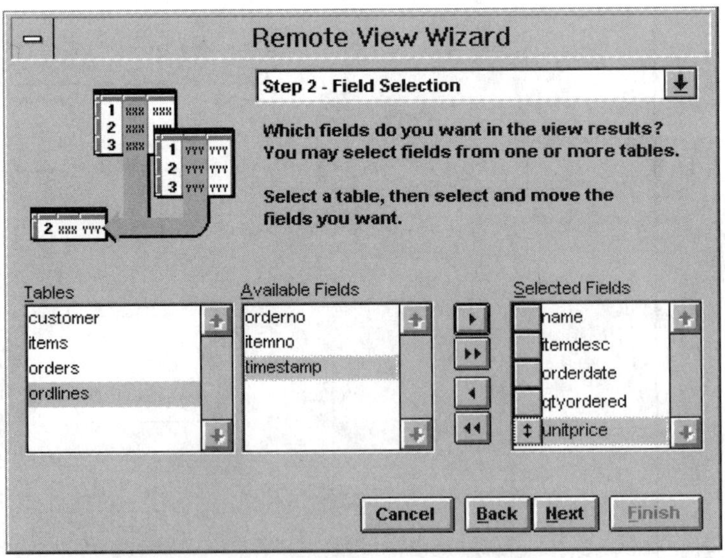

Selecting fields for the view
Figure 20-8.

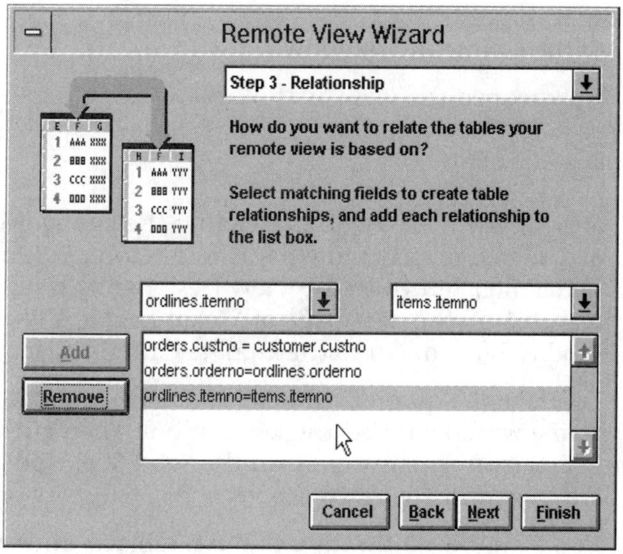

Setting relationships for your view

Figure 20-9.

10. The finish screen is now shown. Click on the Finish button.
11. You are now prompted to name your remote view. Call it **remote1** and click the OK button, and you are again prompted for a SQL Server login.

Once you have successfully logged in, Visual FoxPro will make your remote view.

To see your new view in action type this in the Command window:

```
use remote1
browse
```

And there it is. Now, how to update the records? For demonstration, you can use the Xbase replace command. Click the ESC button to exit the view. Type the following:

```
replace qtyordered with 1
```

This command will put the value, 1, into the qtyordered field of the first record. Start another browse and use the TAB key to move over to the qtyordered column and there is the value of 1.

Now close the browse and the view by clicking ESC again and typing

```
use
```

in the Command window.

Now reopen the view by typing

```
use remote1
```

and browse it. You will notice that the change you made is not there. The qtyordered reverted to what it was before. You need to make the view updatable. Return to the View Designer by highlighting the remote view remote1 on the data page of Visual FoxPro's Project Manager. Click the Modify button. Go to the Update Criteria page.

To make the qtyordered field updatable, click to the left of it in the Field Name window under the key symbol. Then click the same field under the Pencil icon. Finally, click on the Send SQL Updates check box. The changes are shown in Figure 20-10.

You can now go through the use, replace, and browse cycle again to verify that the updates are taking place.

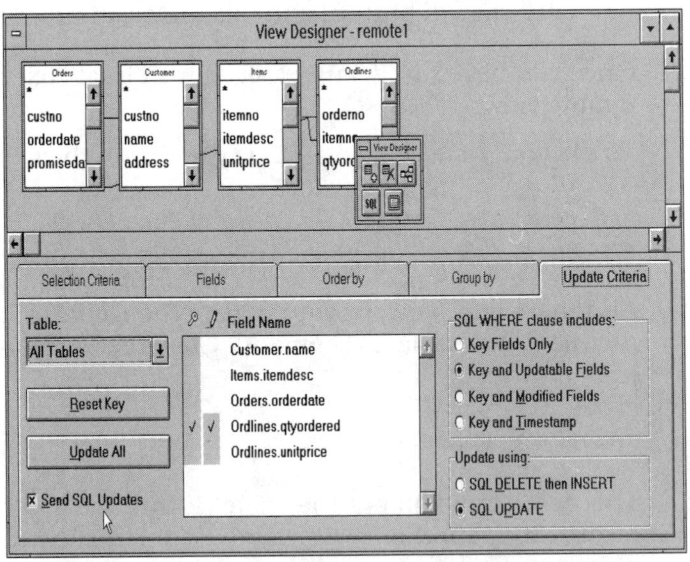

Making qtyordered updatable

Figure 20-10.

Queries

A query is identical to a view, except in this respect: a view can be made updatable (that is, you can modify data in a view), but you cannot update a query. Visual FoxPro gives you a set of options for directing the results of a query. In this chapter, you have been looking at the data through a browse window. With the Query window, you can send the data to a report or a form or a cursor.

As with a view a query is a named relationship stored in the database. By giving it a name, you can call it anytime you need it. Do not confuse a query, a named entity, with a query as in Structured Query Language. The command

```
select * from customer
```

is a query in the second sense. A command like this

```
create query myquery as;
select * from customer
```

is a query in the first sense.

Cursors

This is another confusing term, since there are mouse cursors, I-beam cursors, and so forth that apply to input devices. SQL has a cursor and it has no relationship to the more familiar cursors.

You've already heard that a view is a table—that is, a flat file. You also learned that a query is a read-only view. Neither is required to be an actual file, just to act like one. A cursor is a file; it is given a temporary filename and exists until the view or query that creates it is closed.

Performance issues

You can control how Visual FoxPro uses data by setting the properties of the view or cursor. A good example is row buffering. If you have a large dataset you can wait quite a while for data to be found on the database server and sent back to you. Many times you will be dealing with this data in smaller chunks, such as a browse listing. By instructing Visual FoxPro, through the dbsetprop and cursorsetprop functions, you can have it return your results before it has completed its assembly.

This gives the impression of performance, and your users will like it. There are a number of settings on these commands, and you should review them in the User's Guide.

Finally, on this subject, we again urge you to try your program on live or large datasets. It is easy to get lulled into thinking that your program goes smoothly, when it will choke up on the network when users get hold of it. This is especially so when using database servers because their own complexity can cause them to be poorly tuned for the purpose.

21

Validation, Triggers, and Referential Integrity

In this chapter, we will discuss how validation has changed from a being a part of your program to being a part of your database. Two tools new to Xbase, triggers and referential integrity, add to Visual FoxPro's data-handling capabilities.

These three techniques will help you keep the data in your database clean. We examine each and cover some of the applications and implications.

Data Validation

Validation is the process that you use to determine that an entry is valid. For instance, in an order line-item table such as ordlines from the HiPrice Snacks example, you would not want a quantity ordered of less than one. Actually you might, but for the example, the rule is no orders for negative amounts or zero. First, the way it used to be.

The Xbase Way

dBASE III marked the real entry of dBASE into the PC field. dBASE II was a port from CP/M, and there was no dBASE I (an early example of version inflation). In order for a program to verify that valid values had been selected by the user, you had to wait until the values were all entered and then examine each one for validity and display an error message as necessary.

One of the main features of the original Foxbase and Clipper products was the validation clause. This allowed your programs to check a value as it was being entered. Using validation, you could have the program immediately inform the user that a value was bad before data entry went any further.

This was a major improvement, but it still meant that every part of the program that touched a given value needed a separate validation clause, and if the criteria were changed then all the validations needed to be too. The next step in the Xbase world is here now: data dictionaries. This term encompasses the idea that you should define validation at the level of the table and let it do the validating for you.

The Database Server Way

Database servers have been moving along in the direction of a data dictionary—that is, a set of rules that control how information is stored and validated. With this release of Visual FoxPro, data dictionaries are brought to the Xbase arena. This gives your programs new tools that will make creating and administering a system much easier.

To demonstrate, highlight the ordlines table in the HiPrice project. Click the Modify button and move the cursor down to the qtyordered line, as seen in Figure 21-1.

On the lower left of the Table Designer, you see four fields: Validation Rule, Validation Text, Default Value, and Caption.

Validation Rule is a logical expression—that is, one that is either true or false. A true response from the rule will allow the value to be entered. A false

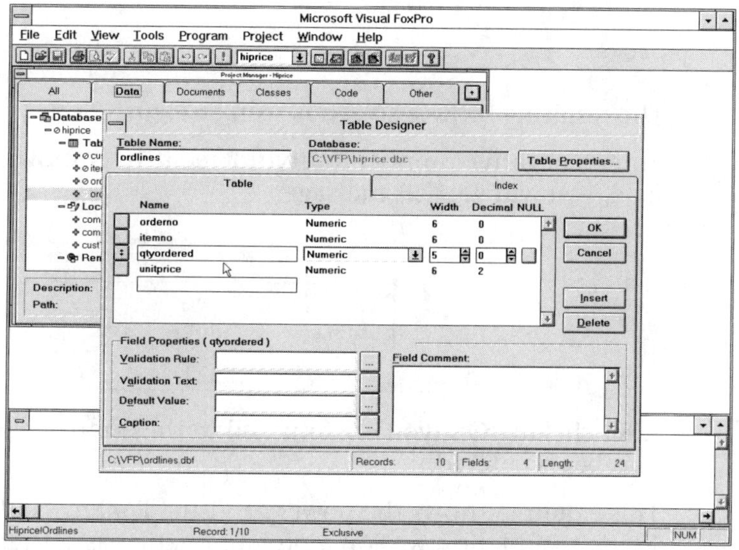

Selecting qtyordered

Figure 21-1.

result from the expression will display a warning with the text in Validation Text and not allow the value to remain.

Enter this rule in the Validation Rule of qtyordered:

```
qtyordered > 0
```

Put a message like this in Validation Text:

```
"Value must be one or more."
```

The two fields should look like this:

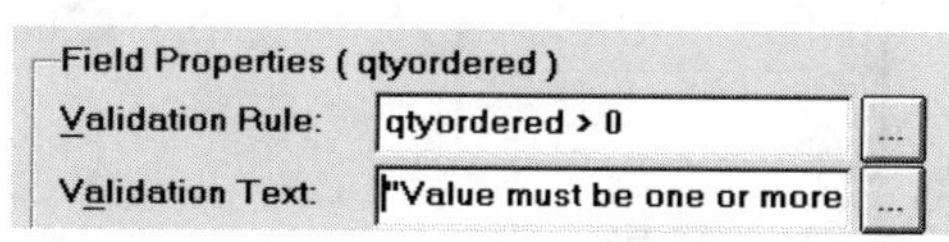

Click the OK button and answer YES to Make Structures Permanent?

Now open the table:

```
use ordlines
```

and browse it:

```
browse
```

The resulting browse screen is seen in Figure 21-2.

Enter a negative number in qtyordered (–10 is shown). Once you leave the field, you will get this message:

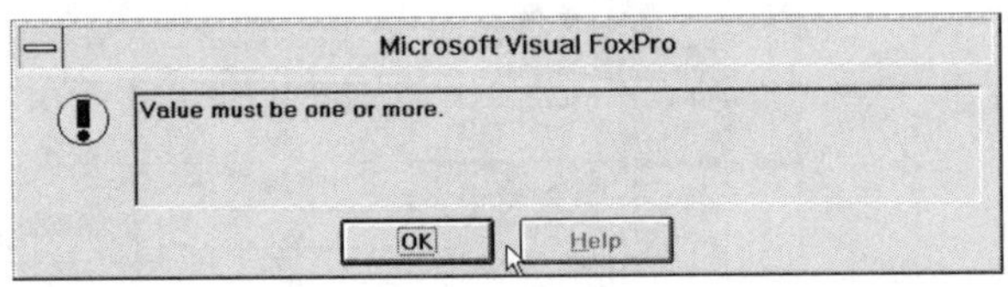

After clicking OK, you are returned to the errant field until a positive number is entered.

This example shows the power of Visual FoxPro's data dictionary. Since Xbase's validation was on a programmatic basis, there was no way to prevent improper values from being entered in a browse or interactively at the command prompt. With Visual FoxPro, even the old DBF format can now benefit from field-level validation.

The last two items to cover on the Table Designer are Default Value and Caption. Default Value lets you specify the value that a field starts with. If

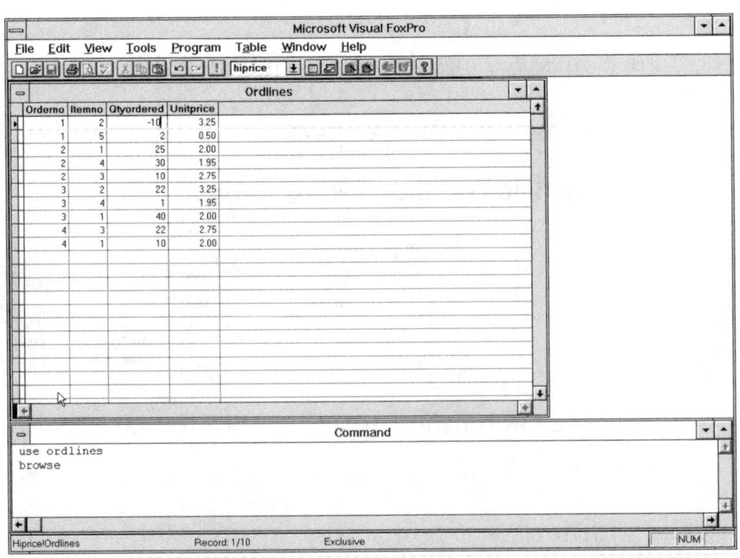

Browsing ordlines
Figure 21-2.

you add a new record, the Default Value is what a field's value will be set to initially. For example, if you had a date field, you might want to set it to be today's date.

Caption is the way a field is titled on a form. For instance, in Chapter 11 you created a screen form with a grid for ordlines. One grid column was called qtyordered, since that was the name of the field. In order to change it to the more readable caption of Qty Ordered, you changed the Caption property of that grid column.

You can also change it for all appearances by setting the Caption for this field here in the Table Designer.

Record-Level Validation

In addition to validation for field values, you can also specify a record validation rule and text. It works just like field validation except that it is triggered when you move off of the record.

Record validation rules, like field rules, are not checked unless the item is modified. You can move around in a table without having to validate data with each move. We will return to record validation after discussing triggers.

Triggers

Distilled to its essence, there are only three things you can do to a record in a table: Delete it, modify it, or create it. Triggers let you control what happens at each of these events. For instance, in an order system, you can use an insert trigger to determine whether a customer's credit is OK before an order for them is entered.

Update, Insert, and Delete

Each of these events can be associated with a procedure. As with validation clauses, the return value has to be logical, true to go ahead or false to abort the operation. In this sense, a trigger is a record, as opposed to field-level, validation.

In many cases you do not need to control the action, you just want to make sure that some step takes place. In other words, you will not be ruling on whether a transaction can occur; you might just want to print the order or notify the credit manager about it.

Triggers are mostly used for Referential Integrity, though the others can be used for this purpose. You can also use the delete trigger for displaying an "Are you sure?" message.

Cannot Change Record Value

A trigger cannot, itself, modify the record that triggered it. Suppose you wanted to add an extended price field to the ordlines table. Since extended price is the product of qtyordered and unitprice, you might think an insert trigger is the ideal time to have your system calculate this value and put it in the extended price field.

You cannot do this. A trigger cannot change a value in its own record. The reason is that the change will cause the update trigger to be called. The update trigger will change the value, calling itself again recursively. The result is a locked-up computer.

Making a Trigger

The ordlines table will again be used as an example. Instead of writing a procedure, you will just enter a false value for the update trigger. This is not as useless as it seems. Many times, for security, integrity, or auditing reasons, you will not want to allow a record such as an order to be modified once it has been entered. Setting the trigger to false will accomplish this.

Again select the ordlines table and click the Modify button in Project Manager. Figure 21-3 shows the Table Designer.

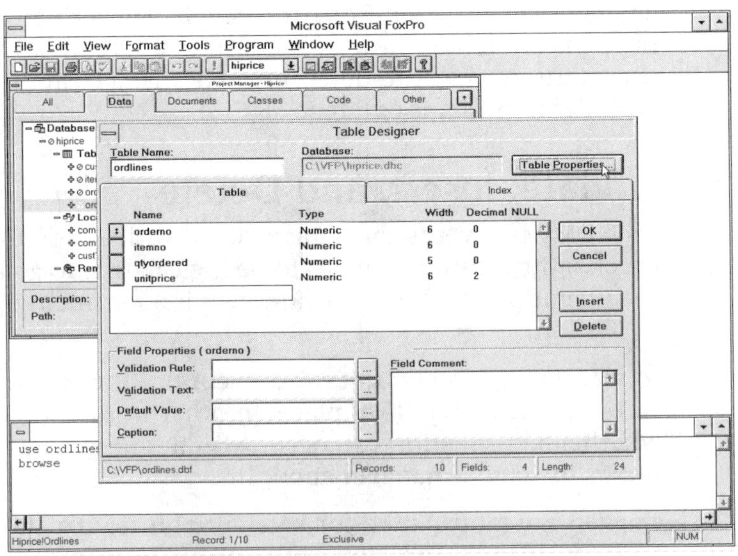

Selecting table properties
Figure 21-3.

Click the Table Properties button in the top right corner. You are now in the Table Properties dialog box. Here, you can see the validation rule and text, the triggers, and the comment. In the UPDATE Trigger field enter the logical false:

```
.f.
```

It should look like this:

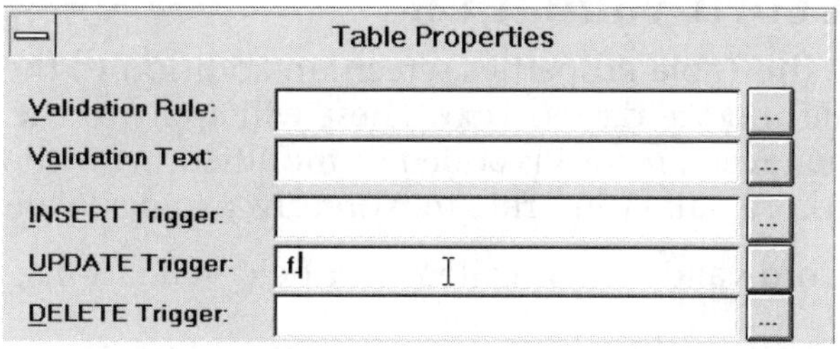

Click the OK button on the Table Properties. Click OK on the Table Designer and select Yes for making changes permanent.

To test this trigger, type the following two commands in the Command window:

```
use ordlines
browse
```

Now select a field in the browse window, say qtyordered, and change the value. When you move the cursor down to the next record, you should see this message:

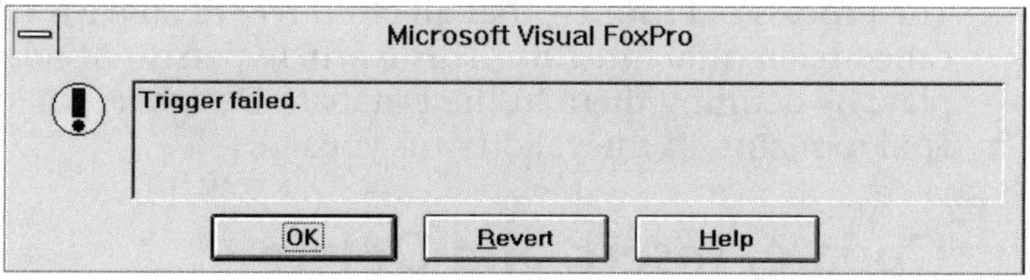

If you select the OK button, you may be shocked to find that the changed value is still there in the browse window. Close the window and browse it again, and you will see that it was not actually changed. Clicking the Revert button on the warning dialog box will cause the value to appear as it was.

Validation Before Triggers

You now have a field validation rule for qtyordered, greater than zero, and a record trigger. Which comes first? Validation—first field, then record.

To demonstrate, browse ordlines again and enter a negative number in qtyordered. You will now see the validation text for qtyordered. The trigger is not called because the validation rule sends the change back as unacceptable.

Record Validation

On the Table Properties screen, in addition to the triggers was a Validation Rule and Validation Text. These will apply to the whole record and are called whenever a record is added or modified. As with field validation and triggers, a record validation rule must return a logical value.

Record validation is called after field validations, if any, and before triggers.

Caution: Do not move the record pointer; that is, do not move to another record in the table being validated. This can cause strange and harmful behavior.

Referential Integrity

One of the biggest problems you can get into is losing the integrity of your data tables. Say the orders table contains a customer number that relates to a customer in the customer table. If this customer gets deleted or has his or her customer number changed, all the orders for that record are orphaned; that is, there is no longer a valid customer record for those orders.

The process of ensuring that all child records have a valid parent record is called referential integrity. This is where persistent relationships come into play. By defining them in the Database Designer, you can then let Visual FoxPro maintain the validity for you.

Update, Insert, and Delete

There are basically three types of action that can cause referential integrity problems: when a record is modified, created, or deleted. It is no accident that these relate to the three triggers that Visual FoxPro offers. Triggers are most often used for referential integrity.

Each of these three actions can trigger one of three responses:

- Ignore it, don't do anything.
- Don't allow the change if there are child records.
- Or "cascade" the updates; that is, make the same change in all child records.

Making a Referential Integrity Rule

Visual FoxPro has a referential integrity builder. Here, you will call on the database created for HiPrice and create a referential integrity rule for updates of the customer number in the customer table and its child, the order table.

First, highlight the HiPrice database in the Visual FoxPro Project Manager, as seen in Figure 21-4, and click the Modify button.

You are taken into the Database Designer. Right-clicking on a blank area of the designer brings up this menu:

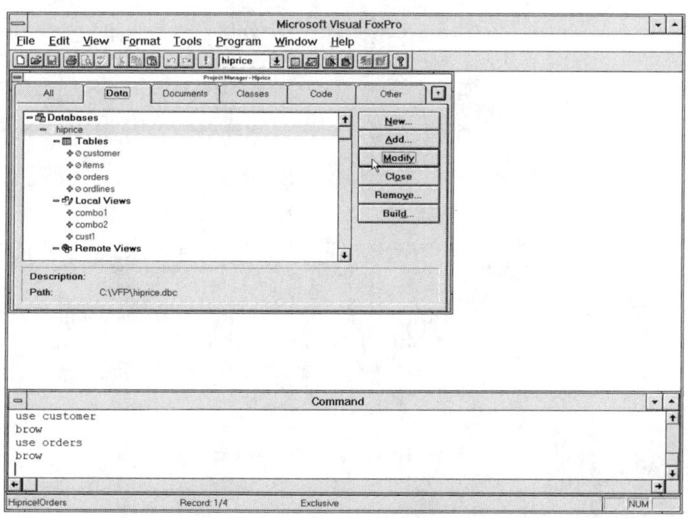

Selecting the HiPrice database
Figure 21-4.

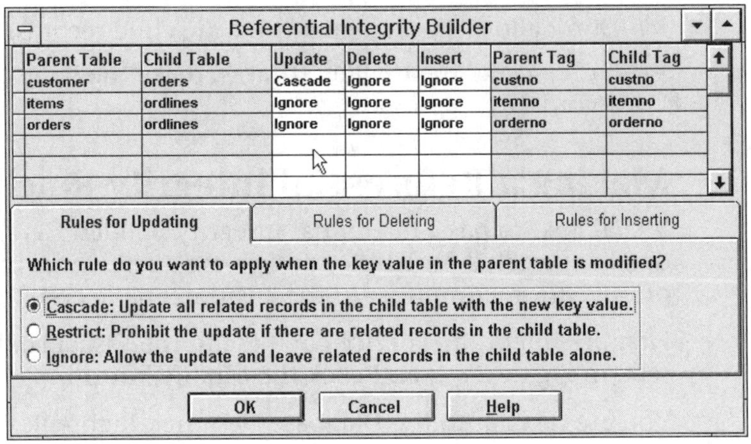

Referential Integrity Builder
Figure 21-5.

Select Referential Integrity and you are dropped into the Referential Integrity Builder. There are tabs for inserting, deleting, and updating. Select the Update tab and highlight the relation where the parent is customer and the child is orders. Press the button for cascading updates. This is seen in Figure 21-5.

Clicking the OK button brings up this dialog box:

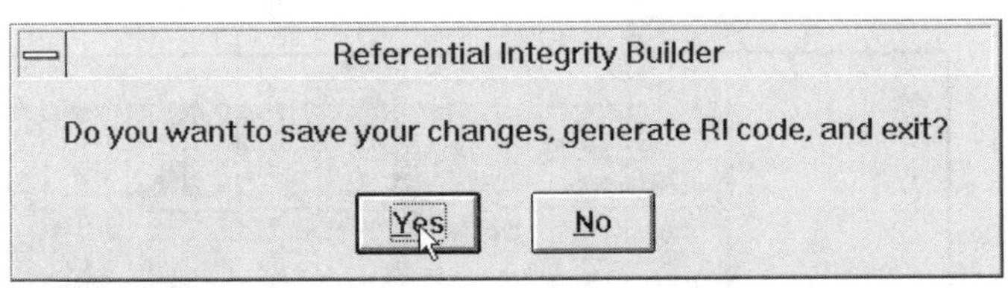

Click OK and the final dialog box asks once more if you really want to do this:

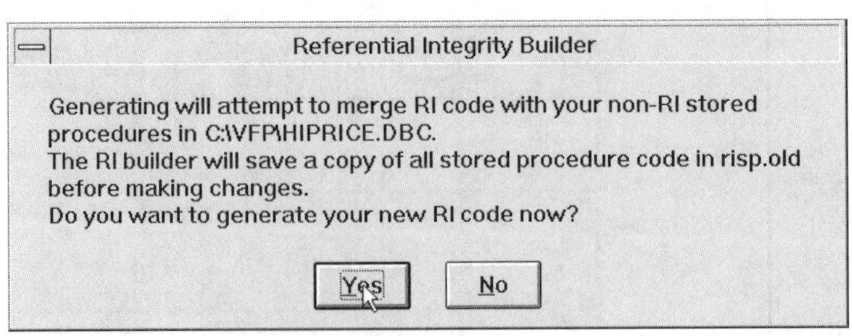

After Visual FoxPro has generated the code to enforce your rule, you are returned to the Database Designer. Close it and type these commands in the Command window:

```
use customer
browse
```

Change the customer number (custno) of the first customer to 5. Close the browse by hitting CTRL-F4. Notice that you did not even open orders. Open it now and look:

```
use orders
browse
```


The orders for customer number 1 have been changed to customer 5.

Cascading updates are one example of using referential integrity to keep your data good. By defining the relationships and actions in the database, you can be sure that related data will stay current even if the updates are not made programmatically.

part 6

Appendixes

A

Differences Between FoxPro 2.6 and Visual FoxPro 3.0

The following sections list and describe the important differences between FoxPro 2.6 and Visual FoxPro 3.0 in the areas of:

- Language
- Tables and Databases
- Interfaces
- Keystrokes
- Menus
- Tools
- Screens
- Reports and Labels
- Functionality

Language Differences

The Visual FoxPro language comprises both new commands and FoxPro 2.6 commands, which are included for backward compatibility. You also need to be aware that many FoxPro 2.6 commands and functions have enhanced or changed functionality as implemented in Visual FoxPro.

Another enhancement is that Visual FoxPro allows long names for windows, objects, tables, and variables. You can use up to 254 characters, except for field names in free tables and index tags.

FoxPro 2.6 Clause, Command, Function, or Feature	Visual FoxPro Command, Function, Property, Event, or Method
@ ... GET DEFAULT	Default property
@ ... GET MESSAGE cMessageText	StatusBarText property
@ ... SAY	Left property, Top property
@ ... SAY FUNCTION, any @ ... GET FUNCTION	Format property
@ ... SAY PICTURE	Image control and OLE Bound control
AFIELDS( )	AFIELDS( ) now provides 11 columns of information
Color	ColorSource property, BackColor and ForeColor properties
Color scheme	ForeColor property, BackColor property, and ColorScheme property
Date data type	Date data type and DateTime data type
DBCONNECT	SQLCONNECT( ) function
DBEXEC	SQLEXEC( ) function
DEACTIVATE MENU	Deactivate event
DEACTIVATE POPUP	
DEACTIVATE WINDOW	
DEFINE WINDOW CLOSE	Closable property
DEFINE WINDOW FLOAT	Movable property
DEFINE WINDOW HALFHEIGHT	HalfHeightCaption property
DEFINE WINDOW ICON FILE	Icon property
Font (Text Menu)	FontName property

Font size (Font dialog)	FontSize property
Font style bold (Font dialog)	FontBold property
Font style italic (Font dialog)	FontItalic property
Height	Height property
Horizontal position (Screen Layout dialog)	Left property
MODIFY SCREEN	MODIFY FORM command
MODIFY STRUCTURE	TABLE Designer
MOVE WINDOW CENTER	AutoCenter property
Numeric data type, Float field type, Integer field type, Double field type, and Currency data type	—
Picture	InputMask property
READ ACTIVATE	ReadActivate event
READ CYCLE	ReadCycle property
READ DEACTIVATE	ReadDeactivate event
READ LOCK	ReadLock property
READ NOMOUSE	ReadMouse property
READ SAVE	ReadSave property
READ SHOW	ReadShow event
READ TIMEOUT	ReadTimeout property
READ VALID	ReadValid event
READ WHEN	ReadWhen event
Screen Name	Name property
SET BORDER	BorderStyle property
SET NOCPTRANS	*See* Preventing Translation of Data in Character or Memo Fields
SHOW GET, SHOW GETS	Refresh method
Size (Screen Layout dialog)	Height, and Width properties
Style (Font dialog)	FontBold, FontItalic, FontUnderline properties. FontShadow property, FontOutline property, FontStrikeThru property

Terminate on selection (Screen Builder)	TerminateRead property
Title (Screen Builder)	Caption property
Valid (Screen Builder)	Click event, DblClick event, LostFocus event, Valid event
Valid Error	ErrorMessage event
Vertical position (Screen Layout dialog)	Top property
When (Screen Builder)	GotFocus event, When event
Width (Screen Builder)	Width property

Table and Database Differences

Visual FoxPro tables are structured differently than in previous versions and Visual FoxPro adds a new structural element: the database. Though FoxPro 2.6 tables are fully functional in Visual FoxPro, if you modify the table structure of FoxPro tables, they are saved as Visual FoxPro tables.

FoxPro 2.6 Feature or Functionality	Visual FoxPro Feature or Functionality
Character field with NOCPTRANS characteristic	Character (BINARY) field type. *See* Data and Field Types.
General field size	Now 4 bytes. *See* General Field Type.
Memo field size	Now 4 bytes. *See* Memo Field Type.
Memo field with NOCPTRANS characteristic	Memo (BINARY) field type. *See* Data and Field Types.
Numeric field	Currency data type, Double field type, Float field type, Integer field type, or Numeric data type
OLE data in a General field	OLE Bound control

Visual FoxPro tables can accept null values. To prevent errors generated by attempts to store null values to FoxPro 2.6 variables or to Visual FoxPro controls, initialize variables or arrays. To prevent users from attempting to store null values to tables, you can disable the NULL-entry key combination by using the following statement:

```
ON KEY LABEL CTRL+0 *
```

The structure of Visual FoxPro screen (.SCX), report (.FRX), and label (.LBX) files differs from the structure of FoxPro 2.6 files. For details on the structure of Visual FoxPro table files created in the Form, Report, and Label Designers, see Table Structures of Table Files in your Visual FoxPro On-line Help.

Interface Differences

In addition to changes in the Visual FoxPro interface, such as keystroke, menu, and tool differences, you need to know about changes to Visual FoxPro screens, reports, and labels. In the following section you can find information on these topics:

- Keystrokes
- Menus
- Tools
- Screens
- Reports and Labels

Keystroke Differences

Visual FoxPro has redefined some FoxPro 2.6 navigation key combinations as shown in the following table:

FoxPro 2.6 Key Combination	Visual FoxPro Key Combination	Definition or Difference
—	CTRL+N	Create a new file
CTRL+N	CTRL+Y	Add a record to a Browse window
CTRL+O	CTRL+E	DO program in edit window

You can insert null values into null-enabled fields with CTRL+0. If you don't want your users to store null values to variables, disable this key combination with the following command:

```
ON KEY LABEL Ctrl+0 *
```

In Visual FoxPro, the TAB key navigates between controls; therefore, you cannot tab through the options in a list box. Instead, use the arrow keys.

Menu Differences

Visual FoxPro only displays menus which have active options. Some menu items are in different locations in Visual FoxPro. The following table shows differences between FoxPro 2.6 and Visual FoxPro:

FoxPro 2.6 Menu Command	Visual FoxPro Menu Command
1 1/2 Space (Text Menu)	1 1/2 Space (Format Menu)
Append (Record Menu)	Append Records (Table Menu)
Append From (Database Menu)	Import (File Menu)
Beautify (Program Menu)	Documenting Wizard (Tools Menu) - Professional Edition only
FoxDoc (Program Menu)	Documenting Wizard (Tools Menu) - Professional Edition only
Browse (Record Menu)	Browse (View Menu)
Change Links (Edit Menu)	Links (Edit Menu)
Copy To (Database Menu)	Export (File Menu)
Debug (Program Menu)	Debug Window (Tools Menu)
Delete (Record Menu)	Delete Records (Table Menu)
Double Space (Text Menu)	Double Space (Format Menu)
Enlarge (Text Menu)	Enlarge Font (Format Menu)
Find Again (Edit Menu)	Find (Edit Menu)
Replace and Find Again (Edit Menu)	Replace (Edit Menu)
Replace All (Edit Menu)	—
Font (Text Menu)	Font (Format Menu)
Generate (Program Menu)	Visual FoxPro generates only menus
Goto (Record Menu)	Go To Record (Table Menu)
Indent (Text Menu)	Indent (Format Menu)
Locate (Record Menu)	Go To Record (Table Menu)
Macros (Program Menu)	Macros (Tools Menu)
Pack (Database Menu)	Remove Deleted Records (Database Menu)
Printer Setup (File Menu)	Page Setup (File Menu)

Recall (Record Menu)	Recall Records (Table Menu)
Reduce (Text Menu)	Reduce Font (Format Menu)
Reindex (Database Menu)	Rebuild Indexes (Table Menu)
Rebuild Indexes (Database Menu)	Replace (Record Menu)
Replace Field (Table Menu)	—
Report (Database Menu)	Print (File Menu)
Label (Database Menu)	Print (File Menu)
Single Space (Text Menu)	Single Space (Format Menu)
Spelling (Text Menu)	Spelling (Tools Menu)
Trace (Program Menu)	Trace Window (Tools Menu)
Undent (Text Menu)	Remove Indent (Format Menu)

Tool Differences

Visual FoxPro has changed some FoxPro 2.6 tools, giving some of them both new names and new functionality. The following table describes these changes:

FoxPro 2.6 Tool	Visual FoxPro Tool
Catalog Manager	Project Manager
Project Manager	Project Manager
Screen Builder	Form Designer
Align (Object Menu)	Layout toolbar
Screen Builder Toolbox	Form Controls toolbar
Control dialogs and screen layout dialogs	Properties window
Menu Builder	Menu Designer
RQBE	Query Designer
Report Writer	Report Designer
Label Designer	Label Designer
View window options	Tools Menu items
Transporter	Conversion Options dialog box
Browse window	Grid Control

Screen Differences

Visual FoxPro can run unconverted FoxPro 2.6 screens (.SPR) files. However, Visual FoxPro forms, instead of using code snippets, use code in events and methods, and properties settings as shown in the following table:

FoxPro 2.6 Screen Feature	Visual FoxPro Property, Method, or Event
#DEFINE, #INSERT preprocessor statements	Global include file called by new .SPR file
#Section 1 Setup code	Form set Load event
#Section 2 Setup code	Form Load event
Cleanup code except procedures	Unload event
Code snippets	Method and event code and properties
Constants	Resolved only in method and event code. *See* Checking the .SPR File
Overlapping @ ... GET	ZOrder Method and ActiveForm and ActiveControl properties

Report and Label Differences

Visual FoxPro can use unconverted FoxPro 2.6 reports and labels; however, Visual FoxPro reports and labels are preferable because they enable you to set and control their data environment and establish report content using report variables.

FoxPro 2.6 Report or Label Feature	Visual FoxPro Report or Label Feature
Memo field size	Now 4 bytes. *See* Memo field type.
REPORT TO FILE	REPORT TO FILE ASCII creates simple text file.
REPORT ENVIRONMENT and LABEL ENVIRONMENT	Data Environment (View Menu).

Functional Differences

Visual FoxPro functionality is, in some cases, different than FoxPro 2.6. The following table summarizes some major differences:

Feature	FoxPro 2.6 Behavior	Visual FoxPro Behavior
CLEAR ALL	Releases everything except system memory variables.	Releases everything except objects currently in use and system memory variables.
Consecutive @ ... GET commands that create overlapping controls.	Controls are overlapped from top (first defined) to bottom (last defined).	Controls are overlapped from bottom to top. To change, *see* Checking Code After Conversion.
@ ... GET controls	Accept data only up to the size of the associated field.	Accepts data up to the size of the control mask. Use an input mask to restrict input to the field size.

B

Running Existing FoxPro 2.6 Resources

If you want to run or update existing FoxPro 2.6 projects or files in Visual FoxPro, you have several choices. Many files developed in previous versions of FoxPro can run, as is, in Visual FoxPro. You also have the option of converting these files to the new Visual FoxPro format; or you can re-structure both files and applications to apply Visual FoxPro's powerful object-oriented features.

Here is how:

<table>
<tr><th>To</th><th>Do This</th></tr>
<tr><td>Run files designed in previous versions of FoxPro</td><td>Use the DO command with any FoxPro 2.6 .SPR, .QPR, or .MPR file. You can open some FoxPro 2.6 files in Visual FoxPro without converting them.<ul><li>FoxPro 2.6 queries (.QPR files) automatically open in the Query Designer without being converted.</li><li>FoxPro 2.6 menus (.MNX files) automatically open in the Menu Designer without being converted.</li><li>FoxPro 2.6 tables (.DBF files) automatically open in the Table Designer without being converted. Visual FoxPro converts tables only if you add a new data type, enable null values in any field, or add the table to a database.</li></ul></td></tr>
<tr><td>Convert FoxPro 2.6 files to Visual FoxPro</td><td>Select the FoxPro 2.6 file from the File menu, click Open, then click OK.
-Or-
Use a MODIFY command, such as MODIFY SCREEN or MODIFY FORM, and the Conversion Options dialog box appears.</td></tr>
<tr><td>Re-structure files to use Visual FoxPro features</td><td>Additional changes to your converted files are necessary if you are to take full advantage of Visual FoxPro's powerful features. Before redesigning your application, review the following Visual FoxPro features:<ul><li>New commands and functions, base classes, properties, events, and methods.</li><li>Enhanced multi-user support.</li><li>Improved connectivity.</li></ul></td></tr>
</table>

C

Visual FoxPro Language Overview

This appendix provides information about the following Visual FoxPro language topics:

- Data and Field Types
- Storing Data
- Operators
- Building Expressions
- Manipulating Data

Data and Field Types

Visual FoxPro data always has a specific data type: This is a description of permissible values, ranges, and sizes of values. After you specify a data type, Visual FoxPro efficiently stores and manipulates the data. Variables and arrays comprise subsets of the available Visual FoxPro data types. Some data types are available only for fields in a table. To add, programmatically, fields of a specific type to a table, you must indicate the field type with a letter abbreviation.

Visual FoxPro Data Types

Data Type	Description	Size	Range
Character	Any text.	1 byte per character to 254	Any characters
Currency	Monetary amount.	8 bytes	- 922337203685477.5808 to 922337203685477.5807
Date	Chronological data consisting of month, year, and date.	8 bytes	01/01/100 to 12/31/9999
DateTime	Consisting of month, year, date, and time.	8 bytes	01/01/100 to 12/31/9999, plus 00:00:00 a.m. to 11:59:59 p.m.
Logical	Boolean value of true or false.	1 byte	True .(T.) or False (.F.)
Numeric	Integers or fractions.	8 bytes in memory; 1 to 20 bytes in table	- .9999999999E+19 to .9999999999E+20
Memo (Binary)	Any memo field data you want to maintain without change across code pages.	4 bytes in table	Limited by available memory

Visual FoxPro Field Types

Field Type	Description	Size	Range
Double	A double-precision floating-point number.	8 bytes	+/-4.94065645841247E -324 to +/-1.79769313486232E 308
Float	Same as Numeric.	8 bytes in memory; 1 to 20 bytes in table	- .9999999999E+19 to .9999999999E+20
General	Reference to an OLE object.	4 bytes in table	Limited by available memory
Integer	Integer values.	4 bytes	-2147483647 to 2147483646
Memo	Reference to a block of data.	4 bytes in table	Limited by available memory
Character (Binary)	Any character data you want to maintain without change across code pages.	1 byte per character to 254	Any characters

Character Data Type

Use the Character data type to include letters, numbers, spaces, symbols, and punctuation. Character fields or variables store text information such as: names, addresses, and numbers not used in mathematical calculations. For more information about the specifications for this type, see Data Types and Field Types in the tables above.

Tip: Phone numbers and zip codes, even though they are comprised mostly of numbers, are handled as Character values.

Currency Data Type

Select the Currency data type rather than Numeric to store monetary values. If you specify more than four decimal places in a currency expression, Visual FoxPro automatically rounds to four places.

Tip: To assign the Currency data type, use the dollar sign: cash = $5.13; bigcash = $124334.87654. In this example, Visual FoxPro internally rounds the variable bigmoney to 124334.8765.

Date Data Type

Select the Date data type if you need to store dates *without* time values. A Date value is stored in the "yyyymmdd" character format.

To assign Date values, enclose the date value in braces:

```
dLastAppointment = {10/14/94}
```

To assign blank Date values, use braces alone or with a space or forward slash, as in the following examples.

```
STORE {} to dBlankdate0
STORE { } to dBlankdate1
STORE {/} to dBlankdate2
```

When you use Date and DateTime data types, these rules always apply:

- {00:00:00AM} is equivalent to {12:00:00AM}, Midnight
- {00:00:00PM} is equivalent to {12:00:00PM}, Noon
- {00:00:00} to {11:59:59} is equivalent to {12:00:00AM} to {11:59:59AM}
- {12:00:00} to {23:59:59} is equivalent to {12:00:00PM} to {11:59:59PM}

DateTime Data Type

Use the DateTime data type if you need to store values either as dates, as times, or both. A DateTime value is stored in eight bytes: two four-byte integers. The first four bytes represent the date. The remaining four bytes represent the time in milliseconds from midnight. DateTime values can contain both a date and a time, or only a date or only a time. If you specify no date value, Visual FoxPro adds a default date of December 30, 1899. If you specify no time value, Visual FoxPro adds a default time of midnight.

For more information about the specifications for this type, see the tables of Data and Field Types.

In both Date and DateTime data types, the following rules apply:

- {00:00:00AM} is equivalent to {12:00:00AM}, Midnight
- {00:00:00PM} is equivalent to {12:00:00PM}, Noon
- {00:00:00} to {11:59:59} is equivalent to {12:00:00AM} to {11:59:59AM}
- {12:00:00} to {23:59:59} is equivalent to {12:00:00PM} to {11:59:59PM}

Double Field Type

Use Double data instead of Numeric when you need more accuracy, a fixed amount of storage in your table, or true floating-point values. For more information about the specifications for this type, see the tables of Data and Field Types.

Float Field Type

The Float data type is included for compatibility, functionally equivalent to Numeric.

General Field Type

The General field comprises a ten-byte reference to the contents of the actual field created by another application, such as a spreadsheet, a word processor document, or a picture. The type and extent of data, however, depend on the OLE server that created the object *and* whether you link or embed the OLE object. If you link an OLE object, the table contains only the reference to the data and to the application that created it. If you embed an OLE object, the table contains a copy of the data as well as a reference to the application that created it. The size of a General field is limited only by the amount of available disk space. Use General fields to store OLE objects.

Integer Field Type

Use the Integer field type to store non-decimal numeric values when performance and table storage limitations are important. The integer field type is stored as a four-byte binary value in tables; therefore, it requires less memory than other numeric data types because binary value requires no ASCII conversion.

Logical Data Type

Logical data types are an efficient way to store information that comprises only two values. Logical data is stored as true (.T.) or false (.F.).

Memo Field Type

The Memo field type stores blocks of data. A Memo field contains a ten-byte reference to the actual contents of the memo. The actual size of memos, however, depends on the amount of data you enter into them. Data from Memo fields of records in a table are stored in a separate file with the same name as the table and an .FPT extension. Memo fields are limited only by the amount of available disk space.

Numeric Data Type

Numeric data indicates magnitude. Numeric values comprise digits from 0 to 9 and an optional sign and decimal point.

Scope of Data Containers

The following table summarizes differences in scope between data containers.

Container	Scope	Example
Constants	Private	#DEFINE ERRSTR "Error!"
Variables	Public, private, or local	Var = 7
Arrays	Public, private, or local	ArrayName[1,1] = 'John Brown'
Fields	Permanent storage, accessible while the table containing the records is open	REPLACE name WITH 'John Brown'
Object Properties	Referenced through the object and the object's container hierarchy	txtCustomer.Value = 'John Brown'

Constants

A constant is a named item that retains its value throughout all operations. The value pi, 3.1415926535, is an example of a numeric constant; the letter "A" is an example of a character constant.

Variables

A variable is stored at a memory location and its value can change programmatically. A variable may contain any data type value and you can change a variable's value at any time. To create a variable, store a value to it using the STORE command or using the = (equal) operator.

Variables exist only while your application is running or during the Visual FoxPro session in which they are created. To specify a variable's scope, you use the keyword: LOCAL, PRIVATE, or PUBLIC.

Arrays

An array is an ordered series of data values, called elements. Arrays exist in memory and are referenced by number, so they afford fast, easy access and manipulation. You can also use SCATTER, GATHER, COPY TO ARRAY, and APPEND FROM ARRAY to move field values to and from various array elements.

Fields

A field is a specific *named* location in a data record. Fields contain a particular type of data and can comprise any Visual FoxPro data type or field type. Name field data types are established at design time in the Table Designer, or at run time with the CREATE TABLE command.

Records

A record is a set of fields that comprises the structure of a table. Records can have up to 255 fields. All records in a table contain the same set of fields. The data type for each field is the same for all records in a table. Although the content of fields may differ from record to record, the size of a field is the same for all records in a table.

Objects

An object is an instance of a class. A class is a description of the data and behavior characteristics of a group of objects. Visual FoxPro objects can be forms, form sets, or controls. Use Visual FoxPro objects to implement consistent, dependable behavior throughout your application, to reduce the amount of code, and to increase the reusability of code.

Operators

Operators allow you to manipulate data of the same type. Visual FoxPro operators are grouped by the following data types and functions:

- Character Operators
- Date and DateTime Operators
- Logical Operators
- Relational Operators
- Numeric Operators

Character Operators

You can join and compare character data using the character operators +, –, and $. The following table lists the character expression operators in order of precedence:

Operator	Action	Code
+	Concatenation. Joins two strings, a string and a field, or a string and a memory variable.	? 'Good ' + 'morning'
–	Concatenation. Removes trailing blanks from the element preceding the operator, then joins two elements.	? customer.first – customer.last
$	Comparison. Seeks one character expression within another.	? 'father' $ 'grandfather' ? 'Main' $ customer.address

Date and Time Operators

The following operators act on dates and times.

Operator	Action	Code
+	Addition	tNewTime = tTime1 + nSeconds; dNewDate = dDate1 + nDays
–	Subtraction	nSeconds = tTime1 – tTime2; tNewTime = tTime1 – nSeconds; dNewDate = dDate1 – nDays

Logical Operators

The following table lists the logical operators in order of precedence.

Operator	Action	Code
( )	Group subexpressions	cVar AND (cVar2 AND cVAR3)
NOT, !	Logical negative	IF NOT cVarA = cVarB; IF ! nVar1 = nVar2
AND	Logical AND	lVar0 AND lVar9
OR	Logical inclusive OR	lVarX OR lVarY

Relational Operators

The following table lists the relational operators.

Operator	Action	Code
<	Less than	? 23 < 54
>	Greater than	? 1 > 2
=	Equal to	? cVar1 = cVar 20
<>, #, !=	Not equal to	? .T. <> .F.
<=	Less than or equal to	? {01/01/92} <= {01/01/92}
>=	Greater than or equal to	? 32 >= nHisAge
==	Character string comparison	? status == "Open"

Numeric Operators

The following table lists the numeric operators in order of precedence.

Operator	Action	Code
( )	Group subexpressions	(4-3) * (12/nVar2)
**, ^	Exponentiation	? 3 ** 2; ? 3 ^ 2
*, /	Multiplication and division	? 2 * 7; ? 14 / 7
%	Modulus (remainder)	? 15 % 4
+, -	Addition and subtraction	? 4 + 15

Creating Expressions

Visual FoxPro Naming Rules

Data containers and some parameters to commands and functions require a name. When you create a name in Visual FoxPro, the following rules apply:

- Use only letters, underscores, and numbers.
- Begin the name with a letter or underscore.
- Use 1 to 254 characters, except for field names in free tables and index tags—they can be 10 characters at most.
- Avoid words reserved by Visual FoxPro.
- File names must follow your operating system's conventions.

Creating Character Expressions

You should compose character expressions by combining character operators with the following Visual FoxPro elements:

- Character fields.
- Functions that return character values.
- Variables and array elements that contain character data.
- Character constants, called string literals.

You can embed a quotation mark in a character string by enclosing the character string using another, different, string delimiter pair, either [ ] or ' '.

Creating Date Expressions

Assemble date expressions by combining date operators with the following Visual FoxPro elements:

- Date or DateTime fields.
- Functions that return dates or dates and times.
- Variables and array elements that contain dates or times.
- Date and DateTime constants.

Visual FoxPro treats an invalid date as an empty date.

Creating Numeric Expressions

Assemble numeric expressions by combining numeric operators with the following Visual FoxPro elements:

- Numeric type fields.
- Functions that return numeric values.
- Memory variables and array elements that contain numeric data.
- Numeric constants.

Creating Logical Expressions

Assemble logical expressions by combining logical operators with the following Visual FoxPro elements:

- Logical type fields.
- Functions that return logical values.
- Variables and array elements that contain logical values.
- Any expression that evaluates to a logical value.

Visual FoxPro evaluates logical expressions from left to right, and only for as long as necessary.

Creating Name Expressions

Some Visual FoxPro commands and functions require that you supply a name. Although a name cannot be a memory variable or an array element, you can create a name expression that substitutes the value of a Character variable or array element as the name. When you store the name to a variable or an array element, you can substitute this name into a command or function by enclosing the memory variable in parentheses. To use a list of names, separate the names with commas. A name is not an expression, a variable or array element, or a field. A name should not be surrounded by quotation marks. Otherwise, names follow the Visual FoxPro naming rules. For example, the REPLACE command requires a field name. You can store a field name to a variable and use a name expression in REPLACE where the field name occurs:

```
STORE 'city' TO cVarCity
REPLACE (cVarCity) WITH 'Paris'
```

Manipulating Data

Macro Substitution

You can replace names with memory variables using macro substitution. When using macro substitution, you place the ampersand (&) before the variable to tell Visual FoxPro to use the value of the variable as a name. Use a period (.) to end the macro substitution expression.

For example, the following print statement produces "FoxPro":

```
x = "Fox"
? "&x.Pro"
```

Working with User-Defined Functions

When creating a function or a procedure, use the FUNCTION or PROCEDURE command to assign a name. Any number of statements may allow the first line. Use the PARAMETERS statement as the first executable line of a stand-alone UDF that receives parameters. If a UDF returns values to the calling program, end it with a RETURN statement. You can call UDFs as procedures or as functions and you can pass up to 24 parameters to them.

Calling a Procedure

To call a procedure, use the DO command followed by the procedure name. For example:

```
DO cMyUDF
```

Calling a Function

To call a function, use the = (equal) operator, followed by the function name and parentheses that contain any parameters you pass to the function. For example:

```
=cMyUDF()
=cMyUDF(p1,p2)
```

If you omit the RETURN statement in a UDF, the default return value is true (.T.).

Passing Parameters by Value or by Reference

You can pass variables or array elements as parameters by reference or by value. To change parameters passed to and returned from a UDF, pass by reference. To maintain the original value of parameters passed to a UDF, even if the UDF changes the values within the UDF, pass by value. By default, Visual FoxPro passes parameters to UDFs by value. Objects are always passed by reference.

Passing Parameters by Reference

You can use the SET command to pass parameters by reference. To pass parameters by reference, do either of the following:

- Type the following command before calling the UDF:

```
SET UDFPARMS TO REFERENCE
```

- Use the @ token to pass a variable or array by reference as shown:

```
? "UDF value: " + STR(plusone(@nX))
```

Passing Parameters by Value

To pass parameters by value, do either of the following:

- Type the following command before calling the UDF:

```
SET UDFPARMS TO VALUE
```

- Use parentheses to pass a variable or array by value, as in the following example:

```
? 'UDF value: ' + STR(plusone((nX)))
```

Working with Fields and Records

You can access data in fields by specifying one or more records containing target data. You can also use a record pointer to access a particular record through the GOTO command, or you can access fields in several records by identifying the records with a Scope, FOR, or WHILE clause in a command.

See	To
Scope Clauses	Specify a record range
FOR Clauses	Find records that match a logical condition
WHILE Clauses	Operate on records while a logical condition is true

Scope Clauses

If a Visual FoxPro command has a Scope clause, you can specify a record range for the command to act on by replacing Scope with one of the clauses in the following table.

Scope Clause	Effect
ALL	Command affects all records in the table.
NEXT nExpr	Command affects a range of records beginning at the current record and continuing for the specified number of records. For instance, the following example acts on the current record and the two following records: REPLACE status WITH "open" NEXT 3
RECORD nNumber	Command affects only the specified record number. The following example acts on record five: REPLACE status WITH "open" RECORD 5
REST	Command affects a range of records beginning with the current record and ending with the last record in the table. The following example stores a null value in the remaining records: REPLACE status WITH .NULL. REST

FOR Clauses

FOR clauses cause a command to act on each record that meets the specified logical condition. FOR clauses have the following syntax:

```
FOR cExpr
```

The following example stores low balance in the alert field of all records that contain less than 500 in the total field:

```
REPLACE alert WITH "low balance" FOR total < 500
```

The following table lists commands in which you can use a FOR clause:

Commands That Use FOR Clauses		
APPEND FROM ARRAY	COUNT	LIST
APPEND FROM	DEFINE PAD	LOCATE
AVERAGE	DELETE	RECALL
BLANK	DISPLAY	REPLACE FROM ARRAY
BROWSE	EXPORT	REPLACE
CALCULATE	FOR( )	REPORT
CHANGE	INDEX	SCAN...ENDSCAN
COPY TO ARRAY	JOIN	SORT
COPY TO	LABEL	SUM

WHILE Clauses

WHILE clauses make a command to act on each record as long as the logical expression contained in the while clause evaluates as true (.T.). The first time the expression evaluates as false (.F.), the command ceases without affecting any remaining records. This expression is typically used with a table that has been sorted or indexed on a field or fields included in the WHILE expression. For example: the following code navigates through indexed table to locate the first record that meets the condition, then the REPLACE command acts on those records that meet the WHILE condition:

```
USE Mytable INDEX street
LOCATE FOR UPPER(street) = "MAIN"
REPLACE street WITH "Maine" WHILE UPPER(street) = "MAIN"
```

The following table lists commands in which you can use a WHILE clause:

Commands That Use WHILE Clauses		
AVERAGE	COUNT	RECALL
BLANK	DELETE	REPLACE
BROWSE	DISPLAY	REPLACE FROM ARRAY
CALCULATE	EXPORT	REPORT
CHANGE	LABEL	SCAN ... ENDSCAN
COPY TO	LIST	SORT
COPY TO ARRAY	LOCATE	SUM

Working with Arrays

Arrays provide a quick way to order information. After information is in an array, you can easily search, sort, and perform data manipulation. To get information to and from arrays, transfer data to a table or transfer data from a table to an array. Visual FoxPro makes no size or data type restrictions on array contents. The only restriction on size is the amount of memory available. Unlike tables, arrays cease to exist when an application ends.

Transferring Data From a Table to an Array

The following Visual FoxPro commands transfer data from a table to an array:

- SCATTER transfers data from a single table record to an array.
- COPY TO ARRAY transfers data from a series of records to an array.
- SELECT - SQL can transfer the results of a query to an array.

Transferring Data From an Array to a Table

The following Visual FoxPro commands transfer data from an array to a table:

- GATHER transfers data from an array to a single table record.
- APPEND FROM ARRAY adds new records to a table and fills the records with data from an array.
- INSERT - SQL appends a single new record to a table and fills the record with data from an array.

Arrays and SELECT - SQL

To send SELECT - SQL query results to an array, specify the INTO ARRAY clause with an array name. If the array doesn't exist, it is automatically created. If the array does exist, it is redimensioned automatically to accommodate the query results. Here's an example:

```
SELECT DISTINCT a.cust_id, a.company, b.amount ;
   FROM customer a, payments b ;
   WHERE a.cust_id = b.cust_id INTO ARRAY results
DISPLAY MEMORY LIKE results
```

Working with Classes and Objects

Visual FoxPro provides two special operators for object programming: the dot operator (.) and the scope resolution operator (::). Visual FoxPro also adds commands that enable you to define a class, and to create and add objects to a class as described in the following table:

Operator, Command, Function	Description
. (Dot operator)	Scopes objects to their parents and properties, events, and methods to objects.
:: (Scope resolution operator)	Calls a parent class method from within the subclass.
CREATEOBJECT( )	Creates an object from a class, a subclass, or an OLE object.
DEFINE CLASS	Creates a class definition.
ADD OBJECT	Adds an object based on an existing class or subclass at design time.
GETOBJECT( )	Returns an OLE object.

Handling Null Values

Null values are

- Equal to the absence of any value.
- Different than zero, the empty string (""), or blank.
- Sorted ahead of other data.
- Propagated in calculations and most functions.

Null values affect the behavior of commands and functions, logical expressions, and parameters as shown in the table below:

To Use Null Values In	See
Commands and functions	Behavior of Null Values in Commands and Functions
Expressions	Behavior of Null Values in Logical Expressions
Parameters	Using NULL as a Parameter

Behavior of Null Values in Commands and Functions

The following table describes how commands and functions interpret null values:

Data Type	Behavior
Logical	Most logical expressions that evaluate to .NULL.. return .NULL. or generate an error. EMPTY( ), ISBLANK( ), and ISNULL( ) are exceptions.
Numeric	Numeric expressions that evaluate to .NULL. return .NULL.
Date	Date expressions containing null values return .NULL.

Behavior of Null Values in Logical Expressions

In most cases, Null values persist through expressions. The following table describes the behavior of null values in logical expressions:

Logical Expression	Result if x=TRUE	Result if x=FALSE	Result if x=.NULL.
x AND .NULL.	.NULL.	FALSE	.NULL.
x OR .NULL.	TRUE	.NULL.	.NULL.
NOT x	FALSE	TRUE	.NULL.

When a conditional expression encounters a null value, the condition fails, because .NULL. is not true (.T.). For example, a FOR clause that evaluates to .NULL. is treated as false (.F.). Note that null values are treated as .NULL. until the entire expression is evaluated.

Using NULL as a Parameter

The following general rules apply to null values passed to commands and functions:

- Commands generate errors when passed a null value.
- Functions that accept .NULL. as a valid value propagate .NULL. to the result.
- Functions that accept parameters that could be numeric values generate an error if you supply .NULL. for those parameters.
- ISBLANK( ), ISDIGIT( ), ISLOWER( ), ISUPPER( ), ISALPHA( ), and EMPTY return false (.F.) when passed a null value. ISNULL( ) returns true (.T.) when passed a null value.
- The commands INSERT - SQL and SELECT - SQL process null values through the IS NULL and IS NOT NULL clauses and, in the case of INSERT, UPDATE, and REPLACE, place null values into records.
- SQL Aggregate functions ignore instead of propagate null values.
- Visual FoxPro aggregate functions only propagate .NULL. if all supplied values are null values; otherwise, any null value is ignored.

Macro File Format (.FKY)

File Header

Byte Offset	Description
01-03	Signature, Hex 79FF
04-15	Ignored
16-17	Number of macros (binary)
18-end	The macros

Individual Macros

Byte Offset	Description
00-19	Macro name
20-21	Macro length (in keystrokes, binary)
22-23	Keystroke (two bytes, binary)
24-end	Macro keystrokes

Memo File Structure (.FPT)

Memo files contain one header record and any number of block structures. The header record contains a pointer to the next free block and the size of the block in bytes. The size is determined by the SET BLOCKSIZE command when the file is created. The header record starts at file position zero and occupies 512 bytes. The SET BLOCKSIZE TO 0 command sets the block size width to 1. Following the header record are the blocks that contain a block header and the text of the memo. The table file contains block numbers that are used to reference the memo blocks. The position of the block in the memo file is determined by multiplying the block number by the block size (found in the memo file header record). All memo blocks start at even block boundary addresses. A memo block can occupy more than one consecutive block.

Memo Header Record

Byte Offset	Description
00-03	Location of next free block*
04-05	Unused
06-07	Block size (bytes per block)*
08-511	Unused

*Integers stored with the most significant byte first

Memo Block Header and Memo Text

Byte Offset	Description
00-03	Block signature* (indicates the type of data in the block) a) 0 - picture (picture field type) b) 1 - text (memo field type)
04-07	Length* of memo (in bytes)
08-n	Memo text (n = length)

*Integers stored with the most significant byte first.

Naming Conventions

This section covers the following types of Visual FoxPro naming conventions:

- Variable Naming Conventions
- Object Naming Conventions
- Constant Naming Conventions
- Window Naming Conventions

Variable Naming Conventions

[Scope]TypeName

Follow this suggested format for naming variables.

Scope Optional. Specifies the range of reference for the variable. For example, local variables can be referenced only within the procedure where they were defined. Public variables are accessible from anywhere in the application. The choices for Scope are

Scope	Description	Example
l	Local	lnCounter
p	Private (default)pnStatus	—
g	Public (global)	gnOldRecno
t	Parameter	tnRecNo

C

Type Specifies the data type for the variable. The choices for Type are:

Type	Description	Example
a	Array	aMonths
c	Character	cLastName
y	Currency	yCurrentValue
d	Date	dBirthDay
t	Datetime	tLastModified
b	Double	bValue
f	Float	fInterest
l	Logical	lFlag
n	Numeric	nCounter
o	Object	oEmployee
u	Unknown	uReturnValue

The scope prefix is recommended but not required. In some cases, explicit scoping does not apply. For example, in the main program of a stand-alone application, there is no difference in visibility for variables scoped as PUBLIC or PRIVATE. The type prefix is always relevant and is required in sample programs.

Object Naming Conventions

PrefixName

Follow this suggested format for naming objects. The choices for Prefix are

Prefix	Object	Example
chk	CheckBox	chkReadOnly
cbo	ComboBox	cboEnglish
cmd	CommandButton	cmdCancel
cmg	CommandGroup	cmgChoices
cnt	Container	cntMoverList
ctl	Control	ctlFileList
<user-defined>	Custom	user-defined
edt	EditBox	edtTextArea
frm	Form	frmFileOpen
frs	FormSet	frsDataEntry
grd	Grid	grdPrices
grc	Column	grcCurrentPrice
grh	Header	grhTotalInventory
img	Image	imgIcon
lbl	Label	lblHelpMessage
lin	Line	linVertical
lst	ListBox	lstPolicyCodes
olb	OLEBoundControl	olbObject1
ole	OLE	oleObject1
opt	OptionButton	optFrench
opg	OptionGroup	opgType
pag	Page	pagDataUpdate
pgf	PageFrame	pgfLeft

Prefix	Object	Example
sep	Separator	sepToolSection1
shp	Shape	shpCircle
spn	Spinner	spnValues
txt	TextBox	txtGetText
tmr	Timer	tmrAlarm
tbr	ToolBar	tbrEditReport

Table Field Naming Conventions

Alias.TypeName

Follow this suggested format for naming fields in tables. These conventions are recommended, not required.

Type Specifies the data type for a field in a table. The choices for Type are

Type	Description	Example
c	Character	Customer.cLastName
d	Date	Customer.dBirthDay
t	Datetime	Customer.tLastMod
b	Double	Customer.bRate
f	Float	Customer.fValue
g	General	Customer.gPicture
l	Logical	Customer.lSellMail
m	Memo	Customer.mComments
y	Currency	Customer.yYearTDate
n	Numeric	Customer.nItems
i	Integer	Customer.iCustID

Constant Naming Conventions

NAME

Follow this suggested format for naming constants. Constants are in upper case.

```
#DEFINE MAX_VALUE 10
```

Window Naming Conventions

wName

Follow this suggested format for naming windows. Do not use a prefix on class definitions; use prefixes only when the object is instantiated.

```
DEFINE WINDOW wCustomerInvoices FROM nFirstRow, nFirstColumn TO nLastRow,
nLastColumn
```

D

Visual FoxPro Reserved Words

Reserved words in Visual FoxPro include functions, system memory variables, properties, events, methods, commands, and clauses. When programming, avoid using reserved words as names (for example, as window, table, or field names). Using reserved words as names is a very dangerous practice which can generate syntax errors (when you are lucky). The following list comprises all Visual FoxPro reserved words.

#DEFINE
#ENDIF
#IF
#IFDEF
#IFNDEF
#INCLUDE
#ITSEXPRESSION
#READCLAUSES
#REGION
#SECTION
#UNDEF
#WNAME
.AND.
.F.
.NOT.
.OR.
.T.
@PROCEDURE
ABS
ACCEPT
ACLASS
ACOPY
ACOS
ACTIVATE
ActivateCell
ActiveColumn
ActiveControl
ActiveForm
ActivePage
ActiveRow
ADATABASES
ADBOBJECTS
ADD
AddColumn
AddItem
ADDITIVE
AddListItem
AddObject
ADEL
ADIR
AELEMENT
AERROR
AFIELDS
AFONT
AFTER
AfterCloseTables
AfterDock
AfterRowColChange
AGAIN
AINDENT
AINSTANCE
ALEN
ALIAS
Alignment
_ALIGNMENT
ALL
AllowTabs
ALLTRIM
ALT
ALTER
ALTERNATE
AlwaysOnTop
AMEMBERS
AND
ANSI
ANSITOOEM
ANY
APLABOUT
APP
APPEND
APRINTERS
ARRAY
AS
ASC
ASCAN
ASCENDING
ASCII
_ASCIICOLS
_ASCIIROWS
ASELOBJ
ASIN
ASORT
ASSIST
_ASSIST
ASUBSCRIPT
AT
ATAN
ATC
ATCLINE
ATLINE
ATN2
ATTRIBUTES
AUSED
AutoActivate
AutoCenter
AutoCloseTables
AUTOMATIC
AutoOpenTables
AUTOSAVE
AutoSize
AVERAGE
AVG
BackColor
BackStyle
BAR
BARCOUNT
BARPROMPT
BaseClass
_BEAUTIFY
BEFORE
BeforeDock
BeforeOpenTables
BeforeRowColChange
BEGIN
BELL
BETWEEN
BITAND
BITCLEAR
BITLSHIFT
BITMAP
BITNOT
BITOR
BITRSHIFT
BITSET
BITXOR
BLANK

BLINK
BLOCKSIZE
BOF
BORDER
BorderColor
BorderStyle
BorderWidth
BOTTOM
Bound
BoundColumn
BOX
_BOX
BROWSE
_BROWSER
BRSTATUS
BUCKET
BufferMode
BufferModeOverride
BUFFERS
BUILD
_BUILDER
ButtonCount
Buttons
BY
_CALCMEM
CALCULATE
_CALCVALUE
CALL
CANCEL
CANDIDATE
CAPSLOCK
Caption
CARRY
CASCADE
CASE
CATALOG
CD
CDOW
CDX
CEILING
CENTER
CENTURY
CGA
CHANGE
CHARACTER
CHDIR
CHECK
CheckBox
ChildAlias
ChildOrder
CHR
CHRSAW
CHRTRAN
Circle
CLASS
CLASSLIB
ClassLibrary
CLEAR
CLICK
ClipControls
_CLIPTEXT
CLOCK
CloneObject
ClosableProperty
CLOSE
CloseTables
Cls
CMONTH
CNT
CNTBAR
CNTPAD
CODEPAGE
COL
COLLATE
COLOR
ColorScheme
ColorSource
COLUMN
ColumnCount
ColumnLines
ColumnOrder
Columns
ColumnWidths
COM1
COM2
ComboBox
COMMAND
CommandButton
CommandGroup
Comment
COMPACT
COMPATIBLE
COMPILE
COMPOBJ
COMPRESS
CONFIRM
CONNECTION
CONNECTIONS
CONNSTRING
CONSOLE
CONTAINER
CONTINUE
CONTROL
ControlBox
ControlCount
Controls
ControlSource
_CONVERTER
COPIES
COPY
COS
COUNT
CPCOMPILE
CPCONVERT
CPCURRENT
CPDBF
CPDIALOG
CREATE
CREATEOBJECT
CTOD
CTOT
CURDIR
_CUROBJ
CURRENCY
CurrentControl
CurrentX

CurrentY
CURSOR
CURSORGETPROP
CURSORSETPROP
CursorSource
CURVAL
Curvature
Custom
CYCLE
DATABASE
DATABASES
DataEnvironment
DATASESSION
DataSessionID
DATASOURCE
DATE
DATETIME
DAY
DB4
DBC
DBF
DBGETPROP
DBLCLICK
_DBLCLICK
DBMEMO3
DBSETPROP
DBTRAP
DBUSED
DDE
DDEAbortTrans
DDEAdvise
DDEEnabled
DDEExecute
DDEInitiate
DDELastError
DDEPoke
DDERequest
DDESetOption
DDESetService
DDESetTopic
DDETerminate
DEACTIVATE
DEBUG
DECIMALS
DECLARE
DEFAULT
DEFAULTSOURCE
DEFINE
DELETE
DeleteColumn
DELETED
DeleteMark
DELETETABLES
DELIMITED
DELIMITERS
DESCENDING
DESIGN
Desktop
Destroy
DEVELOPMENT
DEVICE
_DIARYDATE
DIF
DIFFERENCE
DIMENSION
DIR
DIRECTORY
DISABLED
DisabledBackColor
DisabledForeColor
DisabledPicture
DISKSPACE
DISPLAY
DisplayValue
DISTINCT
DLL
DLLS
DMY
DO
Dock
Docked
DockPosition
DocumentFile
DOHISTORY
DOS
_DOS
DoScroll
DOSMEM
DOUBLE
DoVerb
DOW
DOWN
DownClick
DownPicture
DRAG
DragDrop
DragIcon
DragMode
DragOver
DRAW
DrawMode
DrawStyle
DrawWidth
DRIVER
DropDown
DTOC
DTOR
DTOS
DTOT
DUPLEX
DynamicAlignment
DynamicBackColor
DynamicCurrentControl
DynamicFontBold
DynamicFontItalic
DynamicFontName
DynamicFontSize
DynamicFontStrikethru
DynamicFontUnderline
DynamicForeColor
ECHO
EDIT
EditBox
EDITWORK
EGA25
EGA43

EJECT
EMPTY
EMS
EMS64
ENABLED
ENCRYPT
ENCRYPTION
END
ENDCASE
ENDDO
ENDFOR
ENDIF
ENDPRINTJOB
ENDSCAN
ENDTEXT
ENDWITH
ENVIRONMENT
EOF
ERASE
ERROR
ErrorMessage
ESCAPE
EVALUATE
EVENTS
EXACT
EXCEPT
EXCLUSIVE
EXE
EXISTS
EXIT
EXP
EXPORT
EXPRESSION
EXTENDED
EXTERNAL
F11F12
FCHSIZE
FCLOSE
FCOUNT
FCREATE
FDATE
FDOW

FEOF
FERROR
FETCH
FFLUSH
FGETS
FIELD
FIELDS
FILE
FILER
FILES
FILL
FillColor
FillStyle
FILTER
FIND
FirstElement
FIXED
FKLABEL
FKMAX
FLDLIST
FLOAT
FLOCK
FLOOR
FLUSH
FOLDCONST
FONT
FontBold
FontItalic
FONTMETRIC
FontName
FontOutline
FontShadow
FontSize
FontStrikethru
FontUnderline
FOOTER
FOPEN
FOR
FORCE
ForeColor
FOREIGN
FORM

FORMAT
FormCount
Forms
FORMSET
FOUND
FOX2X
_FOXDOC
_FOXGRAPH
FOXPLUS
FPUTS
FREAD
FREE
FREEZE
FROM
FSEEK
FSIZE
FTIME
FULLPATH
FUNCTION
@FUNCTION
FV
FW2
FWEEK
FWRITE
GATHER
GENERAL
_GENGRAPH
_GENMENU
_GENPD
_GENSCRN
_GENXTAB
GET
GETBAR
GETCOLOR
GETCP
GETDIR
GETENV
GETEXPR
GETFILE
GETFLDSTATE
GETFONT
GETNEXTMODIFIED

GETOBJECT
GETPAD
GETPICT
GETPRINTER
GETS
GLOBAL
GO
GOMONTH
GotFocus
GOTO
Grid
GridLineColor
GridLines
GridLineWidth
GROUP
GROW
HALFHEIGHT
HalfHeightCaption
HAVING
HEADER
HeaderHeight
HEADING
HEADINGS
HEIGHT
HELP
HelpContextID
HELPFILTER
HIDE
HideSelection
HIGHLIGHT
HISTORY
HMEMORY
HOME
HOUR
HOURS
HWND
IBLOCK
ICON
ID
IDXCOLLATE
IF
IIF
Image
IMPORT
IN
Increment
IncrementalSearch
INDBC
_INDENT
INDEX
INDEXES
IndexToItemID
INFORMATION
Init
InitialSelectedAlias
INKEY
INLIST
INPUT
InputMask
INSERT
INSMODE
INSTRUCT
INT
INTEGER
INTENSITY
InteractiveChange
INTERSECT
Interval
INTO
IS
ISALPHA
ISBLANK
ISCOLOR
ISDIGIT
ISEXCLUSIVE
ISLOWER
ISMOUSE
ISNULL
ISOMETRIC
ISREADONLY
ISUPPER
ItemBackColor
ItemData
ItemForeColor
ItemIDData
ItemIDToIndex
JOIN
KEY
KEYBOARD
KeyboardHighValue
KeyboardLowValue
KEYCOLUMNS
KEYCOMP
KEYMATCH
KeyPress
KeyPreview
KEYSET
LABEL
LAST
LASTKEY
LDCHECK
LEDIT
LEFT
LeftColumn
LEN
LEVEL
LIBRARY
LIKE
LINE
LINENO
LineSlant
LINKED
LinkMaster
LIST
ListBox
ListCount
ListIndex
ListItem
ListItemID
_LMARGIN
LOAD
LOCAL
LOCATE
LOCFILE
LOCK
LockScreen

LOG
LOG10
LOGERRORS
LONG
LOOKUP
LostFocus
LOWER
LPARAMETERS
LPARTITION
LTRIM
LUPDATE
MAC
_MAC
MACDESKTOP
MACHELP
MACKEY
MACRO
MACROS
MARGIN
MARK
MASTER
MAX
MaxButton
MaxHeight
MaxLeft
MaxLength
MAXMEM
MaxTop
MaxWidth
MBLOCK
MCOL
MD
MDI
MDIForm
MDOWN
MDX
MDY
MEMLIMIT
MEMLINES
MEMO
MEMORY
MEMOS
MEMOWIDTH
MemoWindow
MEMVAR
MENU
MENUS
MESSAGE
MESSAGEBOX
MESSAGES
MIDDLE
MIN
MinButton
MinHeight
MINIMIZE
MINUS
MINUTE
MinWidth
MKDIR
MLINE
_MLINE
MOD
MODAL
MODIFY
MODULE
MONO
MONO43
MONTH
MOUSE
MouseDown
MouseMove
MousePointer
MouseUp
Movable
MOVE
Moved
MoverBars
MOVERS
MRKBAR
MRKPAD
MROW
MTON
MULTILOCKS
MULTISELECT
MVARSIZ
MVCOUNT
MWINDOW
NAME
NDX
NEAR
NEGOTIATE
NewIndex
NewItemID
NEXT
NOALIAS
NOAPPEND
NOCLEAR
NOCLOSE
NOCONSOLE
NOCPTRANS
NODATA
NoDataOnLoad
NODEBUG
NODELETE
NODUP
NOEDIT
NOEJECT
NOENVIRONMENT
NOFLOAT
NOFOLLOW
NOGROW
NOINIT
NOLGRID
NOLINK
NOLOCK
NOLOG
NOMARGIN
NOMDI
NOMENU
NOMINIMIZE
NOMODIFY
NOMOUSE
NONE
NOOPTIMIZE
NOORGANIZE
NOOVERWRITE

NOPROMPT
NOREAD
NOREFRESH
NOREQUERY
NORGRID
NORMAL
NORMALIZE
NOSAVE
NOSHADOW
NOSHOW
NOSPACE
NOT
NOTE
NOTIFY
NOUPDATE
NOVALIDATE
NOVERIFY
NOWAIT
NOWINDOW
NOWRAP
NOZOOM
NPV
NTOM
NULL
NUMBER
NumberOfElements
NUMLOCK
NVL
OBJECTS
OBJNUM
OBJTOCLIENT
OBJVAR
OCCURS
ODOMETER
OEMTOANSI
OF
OFF
OLDVAL
OLE
OLEClass
OLEOBJECT
OLEOBJECTS
OLETypeAllowed
ON
OneToMany
ONLY
OPEN
OpenTables
OpenWindow
OPTIMIZE
OptionButton
OptionGroup
OR
ORDER
ORIENTATION
OS
OUTPUT
OUTSHOW
OVERLAY
OVERWRITE
PACK
PAD
PADL
PADRPADC
_PADVANCE
PAGE
PageCount
PageFrame
PageHeight
_PAGENO
PageOrder
Pages
PageWidth
Paint
PALETTE
PANEL
PanelLink
PAPERLENGTH
PAPERSIZE
PAPERWIDTH
PARAMETERS
Parent
ParentAlias
ParentClass
PARTITION
PASSWORD
PasswordChar
PATH
PATTERN
PAUSE
PAYMENT
_PBPAGE
PCOL
_PCOLNO
_PCOPIES
PDOX
_PDRIVER
PDSETUP
_PDSETUP
_PECODE
_PEJECT
PEN
_PEPAGE
PFS
PI
PICTURE
PIXELS
PLAIN
PLAY
_PLENGTH
_PLINENO
_PLOFFSET
POINT
POP
POPUP
POPUPS
_PPITCH
_PQUALITY
PRECISION
PREFERENCE
_PRETEXT
PREVIEW
PRIMARY
Print
PRINTER
PRINTJOB

PRINTQUALITY
PRINTSTATUS
PRIVATE
PRMBAR
PRMPAD
PROCEDURE
@PROCEDURE
PROCEDURES
PRODUCTION
PROGRAM
ProgrammaticChange
PROGWORK
PROJECT
PROMPT
PROPER
PROW
PRTINFO
_PSCODE
PSet
_PSPACING
PUBLIC
PUSH
PUTFILE
PV
_PWAIT
QUERY
QUIT
RAND
RANDOM
RANGE
RangeHigh
RangeLow
RAT
RATLINE
RD
RDLEVEL
READ
ReadActivate
READBORDER
ReadCycle
ReadDeactivate
READERROR
ReadExpression
READKEY
ReadLock
ReadMethod
ReadMouse
ReadObject
ReadOnly
ReadSave
ReadShow
ReadTimeout
ReadValid
ReadWhen
RECALL
RECCOUNT
RECNO
RECORD
RecordMark
RecordSource
RecordSourceType
RECOVER
RECSIZE
REDIT
REFERENCE
REFERENCES
REFRESH
REGIONAL
REINDEX
RELATION
RelationalExpr
RELATIVE
RelativeColumn
RelativeRow
RELEASE
ReleaseType
REMOTE
REMOVE
RemoveItem
RemoveListItem
RemoveObject
RENAME
REPLACE
REPLICATE
REPORT
REPROCESS
REQUERY
REQUIRED
Reset
Resizable
Resize
RESOURCE
REST
RESTORE
RESTRICT
RESUME
RETRY
RETURN
RGB
RIGHT
RightClick
RLOCK
_RMARGIN
RMDIR
ROLLBACK
ROUND
ROW
RowHeight
ROWSET
RowSource
RowSourceType
RPD
RTOD
RTRIM
RUN
RUNSCRIPT
RUNTIME
SAFETY
SAME
SAMPLE
SAVE
SaveAs
SaveAsClass
SAY
SCALE
ScaleMode

SCAN
SCATTER
SCHEME
SCOLS
SCOREBOARD
SCREEN
_SCREEN
SCREENS
SCROLL
ScrollBars
Scrolled
SDF
SEC
SECONDS
SEEK
SELECT
Selected
SelectedBackColor
SelectedForeColor
SelectedID
SelectedItemBackColor
SelectedItemForeColor
SELECTION
SelectOnEntry
SelLength
SelStart
SelText
SEPARATOR
SET
SetAll
SETFLDSTATE
SetFocus
SHADOWS
Shape
SHARED
SHEET
SHELL
_SHELL
SHIFT
SHOW
ShowTips
SHUTDOWN
SIGN
SIN
SINGLE
Sizable
SIZE
SKIP
SKPBAR
SKPPAD
SOME
SORT
Sorted
SORTWORK
SOUNDEX
SPACE
Sparse
SpecialEffect
_SPELLCHK
SPINNER
SpinnerHighValue
SpinnerLowValue
SQL
SQLCANCEL
SQLCOLUMNS
SQLCOMMIT
SQLCONNECT
SQLDISCONNECT
SQLEXEC
SQLGETPROP
SQLMORERESULTS
SQLROLLBACK
SQLSETPROP
SQLSTRINGCONNECT
SQLTABLES
SQRT
SROWS
STANDALONE
_STARTUP
STATUS
StatusBarText
STD
STEP
STICKY
STORE
STR
STRETCH
STRING
STRTRAN
STRUCTURE
STUFF
STYLE
SUBCLASS
SUBSTR
SUM
SUMMARY
SUSPEND
SYLK
SYS
SYSFORMATS
SYSMENU
SYSMENUS
SYSMETRIC
SYSTEM
TAB
TabIndex
TABLE
TABLEREVERT
TABLES
TABLEUPDATE
TABS
_TABS
TabStop
TabStretch
TAG
TAGCOUNT
TAGNO
TALK
_TALLY
TAN
TARGET
TEDIT
TerminateRead
TEXT
_TEXT
TextBox

TextHeight
TEXTMERGE
TextWidth
THIS
THISFORM
THISFORMSET
_THROTTLE
TIME
TIMEOUT
Timer
TITLES
TMPFILES
TO
ToolBar
ToolTipText
TOP
TOPIC
TopIndex
TopItemID
TOTAL
TRANSACTION
TRANSFORM
_TRANSPORT
TRAP
TRBETWEEN
TRIGGER
_TRIGGERLEVEL
TRIM
TTOC
TTOD
TTOPTION
TXNLEVEL
TXTWIDTH
TYPE
TYPEAHEAD
UDFPARMS
Undock
UNION
UNIQUE
_UNIX
Unload
UNLOCK
UP
UpClick
UPDATE
UPDATED
UPPER
USE
USED
USERID
USERS
VAL
Valid
VALIDATE
Value
VALUES
VAR
VARREAD
VERB
VERSION
VGA25
VGA50
VIEW
VIEWS
Visible
VOLUME
WAIT
WBORDER
WCHILD
WCOLS
WEEK
WEXIST
WFONT
WHEN
WHERE
WHILE
WIDTH
WINDOW
WindowList
WINDOWS
_WINDOWS
WindowState
WindowType
WITH
_WIZARD
WK1
WK3
WKS
WLAST
WLCOL
WLROW
WMAXIMUM
WMINIMUM
WONTOP
WordWrap
WORKAREA
WOUTPUT
WP
WPARENT
WR1
WRAP
_WRAP
WREAD
WriteExpression
WriteMethod
WRK
WROWS
WTITLE
WVISIBLE
XCMDFILE
XL5
XLS
YEAR
YRESOLUTION
ZAP
ZOOM
Zorder

Index

A

B

C

F

G

H

I

J

K

L

M

T

U

V

W

X

ORDER BOOKS DIR ... ORNE/McGRAW-HILL

For a complete catalog of Osborne's bo ... at 2600 Tenth Street, Berkeley, CA 94710

Call Toll-Free: *1-800-822-8158*
24 hours a day, 7 days a week in U.S. and Canada

Mail this order form to:
McGraw-Hill, Inc.
Customer Service Dept.
P.O. Box 547
Blacklick, OH 43004

Fax this order form to:
1-614-759-3644

EMAIL
7007.1531@COMPUSERVE.COM
COMPUSERVE GO MH

Ship to:

Name ____________________

Company ____________________

Address ____________________

City / State / Zip ____________________

Daytime Telephone: ____________________
(We'll contact you if there's a question about your order.)

ISBN #	BOOK TITLE	Quantity	Price	Total
0-07-88				
0-07-88				
0-07-88				
0-07-88				
0-07-88				
0-07088				
0-07-88				
0-07-88				
0-07-88				
0-07-88				
0-07-88				
0-07-88				
0-07-88				
0-07-88				
	Shipping & Handling Charge from Chart Below			
	Subtotal			
	Please Add Applicable State & Local Sales Tax			
	TOTAL			

Shipping & Handling Charges

Order Amount	U.S.	Outside U.S.
Less than $15	$3.50	$5.50
$15.00 - $24.99	$4.00	$6.00
$25.00 - $49.99	$5.00	$7.00
$50.00 - $74.99	$6.00	$8.00
$75.00 - and up	$7.00	$9.00

Occasionally we allow other selected companies to use our mailing list. If you would prefer that we not include you in these extra mailings, please check here: ☐

METHOD OF PAYMENT

☐ Check or money order enclosed (payable to Osborne/McGraw-Hill)

☐ AMERICAN EXPRESS ☐ DISCOVER ☐ MasterCard ☐ VISA

Account No. ____________________

Expiration Date ____________________

Signature ____________________

In a hurry? Call 1-800-822-8158 anytime, day or night, or visit your local bookstore.

Thank you for your order

Code BC640SL